the SCOTLAND
visitor guide

Colin Baxter Photography, Grantown-on-Spey, Scotland

CONTENTS

Ben Hope and Caisteal Bharraich, Kyle of Tongue, Sutherland

HOW TO USE THIS GUIDE

The Scotland Visitor Guide is split into fourteen chapters, each of which corresponds directly with the VisitScotland regions (Scotland's Tourist Board). Entries are arranged alphabetically, and contain practical information on facilities, opening times, admission, directions, contact telephone number and website plus a short description. A typical entry looks like this one for Stirling Castle (below).

Number

Visitor Attraction

Type of Attraction

121 Stirling Castle

Set dramatically above Stirling on a rock outcrop, and with a number of fascinating architectural features, this is one of Scotland's finest castles.

Map Grid Reference

L5 *Top of Castle Wynd, centre of Stirling.*

Description

Directions

Facilitites

All year round, daily, 9.30am–6pm.
Oct–Mar, 9.30am–5pm.

Tel 01786 450000   www.historic-scotland.gov.uk

Opening Times

Contact details

About the Symbols
A number of symbols have been used throughout the book to represent types of attractions, facilities and whether the entry is associated with the National Trust for Scotland or Historic Scotland. You can find a list of these symbols on the inside cover of this book.

Using the Regional Maps
All entries are clearly marked on a colour-coded regional map at the start of each chapter using the number by the title (in the case of Stirling Castle, 121). You can use the map grid reference (L5) to find the location quickly. Detailed city plans have also been provided for Glasgow and Edinburgh.

Using the Indexes
Two indexes at the back of the book provide easy reference; the first is sectioned into regions and types of attraction, and the second is alphabetical by title.

Special Text
A number of special features appear throughout the guide which highlight top attractions, areas of particular natural beauty including many of Scotland's islands, and events.

GENERAL INFORMATION

TRAVEL INFORMATION

Traveline Scotland
Tel: 0870 608 2608
Provides timetable information for all public transport in Scotland and the rest of Great Britain.

AIRPORT INFORMATION

Aberdeen Airport
BAA Aberdeen
Aberdeen Airport
Dyce
Aberdeen
AB21 7DU
Tel: 0870 040 0006
Web: www.baa.com

Edinburgh Airport
BAA Edinburgh
Edinburgh Airport
EH12 9DN
Tel: 0870 040 0007
Web: www.baa.com

Glasgow Airport
BAA Glasgow
Glasgow Airport
Paisley
Renfrewshire
PA3 2SW
Tel: 0870 040 0008
Web: www.baa.com

Inverness Airport
Terminal Building
Highlands & Islands Airports Limited
Head Office
Inverness Airport
Inverness
IV2 7JB
Tel: 01667 464000
Web: www.hial.co.uk/inverness-airport.html
E-mail: hial@hial.co.uk

For other local airports see regional sections

RAIL

National Rail Enquiries
Tel: 08457 484950

Great North Eastern Railway (GNER)
Web: www.gner.co.uk
E-mail: customercare@gner.co.uk
Route:
operates along Britain's East Coast main line linking England and Scotland

Virgin Trains
Web: www.virgintrains.co.uk
Route:
operates two rail franchises:
West Coast Trains and CrossCountry Trains
West Coast Trains routes include:
London Euston–Scotland
CrossCountry Trains routes include:
Glasgow–Bournemouth
Dundee–Penzance

First ScotRail
Caledonian Chambers
87 Union Street
Glasgow
G1 3TA
Tel: Fares & Train Times: 08457 484950
Telesales: 08457 550033
Customer Relations: 0845 601 5929
Web: www.firstscotrail.co.uk
E-mail: scotrail.enquiries@firstgroup.com
Routes:
operates within Scotland and also Caledonian Sleepers which link Aberdeen, Edinburgh, Fort William, Glasgow and Inverness with London

COACH

National Express Group PLC
Head Office
75 Davies Street
London
W1K 5HT
Tel: Head Office: 0207 529 2000
Timetable Enquiries: 08705 808080
Web: www.gobycoach.com
E-mail: info@natex.co.uk

Rapsons Coaches
1 Seafield Road
Inverness
IVl 1TN
Tel: 01463 710555
Web: www.rapsons.co.uk
Email: info@rapsons.co.uk

Scottish Citylink Coaches Limited
Buchanan Bus Station
Killermont Street
Glasgow
G2 3NP
Tel: 08705 505050
Web: www.citylink.co.uk
E-mail: info@citylink.co.uk

FERRIES

Caledonian MacBrayne
The Ferry Terminal
Gourock
PA19 1QP
Tel: Enquiries: 01475 650100
Vehicle Reservations: 08705 650000
Brochure Hotline: 08705 650000
Web: www.calmac.co.uk
*Routes: Mainland UK to Firth of Clyde Islands &
Peninsulas
Islay, Colonsay & Gigha
Mull & the Inner Hebrides
Skye, Raasay and the Small Isles
The Outer Hebrides*

P&O Irish Sea
Cairnryan
Stranraer
Wigtownshire
DG9 8FR
Tel: 0870 242 4777
Web: www.poirishsea.com
Routes: Mainland UK–Ireland

P&O Scottish Ferries
PO BOX 5
Jamesons Quay
Aberdeen AB11 5NP
Tel: 01224 572615
Web: www.poscottishferries.com
E-mail: passenger@poscottishferries.com
*Routes: Mainland UK–Orkney
Mainland UK–Shetland*

Seacat Scotland
Sea Containers Ferries Scotland Limited
Seacat Terminal
Donegal Quay
Belfast BT1 3AL
Tel: 08705 523523
Web: www.seacat.co.uk
E-mail: belfast.reservations@seacontainers.com
Route: Belfast–Troon

Superfast Ferries
The Terminal Building
Port of Rosyth
Fife KY11 2XP
Tel: 01870 234 870
Web: www.superfastscotland.com
E-mail: info@superfastscotland.com
Route: Rosyth–Zeebrugge

CYCLE

National Cycle Network
Sustrans Scotland
16a Randolph Crescent
Edinburgh EH3 7TT
Tel: 0131 539 8122
Web: www.sustrans.org.uk
E-mail: info@sustrans.org.uk

Detailed regional travel information is located at
the beginning of each chapter.
This includes:
**airport details
bus & coach operators
ferry operators
car hire companies
taxi firms**

Inter-island travel details are also included for
Orkney, Shetland and the Western Isles.

USEFUL ADDRESSES

VisitScotland
23 Ravelston Terrace
Edinburgh EH4 3EU
Tel: 0131 332 2433
Web: www.visitscotland.com
E-mail: info@visitscotland.com

Forestry Commission
231 Corstorphine Road
Edinburgh EH12 7AT
Tel: 0131 334 0303
Web: www.forestry.gov.uk
E-mail: enquiries@forestry.gsi.gov.uk

Historic Scotland
Longmore House
Salisbury Place
Edinburgh EH9 1SH
Tel: 0131 668 8800
Web: www.historic-scotland.gov.uk
E-mail: hs.explorer@scotland.gov.uk

The National Trust for Scotland
Wemyss House
28 Charlotte Square
Edinburgh EH2 4ET
Tel: 0131 243 9300
Web: www.nts.org.uk
E-mail: information@nts.org.uk

Ramblers Association (Scottish Office)
Kingfisher House
Auld Mart Business Park
Milnathort
Kinross KY13 9DA
Tel: 01577 861222
Web: www.ramblers.org.uk
E-mail: enquiries@scotland.ramblers.org.uk

Royal Society for the Protection of Birds
Scotland Headquarters
Dunedin House
25 Ravelston Terrace
Edinburgh EH4 3TP
Tel: 0131 311 6500
Web: www.rspb.org.uk
E-mail: rspb.scotland@rspb.org.uk

Scottish Natural Heritage
12 Hope Terrace
Edinburgh EH9 2AS
Tel: 0131 447 4784
Web: www.snh.org.uk

Scottish Wildlife Trust
Cramond House
off Cramond Glebe Road
Edinburgh EH4 6NS
Enquiries Tel: 0131 312 7765
Bookings Tel: 08701 55 32 55
Web: www.swt.org.uk
E-mail: enquiries@swt.org.uk

Scottish Youth Hostel Association
7 Glebe Crescent
Stirling FK8 2JA
Tel: 01786 891400
Web: www.syha.org.uk
E-mail: info@syha.org.uk

CATERING FOR DISABILITY IN SCOTLAND

Scotland welcomes visitors with disabilities. There are a number of organisations in Scotland designed to aid visitors who need advice and information on visiting Scotland.

Capability Scotland is Scotland's primary disability organisation and can offer help and advice to visitors to Scotland. For further information please contact:

Advice Service Capability Scotland (ASCS)
11 Ellersly Road
Edinburgh
EH12 6HY
Tel: 0131 313 5510
Web: www.capability-scotland.org.uk
E-mail: ascs@capability-scotland.org.uk

Holiday Care is a national charity and the UK's principal provider of travel advice and information for disabled people and their carers. For further information please contact:

Holiday Care
7th Floor
Sunley House
4 Bedford Park
Croydon
Surrey CR0 2AP
Tel: 0845 124 9971
Web: www.holidaycare.org.uk
E-mail: holiday.care@virgin.net

SCOTLAND
chapter regions

SHETLAND

ORKNEY

WESTERN
ISLES

THE
HIGHLANDS
OF SCOTLAND

ABERDEEN
& GRAMPIAN

ANGUS
& DUNDEE

PERTHSHIRE

ARGYLL, THE ISLES,
LOCH LOMOND,
STIRLING &
TROSSACHS

KINGDOM
OF FIFE

EDINBURGH
& LOTHIANS

GREATER
GLASGOW
& CLYDE
VALLEY

SCOTTISH
BORDERS

AYRSHIRE
& ARRAN

DUMFRIES
& GALLOWAY

England

0   30mls
0   40 kms

MAIN TOURIST INFORMATION CENTRES

Aberdeen
23 Union Street
Aberdeen AB11 5BP
Tel: 01224 288828
Web: www.aberdeen-grampian.com
E-mail: info@agtb.org
Open: all year round

Ayrshire & Arran
15 Skye Road
Prestwick KA9 2TA
Tel: 01292 678100
Web: www.ayrshire-arran.com
E-mail: info@ayrshire-arran.com
Open: all year round

Dumfries
64 Whitesands
Dumfries DG1 2RS
Tel: 01387 253862
Web: www.dumfriesandgalloway.co.uk
E-mail: info@dgth.visitscotland.com
Open: all year round

Dundee
21 Castle Street
Dundee DD1 3AA
Tel: 01382 527527
Web: www.angusanddundee.co.uk
E-mail: enquiries@angusanddundee.co.uk
Open: all year round

Dunoon
7 Alexandra Parade
Dunoon PA23 8AB
Tel: 08707 200 629
Web: www.visitscottishheartlands.org
E-mail: info@dunoon.visitscotland.com
Open: all year round

Edinburgh
3 Princes Street
Edinburgh EH2 2QP
Tel: 0845 225 5121
Web: www.edinburgh.org
E-mail: info@visitscotland.com
Open: all year round

Glasgow
11 George Square
Glasgow G2 1DY
Tel: 0141 204 4400
Web: www.seeglasgow.com
E-mail: enquiries@seeglasgow.com
Open: all year round

Inverness
Castle Wynd
Inverness IV2 3BJ
Tel: 01463 234353
Web: www.visithighlands.com
E-mail: info@host.co.uk
Open: all year round ·

Jedburgh
Murray's Green
Jedburgh TD8 6BE
Tel: 08706 080404
Web: www.visitscottishborders.com
E-mail: info@scot-borders.co.uk
Open: all year round

Kirkwall
6 Broad Street
Kirkwall
Orkney KW15 1NX
Tel: 01856 872856
Web: www.visitororkney.com
E-mail: info@otb.ossian.net
Open: all year round

Lewis
26 Cromwell Street
Stornoway
Isle of Lewis HS1 2DD
Tel: 01851 703088
Web: www.visitthehebrides.com
E-mail: stornowaytic@visitthehebrides.co.uk

Oban
Argyll Square
Oban PA34 4AN
Tel: 08707 200 630
Web: www.visitscottishheartlands.org
E-mail: info@oban.visitscotland.com
Open: all year round

Perth
Lower City Mills
West Mill Street
Perth PH1 5QP
Tel: 01738 450600
Web: www.perthshire.co.uk
E-mail: info@perthshire.co.uk
Open: all year round

Shetland
Market Cross
Lerwick
Shetland ZE1 0LU
Tel: 01595 693434
Web: www.visitshetland.com
E-mail: shetland.tourism@zetnet.co.uk
Open: all year round

St Andrews
70 Market Street
St Andrews KY16 9NU
Tel: 01334 472021
Web: www.standrews.com/fife
E-mail: standrewstic@kftb.ossian.net
Open: all year round

Royal Burgh of Stirling
Castle Esplanade
Stirling FK8 1EH
Tel: 08707 200622
Web: www.visitscottishheartlands.org
E-mail: info@rbsvc.visitscotland.com
Open: all year round

SCOTLAND

When tourists first discovered Scotland at the beginning of the Romantic Age even before the end of the eighteenth century, they came first of all for the scenery. A cult of the picturesque developed and is still an important part of a Scottish holiday. Visitors simply enjoy the beauties of the landscape.

However, there is much more to Scotland than simply the views such as the discoveries to be made while touring around, with plenty of opportunities to see a lot in an easy day's drive, such as the Border Abbeys or Perthshire lochs. On the way, there is a choice of attractions to visit. Scotland has more visitor attractions per head of population than any other part of the United Kingdom. Distilleries, especially around the Spey; museums and visitor centres which cover themes as diverse as whaling, mining, textiles, lighthouses or farming life; a heritage of castles and grand mansions: these are just some of the finds awaiting the tourer.

Amongst the country's natural attractions are its wildlife sites: seabird cliffs raucous with gulls and auks in spring and summer; glens filled with the sound of bellowing red deer clashing their antlers in autumn; lowland lochs over which great flights of grey geese gather daily in winter. None of these wildlife highlights are difficult to find. Birdwatchers (and botanists, too) will find plenty to seek out.

As well as activities related to wildlife, the natural setting is a backdrop to a whole range of other things to do. There are more golf courses in Scotland than anywhere else in the world. (After all, the sport originated here on the rabbit-cropped coastal turf – the classic Scottish east-coast links.)

Walking enthusiasts will find a whole range of walks and trails by mountain, moor and woodland. Many are signposted and local advice is readily available. Cyclists can also take advantage of the quiet rural road network, as well as the dedicated cycle trails and signposted national cycle routes. Watersports – from windsurfing to game angling – are also well developed, with a good range of centres.

In Scotland, the great outdoors should be balanced by the city experience and a chance to explore Scotland's contemporary culture. Discover for yourself that Glasgow not only has its own style but also a reputation for friendliness (as well as some of the very best shopping in the UK). No trip to Scotland is complete without taking in the skyline of Edinburgh, simply one of the great capitals of Europe. Aberdeen, Dundee and Inverness also offer a range of cultural options and surprising nightlife.

In short, it is easy to enjoy a wide variety of experiences in Scotland. It could be the most challenging golf courses, the finest seafood or the mellowest malt whiskies. You can board an efficient network of ferries and discover island life or immerse yourself in art and culture in Scotland's cities. Best of all, because so much variety in landscape and activity choice is in quite a small area, you can do all of these things on the same Scottish holiday.

The River Spey and Loch Insh, Strathspey

Hart Fell and Upper Annandale near Moffat

THE SCOTTISH BORDERS

The Scottish Borders, from a southern perspective, are no soft and gentle introduction to Scotland. These rolling hills comprise, at least in part, the old 'Debatable Land', fought over, burnt and raided through the centuries of skirmishing between Scotland and her neighbour.

This is the land of stirring tales from Border ballads, of Border clans and their grim towerhouse strongholds of old – and there is, to this day, a down-to-earth grittiness and frankness about these Border folk, and a huge pride in their communities. This in turn is expressed in the unique Common Ridings, which celebrate the long association of the Borders with horses and horsemanship. Acknowledging the very real needs in times gone by to confirm the boundaries and the security of Border towns, the Common Ridings today instead confirm the identity and spirit of the Border folk. Similarly, local passions run high with the Borders love of rugby – where the Melrose Sevens, for example, are another highlight in the Borders calendar.

Stop by Carter Bar on the main A68 road beyond the Border, or look out from the hilltop by Smailholm Tower, and the breezy uplands seem to roll out forever in smooth domes and flowing curves. On these well-grazed slopes there are sheep, some at least of the Cheviot breed, taking their name from the great sprawl of a hill in whose shadow the Border runs. Elsewhere, the Borders show a more gentle face, with river valleys, fine woodlands and well-tended farms. This is especially true of the eastern borders, around the Merse, the lower valley of the River Tweed, with its rich boulder clay soils.

Another feature of the Border landscape are the great abbeys. Many strands come together here: the monks were also farmers and weavers, tending the flocks and laying the foundations of the Borders textile industry which is still important for the Borderers today. A trip round a woollen mill is a popular visitor activity. The ruined state of the Border abbey, especially the poignant fragment of Kelso Abbey sacked by English forces in the 'rough wooing' of the young Mary Queen of Scots are other reminders of the troubled Border story. At Dryburgh Abbey, Sir Walter Scott lies buried in this peaceful spot by a loop in the river.

Finally, the Scottish Borders were once a Roman centre. The Eildon Hills, their triple summits a landmark throughout the central Borders were the Trimontium of the occupiers. An exhibition at Melrose tells the story of their time here, and of their great fort which once stood at nearby Newstead.

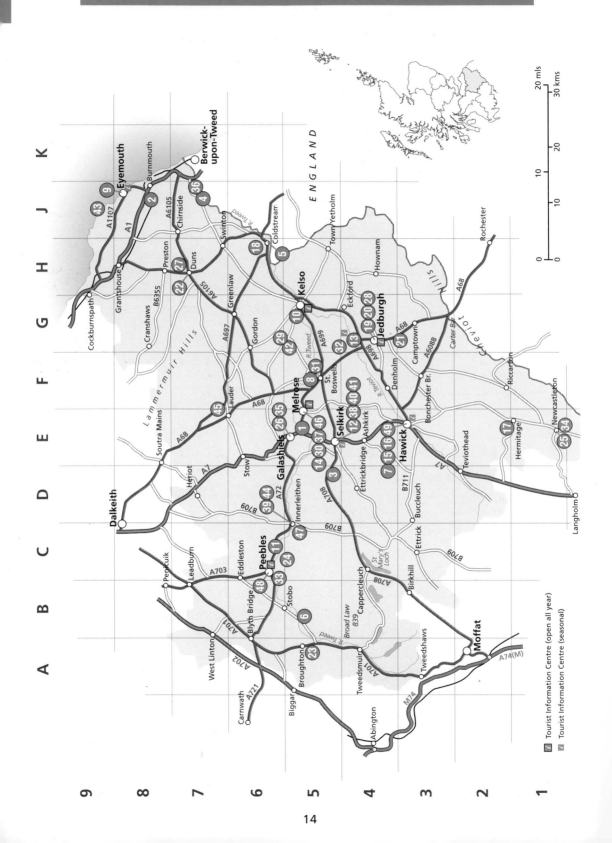

Tourist Information Centre (open all year)

Tourist Information Centre (seasonal)

VISITOR INFORMATION

MAIN TOURIST INFORMATION CENTRE

Jedburgh
Murray's Green
Jedburgh TD8 6BE
Tel: 08706 080404
Web: www.visitscottishborders.com
E-mail: info@scot-borders.co.uk
Open: all year round

YEAR ROUND TOURIST INFORMATION CENTRES

Peebles
High Street
Peebles EH45 8AG
Tel: 08706 080404
Web:
www.visitscottishborders.com
E-mail: info@scot-borders.co.uk

Melrose
Abbey House, Abbey Street
Melrose TD6 9LG
Tel: 08706 080404
Web:
www.visitscottishborders.com
E-mail: info@scot-borders.co.uk

Kelso
Town House, The Square
Kelso TD5 7HF
Tel: 08706 080404
Web:
www.visitscottishborders.com
E-mail: info@scot-borders.co.uk

SEASONAL TOURIST INFORMATION CENTRES

Eyemouth
Tel: 08706 080404
E-mail:
info@scot-borders.co.uk
Open: Apr–end Oct

Harestanes
Tel: 08706 080404
E-mail:
info@scot-borders.co.uk
Open: Apr–end Oct

Hawick
Tel: 08706 080404
E-mail:
info@scot-borders.co.uk
Open: Apr–end Oct

Selkirk
Tel: 08706 080404
E-mail:
info@scot-borders.co.uk
Open: Apr–end Oct

ADDITIONAL INFORMATION

GENERAL TRAVEL INFORMATION
Traveline Scotland
Tel: 0870 608 2608
Provides timetable information for all public transport in Scotland and the rest of Great Britain.

TRAINS

First ScotRail
Caledonian Chambers
87 Union Street
Glasgow G1 3TA
Tel: Fares & Train Times: 08457 484950
Telesales: 08457 550033
Customer Relations: 0845 601 5929
Web: www.firstscotrail.co.uk
E-mail: scotrail.enquiries@firstgroup.com

COACH

National Express Group PLC
75 Davies Street
London W1K 5HT
Tel: 08705 808080
Web: www.gobycoach.com
E-mail: info@natex.co.uk
Route: London–Jedburgh–Edinburgh

BUS

First
395 King Street
Aberdeen AB24 5RP
Tel: 01896 752237
Web: www.firstgroup.com
*Routes: operates an extensive network
throughout The Borders*

CAR HIRE

Bruce Motors, Hawick
Tel: 01450 372287
Web: www.peugeot.co.uk/bruce_motors1
E-mail:
bruce_motors1@peugeotmail.co.uk

Border Autocare & Tyre Services
Tel: 01896 752729

Cook's Car & Van Hire, St Boswells
Tel: 01835 823483
Web: www.cookscarandvanhire.co.uk
E-mail: cooksvan@aol.com

David Harrison, Galashiels
Tel: 01896 759999
Web: www.harrisonfordpeebles.co.uk

David Harrison, Peebles
Tel: 01721 721350
Web: www.harrisonfordpeebles.co.uk

Mansfield Motors, Hawick
Tel: 01450 374041

TAXIS

AH Taxis, Hawick
Tel: 01450 374114

Clan Cabs, Galashiels
Tel: 01896 756796

Cook's Taxis, Kelso
Tel: 01573 226826

D&G Taxis, Hawick
Tel: 01450 377925

Kwik Cab Taxis, Kelso
Tel: 01573 225451

Peter Hogg Taxis, Jedburgh
Tel: 01835 863755

Reiver Taxis, Galashiels
Tel: 01896 755755

R&D Taxis, Galashiels
Tel: 01896 758808

Abbotsford House

1 Abbotsford House

Abbotsford was built by Sir Walter Scott, the nineteenth century novelist and author of classics like Rob Roy and Ivanhoe. Situated on the banks of the River Tweed, the house contains a collection of historic relics, weapons and armour, along with a library containing over 9000 rare volumes. Visitors can see Scott's study, library, drawing room, armouries and dining room.

E5 *Two miles W of Melrose on B6360.*

P WC 🍴 🏛 🔭 🚶 🎫 ££

⊕ Third Mon in Mar–Oct, Mon–Sat, 9.30am–5pm. Mar, Apr, May & Oct, Sun, 2–5pm; Jun–Sept, Sun, 9.30am–5pm.

Tel 01896 752043
www.melrose.bordernet.co.uk/abbotsford

2 Ayton Castle

Scottish Baronial Castle built in 1846 with some fine interiors. Conducted tours & woodland walks.

J8 *On A1, Seven miles N of Berwick-upon-Tweed.*

P WC ♿ £

⊕ Mid May–Mid Sept, Sat–Sun, 2–5pm.

Tel 01890 781212

3 Bowhill House and Country Park

Bowhill, the home of the Duke of Buccleuch, contains an art collection, miniatures, porcelain, silver and tapestries, along with Queen Victoria and Sir Walter Scott relics and a Victorian kitchen. The surrounding country park has woodland walks, an adventure playground & 72 seat theatre.

D5 *Three miles W of Selkirk on A708.*

P WC ♿ 🍴 🏛 E AV 🔭 🚶 🎫 ££

⊕ House: Jul only, 1–5pm. Park: Easter, daily, 11am–5pm; May & June, weekends & bank holidays only, 11am–5pm. Jun–Aug, daily, 11am–5pm. Aug daily except Fri, 11am–5pm.

Tel 01750 22204   www.bowhill.org.uk

4 Chain Bridge Honey Farm   ★

Learn about the life of the honeybee and see a collection of restored vehicles at this honey farm.

J7 *At Horncliffe W of Berwick-upon-Tweed.*

WC ♿ 🍴 🏛 E Free

⊕ Apr–Oct, Mon–Sat, 10.30am–5pm; Sun 2–5pm. Nov–Mar, Mon–Fri, 9am–5pm.

Tel 01289 386362   www.chainbridgehoney.co.uk

5 Coldstream Museum

A museum focusing on local history,
with a programme of changing exhibitions.

H6 *Market Square, Coldstream,*
eight miles NE of Kelso on A698.

& E [AV] ⏃ Free

🕐 Apr–Sept, daily, 10am–4pm; Sun, 2–4pm.
Oct, Mon–Sat, 1–4pm. Closed Sun.

Tel 01890 882630

6 Dawyck Botanic Gardens ✿

With 300 years of tree planting, Dawyck contains
an acclaimed arboretum with mature specimens
of Brewer's Spruce, plus giant trees from North
America, an azalea terrace and various walks.

B5 *On B712, eight miles S of Peebles.*

P [WC] & 🌳 🚻 ⏃ ☼ 🏃 [♿] £

🕐 Feb–Nov, daily, 10am–4pm.
Mar & Oct, daily, 10am–5pm.
Apr–Sept, daily, 10am–6pm.

Tel 01721 760254   www.rbge.org.uk

7 Drumlanrig's Tower Visitor Centre

Housed in an impressive restored fifteenth
century building, the centre relates the history
of Hawick via audio-visual displays.

E3 *Tower Knowe, High Street, Hawick town centre.*

P [WC] & 🚻 E [AV]

🕐 Apr–Oct, Mon–Sat, 10am–5pm;
Jul & Aug, closes 5pm;
Apr–Sep, Sun, 1–4pm.

Tel 01450 377615

8 Dryburgh Abbey ● ✠

Sir Walter Scott and Field Marshall Earl Haig
are buried among the impressive ruins of this
Premonstratensian abbey.

F5 *Five miles SE of Melrose on the B6404.*

P [WC] & 🚻 ⏃ ££

🕐 All year round, daily; reduced hours in winter.

Tel 01896 822381   www.historic-scotland.gov.uk

9 Eyemouth Museum

Includes exhibitions on local industries and
a large tapestry made to mark the 1881
fishing disaster when 189 men perished.

J8 *Entry through TIC, Manse Road, Eyemouth.*

& [♿] £

🕐 Apr–Jun & Sept, Mon–Sat, 10am–5pm;
Sun, 12 noon–3pm. Jul–Aug, Mon–Sat,
10am–5pm; Sun, 12 noon–4pm.
Oct, Mon–Sat, 10am–4pm; Closed Sunday.

Tel 018907 50678

10 Floors Castle

Floors Castle, home of the Duke and Duchess
of Roxburghe, contains fine period French
furniture, plus collections of art, porcelain
and tapestries. Extensive grounds provide
woodland walks and a play area.

G5 *One mile W of Kelso, on A699.*

P [WC] & 🌳 ✕ 🚻 ⏃ ☼ 🏃 [♿] ££

🕐 Mid Mar–End Oct, daily, 10am–4.30pm.
Last admission 4pm.

Tel 01573 223333   www.floorscastle.com

11 Glentress Forest ♠

Features marked forest walks, and a replica
Iron Age roundhouse.

C6 *Three miles E of Peebles on A72.*

P [WC] & ☼ 🏃 Free

🕐 All year round. Car parking charges apply.

Tel 01750 721120   www.forestry.gov.uk

12 Halliwell's House Museum

Tells the story of Selkirk via various displays
including a reconstructed ironmonger's shop
of the 1900s. Robson Gallery houses a variety
of craft and art exhibitions.

E5 *Market Place, Selkirk town centre.*

P & 🚻 E [♿] Free

🕐 Apr–Sept, Mon–Sat, 10am–5pm; Sun,
10am–12 noon. Jul–Aug, Mon–Sat, 10am–5.30pm;
Sun, 10am–12 noon. Oct, Mon–Sat, 10am–4pm.

Tel 01750 20096

13 Harestanes Countryside Visitor Centre ♠

A country park with woodland walks, play
area and wildlife garden, plus exhibitions,
events and activities.

G4 *Ancrum, two miles N of Jedburgh on A68,*
signposted on to B6400.

P [WC] & 🌳 🚻 E ⏃ ☼ 🏃 [♿] Free

🕐 Easter–Oct, daily, 10am–5pm.

Tel 01835 830306

Hermitage Castle

14 Harmony Garden 🌷 ❋

A peaceful walled garden comprising of lawns, herbaceous and mixed borders, vegetable and fruit areas and a display of spring bulbs. The garden is set around an early nineteenth century house (not open) built by Melrose joiner James Waugh.

E5 *Melrose town centre, opposite Melrose Abbey.*

🔔 ♨ £

⊕ Easter–Sept, Mon–Sat, 10am–5pm; Sun, 1–5pm.

Tel 01721 722502
www.nts.org.uk

15 Hawick Cashmere Company ★

Visitors are given the opportunity via a 'viewing gallery' to discover how cashmere is manufactured into a variety of garments; an adjoining shop contains an extensive range of knitwear.

E3 *On Arthur Street, Hawick.*

🅿 🚾 ♿ E ♿ Free

⊕ All year round, Mon–Sat, 9.30am–5pm; Sun, 11am–4pm (May–Oct only).

Tel 01450 371221   www.hawickcashmere.com

16 Hawick Museum and Scott Art Gallery 🏛

The museum is devoted to the social and manufacturing history of the area, while the gallery specialises in nineteenth and twentieth century Scottish art, with changing exhibitions.

E3 *Wilton Lodge Park, Hawick.*

🚾 ♿ ♿ E 🔔 ♨ 👫 Free

⊕ Apr–Sept, Mon–Fri, 10am–12 noon & 1–5pm; Sat & Sun, 2–5pm. Oct–Mar, Mon–Fri, 1–4pm; Sun, 2–4pm.

Tel 01450 373457

17 Hermitage Castle 🅱 🏰

Dating from the fourteenth century and restored in the nineteenth century, this fortress is associated with the de Soulis, the Douglases and Mary Queen of Scots. The Hermitage Chapel is situated nearby.

E2 *On B6399, 5.5 miles NE of Newcastleton.*

🅿 🔔 £

⊕ Apr–Sept, daily, 9.30am–6.30pm.

Tel 01387 376222   www.historic-scotland.gov.uk

18 Hirsel Country Park

Visitors can make use of nature trails, playground, an information centre and museum.

H6 *Two miles N of Coldstream off A697.*

🅿 ♿ ☕ ⛪ ⛱ ☀ 🚶 🎫 £

🕐 All year, dawn–dusk.

Tel 01890 882834   www.hirselcountrypark.co.uk

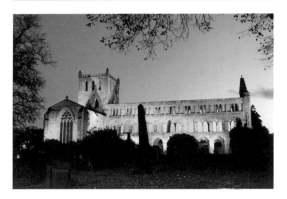

19 Jedburgh Abbey

Impressive ruins of a twelfth century abbey founded by David I. Various items found during excavations, including the 'Jedburgh comb', are on display.

G4 *Jedburgh, on the A68.*

🅿 ♿ ⛪ E AV ⛱ ££

🕐 Apr–Sept, daily, 9.30am–6.30pm.
Oct–Mar, daily, 9.30am–4.30pm.

Tel 01835 863925   www.historic-scotland.gov.uk

20 Jedburgh Castle Jail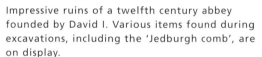

A museum telling the history of Jedburgh, housed in a nineteenth century reform prison building.

G4 *Castlegate, Jedburgh, on the A68.*

🅿 ⛪ E AV ⛱ £

🕐 Mar–Oct, Mon–Sat, 10am–4.30pm; Sun, 1–4pm.

Tel 01835 863254

21 Jedforest Deer and Farm Park

A working farm with rare breeds and deer herds, offering ranger led activities, walks for all ages and tractor rides during warm months. Also on offer are daily displays of birds of prey, and indoor and outdoor play areas.

G3 *On A68, five miles S of Jedburgh.*

🅿 ♿ ☕ ⛪ E ⛱ ☀ 🚶 🎫 ££

🕐 Daily, Easter–Aug, 10am–5.30pm.
Sept–late Oct, 11am–4.30pm.

Tel 01835 840364
www.aboutscotland.com/jedforest/

22 Jim Clark Room

A museum relating to world motor racing champion Jim Clark.

H7 *Newtown Street, Duns.*

♿ ⛪ E AV £

🕐 Apr–Sept, Mon–Sat, 10.30am–1pm & 2–4.30pm;
Sun, 2–4pm. Oct, Mon–Sat, 1–4pm.

Tel 01361 883960

23 John Buchan Centre

A centre devoted to John Buchan, lawyer, politician, soldier, historian, biographer, Governor-General of Canada and, most famously, novelist, his best known work being the thriller, The Thirty-Nine Steps.

A5 *S end of Broughton on A701.*

🅿 ♿ E £

🕐 Easter weekend & May–mid Oct, daily, 2–5pm.

Tel 01899 221050

24 Kailzie Gardens

Set in the Tweed Valley, the gardens contain a walled garden, greenhouses, formal rose garden, herbaceous borders, walks and massed bulbs.

C6 *Two miles E of Peebles on B7062.*

🅿 ♿ ☕ ✕ ⛪ E AV ⛱ 🚶 £

🕐 March–Oct, daily, 10am–5.30pm;
Winter, 10am–dusk.

Tel 01721 720007

25 Liddesdale Heritage Centre Museum

A museum telling the history of Liddesdale and its people, with a commemorative bi-centenary tapestry created by local needleworkers, and a collection of Waverley Line railway memorabilia.

E1 *South Hermitage Street, Newcastleton.*

♿ £

🕐 Easter–end Sept, daily, 1.30–4.30pm.
Closed Tuesday.

Tel 01387 375283
www.liddesdaleheritagecentre.scotshome.com

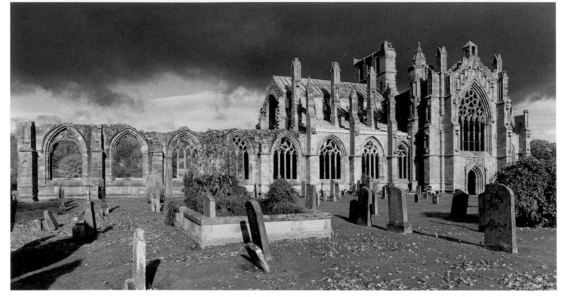

Melrose Abbey

26 Lochcarron Cashmere and Wool Centre ★

Visitors can tour the cashmere woollen mill and see a museum depicting the history of Galashiels.

E5 *Huddersfield Street, Galashiels.*

🅿 ♿ ⚓ E ♿ £

🕐 Jan–Dec, Mon–Sat, 9am–5pm; Jun–Sept, also Sun, 12 noon–5pm. Tours: all year round, Mon–Thur, 10.30am, 11.30am, 1.30pm, 2.30pm. Fri, 10.30 & 11.30am, excluding Public Holidays.

Tel 01896 751100   www.lochcarron.com

27 Manderston 🏰 ❀

An Edwardian country house featuring opulent state rooms, a unique silver staircase, stable, a marble dairy and 56 acres of formal and woodland gardens.

H7 *Two miles E of Duns off A6105.*

🅿 ♿ ☕ ⚓ ⛱ 🧗 ££

🕐 House: Mid May–Sept, Thur & Sun, 2–5pm; also late May & Aug Bank Holiday Mon. Grounds: open until dusk.

Tel 01361 883450   www.manderston.co.uk

28 Mary Queen of Scots Visitor Centre 🏰

This museum, focusing on Mary Queen of Scots, is housed in a sixteenth century building where she once stayed.

G4 *Queen Steet, Jedburgh, on A68.*

♿ ⚓ E AV £

🕐 Mar–Nov, Mon–Sat, 10am–4.30pm; Sun, 11am–4.30pm.

Tel 01835 863331

29 Mellerstain House 🏰

This Georgian house, designed by Robert and William Adam, contains impressive plaster ceilings, period furniture and an art collection.

G5 *On the A6089 S of Gordon.*

🅿 ♿ ☕ ⚓ 🌿 🧗 ♿ ££

🕐 May–Sept, daily except Tues & Sat. Oct, Sat–Sun only. House: 12.30–5pm, last admission 4.15pm. Grounds: 11.30am–5.30pm. Groups by appointment.

Tel 01573 410225   www.mellerstain.com

30 Melrose Abbey ✝

Melrose Abbey, founded by David I in 1136, was virtually destroyed by Richard II's English army in 1385, the remains are largely the result of rebuilding work carried out from the fourteenth century. A casket containing Robert the Bruce's heart is believed to be buried at the abbey.

E5 *Abbey Street, Melrose, off the A6 or A68.*

🅿 ♿ ♿ ☕ E ⛱ ££

🕐 Apr–Sept, daily, 9.30am–6.30pm. Oct–Mar, daily, 9.30am–4.30pm.

Tel 01896 822562   www.historic-scotland.gov.uk

31 Mertoun Gardens ❖

The gardens are set in 26 acres of grounds and contain fine trees, herbaceous plants and flowering shrubs. There is also a well preserved circular dovecot thought to be the oldest in the country.

F5 *Two miles E of St Boswells on B6404.*

P WC ❀ £

🕐 Apr–Sept, weekends, 2–6pm.
Mon public holidays, 2–6pm.

Tel 01835 823236

32 Monteviot House Gardens ❖

The garden is made up of a number of areas, from a box-hedged herb garden to a view of the river below, down through a terraced rose garden into a river garden. A water garden features three islands linked by wooden bridges, leading to an arboretum.

F4 *Four miles N of Jedburgh on B6400.*

P WC ♿ ❀ £

🕐 Apr–Oct, 12 noon–5pm (last admission 4.45pm).

Tel 01835 830380 (mornings)

33 Neidpath Castle ♜

A fourteenth century castle converted to a tower house, with fine views from the parapets, a pit prison, draw well and batiks depicting the life of Mary Queen of Scots.

C6 *One mile W of Peebles on A72.*

P WC ⛪ E ⛺ ❀ 👫 £

🕐 Easter weekend, May–Sept, Mon–Sat, 10.30am–5pm; Sun, 12.30–5pm.

Tel 01721 720333

34 Newcastleton Forest ⛺

A large forest with waymarked routes and an unmanned information centre.

E1 *Two miles E of Newcastleton, off B6357.*

P WC E ⛺ ❀ 👫 Free

🕐 All year round.

Tel 01750 721120   www.forestry.gov.uk

35 Old Gala House and Scott Gallery 🏛

Visitors can learn the 500-year history of the house, its inhabitants and the development of the town of Galashiels.

E5 *Centre of Galashiels off A7/A72.*

P WC ♿ ☕ ⛪ E AV ❀ Free

🕐 Apr–May & Sept, Tue–Sat, 10am–4pm.
Jun–Aug, Mon–Sat, 10am–4pm; Sun, 1pm–4pm.
Oct, Tue–Fri, 1–4pm; Sat, 10am–4pm.

Tel 01750 20096

36 Paxton House ♜

Paxton House, built from 1758-62 to the design of John and James Adam, is one of the finest Palladian houses in Scotland. In 1811, George Home added one of the first purpose-built picture galleries in a Scottish country house which now provides the setting for over 70 paintings on loan from the National Galleries. Visitors can also make use of the gardens, walks and a children's adventure playground.

J7 *Three miles W of A1, turning off at Berwick-Upon-Tweed.*

P WC ♿ ☕ ⛪ E ⛺ ❀ 👫 ££

🕐 House: Easter–Oct, daily, 11am–5pm (last tour 4.15pm). Grounds and gardens: 10am–sunset.

Tel 01289 386291   www.paxtonhouse.com

37 Priorwood Garden ♕ ❖

This garden produces plants for use in dried flower arrangements, and has an orchard containing historic apple varieties, plums, damson, greengage and pears.

E5 *Melrose, off A6091, adjacent to the Abbey.*

♿ ⛪ ⛺ 📧 £

🕐 Jan–Mar, Mon–Sat, 12 noon–4pm;
Apr–24 Dec, Mon–Sat, 10am–4pm;
Sun, 1–5pm.

Tel 01896 822493   www.nts.org.uk

38 Robert D Clapperton Daylight Photographic Studio 🏛

An original daylight photographic studio dating from 1867. The small family owned museum has been in existence in Selkirk since 1867, trading under the founder's name, Robert D Clapperton for three generations. The studio is set up as a working museum with many photographic artefacts and a large negative archive.

E5 *From Selkirk Market Place travel E along the High Street. Museum is 700m on the right.*

E £

🕐 May–Aug, Fri–Sun, 2pm–4pm.
Other times by arrangement.

Tel 01750 20523
www.scottishbordercamera.org.uk

Smailholm Tower

39 Robert Smail's Printing Works

This restored printing works demonstrates old printing techniques and includes an office, paper store with reconstructed water wheel, and composing and press rooms. Historic items and photographs give an insight into life in Innerleithen.

C5 *Innerleithen High Street, on A72, 6 miles E of Peebles.*

⛪ E ♿ £

🕐 Easter Fri–Mon & Jun–Sept, Thur–Mon, 12 noon–5pm; Sun, 1–5pm

Tel 01896 830206   www.nts.org.uk

40 Selkirk Glass Visitor Centre ★

Visitors can witness glass blowing demonstrations at this paperweight factory.

E5 *On A7, one mile N of Selkirk.*

P WC ♿ ⛪ ☕ ✕ E 🌱 ♿ Free

🕐 Mon–Sat, 9am–5pm; Sun, 11am–5pm. Glass blowing demonstrations, Mon–Sat.

Tel 01750 20954

41 Sir Walter Scott's Courtroom 🏛

Sir Walter Scott served as the Sheriff of Selkirkshire in this nineteenth century former town house and Sheriff Court.

E5 *Market Place, Selkirk town centre.*

E Free

🕐 Apr–Sept, Mon–Fri, 10am–4pm; Sat, 10am–2pm. May–Aug, Sun, 10am–2pm. Oct, Mon–Sat, 1–4pm.

Tel: 01750 20096

42 Smailholm Tower 🏰

A sixteenth century tower house containing an exhibition of tapestries and figures relating to Sir Walter Scott's Minstrelsy of the Scottish Borders.

G5 *Smailholm, six miles W of Kelso off the B6937, on the B6404.*

P ⛪ E £

🕐 Apr–Sept, daily, 9.30am–6.30pm. Oct–Mar, Sat & Sun, 9.30am–4.30pm.

Tel 01573 460365   www.historic-scotland.gov.uk

43 St Abb's Head · 🐦

A high cliff face is the home to a variety of bird colonies including guillemots, kittiwakes, razorbills, shags, puffins and herring gulls, while the surrounding waters form Scotland's first marine nature reserve. Visitors can view nesting seabirds via a camera link in the centre.

J9 *Two miles N of Coldingham off A1107.*

P WC ♿ ☕ E ♟ £

🕐 Reserve: all year round. Centre: Apr–Oct, daily, 10am–5pm (groups by appointment only).

Tel 01890 771443   www.nts.org.uk

44 St Ronan's Well Interpretive Centre 🏛

Wells, exhibition and garden at an historic spa built in 1828; displays describe St Ronan's Border Games and the legend of St Ronan.

C5 *Turn left on Innerleithen High Street, heading E towards Galashiels, and follow signs.*

P WC ♿ E ⛱ 🌱 ♟ Free

🕐 Easter–Oct, Mon–Fri, 10am–1pm & 2–5pm. Apr–Oct, Sat, 10am–1pm & 2–5pm.

Tel 01721 724820

Thirlestane Castle

45 Thirlestane Castle

The historic seat of the Earls and Duke of Lauderdale, Thirlestane features fine seventeenth century ceilings, pictures, furniture, historic toys and country life displays, along with woodland walks and an adventure playground.

E7 *Off A68 at Lauder.*

E ££

Good Friday, Easter Sun & Mon; May, Jun–mid Sep, Sun, Wed–Fri; Jul–Aug, Sun–Fri; Open from 10.30am last admission 2.30pm.

Tel 01578 722430 www.thirlestanecastle.co.uk

46 Three Hills Roman Heritage Centre

An exhibition devoted to life on the Scottish Roman frontier, with artefacts, models and a video, plus guided walks.

E5 *Market Square, Melrose town centre.*

E £

Easter–Oct, daily, 10.30am–4.30pm.

Tel 01896 822651
www.trimontium.freeserve.co.uk

47 Traquair House

The oldest inhabited house in Scotland, Traquair dates back to the twelfth century and has been visited by 27 Scottish monarchs. Visitors can see secret stairs, cellars, books, embroideries and letters from former times, and sample a tipple in the brewery museum. Also on offer is a walled garden, maze and craft workshops.

C5 *On B709, 1.5 miles S of Innerleithen.*

££

House: daily, Easter–Sept, 12 noon–5pm; Jun–Aug, opens 10.30am (last admission 5pm); Oct, 11am–4pm.
Group guided tours outwith these hours can be arranged in advance.

Tel 01896 830323 www.traquair.co.uk

48 Tweeddale Museum and Gallery

Museum of local history and gallery of contemporary art.

C6 *High Street, Peebles.*

E Free

Mon–Fri, 10am–12 noon & 2–5pm.
Easter–Oct, also Sat, 10am–1pm & 2–5pm.

Tel 01721 724820

49 Wrights of Trowmill Ltd

Visitors can tour this working weaving mill and learn how cloth is manufactured.

E3 *Trowmill, Hawick.*

Free

Factory: Mon–Thur, 9am–4pm; Fri, 9am–11.30am.
Shop: Mon–Sat, 9.30am–5pm; Sun, 10am–5pm.

Tel 01450 372555

Threave Castle near Castle Douglas

Rockcliffe near Dalbeattie on the Solway Firth

DUMFRIES AND GALLOWAY

Unaccountably bypassed in some visitors' itineraries around Scotland, Scotland's south-west truly deserves the label of 'undiscovered country'. Like the Scottish Borders it is a substantial area – a full 100 miles (160km) from turning west at Gretna to the former ferry port for Ireland at Portpatrick. Like the Scottish Borders it has plenty of character, especially in its distinctive towns, many of which seem to specialise in painted frontages in picture-postcard pastel shades, such as Kirkcudbright, which are highly attractive to the visitor.

The warming waters of the Gulf Stream (more correctly, the North Atlantic Drift) bring a softness to the Lowland landscape, characterised by a vivid greenness (seen again in Ayrshire) in the fields, where typically belted Galloway cattle wade through the rich grazings. The mild airs also make Galloway gardens thrive, and these are one of the area's specialities, with notably tender species such as cabbage palms and tree ferns to be seen at places like Logan Botanic Garden *(see p32)*.

Beyond the south-facing Solway edge, there is always the sense of the hills as a background. This is where Galloway springs one of its many surprises. There are substantial upland areas, with parts of the Galloway Forest Park, notably around Loch Trool, offering stretches of scenery with heather slopes, birch and pine, which rival the Trossachs in scale and in the harmonious setting of woodland and water. The Merrick, highest mainland point in the Southern Uplands at 843 m (2765 ft), is a day-long expedition on foot from the road-end at Glen Trool.

The rural byways – aside from the hectic dash of the A75 – are ideal territory for relaxed touring (by car or bike). There are coastal loops to explore by way of places like Dundrennan Abbey, where Mary Queen of Scots spent her last night in Scotland, or Rockcliffe with its attractive coastal scenery. Similarly, the upland roads give a real sense of the empty spaces in the hills with their endless blocks of conifers.

Mary Queen of Scots gave her name to one such route, the Queen's Way, a former pilgrims' road on its way to Whithorn. This route twists through the moors and upland plantings between New Galloway and Newton Stewart.

As well as the Stewart queen, other historical figures met while Galloway touring include Robert the Bruce. Two separate inscribed stones – one at Clatteringshaws on the Queens Way, the other at Glen Trool – recall the struggles of the Scots' Wars of Independence. The area's main town of Dumfries is closely associated with Robert Burns, who spent the final years of his life there.

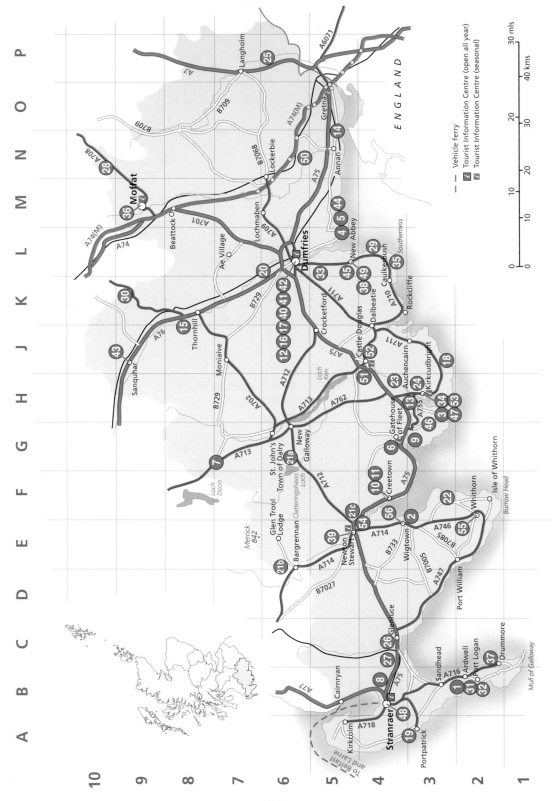

Vehicle ferry
Tourist Information Centre (open all year)
Tourist Information Centre (seasonal)

VISITOR INFORMATION

MAIN TOURIST INFORMATION CENTRE

Dumfries
64 Whitesands
Dumfries DG1 2RS
Tel: 01387 253862
Web: www.dumfriesandgalloway.co.uk
E-mail: info@dgtb.visitscotland.com
Open: all year round

YEAR ROUND TOURIST INFORMATION CENTRE

Stranraer
Harbour Street
Stranraer DG9 7RA
Tel: 01776 702595
Web: www.dumfriesandgalloway.co.uk
E-mail: stranraer@visitscotland.com
Open: all year round

SEASONAL TOURIST INFORMATION CENTRES

Castle Douglas
Tel: 01556 502611
E-mail: castledouglas@
visitscotland.com
Open: Apr–Oct

Gretna Green
Tel: 01461 337834
E-mail: gretnagreen@
visitscotland.com
Open: All year

Moffat
Tel: 01683 220620
E-mail: moffat@
visitscotland.com
Open: Apr–Oct

Gatehouse of Fleet
Tel: 01557 814212
E-mail: gatehouseoffleet@
visitscotland.com
Open: Apr–Oct

Kirkcudbright
Tel: 01557 330494
E-mail: kirkcudbright@
visitscotland.com
Open: Feb–Nov

Newton Stewart
Tel: 01671 402431
E-mail: newtonstewart@
visitscotland.com
Open: Apr–Oct

ADDITIONAL INFORMATION

GENERAL TRAVEL INFORMATION

Traveline Scotland
Tel: 0870 608 2608
Provides timetable information for all public transport in Scotland and the rest of Great Britain.

TRAINS

First ScotRail
Caledonian Chambers
87 Union Street
Glasgow G1 3TA
Tel: Fares & Train Times:
08457 484950
Telesales:
08457 550033
Customer Relations:
0845 601 5929
Web: www.firstscotrail.co.uk
E-mail: scotrail.enquiries
@firstgroup.com

COACH

Scottish Citylink Coaches
Limited
Buchanan Bus Station
Killermont Street
Glasgow G2 3NP
Tel: 08705 505050
Web: www.citylink.co.uk
E-mail: info@citylink.co.uk
Route: Dumfries–Glasgow

BUS

Stagecoach Western Buses
Head Office

Sandgate Bus Station
Ayr KA7 1DD
Tel: 01387 253496
Web: www.stagecoachbus.com
E-mail: customerservices@
stagecoachbus.com
*Routes: operates an extensive
network throughout Dumfries
& Galloway and also
Dumfries–Edinburgh
Dumfries–Glasgow*

McEwan Coach Services
Head Office
22 Whitesands
Dumfries DG1 2RR
Tel: 01387 256533
*Routes: Dumfries–Edinburgh
Dumfries–Kirkcudbright
Dumfries–Stranraer*

FERRIES

P&O Irish Sea
Cairnryan
Stranraer
Wigtownshire DG9 8FR
Tel: 0870 242 4777
Web: www.poirishsea.com
Route: Cairnryan–Larne

Stena Line UK Limited
Charter House
Park Street
Ashford
Kent TN24 8EX
Tel: 08705 707070
Web: www.stenaline.com
E-mail: info.uk@stenaline.com
Route: Stranraer–Belfast

CAR HIRE

Arnold Clark, Dumfries
Tel: 01387 247151
Web: www.arnoldclark.co.uk
E-mail:
central.reservations@arnold
clark.co.uk

GK Group Peugeot Rental,
Stranraer
Tel: 01776 889701

Hertz Rent A Car, Stranraer
Tel: 01776 706622
Web: www.hertz.co.uk

Enterprise Rent a Car,
Unit 2
St Marys Industrial Estate
Dumfries
Tel: 01387 266246

TAXIS

Alba Taxis, Dumfries
Tel: 01387 259555

Cairn Taxis, Dumfries
Tel: 01387 720720

Calside Taxis, Dumfries
Tel: 01387 710710

County Mini Cabs, Dumfries
Tel: 01387 269269

Cresswell Taxis, Dumfries
Tel: 01387 255139

Gibb's Taxis, Sanquhar
Tel: 01659 67176

Thomson Taxis, Annan
Tel: 01461 205020

Star Taxis, Dumfries
Tel: 01387 253336

Warbeck's Taxis, Lockerbie
Tel: 01387 810676

Caerlaverock Castle

1 Ardwell Gardens

Formal and informal gardens surrounding an eighteenth century country house (not open to the public) featuring azaleas, camellias and rhododendrons, a walled garden, summer bedding and herbaceous borders.

B2 *On A716, ten miles S of Stranraer.*

🅿 WC 🌿 🚶 £

🕐 Apr–Sept, daily, 10am–5pm.

Tel 01776 860227

2 Bladnoch Distillery Visitor Centre

Housed in a building dating from 1817, this is Scotland's most southerly distillery. Whisky production recommenced here in 2000. Visitors can take a guided tour, enjoy a dram and hear live music during the summer months.

E3 *One mile S of Wigtown, on A714.*

🅿 WC ☕ 🏛 E AV 🚶 £ £

🕐 All year, Mon–Fri, 9am–5pm.
Jul–Aug, Sat, 11am–5pm;
Sun, 12 noon–5pm.

Tel 01988 402605   www.bladnoch.co.uk

3 Broughton House and Garden 🏆 ❈ 🏛

This eighteenth century house was purchased by artist E A Hornel who added on a gallery and studio. Visitors can see paintings by Hornel and various other artists, plus a collection of Scottish books. The garden, with its Japanese influences, runs down as far as the Dee estuary.

H3 *High Street, Kirkcudbright.*

E £££

🕐 House & Garden: Apr–Jun & Sep–Oct, daily, 12 noon–5pm. Jul–Aug, daily, 10am–5pm. Garden only: Feb–Apr, daily, 11am–4pm.

Tel 01557 330437   www.nts.org.uk

4 Caerlaverock Castle 🏰

Caerlaverock, a striking moated castle, was built over 700 years ago to a unique triangular plan. Demolished then rebuilt between the fourteenth and seventeenth centuries, remaining features of interest include the twin-towered gatehouse and the Nithsdale Lodging, a seventeenth century Renaissance house within the courtyard. Also on offer is a children's adventure park and model seige engines.

L5 *Eight miles SE of Dumfries on the B725.*

🅿 WC ♿ 🌿 🏛 E 🚶 £££

🕐 Apr–Sept, daily, 9.30am–6.30pm.
Oct–Mar, daily, 9.30am–4.30pm.

Tel 01387 770244   www.historic-scotland.gov.uk

5 Caerlaverock Reserve

This reserve, run by the Wildfowl and Wetlands Trust, attracts large numbers of barnacle and pink footed geese, whooper and Bewick's swans and several species of ducks which can all be viewed from hides and observation points.

M5 *Off B725, nine miles SE of Dumfries.*

🅿 WC ♿ 🌿 🏛 🚶 Free

🕐 All year round, daily, 10am–5pm.

Tel 01387 770275   www.swt.org.uk

6 Cardoness Castle 🏰

Ruins of a fifteenth century tower house, offering good views over Fleet Bay.

G4 *One mile SW of Gatehouse of Fleet on the A75.*

🅿 🏛 E 🚶 £

🕐 Apr–Sept, daily, 9.30am–6.30pm;
Oct–Mar, Sat & Sun, 9.30am–4.30pm.

Tel 01557 814427   www.historic-scotland.gov.uk

7 Carsphairn Heritage Centre 🏛

A typical Galloway bothy, purpose-built as a heritage centre, with a permanent display and local themed exhibitions. Leaflets and booklets are available, along with Internet access.

G7 *On A713, 25 miles NW of Castle Douglas.*

🅿 WC ♿ E 🚶 £

Apr–May, Sat & Bank Holidays, 10.30am–5pm;
Sun, 2–5pm.
Jun–Sept, Thur–Tue, 10.30am–5pm; Sun, 2–5pm.
Tel 01644 460653
wwwcarsphairnheritage.co.uk

8 Castle Kennedy Gardens

The gardens, extending for 75 acres, are set
around Lochinch Castle and the ruins of Castle
Kennedy. The terraces and embankments were
built mostly in the eighteenth century, and
among the avenues, wooded garden areas
and formal beds are impressive arrays of
rhododendrons, azaleas and embothriums.
Other features include a Monkey Puzzle
Avenue, and a two-acre circular lily pond.

B4   *Five miles E of Stranraer on A75.*

Easter–Sept, daily, 10am–5pm.
Tel 01776 702024
www.castlekennedygardens.co.uk

9 Cream O' Galloway Visitor Centre ★

This family run farm makes a range of organic
ice cream; as well as watching the production
process, visitors can make use of nature walks
and an extensive adventure playground.

G3   *Signposted on Sandgreen Road,
1.5 miles S of A75 near Gatehouse of Fleet.*

Daily, Feb–Mar, 10am–4pm. Apr–Aug, 10am–6pm.
Sep–Oct, 10am–5pm.
Nov–Mar, Sat–Sun, 10am–4pm. Closed Dec & Jan.
Tel 01557 814040
www.creamogalloway.co.uk

10 Creetown Gem Rock Museum

A worldwide collection of gemstones, crystals,
minerals and fossils including a fossilised
dinosaur egg and meteorites from outer space.
A crystal cave features an ultra-violet display.

F4   *Off A75 at Creetown, 11 miles W of Gatehouse
of Fleet.*

Easter–Sept, daily, 9.30am–5.30pm.
Oct & Nov, 10am–4pm. Dec–Feb, weekends only,
10am–4pm or by appointment.
Tel 01671 820357
www.gemrock.net

11 Creetown Heritage Museum

An exhibition portraying Creetown from its
eighteenth century beginnings as a fishing
hamlet, through the growth and decline of its
granite quarries, to the present day. Displays
include old photographs, village shop, war
memorabilia, information on Wigtown Bay
Nature Reserve and work by local artists.

F4   *St John's Street, Creetown, off the A75.*

Easter–Jun & Sept–Oct, Sun–Tue,
Thur & Fri, 11am–4pm. Jul–Aug, daily, 11am–4pm.
Tel 01671 820471
www.creetown-heritagemuseum.com

12 Crichton Estate

Formerly an Edwardian psychiatric hospital and now
a conservation site, the Crichton estate consists of
34 hectares of parkland and gardens. Attractions
include the Crichton Memorial Church, rock garden
and an arboretum museum which exhibits patients'
artwork dating from 1839 and topical displays.

L6   *South side of Dumfries.*

Free

Museum closed for refurbishment. Please call for
details of re-opening. Cafe: all year round, Mon–Fri,
10am–6pm; Sun, 11am–6pm. Bar: daily, 11am–11pm.
Tel 01387 247544   www.crichton.org.uk

13 David Coulthard Museum

A museum devoted to motor racer David
Coulthard, exhibiting cars, trophies and suits.

H3   *On the A75 at Burnbrae by Twynholm.*

Apr–Oct, daily (closed Wed), 10am–4pm.
Jun–Sept, daily, 10am–4pm.
Tel 01557 860050
www.davidcoulthardmuseum.com

14 Devil's Porridge

An exhibition telling the story of the secret
munitions factory built during the First World War;
devil's porridge refers to the explosive paste that
was mixed by hand and put into shells and bullets.

N5   *St John's Church, Dunedin Road, Eastriggs,
four miles E of Annan on B721.*

Easter, Fri–Mon, 10am–4pm. May–Oct, Mon–Sat,
10am–4pm; Sun, 12 noon–4pm.
Tel 01461 40460   www.devilsporridge.co.uk

15 Drumlanrig Castle Gardens and Country Park

Drumlanrig, the Dumfriesshire home of the Duke of Buccleuch and Queensferry KT, contains fine furniture and paintings including works by Rembrandt and Leonardo da Vinci. Robert the Bruce, Mary Queen of Scots and Robert Burns all have associations with the castle.

K8   *On the A76, four miles N of Thornhill.*

P [WC] & ☕ ⛪ E [AV] 🅿 ⛷ 🚶 [£] ££

⏲ Gardens & Park: Easter–Sept, daily, 11am–5pm.
Castle: May–Sept, daily, 12 noon–4pm.
Closed Fri, May & June.

Tel 01848 330248   www.drumlanrigcastle.org.uk

16 Dumfries and Galloway Aviation Museum

A collection of aircraft and memorabilia set around the original control tower of the former RAF Dumfries. The exhibits include a Gloster Meteor T7, De Havilland Vampire T11 and Supermarine Spitfire Mk11, recovered from the waters of Loch Doon. Also on display are flying clothing from both World Wars, and objects recovered from various crash sites.

L6   *Heathhall Industrial Estate, on A701, NE of Dumfries town centre.*

P [WC] & ☕ ⛪ E [AV] 🅿 ⛷ 🚶 £

⏲ Easter–Oct, weekends, 10am–5pm.
Telephone for other hours in high season.

Tel 01387 251623
www.dumfriesaviationmuseum.com

17 Dumfries Museum and Camera Obscura

A museum telling the history of Dumfries and Galloway, with fossil footprints left by prehistoric animals, wildlife, tools and weapons, carvings and items from a Victorian farm, workshop and home. The camera obscura, installed in 1836, is on the top floor of the old windmill tower and gives a panoramic view of Dumfries and the surrounding countryside. Entry to the museum is free, but there is an admission to the camera obscura.

L6   *The Observatory, Dumfries town centre.*

P [WC] & ⛪ E ⛷ £

⏲ Apr–Sept, Mon–Sat, 10am–5pm; Sun, 2–5pm.
Oct–Mar, Tue–Sat, 10am–1pm & 2–5pm.
Camera Obscura weather permitting.

Tel 01387 253374
www.dumfriesmuseum.demon.co.uk

18 Dundrennan Abbey

The ruins of Dundrennan, a Cistercian abbey founded in 1142 by David I, are set in tranquil surroundings, and include impressive Gothic and Romanesque arches plus the thirteenth century frontage of the chapter house. Mary Queen of Scots spent her last night on Scottish soil here in May 1568.

J3   *On the A711, 6.5 miles SE of Kirkcudbright.*

P & £

⏲ Apr–Sept, daily, 9.30am–6.30pm.
Oct–Mar, Sat & Sun, 9.30am–4.30pm.

Tel 01557 500262
www.historic-scotland.gov.uk

19 Dunskey Garden and Woodland Walks

A restored eighteenth century walled garden, offering a variety of scenic woodland walks.

A3   *Portpatrick on the A77, SW of Stranraer.*

P & ☕ ⛪ ⛷ 🚶 £

⏲ End Mar–Oct, daily, 10am–5pm.
Winter by arrangement.

Tel 01776 810211   www.dunskey.com

20 Ellisland Farm

Robert Burns lived and farmed here between 1788–1791, also writing some of his most famous works including *Tam O'Shanter*.

L6   *On A76 six miles NW of Dumfries.*

P [WC] & ⛪ 🅿 ⛷ £

⏲ Apr–Sept, Mon–Sat, 10am–5pm; Sun, 2–5pm.
Oct–Mar, Tue–Sat, 10am–5pm.

Tel 01387 740426   www.ellislandfarm.co.uk

21 Galloway Forest Park

Stretching for 300 square miles, Galloway Forest Park comprises varying landscapes and wildlife, and offers visitors a number of walks, cycle routes and forest drives.

Tel 01671 402420   www.forestry.gov.uk

21a Clatteringshaws Visitor Centre

Contains displays on local wildlife, history and forest development.

G6   *Six miles W of New Galloway, in Galloway Forest Park.*

P [WC] & ☕ ♨ E ⌐ 🌿 🚶 ♿ Free

🕐 Mar 26–Sept 25, daily, 10.30am–5pm.
Sept 26–Oct 30, daily, 10.30am–4.30pm.

Tel 01644 420285   www.forestry.gov.uk

21b Glen Trool Visitor Centre

Along with walks and cycle routes, visitors
can climb the Merrick, the highest peak in
southern Scotland, and see Bruce's Stone,
a memorial to Robert the Bruce's victory
over the English.

E6   *Bargrennan, off A714,*
twelve miles N of Newton Stewart.

P [WC] & ☕ 🌿 🚶 Free

🕐 Mar 26–Sept 25, daily, 10.30am–5pm.
Sept 26–Oct 30, daily, 10.30am–4.30pm.

Tel 01671 402420   www.forestry.gov.uk

21c Kirroughtree Visitor Centre

Includes a play area and information on trails,
cycle routes and wildlife.

F5   *Off A75 at Palnure,*
three miles E of Newton Stewart.

P [WC] & ☕ ♨ ⌐ 🚶 ♿ Free

🕐 Mar 26–Sept 25, daily, 10.30am–5pm.
Sept 26–Oct 30, daily, 10.30am–4.30pm.
Nov 5–Dec 11, Sat–Sun, 11am–4pm.

Tel 01671 402165   www.forestry.gov.uk

22 Galloway House Gardens ❋

Woodland and formal gardens with various
scenic walks, leading down to the shore and
a sandy bay.

F3   *Garlieston, S of Newton Stewart on the B7004.*

P & ⌐ 🌿 🚶 £

🕐 Mar–Oct, daily, 9am–5pm.

Tel 01988 600680
www.gallowayhousegardens.org.uk

23 Galloway Hydro Visitor Centre ★

Visitors are given guided tours of this 1930s
operational power station. Of interest is a dam,
fish pass, video, office recreated in 30s style and
exhibition on how power is generated.

H4   *At Tongland Power Station, on A711,*
two miles N of Kirkcudbright.

P [WC] & ☕ ♨ E [AV] ⌐ 🌿 🚶 £

🕐 May–Sept, Mon–Fri, 9.30am–5pm.

Tel 01557 330114   www.scottishpower.com

24 Galloway Wildlife Park 🐘

A zoological park and wild animal conservation
centre housing nearly 200 animals including
pandas, monkeys, lynx and Scottish wildcats.
Free activities and guided tours are arranged
for weekends and school holidays.

H3   *One mile E of Kirkcudbright on B727.*

P [WC] & ☕ ♨ ⌐ 🌿 ££

🕐 Mid Mar–Oct, daily, 10am–dusk, last
admission 5pm. Nov–Mar, Sat & Sun, 10am–4pm.

Tel 01557 331645   www.gallowaywildlife.co.uk

25 Gilnockie Tower 🏰

This Border Reivers Tower, standing
at 60 ft high, is associated with Johnie
Armstrong of Gilnockie, and acts as a centre
for the Clan Armstrong. Guided tours take
visitors round all four floors (connected by
a wheel staircase), the museum, Clan Room
and the elaborate parapet.

P6   *Two miles N of Canonbie on A7*
at Hollows village.

P [WC] ♨ 🌿 ££

🕐 Easter–Sept, daily, from 2.30pm;
other times by appointment.

Tel 013873 71876   www.armstrong-clan.co.uk

26 Glenluce Abbey 🏛 ✚

Cistercian abbey founded around 1192, and
set in a peaceful valley alongside a sixteenth
century chapter house. Various items of interest
found at the abbey are also on display.

C4   *Two miles NW of Glenluce village off the A75.*

P & ☕ ♨ E £

🕐 Apr–Sept, daily, 9.30am–6.30pm.
Oct–Mar, Sat & Sun, 9.30am–4.30pm.

Tel 01581 300541   www.historic-scotland.gov.uk

27 Glenwhan Gardens ❋

The effects of the Gulf Stream allow exotic
plants to thrive in these gardens which are
set in a commanding position with views
over Luce Bay and the Mull of Galloway.
New wildflower walk for 2005.

C4   *Dunragit, seven miles E of Stranraer.*

P [WC] & ☕ ✕ ♨ ⌐ 🌿 🚶 ♿ ££

🕐 Mar–Oct, daily, 10am–5.30pm.

Tel 01581 400222
www.glenwhangardens.co.uk

28 Grey Mare's Tail

A dramatic 61 m (200 ft) hillside waterfall.
A visitor centre with CCTV facility gives views
of a peregrine falcon nest site.

N10 *On A708, ten miles NE of Moffat.*

P ⁂ Free

☺ Open all year.
Visitor centre: Jun–Aug, Thur–Mon,12 noon–4pm.

Tel 01556 502575   www.nts.org.uk

29 John Paul Jones Museum

A museum devoted to John Paul Jones,
'The Father of the American Navy', situated
amidst woodland with views over the Solway
and Lake District. The cottage is furnished
in the style of the 1700s and rooms include
a reconstruction of his ship's cabin.

L4 *On Arbigland Estate, near Kirkbean,
13 miles SW of Dumfries on A710.*

P WC ❀ 🏛 E AV 🎪 ⁂ 🏧 £

☺ Apr, May, Jun & Sept, Tue–Sun, 10am–5pm.
Jul–Aug, daily, 10am–5pm.

Tel 01387 880613   www.jpj.demon.co.uk

30 Leadhills and Wanlockhead Railway ★

Visitors can travel on Britain's highest adhesion
railway travelling to 1500ft above sea level
linking Scotland's highest villages, Leadhills and
Wanlockhead, which were at the centre of
Scotland's lead mining industry.

K9 *44 miles south of Glasgow off M74 J13
southbound or J14 northbound. Also from A76 south
of Sanquhar.*

P WC ❀ 🏛 E 🎪 ⁂ £

☺ Easter weekend, May & Aug Bank Holiday.
May–Sep, Sat & Sun. Trains run from 11am–5pm.

Tel 01573 223691   www.leadhillsrailway.co.uk

31 Logan Botanic Garden ❀

Set in a mild climate washed by the Gulf Stream,
Logan contains an excellent collection of exotic
plants. Features include a walled garden with
tree ferns, palms and borders, and a woodland
area with a Gunnera bog.

B2 *Off B7065, 14 miles S of Stranraer.*

P WC ❀ ✕ 🏛 ⁂ 🎪 🏧 ££

☺ Daily, Mar & Oct, 9.30am–6pm.
Apr–Sept, 10am–6pm. Other times by arrangement.

Tel 01776 860231   www.rbge.org.uk

32 Logan Fish Pond Marine Life Centre

A Victorian fish larder containing live sea fish,
set in an adapted rock formation on the shore.
Visitors can also see touch pools, a cave
aquarium and restored bathing hut.

B2 *Fourteen miles S of Stranraer, off B7065,
one mile from Logan Botanic Gardens.*

P 🏛 ⁂ 🎪 ££

☺ Feb–Sept, daily, 10am–5pm. Oct, 10am–4pm.

Tel 01776 860300   www.loganfishpond.co.uk

33 Mabie Farm Park ★

A play farm for children with grass sledging,
water slides, quad bikes, pedal go-karts,
donkey/pony rides and a pets corner.

L5 *Off A710, 4.5 miles S of Dumfries.*

P WC ❀ ☕ 🏛 ⁂ 🎪 ££ 🏧

☺ Mid Mar–Oct, daily, 10am–5pm.

Tel 01387 259666   www.mabiefarm.co.uk

34 MacLellan's Castle

Thomas MacLellan of Bombie, a past provost
of Kirkcudbright, built this town house in 1577.
Although now without a roof, the remains
are well preserved and have retained a host
of interesting architectural features.

H3 *In Kirkcudbright on the A711.*

£

☺ Mid Mar–Sept, daily, 9.30am–6.30pm.

Tel 01557 331856   www.historic-scotland.gov.uk

35 Mersehead Nature Reserve

An RSPB reserve running along the north Solway
shore, and featuring waders, wintering wildfowl
and other wildlife. Visitors can make use of an
information centre, trails and a hide.

L4 *On A710, eighteen miles SW of Dumfries.*

P WC ❀ E 🏃 Free

☺ All year round, daily, dawn to dusk.

Tel 01387 780298   www.rspb.org.uk

36 Moffat Museum

Tells the story of Moffat through the ages,
from early history and geography, to the rise
of the Spa and changing economy of today.

M9 *Moffat town centre, opposite the church gates.*

E Free

🕐 Easter & from Whit weekend–Sept, Thur–Tue,
10.45am–4.15pm. Sun, 1.15–4.15pm.

Tel 01683 220868/220980

---

37 Mull of Galloway Visitor Centre

A visitor centre and lighthouse on Scotland's
most southerly point and one of the country's
most important wildlife sanctuaries. Visitors
can see live video links of seabirds via cameras
mounted on the cliffs or climb the 115 steps
to the top of the lighthouse.

C2   22 miles S of Stranraer off the A716 at Drummore

P WC & ♥ E AV ☼ 林 £

🕐 Visitor Centre: Apr–Sep, daily, 10am–4pm.
Lighthouse: Apr–Sep, Sat–Sun, 10am–3.30pm.

Tel 01776 830682   www.mull-of-galloway.co.uk

38 New Abbey Corn Mill

This eighteenth century water-powered oatmeal
mill has been fully restored, and now provides
demonstrations for visitors during the summer
months. Also on offer are informative displays
and a video on milling.

L5   New Abbey, on the A710, eight miles S of Dumfries.

🏛 E AV 🎫 £

🕐 Easter–Sept, daily, 9.30am–6.30pm.
Oct–Mar, Sat–Wed, 9.30am–4.30pm.

Tel 01387 850260   www.historic-scotland.gov.uk

---

39 Newton Stewart Museum 🏛

A former church now containing a wealth of local
items from past years, illustrating the natural and
social history of Newton Stewart and Galloway.

E5   York Road, Newton Stewart.

P & 🏛 E £

🕐 Easter–Oct, daily, 2–5pm.
Other times by arrangement.

Tel 01671 402472

---

40 Old Bridge House 🏛

The Old Bridge House, a sandstone building
erected in 1660 and built into the Devorgilla
Bridge itself, is the town's oldest house.
Now a museum, visitors can see the family
kitchen, nursery and bedroom of a Victorian
home, along with an early dentist's surgery.

L6   Mill Road, Dumfries town centre,
at end of Devorgilla Bridge.

🏛 E ☼ Free

🕐 Apr–Sept, Mon–Sat, 10am–5pm; Sun, 2–5pm.

Tel 01387 256904

www.dumfriesmuseum.demon.co.uk

---

41 Robert Burns Centre 🏛

Situated in an eighteenth century watermill,
the centre tells the story of Robert Burns'
last years spent in Dumfries. The exhibition
features his original manuscripts and
belongings, and a scale model of Dumfries
in the 1790s. The centre also contains a
cinema, displays of work by local artists
and an audio-visual presentation.

L6   Mill road, west bank of River Nith, Dumfries.

P WC & ✗ 🏛 E AV 🎞 ☼ 🎫 £

🕐 Apr–Sept, Mon–Sat, 10am–8pm; Sun, 2–5pm.
Oct–Mar, Tue–Sat, 10am–1pm & 2–5pm.

Tel 01387 264808

www.dumfriesmuseum.demon.co.uk

---

42 Robert Burns House 🏛

The house where Robert Burns spent the
last few years of his life and died in aged
37 in 1796. Visitors can see his study with
desk and chair, the famous Kilmarnock and
Edinburgh editions of his work, original
manuscripts and various items belonging
to himself and his family.

L6   Burns Street, W of Brooms Road, Dumfries.

🏛 E 🎫 Free

🕐 Apr–Sept, Mon–Sat, 10am–5pm; Sun, 2–5pm.
Oct–Mar, Tue–Sat, 10am–1pm & 2–5pm.

Tel 01387 255297

www.dumfriesmuseum.demon.co.uk

43 Sanquhar Tolbooth Museum

Situated in an eighteenth century tolbooth, the museum tells the story of Sanquhar's famous knitting tradition, local mining, Sanquhar jail, and how the ordinary people of Upper Nithsdale lived and worked.

J9 *High Street, Sanquhar town centre, on A76.*

🏛 E AV Free

🕓 Apr–Sept, Tue–Sat, 10am–1pm & 2–5pm; Sun, 2–5pm.

Tel 01659 50186
www.dumfriesmuseum.demon.co.uk

44 Savings Banks Museum 🏛

Housed in the building where savings banks began in 1810, the museum traces the life of the Rev. Henry Duncan DD, 'Father' of savings banks and restorer of the Ruthwell Cross, a renowned medieval monument. Displays include an international collection of savings boxes, bank notes and coins, and a beeswax model of the Ruthwell Cross.

M5 *Ruthwell on B724 off A75, E of Dumfries.*

P E Free

🕓 Apr–Sept, daily, 10am–1pm & 2–5pm. Oct–Mar, closed Sun & Mon. Group visits by appointment.

Tel 01387 870640
www.lloydstsb.com/savingsbanksmuseum

45 Shambellie House Museum of Costume 🏛

Shambellie, a beautiful Victorian house set in wooded grounds, offers visitors a chance to see period clothes, from the 1850s to the 1950s, in appropriate room settings with accessories, furniture and decorative art. Also houses temporary costume exhibitions.

L5 *New Abbey, seven miles S of Dumfries on A710.*

P WC 🍴 🏛 E 🎋 ⚡ 🖼 £

🕓 Easter–Oct, daily, 10am–5pm.

Tel 01387 850 375   www.nms.ac.uk/costume

46 Steading Gallery and Studio ★

A collection of contemporary paintings by Scottish artists, with changing exhibitions and a sculpture garden.

G3 *On the B727 at Borgue, six miles SW of Kirkcudbright off A755.*

P ♿ 🏛 Free

🕓 End May–End Sept, Apr & Dec, Wed–Sun, 1–5pm.

Tel: 01557 870464
www.artandcraftsouthwestscotland.com

47 Stewartry Museum 🏛

A collection of exhibits relating to the social and natural history of the Stewartry area.

H3 *On the A711 at Kirkcudbright.*

WC 🏛 E 🎋 Free

🕓 All year round, Mon–Sat (times vary); Jun–Sept, Sun, 2–5pm.

Tel 01557 331643
www.dumfriesmuseum.demon.co.uk

48 Stranraer Museum 🏛

Set in the old Town Hall, the museum tells the story of Wigtownshire. On display is one of Scotland's oldest ploughs, plus displays on archaeology, local history and farming.

B4 *George Street, Stranraer town centre.*

WC ♿ 🏛 E Free

🕓 Mon–Fri, 10am–5pm; Sat closed 1–2pm.

Tel 01776 705088
www.dumfriesmuseum.demon.co.uk

49 Sweetheart Abbey ✠

Remains of a late thirteenth century and early fourteenth century Cistercian abbey founded by Devorgilla, Lady of Galloway, in memory of her husband John Balliol. Devorgilla was buried here along with a casket containing her husband's embalmed heart.

L5 *New Abbey, seven miles S of Dumfries on A710.*

🅿 ♿ £

🕐 Apr–Sept, daily, 9.30am–6.30pm.
Oct–Mar, Sat–Wed, 9.30am–4.30pm.

Tel 01387 850397

www.historic-scotland.gov.uk

50 Thomas Carlyle's Birthplace 🌿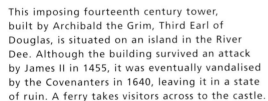

Writer and historian Thomas Carlyle was born here in 1795. The house is furnished in the style of the era, and contains portraits and some of Carlyle's belongings.

N6 *Ecclefechan, off M74, 5.5 miles SE of Lockerbie.*

🅿 ££

🕐 May–Sept, Thu–Mon, 1–5pm.

Tel 01576 300666   www.nts.org.uk

51 Threave Castle 🏰

This imposing fourteenth century tower, built by Archibald the Grim, Third Earl of Douglas, is situated on an island in the River Dee. Although the building survived an attack by James II in 1455, it was eventually vandalised by the Covenanters in 1640, leaving it in a state of ruin. A ferry takes visitors across to the castle.

J4 *On the A75, three miles W of Castle Douglas.*

🅿 🚾 ⛱ £

🕐 Apr–Sept, daily, 9.30am–6.30pm.

Tel 0131 668 8800   www.historic-scotland.gov.uk

52 Threave Garden and Estate 🌿 🌸 🐦

The garden contains herbaceous borders and a heather garden, and produces colourful displays of daffodils in the spring. Visitors can follow various marked trails round the estate, which is also a wildfowl refuge, and view birds from a series of bird hides.

J4 *One mile W of Castle Douglas on the A75.*

🅿 🚾 ☕ ✕ ⛱ ☀ 🚶 £££

🕐 Estate and garden, all year, daily, 9.30am–sunset. Visitor and countryside centres: Apr–Oct, daily, 9.30am–5.30pm. Feb–Mar, Nov–Dec, daily, 10am–4pm.

Tel 01556 502575   www.nts.org.uk

53 Tolbooth Arts Centre

Visitors can learn about the Kirkcudbright artists' colony via an audio-visual presentation and exhibition of paintings by important Kirkcudbright artists.

H3 *Kirkcudbright town centre, on the A711.*

🚾 ♿ ☕ ⛱ E 📽 £

🕐 May–Sept, Mon–Sat, 11am–5pm; Sun, 2–5pm. July–Aug, Mon–Sun, 10am–5pm; Sun, 2–5pm. Oct–Apr, Mon–Sat, 11am–4pm; Sun, 2–5pm.

Tel 01557 331556

www.dumfriesmuseum.demon.co.uk

54 Tropic House ★

Visitors can see free flying exotic butterflies in a covered tropical setting of plants and ponds, plus a display of insect eating plants.

E4 *One mile S of Newton Stewart on A714.*

🅿 🚾 ♿ ☕ ⛱ E ⛱ 🚶 £

🕐 Jul–Sept, daily, 10am–7pm. Oct–Mar, 11am–3pm. Easter–Jun, 10am–5pm.

Tel 01671 404050   www.tropichouse.co.uk

55 Whithorn Priory and the Monreith Cross

One of the earliest Christian sites, Whithorn was founded by St Ninian in the fifth/sixth century; a Premonstratensian priory was added in the twelfth century. A museum houses various Christian carvings including the Latinus stone, the earliest Christian memorial in Scotland, and the Monreith Cross, carved here around the eleventh century.

F2 *Whithorn, on the A746, S of Newton Stewart.*

🚾 ♿ ☕ ⛱ E 📽 ⛱ 🚶 £

🕐 Apr–Oct, daily, 10.30am–5pm.

Tel 01988 500508   www.historic-scotland.gov.uk

56 Wigtown: Scotland's Book Town ★

Hailed as Scotland's only national 'book town'. Wigtown contains around twenty shops, selling a huge variety of new and antiquarian titles. For information on book readings, festivals and fairs, contact the Book Town Office on the number below.

E4 *On A714, eight miles S of Newton Stewart.*

🕐 Book shops open all year round, though some have restricted hours in Jan & Feb.

Tel 01988 402036

www.wigtown-booktown.co.uk

AYRSHIRE AND ARRAN

Down in the south-west corner of Scotland, Galloway becomes Ayrshire. At first, the same sense prevails of a land of bare hills, curlew-haunted moorland and dark conifer woods, all tucked away and out of the mainstream. Explore the lonely valleys of Carrick and such places as Barr, tucked in the woodlands by the River Stinchar, to sample a decidedly unhurried quality.

Further north the ambience changes, the cliff-girt coastline of Galloway gradually giving way to the gentler shores to the north. The tang of the sea is in the air, the island-hump of Ailsa Craig is prominent offshore, while the Firth of Clyde is punctuated by yacht sails, at least at weekends. Inland, the hawthorn hedges and glossy dairy cattle are reminders of the prosperous farmland once worked by a ploughman poet whose fame went round the world. Down by the sea, parts of Ayrshire seem to be a chain of well manicured golf courses, as the old county falls gradually into the sway of Glasgow and the Clydeside conurbation (as geographers would call it). Hereabouts, there are still hints of the Clyde coast's heyday as a former holiday playground for Scotland's largest city.

The leisure resort air is even more prevalent on the island of Arran. Its distinctive profile, whose highest point is the peak of Goat Fell, is sometimes called 'the sleeping warrior'. The island itself is referred to as 'Scotland in miniature' as the Highland Boundary Fault runs through it.

Travel around Ayrshire and Arran and there are Vikings to be encountered at Largs – at least in the local attraction Vikingar! which tells the story of the Battle of Largs in 1263 (see p45). This event broke the power of the Scandinavian invaders in this part of Scotland. Robert Burns prevails around Ayr, notably at Alloway, where his birthplace cottage is still a place of pilgrimage and, like several other venues, is in the Burns National Heritage Park (see p42). At Mauchline, perched on a broad ridge east of Ayr, he spent his early married life, and his house has been preserved in period. Even US President Roosevelt has a presence in this part of Scotland: for his war-time leadership, a flat was given to him on behalf of the Scottish people, in the sumptuous Culzean Castle, on the coast south of Ayr. Along with its country park, Culzean is the National Trust for Scotland's most popular attraction (see p42).

Machrie Moor Stone Circle, Isle of Arran

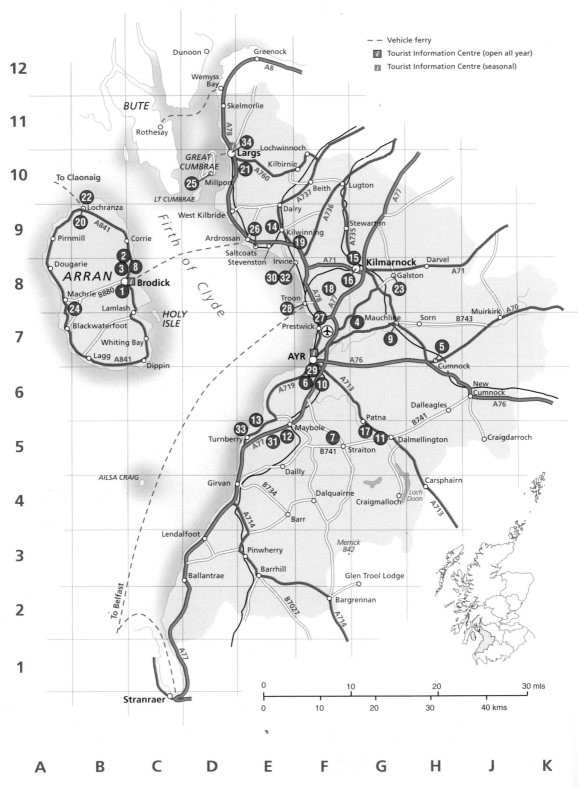

Vehicle ferry
Tourist Information Centre (open all year)
Tourist Information Centre (seasonal)

Dunoon
Greenock
Wemyss Bay
A8
Skelmorlie
BUTE
Rothesay
Lochwinnoch
Largs
GREAT CUMBRAE
Kilbirnie
Millport
LT CUMBRAE
Beith
Lugton
A737
Dalry
A760
Stewarton
A736
A735
A77
To Claonaig
Lochranza
A841
West Kilbride
Kilwinning
Corrie
Ardrossan
Pirnmill
Saltcoats
Stevenston
Irvine
Dougarie
ARRAN
Brodick
A71
Kilmarnock
Darvel
Machrie B880
Galston
A71
Lamlash
HOLY ISLE
Troon
Muirkirk
A70
Blackwaterfoot
Prestwick
A78
A77
Mauchline
Sorn
B743
Whiting Bay
Lagg
A841
Dippin
AYR
A76
Cumnock
Firth of Clyde
New Cumnock
A719
A713
A76
AILSA CRAIG
Patna
Dalleagles
B741
Craigdarroch
Turnberry
Maybole
Straiton
Dalmellington
Craigmalloch
To Belfast
A77
A71
B741
Dailly
Carsphairn
Girvan
B734
Dalquairne
Loch Doon
A713
Barr
Lendalfoot
A714
Merrick 842
Pinwherry
Ballantrae
Barrhill
Glen Trool Lodge
B7027
Bargrennan
A714
Stranraer

0   10   20   30 mls
0   10   20   30   40 kms

A   B   C   D   E   F   G   H   J   K

VISITOR INFORMATION

MAIN TOURIST INFORMATION CENTRES

Ayr
22 Sandgate
Ayr
Ayrshire KA7 1BW
Tel: 01292 678100
Web: www.ayrshire-arran.com
E-mail: info@ayrshire-arran.com
Open: all year round

Brodick
The Pier
Brodick
Isle of Arran KA27 8AU
Tel: 01292 678100
Web: www.ayrshire-arran.com
E-mail: info@ayrshire-arran.com
Open: all year round

General Enquiries
Ayrshire & Arran
15 Skye Road
Prestwick KA9 2TA
Tel: 01292 678100
Web: www.ayrshire-arran.com
E-mail: info@ayrshire-arran.com

SEASONAL TOURIST INFORMATION CENTRE

Largs
KA30 8BQ
Tel: 01292 678100
E-mail: info@ayrshire-arran.com
Open: Apr–Oct

ADDITIONAL INFORMATION

GENERAL TRAVEL INFORMATION
Traveline Scotland
Tel: 0870 608 2608
Provides timetable information for all public transport in Scotland and the rest of Great Britain.

AIR TRAVEL
Glasgow Prestwick International Airport, Aviation House
Prestwick
Ayrshire KA9 2PL
Tel: 01292 511000 Web: www.gpia.co.uk E-mail: mcphersong@gpia.co.uk

TRAINS

First ScotRail
Caledonian Chambers
87 Union Street
Glasgow G1 3TA
Tel: Fares & Train Times:
08457 484950
Telesales: 08457 550033
Customer Relations:
0845 601 5929
Web: www.firstscotrail.co.uk
E-mail: scotrail.enquiries
@firstgroup.com

BUS

Stagecoach Western Buses
Head Office
Sandgate Bus Station
Ayr KA7 1DD
Tel: 01292 613700
Web: www.stagecoachbus.com
E-mail:
customerservices@ssne.co.uk
*Routes: operates an extensive
network throughout Ayrshire
& Arran*

FERRIES

Seacat Scotland
Sea Containers Ferries Scotland
Limited
Seacat Terminal
Donegal Quay
Belfast BT1 3AL
Tel: 08705 523523
Web: www.steam-packet.com
E-mail: belfast.reservations@
seacontainers.com
Route: Troon–Belfast

Inter island ferries

Caledonian MacBrayne
The Ferry Terminal
Gourock PA19 1QP
Tel: Enquiries: 01475 650100
Vehicle Reservations:
08705 650000
Brochure Hotline:
01475 650288
Web: www.calmac.co.uk
*Routes: Lochranza (Arran)–
Claonaig (Kintyre)
Ardrossan–Brodick (Arran)
Largs–Cumbrae Slip*

CAR HIRE

Arran Transport Limited
Brodick, Isle of Arran
Tel: 01770 302121
E-mail: ukfilter@lineone.net

Arnold Clark Car Rental, Ayr
Tel: 01292 270037
Web: www.arnoldclark.co.uk

Compass Self Drive, Kilmarnock
Tel: 01563 537799
E-mail: enquiries@
compass-selfdrive.co.uk

Eurodrive Vehicle Rental, Ayr
Tel: 01292 619192

Kerr & Smith Limited,
Cumnock
Tel: 01290 422440
Web: www.kerrandsmith.co.uk
E-mail:
cumnock@kerrandsmith.co.uk

Whiting Bay Garage
Whiting Bay, Isle of Arran
Tel: 01770 700345

TAXIS

Streamline Taxis, Prestwick
Tel: 01292 280000

Brisbane Taxis, Largs
Tel: 01475 689990

Cowan's Taxis, Ayr
Tel: 01292 591352

Eddie's Cabs, West Kilbride
Tel: 01294 822812

Gribben's Central Taxis, Ayr
Tel: 01292 267655

Herbie's Taxis, Largs
Tel: 01475 689689

Premier Taxis, Saltcoats
Tel: 01294 474747

West Coast Taxis, Saltcoats
Tel: 01294 605605

Whiting Bay Garage
Tel: 01770 700345

ARRAN

The island of Arran is reached by regular ferry services from Ardrossan in Ayrshire, though a summer-only service also links it to Kintyre from Lochranza in the north. The ridges, whose highest point is Goat Fell, gives the northern half of the island a Highland ambience. The high granite mass is much cut into by ancient glacier troughs, giving poor acid soils and moorlands, as well as many crags and ridges, and a narrow coastal strip.

The southern end of Arran is gentler, with sheep runs, as well as the regular enclosed farmland, though the exposure to southerly gales up the Firth gives the trees there a wind-carved look. More sheltered and extensive woodlands can be found on the east coast, especially around the main settlement of Brodick, which straggles along the bay with its promenade and beach.

Most of the settlement on Arran is on the coastal strip, at places like Lochranza, where the shallows of the sea loch, guarded by the tower of Lochranza Castle, spill into the lower reaches of a glen created by glaciers long ago.

1 Arran Aromatics ★

Visitors can see the preparation of toiletries and candles, along with the production and tasting of various cheeses.

C8 *One mile from Brodick ferry terminal on A841.*

P WC & ☕ ✕ ⊞ ☼ Free

⏲ Daily, Mar–Sept, 9.30am–5.30pm.
Oct–Feb, daily, 9.30am–5pm.

Tel 01770 302595   www.arranaromatics.com

2 Arran Brewery ★

Arran's first working commercial brewery, established in 2000, lets visitors see the processes, ingredients used and taste the final product of this award-winning beer.

B8 *Two miles NE of Brodick on A841, Arran.*

P & ⊞ ⊞ ⊼ ☼ £

⏲ Summer: Mon–Sat, 10am–5pm;
Sun, 12.30pm–5pm.
Winter: Wed–Mon, 10am–3.30pm.

Tel 01770 302353   www.arranbrewery.com

3 Arran Heritage Museum 🏛

A museum featuring local social history, archaeology and geology, plus hands-on exhibits suitable for children. Special events and demonstrations are held on Sundays (see local press or check website for details).

C8 *On A841 coast road at Rosaburn, N of Brodick.*

P WC & ☕ ⊞ E AV ⊼ ☼ £

⏲ Apr–Oct, daily, 10.30am–4.30pm.

Tel 01770 302636   www.arranmuseum.co.uk

4 Bachelors' Club 👤 🏛

Robert Burns spent time in this seventeenth century house attending a debating club, dancing lessons and his initiation into Freemasonry.

G7 *Tarbolton, off A719, on B730,*
eight miles NE of Ayr.

££

⏲ Apr–Sept, Fri–Tue, 1–5pm. Last admission 4.30pm.

Tel 01292 541940   www.nts.org.uk

Brodick Castle, Garden and Country Park

5 Baird Institute

Cumnock Pottery and Mauchline Boxware feature strongly at this museum, along with an exhibition on Keir Hardie, founder of the Labour Party, who spent many years in Cumnock.

H7 *Lugar Street, Cumnock, 15 miles E of Ayr on A70.*

E Free

⊕ All year round, Thur–Sat, 11am–5pm.

Tel 01290 421701   www.east-ayrshire.gov.uk

6 Belleisle Estate and Garden

An estate comprising of golf courses, parkland and gardens plus an aviary, pets and deer park.

F6 *Alloway, two miles S of Ayr on the B77024.*

🅿 ♿ 🚻 🍴 🚶 Free

⊕ Easter–Oct, 8am–8pm. Nov–Mar, 8am–4.15pm. Tearoom: summer only.

Tel 01292 441025   www.south-ayrshire.gov.uk

7 Blairquhan

This private regency house, designed by William Burns for Sir David Hunter Blair, contains a collection of fine furniture and paintings, particularly of the Scottish Colourists. Visitors can also make use of the extensive grounds with walks, woodland and a walled garden.

F5 *Head S of Maybole on B7023; turn off on B741 and head E for three miles.*

🅿 🚻 ♿ 🛖 🌿 🚶 ♿

⊕ Mid Jul–mid Aug, daily (except Mon), 1.30–4.15pm.

Tel 01655 770239

www.blairquhan.co.uk

8 Brodick Castle, Garden and Country Park

This sandstone castle, built on the site of a Viking fortress, has parts dating from the thirteenth century; contents include silver, porcelain, paintings and sports trophies. The gardens contain a rhododendron collection and an array of exotic plants, while various woodland walks pass by gorges, ponds and the coast. Other facilities include a countryside centre, nature display room and adventure playground.

C8 *Two miles NE of Brodick on A841, Arran.*

🅿 🚻 ♿ 🛖 ✕ 🏛 🍴 🚶 ♿ £££

⊕ Castle: Apr–Sep, daily, 11am–4.30pm. Oct, daily, 11am–3.30pm (last entry 30 mins before closing), telephone for winter hours. Reception Centre & Shop: Apr–Oct, daily, 10am–4.30pm. Garden & country park: all year round, daily, 9.30am–sunset.

Tel 01770 302202   www.nts.org.uk

Culzean Castle and Country Park

9 Burns House Museum

Along with a Burns room and exhibition, visitors can see a curling display and collection of Mauchline Boxware.

G7 *Mauchline, 12 miles NE of Ayr on B743.*

P WC ⛪ E AV ⊓ Free

🕑 Easter-Oct, Tue–Sat, 10am–5pm.

Tel 01290 550045   www.east-ayrshire.gov.uk

10 Burns National Heritage Park

Gives an insight into the life and works of Robert Burns. The park consists of the cottage where Burns was born, a museum, Tam o' Shanter Experience Visitor Centre and the Burns Monument. Enthusiasts of the poem *Tam o' Shanter* can also see Brig o'Doon, a fifteenth century arch bridge, and Kirk Alloway, a ruined church, both of which feature in the poem.

F6 *Two miles S of Ayr, on A77 Glasgow/Stranraer road.*

P WC ♿ ⛴ ✗ ⛪ E AV ♨ £ ££

🕑 Burns Cottage, Museum and the Tam O'Shanter Experience: Apr–Sept, 10am–5.30pm. Oct–Mar, 10am–5pm (last entry 1 hour before closing).

Tel: 01292 443700   www.burnsheritagepark.com

11 Cathcartston Visitor Centre

Old photographs and maps of the Doon valley feature prominently at this museum dedicated to local history.

G5 *Cathcartston near Dalmellington; turn off the A713 to the B741 SE of Ayr.*

P E Free

🕑 All year, Thur–Sat, 11am–5pm.

Tel 01292 550633   www.east-ayrshire.gov.uk

12 Crossraguel Abbey

Founded in the thirteenth century, then destroyed during the Wars of Independence, the current remains of this Cluniac monastery are the result of rebuilding over the following three hundred years. The ruins, which are very well preserved, comprise of a church, cloister, chapter house and domestic premises.

E5 *Two miles S of Maybole on the A77.*

P WC E ⊓ £

🕑 Apr–Sept, daily, 9.30am–6.30pm.

Tel 01655 883113   www.historic-scotland.gov.uk

13 Culzean Castle and Country Park

This once simple fortified tower house, set on clifftops overlooking the Firth of Clyde, was transformed by Robert Adam into a stylish eighteenth century residence for David Kennedy,

10th Earl of Cassillis. Along with fine paintings and furniture, visitors can see a weaponry display and Georgian-style kitchen. The country park, created in 1969, and Scotland's first, consists of miles of extensive woodland, a walled garden, deer park, swan pond and adventure park.

E5 *Twelve miles S of Ayr on A719.*

P WC & ♥ ✕ ⊞ E 🪑 🎿 🥾 ££

🕑 Castle: Apr–Oct, daily, 10.30am–5pm (last admisssion 4pm). Visitor Centre: Apr–Oct, daily, 9.30am–5.30pm. Nov–Mar, Sat–Sun, 11am–4pm. Walled Garden: closes at 4pm. Country Park: all year, daily, 9.30am–sunset.

Tel 01655 884455 www.culzeancastle.net

---

14 Dalgarven Mill and Museum 🏛

Adjacent to Dalgarven, a restored water mill set by the river Garnock, is a museum dedicated to Ayrshire country life, with rural tools, photographs and artefacts. Also on display are costumes dating from the eighteenth century, with fine examples of Ayrshire whitework.

E9 *Off the A738, on the A737 between Dalry and Kilwinning.*

P WC & ♥ E ££

🕑 Easter–Oct, Tue–Sun, 10am–5pm. Nov–Easter, Tue–Fri, 10am–4pm; Sat & Sun, 10am–5pm.

Tel 01294 552448 www.dalgarvenmill.org.uk

---

15 Dean Castle and Country Park 🏰 ♣

The stronghold of the Boyds of Kilmarnock for 400 years, Dean Castle now houses collections of arms and armour, musical instruments and Burns manuscripts. On offer in the country park is a visitor centre with Discovery Room, an adventure playground, riding centre, rare breeds and children's area with ducks, geese and birds.

G8 *Twenty minute walk from Kilmarnock Railway Station; signposted from A77, S of Glasgow.*

P ♥ E 🥾 Free

🕑 Castle: Telephone for entry details. Visitor Centre: Apr–Sept, 12 noon–5pm. Oct–Mar, 12 noon–4pm.

Tel 01563 522702 www.deancastle.com

---

16 Dick Institute 🏛

Temporary and permanent exhibitions cover two floors of this Victorian building. Fine art, social and natural history collections are upstairs, while galleries downstairs house temporary arts and crafts displays.

G8 *Elmbank Avenue, Kilmarnock town centre.*

P WC & ⊞ E Free

🕑 All year, Tue–Sat, 11am–5pm.

Tel 01563 554343

---

17 Dunaskin Heritage Centre 🚂 🏛

Visitors can take guided tours of the Craigton Mine Experience, and a 1914 ironworker's cottage, and try two self-guided walks with electronic hand-held wand. Also on offer is an audio-visual presentation, interactive computer quiz and the tallest playtower in Britain. During the summer months, the Ayrshire Railway Preservation Group operate a working steam train on most Sundays in July and August.

G5 *Twelve miles S of Ayr on A713.*

P WC & ♥ ✕ ⊞ E AV 🪑 🎿 🥾 ££

🕑 Easter–Oct, daily, 10am–5pm.

Tel 01292 531144 www.dunaskin.co.uk

---

18 Dundonald Castle

This imposing fourteenth century tower house, built by Robert II, stands by the village of Dundonald, and incorporates parts of an earlier castle destroyed during the Wars of Independence.

F8 *Dundonald, on B730, between A77 and A759, SW of Kilmarnock.*

P WC ♥ ⊞ E £

🕑 Apr–Sept, daily, 10am–5pm.

Tel 01563 850201 www.historic-scotland.gov.uk

---

19 Eglinton Country Park ♣

Leisure and recreational facilities include fishing, horse riding, cycling and walking routes, play areas and a ranger-led programme of events. An interpretation hall tells the story of the estate, once the seat of the Montgomery family, and site of the Eglinton Tournament.

F9 *Off the Eglinton Interchange, on A76 between Irvine and Kilwinning.*

P WC & ♥ ⊞ E 🪑 🥾 Free

🕑 Park: all year round, dawn–dusk. Visitor Centre: Apr–Oct, daily, 10am–4.30pm.

Tel 01294 551776

20 Isle of Arran Distillery

Visitors can learn how the Isle of Arran single malt whisky is produced via a tour, audio-visual presentation and exhibition.

B9 *Lochranza, fourteen miles NW of Brodick on A841, Arran.*

P WC & ♥ ✗ 🏛 E AV ⛱ ☼ 🎫 ££

⊕ All year, daily (tours every hour on the half hour from 10.30am). Shop: 10am–6pm. Restaurant: 10am–5pm.

Tel 01770 830264   www.arranwhisky.com

21 Kelburn Castle and Country Park 🏰 ♣

Kelburn Castle, home of the Earls of Glasgow, is surrounded by extensive parkland; activities include walks, horse riding, ranger's workshop, pets' corner, play areas and the Secret Forest adventure area.

E10 *Off A78, two miles S of Largs.*

P WC ✗ 🏛 E AV ⛱ ☼ 🎫 ££

⊕ Easter–Oct, daily, 10am–6pm. Castle: July–mid Sept.

Tel 01475 568685
www.kelburncountrycentre.com

22 Lochranza Castle 🏛 🏰

A tower house, thought to be a sixteenth century version of an earlier building.

B10 *Off the A841, north coast of Arran.*

P Free

⊕ Key available for the property at the following times: Apr–Sept, daily, 9.30am–6.30pm.

Tel 0131 668 8800
www.historic-scotland.gov.uk

23 Loudoun Castle Theme Park ♣

Stretching for 500 acres, the theme park offers a selection of exciting rides including a roller coaster, carousel, Drop Zone, road trains, games, karting, pony rides and woodland walks.

G8 *Galston on the A719, between the A77 and A71.*

P WC & ♥ ✗ 🏛 ⛱ ☼ 🎫 ££

⊕ Easter–Sept, daily, 10am–5pm (times may change, please telephone for details).

Tel 01563 822296   www.loudouncastle.co.uk

24 Machrie Moor Stone Circles 🏛 🗿

An important Bronze Age site featuring the remains of five stone circles. A short distance northwards lie the Moss Farm Road stone circle and cairn, while about a mile north again is the Auchagallon stone circle.

A8 *Near Tormore, off A841, W side of Arran; 1.5 mile walk to site.*

Free

⊕ All year round.

Tel 0131 668 8800   www.historic-scotland.gov.uk

25 Museum of the Cumbraes 🏛

Visitors can learn about life on the Cumbraes via displays of old photographs and artefacts.

D10 *Millport, on B899, on the Isle of Cumbrae; a ferry runs from Largs.*

WC & E ⛱ Free

⊕ Thur–Mon, 10am–5pm. Closed for lunch, 1–2pm.

Tel 01475 531191   www.north-ayrshire.gov.uk

26 North Ayrshire Museum 🏛

A museum covering the history of North Ayrshire with displays on archaeology, transport and popular culture. There is also a section showing the maritime history of Ardrossan and a reconstruction of an Ayrshire cottage interior.

E9 *Manse Street, in Saltcoats town centre.*

P WC 🏛 E Free

⊕ Mon–Sat, 10am–1pm & 2–5pm. Closed Wed.

Tel 01294 464174
www.northayrshiremuseums.org.uk

27 Prestwick Golf Course 🏴

Prestwick Golf Club was the birthplace of the Open Championship and, therefore, of professional tournament golf. The land on which the club built its first formal course had originally been granted to the men of Prestwick by King Robert the Bruce of Scotland for services rendered during the Wars of Independence.

F7 *Off A79, adjacent to Prestwick airport.*

🅿 ⓦ ♿ ✕ 🏛 💷

🕐 Booking advisable. Saturday members only. Phone to book on Sundays.

Tel 01292 477404   www.prestwickgc.co.uk

28 Royal Troon Golf Course

Lying at the southern end of the Ayrshire coastline, Royal Troon Golf Club was founded in 1878, evolving into one of the toughest on the Open rota. It boasts not only the longest hole in Open Championship golf but the shortest too, the famous 8th hole known as the 'Postage Stamp'.

F8 *Off A77, 35 miles W of Glasgow.*

🅿 ⓦ ✕ 🏛 💷

🕐 Booking is essential.

Tel 01292 311555   www.royaltroon.co.uk

29 Rozelle House and Gardens

The house, built in the eighteenth century, contains various art exhibits including a series of paintings by Alexander Goudie depicting scenes from Burns' *Tam o' Shanter*. A converted stable block houses changing exhibitions, while the grounds offer woodland walks and a sculpture area with pieces by Henry Moore.

F7 *Monument Road, 2.5 miles from centre of Ayr on the A79.*

🅿 ⓦ 🍴 🏛 E 🪑 ⚇ 🧗 💷 Free

🕐 All year round, Mon–Sat, 10am–5pm; Sun (Apr–Oct only), 2–5pm.

Tel 01292 445447   www.goudie.co.uk

30 Scottish Maritime Museum

A museum focusing on Scotland's seafaring history; along with various exhibits, visitors can see the shipyard worker's tenement flat and historic vessels moored at the harbour.

F8 *Harbourside, Irvine.*

🅿 ⓦ ♿ 🍴 ✕ 🏛 E 🪑 ⚇ £

🕐 Apr–Oct, 10am–5pm. Last admission 4pm.

Tel 01294 278283
www.scottishmaritimemuseum.org

31 Souter Johnnie's Cottage

John Davidson, who featured in Burns' *Tam o' Shanter* as Souter Johnnie, once lived here. Visitors can see furniture of the era, Burns relics, a shoemaker's (souter's) work area and characters from the poem modelled in stone.

E5 *Kirkoswald, on A77, eight miles NE of Girvan.*

🅿 ♿ ££

🕐 Apr–Sept, Fri–Tue, 11.30am–5pm.

Tel 01655 760603   www.nts.org.uk

32 The Vennel Gallery

Adjacent to the Vennel Gallery, with its exhibitions of contemporary art and crafts, is the Heckling Shop where Robert Burns worked and the Lodging House where he lived in 1781.

F8 *Glasgow Vennel, off Townhead, Irvine.*

♿ 🏛 E 📺 £

🕐 Fri–Sun, 10am–1pm & 2–5pm. Wheelchair access to the Gallery and Heckling Shop only.

Tel 01294 275059
www.northayrshiremuseums.org.uk

33 Turnberry Golf Course

Turnberry has hosted both the Amateur Championship and the Open Championship three times apiece. The most famous hole on the Ailsa Course is the 9th, a par-4 known as 'Bruce's Castle' after the nearby remains of a fortress where Scottish king, Robert the Bruce, is said to have sheltered during one of his campaigns.

E5 *Off A77, N of Girvan.*

🅿 ⓦ ♿ ✕ 🏛 E

🕐 Apr–Sept, daily, 7am–7pm. Oct–Mar, daily, 8am–5pm.

Tel 01655 331000   www.turnberry.co.uk

34 Vikingar!

The story of the Vikings in Scotland is brought to life via a series of multi-media exhibits and narrators in full Viking costume.

D10 *Greenock Road, Largs on the A78.*

🅿 ⓦ ♿ 🍴 ✕ 🏛 E 📺 💷 ££

🕐 Daily, Apr–Sept, 10.30am–5pm. Oct–Mar, 10.30am–3.30pm. Nov & Feb, weekends, 10.30am–3.30pm.

Tel 01475 689777
www.vikingar.co.uk

Glasgow University

GLASGOW AND CLYDE VALLEY

As Scotland's largest city and one which had been formerly labelled 'Workshop of the Western World', Glasgow's re-birth as a kind of post-industrial centre has been spectacular. Now it has an image as a happening place with what some commentators describe as its own café society, all helped by its reputation for having friendly locals.

In addition, it is a major retail centre, having never really lost its commercial and entrepreneurial skills. The so-called 'tobacco lords' – the enterprising Glasgow merchants who traded with the Americas – gave way to later Victorian business folk who built the exuberant nineteenth-century architecture which survives in downtown Glasgow today. The Merchant City still thrives in the grid of streets east of Buchanan Street and contributes to the city's sense of vibrancy.

Glasgow artistic and cultural life also thrives and it is the headquarters for many of Scotland's main cultural organisations. The Museum and Art Gallery at Kelvingrove *(see p57)* is a reminder that there has always been a strong cultural strand in the life of the city. (The Hunterian Museum close to Kelvingrove was the first public museum in Scotland.) Now these old-established places are just part of a huge range of cultural and heritage attractions in the city.

Its Gallery of Modern Art, *(see p54)* the former Stirling's Library, a handsome neoclassical building, stands right in the heart of the city. The Burrell Collection in Pollok Park *(see p52)* houses the eclectic collection of a wealthy shipowner, who gifted his life's work to the city. The St Mungo Museum of Religious Life and Art *(see p60)* offers a thought provoking journey through universal themes of life and religion.

As an example of a heritage attraction, The Tall Ship at Glasgow Harbour *(see p61)* was built with local steel on the River Clyde in 1896. The Glenlee represented the final development of the cargo-carrying sailing ship – the kind of 'Clyde-built' vessel which contributed to the city's trade and wealth. Close by, the new Science Centre is a reminder of the future and offers a chance of discovering about modern science through interactive exhibits.

The Glasgow experience also includes exploring the River Clyde. As the river approaches the old town of Lanark, in the wooded setting above a rocky gorge stands New Lanark, a former model textile village *(see p59)*. The story of the founding of this unique social experiment is told on site. On the other side of Glasgow, in the major town of Paisley, the Abbey here was founded in the twelfth century. Also worth visiting is the Paisley Museum and Art Gallery, portraying the origin of the distinctively patterned Paisley shawl.

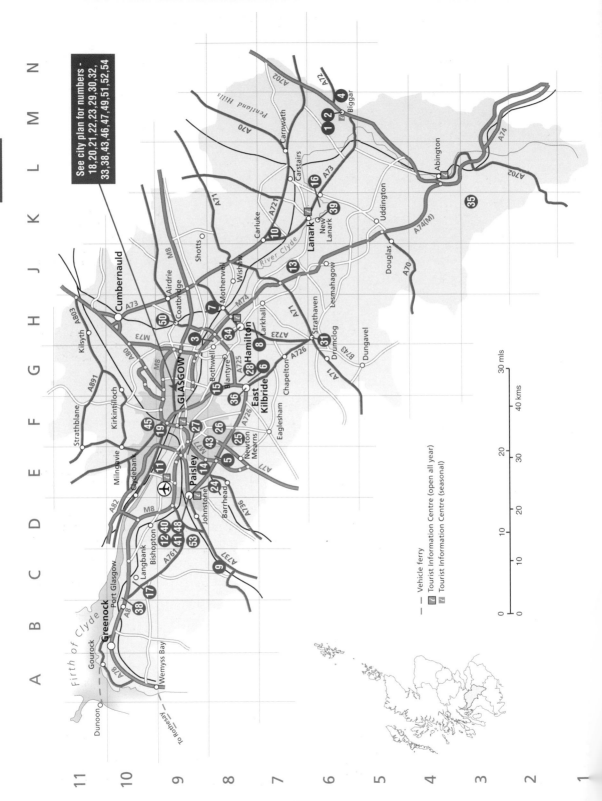

See city plan for numbers -
18, 20, 21, 22, 23, 29, 30, 32,
33, 38, 43, 46, 47, 49, 51, 52, 54

Firth of Clyde

Pentland Hills

River Clyde

GLASGOW

Cumbernauld

Paisley

Greenock

Hamilton

East Kilbride

Lanark

Biggar

Abington

Dunoon
Gourock
Wemyss Bay
To Rothesay
Port Glasgow
Langbank
Bishopton
Johnstone
Barrhead
Clydebank
Milngavie
Strathblane
Kilsyth
Kirkintilloch
Airdrie
Coatbridge
Bothwell
Blantyre
Newton Mearns
Eaglesham
Chapelton
Strathaven
Drumclog
Dungavel
Lesmahagow
Douglas
Uddingston
New Lanark
Carluke
Carstairs
Carnwath
Shotts
Wishaw
Motherwell
Larkhall

Vehicle ferry
Tourist Information Centre (open all year)
Tourist Information Centre (seasonal)

30 mls
40 kms

A702
A72
A73
A74
A74(M)
A70
A71
A721
A723
A726
A71
B743
A73
A70
M8
M73
M74
M77
A803
A891
A82
A80
A761
A737
A736
A726
A725
A78
A8

VISITOR INFORMATION

MAIN TOURIST INFORMATION CENTRE

Glasgow
11 George Square
Glasgow
G2 1DY
Tel: 0141 204 4400
Web: www.seeglasgow.com
E-mail: enquiries@seeglasgow.com
Open: all year round

Abington
Welcome Break
Motorway Service Area
M74, Junction 13
Abington ML12 6RG
Tel: 01864 502436
E-mail: abington@seeglasgow.com
Open: all year round

Glasgow Airport
Tourist Information Desk
Glasgow International Airport
Paisley PA3 2ST
Tel: 0141 848 4440
E-mail: airport@seeglasgow.com
Open: all year round

SEASONAL TOURIST INFORMATION CENTRE

Biggar
155 High Street
Biggar
ML12 6DL
Tel: 01899 221066
Web: www.seeglasgow.com
E-mail: biggar@seeglasgow.com
Open: Easter–Oct

Lanark
Horsemarket
Ladyacre Road
Lanark ML11 7LQ
Tel: 01555 661661
E-mail: lanark@seeglasgow.com
Open: all year round

Paisley
9A Gilmour Street
Paisley PA1 1DD
Tel: 0141 889 0711
E-mail: palsley@seeglasgow.com
Open: all year round

YEAR ROUND TOURIST INFORMATION CENTRES

Hamilton
Road Chef Services
M74, Northbound
Hamilton ML3 6JW
Tel: 01698 285590
E-mail: hamilton@seeglasgow.com
Open: all year round

ADDITIONAL INFORMATION

GENERAL TRAVEL INFORMATION
Traveline Scotland
Tel: 0870 608 2608
Provides timetable information for all public transport in Scotland and the rest of Great Britain.

TRAINS

First ScotRail
Caledonian Chambers
87 Union Street
Glasgow G1 3TA
Tel: Fares & Train Times:
08457 484950
Telesales: 08457 550033
Customer Relations:
0845 601 5929
Web: www.firstscotrail.co.uk
E-mail:scotrail.enquiries@
firstgroup.com

Glasgow–Dundee
Glasgow–Edinburgh
Glasgow–Glasgow Airport
Glasgow–Inverness
Glasgow–Isle of Skye
Glasgow–Oban

COACH

Scottish Citylink Coaches
Limited
Buchanan Bus Station
Killermont Street
Glasgow G2 3NP
Tel: 08705 505050
Web: www.citylink.co.uk
E-mail: info@citylink.co.uk
Routes: Glasgow–Aberdeen
Glasgow–Campbeltown
Glasgow–Dumfries

BUS

First
197 Victoria Road
Glasgow G42 7AD
Tel: 0141 636 3195
Web: www.firstglasgow.co.uk
Route: operates an extensive
bus network throughout
Glasgow

FERRIES

Caledonian MacBrayne
The Ferry Terminal
Gourock PA19 1QP
Tel: Enquiries: 01475 650100
Vehicle Reservations:
08705 650000

Brochure Hotline:
01475 650288
Web: www.calmac.co.uk
Routes: Gourock–Dunoon
(Cowal)
Wemyss Bay–Rothesay (Bute)

Western Ferries (Clyde) Limited
Hunter's Quay
Dunoon
Argyll PA23 8HJ
Tel: 01369 704452
Web:www.westernferries
clyde.co.uk
E-mail: enquiries@
western-ferries.co.uk
Route: Gourock (McInroy's
Point)–Dunoon (Hunter's
Quay)

CAR HIRE

AMK Self Drive, Glasgow
Tel: 0141 950 4200
Web:www.amkselfdrive.co.uk

Arnold Clark, Glasgow
Tel: 0141 334 9501
Web: www.arnoldclark.co.uk

Avis Rent-A-Car, Glasgow
Tel: 0141 842 7599
Web: www.avis.co.uk

Clarkson of Glasgow
Tel: 0141 771 3990
Web: www.carhirescotland.com

Enterprise Rent-A-Car, Glasgow
Tel: 0141 248 4981
Web: www.enterprise.com

Hertz Rent-A-Car, Glasgow
Tel: 0141 248 7736
Web: www.hertz.co.uk

TAXIS

City Private Hire, Glasgow
Tel: 0141 222 2220

Glasgow Taxis Limited,
Glasgow
Tel: 0141 429 7070

Online Radio Cars,
Glasgow
Tel: 0141 550 4040

1 Biggar Gasworks Museum

The last surviving small town coal-gas works in Scotland; the oldest part dates from 1839.

M6 *Gas Works Road, Biggar, off A702.*

P WC E Free

Jun–Sept, daily, 2–5pm.

Tel 01899 221050   www.historic-scotland.gov.uk

2 Biggar Museum Trust

The Trust runs a number of museums in the Biggar area, including the Moat Park Heritage Centre, Gladstone Court Museum with it's Victorian shops and other historical interiors, and Greenhill Covenanters Farmhouse.

M6 *Set around Biggar, on A702.*

Facilities and times vary; please telephone or see website for details.

Tel 01899 221050   www.biggar-net.co.uk

3 Bothwell Castle

This, the largest thirteenth century stone castle in Scotland, consisted of a courtyard surrounded by a series of towers, and suffered great damage during the Wars of Independence. Various additions have been made including a fifteenth century tower, great hall and chapel.

H8 *At Uddingston off the B7071.*

P WC E £

Apr–Sept, daily, 9.30am–6.30pm.
Oct–Mar, Sat–Wed, 9.30am–4.30pm

Tel 01698 816894
www.historic-scotland.gov.uk

4 Broughton Gallery

A privately owned gallery, devoted to exhibiting and selling works from British artists and craft makers. Broughton Place was built in the style of a Scottish tower house by Sir Basil Spence and is set on a hillside above the Tweed valley. The walled garden is also open to visitors.

M6 *Just N of Broughton Village on the A701.*

P WC E Free

Apr–Sept & mid Nov–Christmas, daily (except Wed), 10.30am–6pm.

Tel: 01899 830234   www.broughtongallery.co.uk

5 Burrell Collection

The Burrell Collection, housed within the grounds of Pollok Country Park, is a diverse collection of over 8000 art exhibits. Sir William Burrell was heir to an extensive merchant fleet and a self-trained art collector. When he and his brother sold the business in 1916, he was able to build up his remarkable collection, which was eventually given to the city of Glasgow in 1944.

E8 *Pollok County Park, Pollokshaws Road, Glasgow.*

P WC X E Free

Mon–Thur & Sat, 10am–5pm;
Fri & Sun, 11am–5pm.

Tel 0141 287 2550   www.glasgow.gov.uk

6 Calderglen Country Park

A suitable destination for a family outing, with a children's zoo, play areas, adventure playground, miles of countryside trails and visitor centre.

G7 *S of East Kilbride on A726.*

P WC E Free

Park: dawn–dusk.
Visitor centre: times vary, please check for details.

Tel 01355 236644   www.southlanarkshire.gov.uk

7 Carfin Grotto and Pilgrimage Centre

Built by Roman Catholics in 1922, Carfin Grotto acts as a shrine to St Thérèse of Lisieux. The centre adjacent looks at the history and traditions of pilgrimage around the world.

H8 *Carfin, twelve miles E of Glasgow, off the A73.*

P WC X E AV Free

All year round, daily, 10am–5pm.

Tel 01698 268941

8 Chatelherault Country Park

Chatelherault is an eighteenth century hunting lodge and summer house, originally commissioned by the fifth Duke of Hamilton. Restored in the 1980s, visitors can now see the Duke's Banqueting Hall and Bedroom, along with formal gardens and a museum. Woodland walks provide access to the gorge of the River Avon, ancient oaks and ruined Cadzow Castle. Walks and activities are led by a Ranger Service.

H8 *Enter at village of Ferniegair, on A72.*

P WC E

Visitor Centre: Mon–Sat, 10am–5pm;
Sun, 12 noon–5pm. House: Mon–Thur, 10am–4.30pm; Sun, 12 noon–4.30pm.

Tel 01698 426213

CHARLES RENNIE MACKINTOSH

Glasgow born Charles Rennie Mackintosh (1868-1928) was an architect who influenced European design, but only in recent times has he achieved widespread recognition in his own country. Now acknowledged as a truly original and creative designer, he combined an expression of the modern with a love of the traditional. He is particularly noted for his attention to detail. Wherever possible, furniture and fittings were included as part of the overall design – this was in keeping with his belief that building design should be 'a total work of art to the wholeness of which each contrived detail contributes'.

Recognised as an outstanding talent, and winner of many awards while still at art school, he was able to travel in Europe, financed by the prizes and a scholarship. His early influences included the Pre-Raphaelites, the Japanese, Whistler and Beardsley. The so-called 'Glasgow style' of Mackintosh and others was a recognisable movement by the 1890s. He became a partner in the Glasgow firm of Honeyman and Keppie in 1904 and by the latter years of the 1900s, had designed many interiors, furnishings, fireplaces, etc., for a variety of large homes and public buildings.

In Glasgow, his work includes the masterpiece, the Glasgow School of Art (see p55), as well as the reconstructions at the Hunterian Museum (see p57). Also notable are The Willow Tea Rooms (see p61), in Sauchiehall Street. Sensitively restored, these rooms are remarkable survivors in the commercial heart of Glasgow. They show clearly his design skill, following through a theme down to the finest detail. The former Queen's Cross Church, designed by Mackintosh, houses the

headquarters of Charles Rennie Mackintosh Society, with a small exhibition area and memorabilia (see p59).

The former Glasgow Herald Building in Mitchell Street, an early Mackintosh design (1893) is now restored in a new role as The Lighthouse, Scotland's Centre for Architecture, Design and the City (see p58). Other Mackintosh buildings include the Hill House (see p117), House for an Art Lover (see p56) and Scotland Street School Museum (see p60).

---

9 Clyde Muirshiel Regional Park

Outdoor activities on offer include water sports, mountain bike hire, fishing and woodland walks. Visitors can also see a grotto, maze, fishponds plus informative displays at the visitor centres.

C8 *Off the A737 E of Largs at Lochwinnoch.*

🅿 🚻 ♿ 🍴 🏛 AV 🏞 ⛷ 🚶 ♨ Free

🕐 Apr–Oct, daily, 10am–8pm or dusk.
Nov–Mar, 10am–4pm.

Tel 01505 842882
www.clydemuirshiel.co.uk

10 Clyde Valley Woodlands

A reserve made up of three woodland areas in the Clyde Valley, namely Cleghorn Glen, Cartland Craigs and Jock Gill's Wood. Impressive deciduous clusters of ash, oak and wych elm are home to a variety of birds and other wildlife such as badgers, roe deer and great spotted woodpeckers.

K7 *Off A72, on outskirts of Carluke or A706/A72, outskirts of Lanark.*

⛷ 🚶 Free

🕐 Open access.

Tel 01555 665928   www.snh.org.uk

11 Clydebuilt Scottish Maritime Museum

An exhibition charting the development of Glasgow and the Clyde from 1700 to the present day. The story is told through audio-visuals, computer interactives, hands-on displays, video and temporary exhibitions.

E9 *Beside Braehead Shopping Centre at J25a (westbound) and J26 (eastbound) off the M8. Follow directions to the 'green' car park.*

🅿 📶 ♿ ⛩ E 📺 ££

🕐 Mon–Thur & Sat, 10am–5.30pm; Sun, 11am–5pm.

Tel 0141 886 1013   www.scottishmuseums.org

12 Coats Observatory 🏛

Built by John Honeyman, this Victorian observatory features displays on astronomy, astronautics, meteorology and the history and architecture of the building.

E9 *Oakshaw Street, Paisley.*

📶 Free

🕐 All year round, Tue–Sat, 10am–5pm; Sun, 2–5pm. Oct–Mar, 7–9.30pm, weather permitting.

Tel 0141 889 2013   www.renfrewshire.gov.uk

13 Craignethan Castle 🏰

Set by the River Nethan, Craignethan was originally built by Sir James Hamilton around 1530 and featured a huge rampart, now demolished. Various additions were made over the next few hundred years, including a tower house, still fairly well preserved.

J7 *5.5 miles NW of Lanark off the A72.*

🅿 📶 ☕ ⛩ E £

🕐 Apr–Sept, daily, 9.30am–6.30pm. Oct–Mar, Sat & Sun only, 9.30am–4.30pm.

Tel 01555 860364   www.historic-scotland.gov.uk

14 Crookston Castle 🏰

A unique castle, originating in the fourteenth/fifteenth centuries, with a main building surrounded by four corner towers. It suffered demolition around 1489 while being held by the Stewarts of Darnley.

E9 *Off Brockburn Road, SW of Glasgow city centre.*

Free

🕐 Keys available locally at these times: Apr–Sept, daily, 9.30am–6.30pm. Oct–Mar, Mon–Sat, 9.30am–4.30pm; Sun, 2–4.30pm.

Tel 0131 668 8800   www.historic-scotland.gov.uk

15 David Livingstone Centre

This eighteenth century tenement houses a museum devoted to explorer and missionary David Livingstone, who was born here in 1813. Visitors can learn about his explorations and see a number of personal items.

G8 *Blantyre, off M74 at J5, via A725/A724.*

🅿 📶 ♿ ☕ ⛩ E 📶 ££

🕐 Apr–mid Dec, Mon–Sat, 10am–5pm; Sun, 12.30–5pm.

Tel 01698 823140   www.nts.org.uk

16 Falls of Clyde Wildlife Reserve

The reserve's woodland, which lines both sides of the gorge, is home to a number of wildlife species including warblers, deer, foxes and badgers. The visitor centre offers a ranger service, which provides a number of outdoor activities such as badger watching.

K6 *From M74, follow signs for New Lanark.*

🅿 ⛩ E 📶 📶 Free

🕐 Visitor Centre: daily, Mar–Dec, 11am–5pm; Jan–Feb, 12 noon–4pm. Reserve: summer, daily, 8am–8pm; winter, daylight hours.

Tel 01555 665262   www.swt.org.uk

17 Finlaystone Country Estate ♣

Built in the fourteenth century, and extended in 1760 and 1900, Finlaystone House is currently home to the Chief of the Clan MacMillan. Extensive grounds contain formal gardens, woodland walks, play areas and a visitor centre with a collection of dolls from around the world and the history of the Clan Macmillan.

C10 *On A8, one mile W of Langbank.*

🅿 📶 ♿ ☕ ⛩ E 🍴 📶 📶 £

🕐 Grounds: all year round, daily, 10.30am–5pm.

Tel 01475 540285   www.finlaystone.co.uk

18 Gallery of Modern Art

Four floors of contemporary paintings, sculpture and installations from around the world.

W3 *Queen Street, Glasgow city centre.*

📶 ♿ ☕ ⛩ E 🎦 Free

🕐 Mon–Wed & Sat; 10am–5pm; Thur, 10am–8pm; Fri & Sun, 11am–5pm.

Tel 0141 229 1996   www.glasgow.gov.uk

19 Glasgow Botanic Gardens 🌼

These gardens are best known for their tropical collections including orchids, begonias and tree ferns, while Kibble Palace is home to the temperate plants. The gardens also have an arboretum, herbaceous borders, herb garden, rose and scented garden. Kibble Palace closed until summer 2006 for major refurbishment.

F9 *Corner of Great Western Road, NW of Glasgow city centre.*

🚻 E 🏞 Free

🕐 Garden: 7am–dusk. Glasshouses: winter, daily, 10am–4.15pm; summer, 10am–4.45pm.

Tel 0141 334 2422

20 Glasgow Cathedral 🅱 ✠

Erected between the thirteenth and fifteenth centuries over the supposed site of the tomb of St Kentigern, the cathedral features a vaulted crypt, carved stones and unique stone screen. The lower church contains a shrine dedicated to St Mungo, patron saint of Glasgow.

Y3 *Castle Street, central Glasgow.*

🏛 E Free

🕐 Apr–Sept, Mon–Sat, 9.30am–6pm; Sun, 1–5pm. Oct–Mar, Mon–Sat, 9.30am–4pm; Sun, 1–4pm.

Tel 0141 552 6891   www.historic-scotland.gov.uk

21 Glasgow City Chambers ★

This impressive nineteenth century building is home to the headquarters of Glasgow City Council. The interior features pillars and staircases in marble and granite, mosaic floors and lavishly painted ceilings.

W3 *Off George Square, Glasgow city centre.*

🚻 ♿ Free

🕐 Mon–Fri, 9am–4.30pm; guided tours at 10.30am & 2.30pm. Closed public holidays.

Tel 0141 287 4018   www.glasgow.gov.uk

22 Glasgow School of Art ★

Glasgow School of Art, still a working art school, is Charles Rennie Mackintosh's greatest architectural masterpiece. Guided tours through various corridors to the Gallery, Mackintosh Room and Library, where you can see his unique interiors and furniture.

V4 *Renfrew Street, Glasgow city centre.*

🚻 ♿ ☕ 🏛 E 💷 ££

🕐 Guided tours: Apr–Sept, daily, 10.30, 11 & 11.30am; 1.30, 2 & 2.30pm. Oct–Mar, Mon–Fri, 11am & 2pm; Sat, 10.30 & 11am.

Tel 0141 353 4526   www.gsa.ac.uk

23 Glasgow Science Centre 🏛

This millennium project, situated on the River Clyde, includes three buildings: an IMAX theatre shows educational films on a huge screen, the Science Mall contains exhibits, hands-on demonstrations, and planetarium theatres, while the Glasgow Tower, topping 100 m high, rotates 360°, offering panoramic views.

R3 *Pacific Quay, on south bank of the Clyde.*

🅿 🚻 ♿ ☕ ✗ 🏛 E 📺 🏞 ☼ 💷 ££

🕐 Science Mall open daily, 10am–6pm. Film & show times vary; telephone for details.

Tel 0141 420 5000   www.gsc.org.uk

House for an Art Lover, Glasgow

24 Gleniffer Braes Country Park ♣

Visitors can make use of various marked trails and play areas, and admire views across Paisley and Glasgow.

E9 *Glenfield Road, Paisley off the B775.*

🅿 wc E ⏚ ⚹ ⚹⚹ Free

🕐 Daily, 8am–dusk.

Tel 0141 884 3794   www.renfrewshire.gov.uk

25 Greenbank Garden 🌿 ❀

Greenbank consists of over 15 acres of gardens which contain a range of ornamental plants, annuals, perennials, shrubs and trees.

F8 *Off M77 and A726, follow signs for East Kilbride to Clarkston Toll; six miles S of Glasgow city centre.*

wc ♿ ☕ ⛪ ⏚ ⚹⚹ ££

🕐 Apr–Oct, daily, 11am–5pm.
Nov–Mar, weekends, 2–4pm.

Tel 0141 639 3281   www.nts.org.uk

26 Holmwood House 🌿 🏰

This fine example of Alexander 'Greek' Thomson's domestic design was built in 1857 for James Couper, a local mill owner. An ongoing conservation project has revealed Thomson's decorative work in wood, plaster and marble.

F8 *Netherlee Road, four miles S of Glasgow city centre; signposted from Clarkston Road on B767.*

🅿 wc ♿ ⛪ E ⚹⚹ ££

🕐 Apr–Oct, daily, 12 noon–5pm.
Groups must pre-book.

Tel 0141 637 2129   www.nts.org.uk

27 House for an Art Lover 🏛

A nineties-built house based on a collection of competition entry drawings produced by Charles Rennie Mackintosh nearly a century earlier. Visitors can tour a number of rooms, and compare Mackintosh's original designs with the recreated interiors, furniture and fittings.

F9 *Bellahouston Park, off Dumbreck Road, S of Glasgow city centre.*

🅿 wc ♿ ✕ ⛪ E AV ⚹ ⚹⚹ 💷 ££

🕐 Opening hours vary please telephone for details.

Tel 0141 353 4770
www.houseforanartlover.co.uk

28 Hunter House Museum 🏛

Hunter House tells the story of John and William Hunter, born there in the eighteenth century, who both made their fame and fortune in the world of medicine and science. The New Town display area describes how East Kilbride became Scotland's first 'new town', and features old photographs and slides.

G8 *Maxwellton Road, NE of East Kilbride town centre; off A749 to Calderwood Road.*

🅿 wc ♿ ☕ ⛪ E AV Free

🕐 Apr–Sept, Mon–Fri, 12.30–4.30pm;
weekends, 12 noon–5pm.

Tel 01355 261261

Kelvingrove Art Gallery & Museum

29 Hunterian Museum and Art Gallery incorporating the Mackintosh House

The Hunterian was Scotland's first public museum, founded on Dr William Hunter's collections. The gallery section holds paintings by Rembrandt, Chardin and Stubbs, and Scottish Colourists Fergusson, Peploe, Cadell and Hunter. The gallery also contains the Mackintosh House, which includes a reconstruction of the interiors of Mackintosh's Glasgow home, making use of original designs and furniture.

R6 *The Museum is on University Avenue, and Gallery on Hillhead Street; both are at the university, in the west end of the city.*

wc & ♥ ⊞ E ⊞ Free

⊕ Mon–Sat, 9.30am–5pm; admission charge for the Mackintosh House & closes, 12.30–1.30pm.

Tel: 0141 330 4221   www.hunterian.gla.ac.uk

30 Hutcheson's Hall 🏵 🏛

Built in the beginning of the nineteenth century, this unusual building incorporates statues of George and Thomas Hutcheson who founded Hutchesons' Hospital. Interior features include a collection of portraits and exhibition titled *Glasgow Style*.

X3 *Ingram Street, SE corner of George Square.*

wc & ⊞ E Free

⊕ Gallery and Function Hall: all year round, Mid Jan–mid Dec, Mon–Sat, 10am–5pm.

Tel 0141 552 8391   www.nts.org.uk

31 John Hastie Museum 🏛

Features displays on life in the area, including its agricultural and weaving history.

H6 *Strathaven, on the A71 NE of Kilmarnock.*

& ⊞ E Free

⊕ Apr–Sept, daily, 12.30–4.30pm.

Tel 01357 521257

32 Kelvingrove Art Gallery and Museum

Kelvingrove, with its striking red sandstone facade and grand interiors, is one of Scotland's most popular free attractions. It houses an impressive and hugely varied art collection, silver, ceramics, armour and weaponry, costumes and furniture, plus a large natural history section. Notable artists with works exhibited on the first floor include Rembrandt, Millet, Van Gogh, Renoir, Sisley, Picasso, Rossetti, McTaggart and the Glasgow Boys.

R5 *Kelvingrove, Glasgow.*

P wc & ♥ ✕ ⊞ E AV ⏛ ✲ ⊞ Free

⊕ Closed until 2006 for major refurbishment

Tel 0141 287 2699   www.glasgow.gov.uk

33 Lighthouse

The Lighthouse is Scotland's centre for architecture, design and the city, and is home to the Mack Room (an exhibition based on the life and work of Charles Rennie Mackintosh) and a changing programme of exhibitions and events. Other attractions include an adventure playground for children aged 3–8 years and a viewing tower.

W3 *Mitchell Lane, off Buchanan Street, Glasgow.*

🚾 ♿ ♥ ✕ 🏛 E ☀ ♿ £

🕐 Daily, 10.30am–5pm; except Tue, 11am–5pm & Sun, 12 noon–5pm.

Tel 0141 221 6362
www.thelighthouse.co.uk

34 Low Parks Museum

Two museums in one, housed in historic buildings which were once part of the Duke of Hamilton's estate. The area's history is explored through displays and interactives, while an exhibition gives the history of the Cameronians Regiment.

H8 *Muir Street, Hamilton.*

🅿 🚾 ♿ 🏛 E Free

🕐 Mon–Sat, 10am–5pm; Sun, 12 noon–5pm.

Tel 01698 328232
www.southlanarkshire.gov.uk

35 Museum of Lead Mining

Set in Wanlockhead, Scotland's highest village, the visitor centre has a display of rare minerals and mining artefacts. There are also period cottages, a historic beam engine, Europe's second oldest subscription library and guided tours of a lead mine.

K3 *Wanlockhead, on B797; signposted from M74 and A76.*

🅿 🚾 ♿ ♥ ✕ 🏛 E 🪑 ♿ ♿ ££

🕐 Apr–Oct, daily, 11am–4.30pm.
   Jul & Aug, 10am–5pm.

Tel 01659 74387   www.leadminingmuseum.co.uk

36 Museum of Scottish Country Life

A museum showing how country people lived and worked in Scotland in the past, and how this has shaped the countryside of today. The site includes a new museum housing the national country life collections and the original Georgian farmhouse and working farm at Wester Kittochside.

G8 *Wester Kittochside, East Kilbride.*

🅿 🚾 ♿ ♥ 🏛 E 🪑 ☀ ♿ ♿ £

🕐 Daily, 10am–5pm. Closed Christmas & New Year.

Tel 01355 224181   www.nms.ac.uk/countrylife

37 Museum of Transport

Cars, trains, trams, bicycles, motorbikes, buses and boats are all on display at this museum devoted to the history of transport. Prominent features include a reconstruction of a 1938 Glasgow street, a car showroom and a railway station with a display of Scottish locomotives.

R5 *Bunhouse Road, west side of Kelvingrove Park, Glasgow.*

🚾 ♿ ♥ 🏛 E AV ♿ Free

🕐 Mon–Thur & Sat, 10am–5pm; Fri & Sun, 11am–5pm.

Tel 0141 287 2720

38 Newark Castle

Dating back to the fifteenth century, Newark was once occupied by James IV. The gatehouse tower was later joined to a mansion block.

B10 *Port Glasgow on A8; right at Newark roundabout.*

🅿 🚾 E £

🕐 Apr–Sept, daily, 9.30am–6.30pm.

Tel 01475 741858   www.historic-scotland.gov.uk

39 New Lanark World Heritage Village

Surrounded by native woodlands and close to the Falls of Clyde, this cotton mill village was founded in 1785 and became famous as the site of Robert Owen's model community. Now fully restored as both a living community and visitor attraction. The history of the village is interpreted via a dark ride called *The New Millennium Experience* and the show *Annie McLeod's Story*, plus a shop and millworker's house of the 1820s and 1930s, and the home of Robert Owen himself.

K6 *By Lanark, off A73.*

P WC & 曲 ♥ X E ⊼ ⚹ 終 ⊠ ££

⊕ All year round, daily, 11am–5pm. Closed Christmas and New Year days.

Tel 01555 661345 www.newlanark.org

40 Paisley Abbey

This twelfth century Cluniac Abbey features varying styles of architecture, stained glass windows and restored choir and transept areas.

E9 *In the centre of Paisley.*

WC & ♥ 曲 E Free

⊕ Mon–Sat, 10am–3.30pm; Sun open for services only.

Tel: 0141 889 7654

41 Paisley Museum and Art Galleries

Along with displays of ceramics and nineteenth century Scottish art, visitors can learn about old weaving techniques and see the world's largest collection of Paisley shawls.

E9 *High Street, centre of Paisley.*

WC & 曲 E Free

⊕ Tue–Sat, 10am–5pm; Sun, 2–5pm; public holidays, 10am–5pm.

Tel 0141 889 3151 www.renfrewshire.gov.uk

42 People's Palace

Opened in 1898, the People's Palace tells the local and social history of the city of Glasgow from 1750; lying adjacent is a glasshouse-style building containing the Winter Gardens.

Y1 *Glasgow Green, E of city centre on A749 or A730.*

P WC & ♥ 曲 E AV ⊼ Free

⊕ All year round, Mon–Thur & Sat, 10am–5pm; Fri & Sun, 11am–5pm.

Tel 0141 271 2951 www.glasgow.gov.uk

43 Pollok House

This Georgian house, built by the Maxwell family in 1750, contains a collection of paintings, silver and ceramics. It is set in Pollok Country Park, also the home of the Burrell Collection.

F8 *Pollok Country Park, three miles S of Glasgow, off M77 at J1; follow signs for adjacent Burrell Collection.*

P & ♥ X 曲 E ⊠ £££

⊕ All year, daily, 10am–5pm.

Tel 0141 616 6410 www.nts.org.uk

44 Provand's Lordship

Built in 1471 as part of St Nicholas' Hospital, Provand's Lordship is Glasgow's oldest and only medieval house and contains a collection of historic Scottish furniture. Behind the house is the St Nicholas Garden, a medicinal herb garden designed in 1995.

Y3 *Castle Street, Glasgow city centre. Parking in Glasgow Cathedral car park.*

♥ 曲 Free

⊕ All year, Mon–Thur & Sat 10am–5pm. Fri & Sun, 11am–5pm. Closed 25, 26 & 31 Dec (pm); 1 & 2 Jan.

Tel 0141 552 8819 www.glasgowmuseums.com

45 Queen's Cross Church

A galleried, single-aisled church designed by Charles Rennie Mackintosh in the late nineteenth century. Features of interest include its stained glass and carving on wood and stonework.

F9 *Garscube Road, half a mile W of Glasgow city centre.*

WC & ♥ 曲 E ⊠ £

⊕ Mon–Fri, 10am–5pm; Sun, 2–5pm.

Tel 0141 946 6600 www.crmsociety.com

Winter Gardens, People's Palace

46 Scotland Street School Museum 🏛

Glasgow style stone carving and twin leaded towers feature prominently on this Charles Rennie Mackintosh designed building. Now a museum dedicated to the history of education, displays include classrooms from different eras, a cookery room and changing exhibitions.

T1 *One mile S of city centre opposite Shields Road underground station.*

♿ WC 🍵 ♿ E AV Free

🕐 Mon–Thur & Sat, 10am–5pm;
Fri & Sun, 11am–5pm.

Tel 0141 287 0500   www.glasgow.gov.uk

47 Sharmanka Kinetic Gallery 🏛

A collection of mechanical sculptures, made by Eduard Bersudsky from hundreds of tiny carved figures and pieces of old scrap, move to music and synchronised lighting. Full performances last one hour, and family matinees for 45 minutes. Book in advance by telephone or e-mail.

X2 *King Street, Merchant City, Glasgow city centre.*

♿ ♿ AV £

🕐 Full performances: Thur & Sun, 7pm.
Children's matinee: Sun, 3pm.
Performances can be given for individuals and small groups at other times. Call for details.

Tel 0141 552 7080
www.sharmanka.kinetic@virgin.net

48 Sma 'Shot Cottages 🏛

A group of cottages with a historical theme, including an eighteenth century weaver's cottage containing a working loom.

E9 *George Place, Paisley.*

WC 🍵 ♿ E Free

🕐 Apr–Sept, Wed & Sat, 12 noon–4pm.

Tel: 0141 889 1708   www.smashot.co.uk

49 St Mungo Museum of Religious Life and Art 🏛

A museum and gallery focusing on different religious faiths in Scotland and throughout the world. Visitors can see a diverse collection of exhibits including Salvador Dali's famous painting *Christ of St John of the Cross*, and wander round the unique Zen garden, symbolising the harmony between people and nature.

Y3 *Castle Street, beside Glasgow Cathedral, Glasgow city centre.*

WC ♿ 🍵 ♿ E AV 🌿 £ Free

🕐 All year round, Mon–Thur & Sat, 10am–5pm;
Fri & Sun, 11am–5pm.

Tel 0141 553 2557   www.glasgow.gov.uk

50 Summerlee Heritage Park 🏛

This 22 acre site is based around the site of the nineteenth century Summerlee Ironworks and its branch of the Monklands Canal. The park features an electric tramway offering rides on modern and Edwardian open-topped trams, along with an under-cover exhibition hall with working machinery and period room settings, and a recreated addit mine and miners' cottages.

H9 *W of Coatbridge town centre at Heritage Way, off West Canal Street.*

P WC ♿ 🍵 E ♿ 🌿 👫 Free

🕐 Apr–Oct, daily, 10am–5pm.
Nov–Mar, 10am–4pm.

Tel 01236 431261   www.northlan.gov.uk

Willow Tea Rooms, Glasgow

51 Tall Ship at Glasgow Harbour ★

Built in 1896, the s. v. *Glenlee* is one of the last remaining Clydebuilt sailing ships still afloat. An exhibition describes life on the ship, where she sailed and what cargoes she carried.

Q4 *Next to Glasgow SECC, J19 off M8; signposted.*

P WC E AV ££

Mar–Oct, daily, 10am–5pm.
Nov–Feb, daily, 11am–4pm.

Tel 0141 222 2513 www.thetallship.com

52 Tenement House

A typical lower middle class Glasgow tenement flat of the late nineteenth century, with original furnishings and fittings. A reception flat contains an exhibition on tenement living and the history of tenements in Glasgow.

U5 *Buccleuch Street, near Glasgow School of Art, Glasgow city centre.*

WC E ££

Mar–Oct, daily, 1–5pm (last admission 4.30pm).
Groups by appointment, weekday mornings only.

Tel 0141 333 0183 www.nts.org.uk

53 Weaver's Cottage

A typical eighteenth century handloom weaver's cottage housing a number of looms and weaving equipment, with weekend weaving demonstrations.

D9 *M8 junction 28A, A737, follow signs for Kilbarchan.*

££

Apr–Sept, Fri-Tue, 1–5pm

Tel 01505 705588 www.nts.org.uk

54 Willow Tea Rooms ★

The interior for this tea room on the first floor of the building was initially styled by Charles Rennie Mackintosh; still a tea room, much of the furniture and fittings are now reproductions. Mackintosh also remodelled the facade, creating the unique room-wide window.

V4 *Above Hendersons, Sauchiehall Street, Glasgow city centre.*

WC

Tel 0141 204 5242 www.willowtearooms.co.uk

Edinburgh Castle at dusk

EDINBURGH AND THE LOTHIANS

Edinburgh, with its distinctive cityscape, is simply one of the great capitals of Europe. With its panorama of fortified crag, of Arthur's Seat and the neo-classical columns on Calton Hill, all outlined against the sky, Edinburgh makes a dramatic first impression.

Few other places can match the grandeur of the prospect of castle ramparts from the middle of a busy shopping street. Few cities can offer the experience of more than a hint of wildness and rocky grandeur just a few minutes from the city-centre bustle simply by walking in a royal park. Likewise, there are few other urban street layouts which allow such views northwards than those afforded from, say, George Street, looking over the rooftops to the field-pattern across the Firth in Fife.

Edinburgh, on first impression, seems to be almost theatrical – the skyline a backdrop for some festival production, or perhaps a novel by Sir Walter Scott, or a tale of intrigue by Robert Louis Stevenson. Small wonder it is the setting for the largest cultural festival in the world.

Castle, royal palace and a range of museums which include both the Royal Museum (see p82) and the adjoining Museum of Scotland (see p78) are on the basic list of 'must-sees' for most visitors. The National Gallery of Scotland, the Scottish National Portrait Gallery and the Gallery of Modern Art likewise demand repeat visits. Our Dynamic Earth (see p80) represents the modern, 'high-tech' visitor experience in a presentation on the theme – as its name suggests – of earth science and the varied habitats of our planet. This range of attractions, from Britannia to the Botanics, are only part of the Edinburgh experience. The new Parliament adds a further significance to Edinburgh's role as the nation's capital.

Edinburgh's countryside, the Lothians, surround it on all sides and offer many and varied excursions, from the birthplace of Mary, Queen of Scots at Linlithgow Palace in West Lothian, to the birthplace of John Muir – the founder of the US national parks movement – in Dunbar, in the east. Midlothian is noted for Rosslyn Chapel, the finest piece of medieval stone carving anywhere in Scotland (see p82). Closer at hand are the Pentland Hills, offering a range of walks and an easy escape from the busy city streets. There are fine high-level city views overlooking Swanston, just one of Edinburgh's villages, associated with Robert Louis Stevenson.

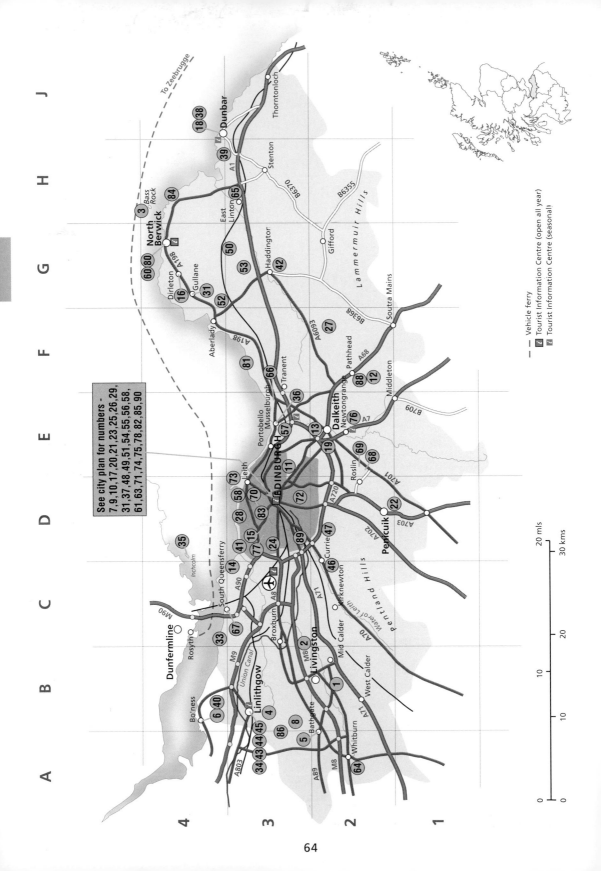

See city plan for numbers –
7, 9, 10, 17, 20, 21, 23, 25, 26, 29, 31, 37, 48, 49, 51, 54, 55, 56, 58, 61, 63, 71, 74, 75, 78, 82, 85, 90

To Zeebrugge

--- Vehicle ferry
⧓ Tourist Information Centre (open all year)
⧓ Tourist Information Centre (seasonal)

20 mls
30 kms
0   10   20
0   10   20   30

Dunbar
Thorntonloch
Stenton
A1
Bass Rock
North Berwick
East Linton
Haddington
Gifford
B6370
B6355
Lammermuir Hills
Soutra Mains
B6368
Dirleton
Gullane
Aberlady
A198
A6093
A68
A7
Pathhead
Newtongrange
Middleton
B709
Tranent
Musselburgh
Portobello
Dalkeith
EDINBURGH
Leith
Roslin
A701
A703
A702
A720
Penicuik
Pentland Hills
A71
Currie
Kirknewton
Balerno
Mid Calder
West Calder
Water of Leith
A70
A71
Whitburn
A89
M8
Livingston
Broxburn
Bathgate
Armadale
Blackburn
Union Canal
M8
M9
Linlithgow
Bo'ness
Rosyth
Dunfermline
M90
South Queensferry
Inchcolm
A90
A8
A803

18/38
39
84
3
65
60/80
16
31
52
50
53
42
27
81
66
36
57
13
12
88
76
19
11
69
68
73
58
70
72
22
28
15
83
77
24
89
47
46
14
41
35
67
33
6
40
4
86
8
5
34/43/44/45
64
1

VISITOR INFORMATION

YEAR ROUND TOURIST INFORMATION CENTRES

Edinburgh International Airport
Tourist & Airport Information Desk
Edinburgh EH12 9DN
E-mail: info@visitscotland.com
Open: all year round

MAIN TOURIST INFORMATION CENTRES

Edinburgh
3 Princes Street
Edinburgh EH2 2QP
Tel: 0131 0845 225 5121
Web: www.edinburgh.org
E-mail: info@visitscotland.com
Open: all year round

North Berwick
Quality Street
North Berwick EH39 4HJ
E-mail: info@visitscotland.com
Open: all year round

SEASONAL TOURIST INFORMATION CENTRES

Dunbar
143 High Street
Open: Easter-Oct

Linlithgow
Burgh Hall
Open: Easter–Oct

Newtongrange
Scottish Mining Museum
Open: Easter–Oct

Old Craighall
Old Craighall Junction, A1
Open: Easter–Oct

ADDITIONAL INFORMATION

GENERAL TRAVEL INFORMATION
Traveline Scotland
Tel: 0870 608 2608
Provides timetable information for all public transport in Scotland and the rest of Great Britain.

AIR TRAVEL

BAA Edinburgh
Edinburgh Airport
Edinburgh EH12 9DN
Tel: 0131 333 1000
Web: www.baa.com

TRAINS

First ScotRail
Caledonian Chambers
87 Union Street
Glasgow G1 3TA
Tel: Fares & Train Times:
08457 484950
Telesales:
08457 550033
Customer Relations:
0845 601 5929
Web: www.firstscotrail.co.uk
E-mail: scotrail.enquiries
@firstgroup.com

COACH

Scottish Citylink Coaches
Limited
Buchanan Bus Station
Killermont Street
Glasgow G2 3NP
Tel: 08705 505050
Web: www.citylink.co.uk
E-mail:
info@citylink.co.uk
*Routes: Edinburgh–Aberdeen
Edinburgh–Dundee
Edinburgh–Glasgow
Edinburgh–Inverness*

*Edinburgh–Isle of Skye
Edinburgh–Glasgow–Stranraer
–Belfast*

BUS

First Edinburgh
14-16 Eskbank Road
Dalkeith EH22 1HH
Tel: 0131 225 3858
Web:
www.firstedinburgh.co.uk
*Routes include:
Edinburgh City Centre
Edinburgh–Falkirk
Edinburgh–Kelso
Edinburgh–Livingstone
Edinburgh–Stirling*

Lothian Buses PLC
Head Office
55 Annadale Street
Edinburgh EH7 4AZ

Travel Centre
Hanover Street
& Waverley Bridge
Tel: 0131 555 6363
Web: www.lothianbuses.co.uk

*Routes: Edinburgh and The
Lothians
Also operates
Edinburgh Tour (City
Sightseeing),
Airlink (shuttle service
between Edinburgh Airport
and the city centre)*

*and Britannia (link between
the city centre and The Royal
Yacht Britannia)*

CAR HIRE

Arnold Clark Car and Van
Rental, Edinburgh
Tel: 0845 607 4500
Web: www.arnoldclark.co.uk

Avis Rent A Car, Edinburgh
Airport
Tel: 0131 344 3900
Web: www.avis.co.uk

Belmont Peugeot, Edinburgh
Tel: 0131 453 6644
Web: www.jmgroup.co.uk

Capital Car and Van Hire,
Edinburgh
Tel: 0131 652 9898
Web: www.121carhire.com
E-mail: info@capital-
carhire.co.uk

Condor Self Drive, Edinburgh
Tel: 0131 229 6333
Web:www.condorself
drive.co.uk
Email:
sales@condorselfdrive.com

Enterprise Rent-A-Car,
Edinburgh
Tel: 0131 442 4440
Web: www.enterprise.com

Ford Rent-A-Car, Edinburgh
Tel: 0131 557 0000
Web: www.rent-ford.com
E-mail: fordrent@aol.com

Good News Car Hire,
Edinburgh
Tel: 0131 557 5964
E-mail: operations
@goodnewsselfdrive.com

Gran Turismo, Edinburgh
Tel: 0131 466 3447
Web: www.granturismo.
demon.co.uk
E-mail: alan@granturismo.
demon.co.uk

Dollar Fifty Car Rental,
Edinburgh
Tel: 0131 337 1319
Web: www.thrifty.co.uk
E-mail:
thrifty.edinburgh@thrifty.co.uk

TAXIS

Accolade City Taxis, Edinburgh
Tel: 0131 557 5718

Computer Cabs, Edinburgh
Tel: 0131 228 2555

Central Radio Taxis, Edinburgh
Tel: 0131 229 2468

City Cabs, Edinburgh
Tel: 0131 228 1211

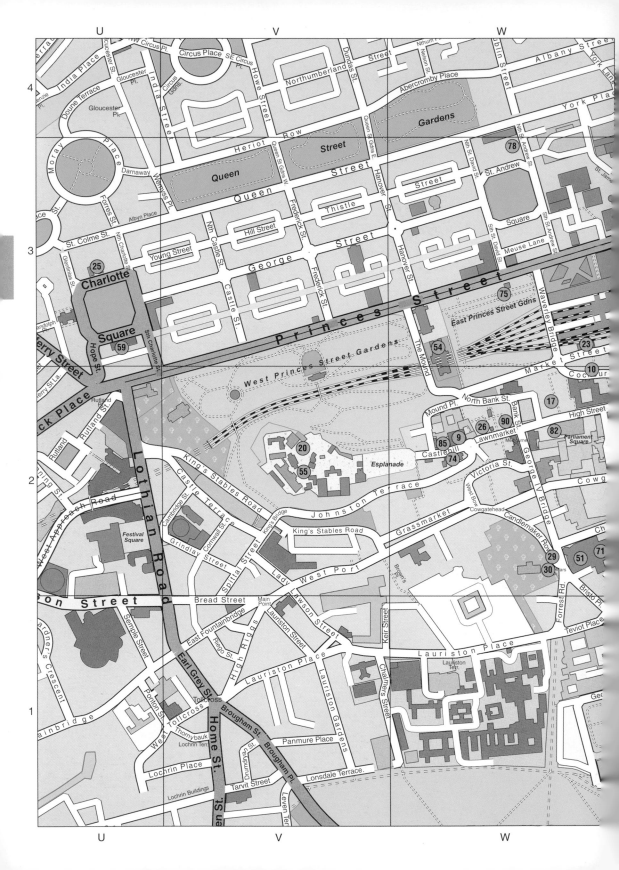

1 Almond Valley Heritage Trust 🏛

A museum exploring the history and environment of West Lothian. The centre includes Livingston Mill with its friendly farm animals, play areas and walks.

B2 *Signposted from J3 on the M8.*

🅿 ♿ 🚻 ☕ ✕ 🎁 E 🎋 🚶 ♿ £

🕐 10am–5pm, daily

Tel 01506 414957   www.almondvalley.co.uk

2 Almondell and Calderwood Country Park ♣

A scenic and tranquil park based around two estates along the River Almond. Facilities include walks, barbecue areas and a ranger service.

C3 *Two miles S of Broxburn; turning signposted off A89 at Broxburn.*

🅿 🚻 ♿ ☕ 🎁 E 🎋 🚴 🚶 Free

🕐 Daily, Summer, 9am–5pm; Winter, 10am–4pm.

Tel 01506 882254   www.beecraigs.com

3 Bass Rock 🦅

Located off the coast of North Berwick in the Firth of Forth, the Bass Rock measures one mile in length, with sheer cliffs dropping down at all sides. Signs of human life include a lighthouse and ruins of a sixteenth century chapel, but the rock is best known as a bird sanctuary, attracting thousands of gannets every year. Visitors can sail round the island on organised boat trips.

H4 *The Bass Rock is three miles off the coast of North Berwick. Boat trips on the* Sula II *leave from North Berwick harbour.*

🚴 ££

🕐 Daily trips run during summer months, weather permitting. Contact operator for timetable.

Tel 01620 892838 (boat operator)

4 Beecraigs Country Park ♣

A country park, set in the Bathgate Hills above Linlithgow, offering a range of activities including walking, riding and cycling routes, park centre, play area and ranger service.

B3 *Two miles S of Linlithgow, close to J3 & 4 off M9.*

🅿 🚻 ♿ ✕ 🎁 🎋 🚴 🚶 ♿ Free

🕐 Daily, throughout the year; times vary.

Tel 01506 844516   www.beecraigs.com

5 Bennie Museum 🏛

Local history museum containing artefacts of social, industrial and historical interest, from Bathgate glass and a Roman coin, to war memorabilia. Three special exhibitions run annually.

A2 *Mansefield Street, Bathgate town centre.*

🚻 ♿ E Free

🕐 Apr–Sept, Mon–Sat, 10am–4pm. Oct–Mar, 11am–3.30pm.

Tel 01506 634944

www.benniemuseum.homestead.com

6 Bo'ness and Kinneil Railway 🚂 and Birkhall Fireclay Mine

The Scottish Railway Exhibition tells the story of the development of railways in Scotland and their impact on the Scottish people. Historic railway buildings, including the station and the train shed, have been relocated from sites all over Scotland. A train journey takes passengers into the West Lothian countryside to Birkhill, where guided tours lead into the underground workings of Birkhill Fireclay Mine, with its ancient fossils.

B4 *Bo'ness, on the S shore of the River Forth, eight miles W of the Forth Road Bridge.*

🅿 🚻 ♿ ✕ 🎁 E 🎋 🚶 ♿ ££

🕐 April–Oct, Sat/Sun 11am–5pm (last admission 4pm). Jul–Aug, Tue–Sun, 11am–5pm (last admission 4pm).

Tel 01506 825855   www.srps.org.uk

7 Brass Rubbing Centre ★

The centre offers a collection of replicas moulded from ancient Pictish stone, rare Scottish brasses and medieval church brasses. Experienced staff show visitors how to do their own rubbings.

X2 *Historical Trinity Apse opposite the Museum of Childhood, Royal Mile, Edinburgh city centre.*

🎁 ££

🕐 Apr–Sept, Mon–Sat, 10am–5pm. Festival opening Sun, 12 noon–5pm. Last rubbing 4pm.

Tel 0131 556 4364

8 Cairnpapple Hill

This important archaeological site was used for burial and ceremonial purposes from around 3000–1400 BC. Visitors can see burial areas, ancient stones and a cairn, along with views to the West.

B3 *Off A706, three miles N of Bathgate.*

P 🏛 E ♿ £

◷ Apr–Sept, daily, 9.30am–6.30pm.

Tel 01506 634622 www.historic-scotland.gov.uk

9 Camera Obscura and World of Illusions ★

Spy on passers-by in the street below and pick them up on your hand in this 150 year old giant camera. Magic Gallery of optical illusions with holograms, stunning rooftop views and live city viewcams.

W2 *Adjacent to the castle, Royal Mile, Edinburgh city centre.*

WC 🏛 E AV ♿ 🔁 ££

◷ Apr–Jun & Sep–Oct, daily, 9.30am–6pm. Jul–Aug, 9.30am–7.30pm. Nov–Mar, daily, 10am–5pm. Last presentation 1 hour before closing.

Tel 0131 226 3709 www.camera-obscura.co.uk

10 Collective Gallery 🏛

A contemporary art gallery which promotes emergent Scottish artists and art forms and provides exhibition space to view their work.

W2 *Cockburn street, off Royal Mile at North Bridge.*

WC ♿ E Free

◷ All year round, Wed–Sun, 12 noon–5pm.

Tel 0131 220 1260
www.collectivegallery.net

11 Craigmillar Castle

This L-plan tower house was expanded in the 15th and 16th centuries, and is very well preserved. Mary, Queen of Scots stayed there after the murder of her secretary David Rizzio at Holyroodhouse.

E3 *Three miles SE of Edinburgh, off the A68.*

P WC ♿ ☕ 🏛 E £

◷ Apr–Sept, daily, 9.30am–6.30pm.
Oct–Mar, Sat–Wed, 9.30am–4.30pm

Tel 0131 661 4445
www.historic-scotland.gov.uk

12 Crichton Castle

The oldest part of Crichton dates back to the fourteenth century, but the most impressive features were added by Francis Stewart, Earl of Bothwell, who built Rennaissance style fireplaces, ceilings and unusual faceted walls.

F2 *Off the A68, three miles SW of Pathhead.*

P £

◷ Apr–Sept, daily, 9.30am–6.30pm.

Tel 01875 320017 www.historic-scotland.gov.uk

13 Dalkeith Country Park ♣

Once home to the Dukes of Buccleuch, the grounds surrounding Dalkeith Palace (not open to the public) contain farm animals, adventure play area, trails and a ranger service.

E2 *Seven miles S of Edinburgh city centre on A68.*

P WC ♿ ☕ 🏛 🍴 ♿ £

◷ Apr–Sept, daily, 10am–6pm.

Tel 0131 654 1666
www.dalkeithcountrypark.com

14 Dalmeny House

Dalmeny, the home of the Earls of Rosebery for over 300 years, contains fine eighteenth century furniture, tapestries, porcelain, portraits by Gainsborough, Raeburn and Reynolds, along with an impressive Napoleonic collection.

C3 *On Firth of Forth, eight miles W of Edinburgh; turn off A90 to B924, Dalmeny/South Queensferry exit.*

P WC ☕ 👥 ££

◷ Jul–Aug, Sun–Tue, 2–5.30pm.
(last admission 4.45pm).

Tel 0131 331 1888 www.dalmeny.co.uk

Edinburgh Castle & city from Salisbury Crags

15 Dean Gallery

Situated near the Scottish National Gallery of Modern Art, the Dean Gallery houses a collection of Dada and Surrealism. Edinburgh-born sculptor Sir Eduardo Paolozzi donated a large body of his work to the National Galleries of Scotland and his collection of prints, drawings, moulds and studio contents are housed here.

D3 *Belford Road, W end of city.*

P WC & 🍴 🏛 E 💷 Free

🕐 All year round, daily, 10am–5pm;
    Thur, 10am–7pm.

Tel 0131 624 6200   www.natgalscot.ac.uk

16 Dirleton Castle 🏰 ❁

Dating from the thirteenth century, and rebuilt in the fourteenth and sixteenth centuries, Direlton is now set in beautiful gardens, which contain the world's longest herbaceous border.

G4 *Dirleton, three miles W of North Berwick on the A198.*

P & 🏛 E ££

🕐 Apr–Sept, daily, 9.30am–6.30pm.
    Oct–Mar, daily, 9.30am–4.30pm;

Tel 01620 850330   www.historic-scotland.gov.uk

17 DOM Art Gallery 🏛

Edinburgh's oldest house, dating from 1480 and set in Advocate's Close off the High Street, provides the venue for a range of works by living European artists.

W2 *Opposite St Giles Cathedral, Royal Mile, Edinburgh city centre.*

WC 🏛 E 💷 £

🕐 All year round, Thur–Tue, 11am–5.30pm.

Tel 0131 225 9271

18 Dunbar Town House Museum 🏛

A local history museum located in a sixteenth century town house, with a hands-on introduction to archaeology.

J4 *High Street, Dunbar town centre.*

🏛 E AV Free

🕐 Apr–Oct, daily, 12.30–4.30pm.
    Nov–Mar, Sat & Sun, 2–4.30pm.

Tel 01368 863734   www.dunbarmuseum.org

19 Edinburgh Butterfly ★
and Insect World

Visitors can wander round an indoor tropical area and observe the natural behaviour of hundreds of butterflies as they feed off flowers and lay their eggs.

E2 *Off Edinburgh city bypass at Gilmerton exit or Sherrifhall Roundabout.*

P WC & 🍴 ✕ 🏛 E AV 🍴 💷 ££

🕐 Summer, daily, 9.30am–5.30pm.
    Winter, daily, 10am–5pm.

Tel 0131 663 4932
www.edinburgh-butterfly-world.co.uk

EDINBURGH CASTLE

The very symbol of Edinburgh, and of Scotland itself, the natural defensive site of Edinburgh Castle has been occupied since at least the Bronze Age. It was an important royal court from the eleventh century, with successive waves of building thereafter. King David II in the mid fourteenth century built the first defences across the east side of the crag to protect the gentler slope.

The castle has been the scene of many warlike episodes. During the Scots Wars of Independence, having been in English hands, it was re-taken by the Scots in 1312 and withstood sieges by King Henry IV of England in 1390 and 1400. The castle was under siege again in 1567, with Sir William Kirkcaldy of Grange holding out on behalf of Mary, Queen of Scots till 1573. Many other dramatic incidents are recorded and the last shots fired in anger were in 1745 as the castle held out against the blockading Jacobite forces of Bonnie Prince Charlie.

There is plenty for today's visitors to see. The much-altered Great Hall of King James IV dates originally from the early fifteenth century. Prominent from the Esplanade, the conspicuous Half Moon Battery was built on the ruins of King David's Tower (destroyed in the long siege of 1576-73). Another conspicuous building is the New Barracks of 1790, which adds to the castle's distinctive profile. The Vaults below, whose best description is in Stevenson's unfinished novel *St Ives*, are dank and atmospheric. The Scottish National War Memorial is a reminder of the sacrifices of the ordinary soldier, while the Honours of Scotland Exhibition displays the Scottish crown, sceptre and sword of state, the oldest surviving regalia in Europe. Visitors can also see the Stone of Scone, the crowning seat of the monarchy which was stolen by King Edward of England in the fourteenth century and returned to Scotland in 1996.

20 Edinburgh Castle

Edinburgh Castle, the capital's most famous sight, contains much of interest including the Stone of Destiny, the Scottish Crown Jewels (Honours of Scotland), Mons Meg, the One o'clock Gun and the National War Museum (see above).

V2 *Top of Royal Mile, Edinburgh city centre.*

🅿 🚾 ♿ ✕ 🏛 E ♨ £££

🕐 Apr–Sept, daily, 9.30am–6pm. Oct–Mar, daily, 9.30am–5pm. Last admission 45 minutes before closing.

Tel 0131 225 9846   www.historic-scotland.gov.uk

21 Edinburgh City Art Centre

Opened in 1980, the City Art Centre houses a range of exhibitions and is home to the city's Scottish art collection, totalling 3,500 works including paintings, photographs, tapestries and sculpture. It regularly showcases temporary exhibitions from around the world.

X3 *Market Street, behind Waverley Station in Edinburgh city centre.*

🚾 ♿ 🍴 E 🖼 Free

🕐 All year round, Mon–Sat, 10am–5pm. Times vary depending on exhibition. Admission for some events.

Tel 0131 529 3993   www.cac.org.uk

EDINBURGH INTERNATIONAL FESTIVAL, FRINGE AND TATTOO

No visitor to Edinburgh in August or early September can fail to notice the impact of the Edinburgh Festival (and its unruly cousin, the Fringe) on Scotland's capital. The atmosphere is dynamic – the city is simply the place to be. The first ever Festival was held in 1947, under an initiative to make Edinburgh an international centre for the arts, an opportunity which had come about because of the difficulties faced by older-established European festivals in the immediate post-war years.

The Festival has always provided a mix of music and drama from Scotland and much further afield. Perhaps its most famous event is the annual Edinburgh Military Tattoo (above), which takes place on the Castle Esplanade throughout the Festival. The Fringe came about as other smaller performing companies, who had not been invited to the 'official' Festival, turned up anyway. Now the combination of Festival and Fringe has created one of the largest arts festival in the world – a major artistic celebration where a host of today's internationally acclaimed media figures took their early steps on the road to fame.

22 Edinburgh Crystal Glasshouse ★

A chance to watch the craftsmen at work and discover the history of Edinburgh Crystal via an interactive exhibition. A VIP Experience (must be booked 24 hours in advance) gives visitors the opportunity to blow and cut glass themselves.

D2 *Take A701 from Edinburgh City Bypass, travelling S to Penicuik.*

🅿 ♿ 🚻 ♿ ✕ ⛪ E 🆎 🍴 🎫 £

⊕ Daily, Mar–Oct from 10am; Nov–Feb from 11am.

Tel 01968 675128   www.edinburgh-crystal.co.uk

23 Edinburgh Dungeon   🏛

An attraction focusing on the darker chapters in Scottish history, such as Burke and Hare and cannibal Sawney Bean, via a combination of live actors, tableaux and special effects.

W3 *Market Street, next to Waverley train station, Edinburgh city centre.*

⛪ 🎫 £££

⊕ Daily, Jul–Aug, 10am–7pm; Nov–Feb, 11am–4pm; Sept–Oct & Mar–Jun, 10am–5pm.

Tel 0131 240 1000   www.thedungeons.com

THE FORTH BRIDGE

In 1873 the foundation stone was laid for a bridge, designed by Sir Thomas Bouch, across the estuary of the River Forth. When Bouch's Tay Bridge fell in 1879, work on the Forth Bridge was abandoned. A contract for a new Forth Bridge was awarded three years later to Tancred, Arrol and Co. To allay public anxiety, steel and not cast iron was used. The new bridge was designed on the cantilever principle (invented in the Far East).

By 1890 the structure was complete with 54,000 tons of steel, 194,000 cubic yards of granite, stone and concrete, plus 7 million rivets. (The Prince of Wales banged in the last one during the opening ceremony.) At 2.5km (1.6 miles) long and 10m (361 ft) to the top of the cantilever it was the largest steel structure of its type in the world at the time. More than a century later it still carries today's high-speed trains on the east coast main line. Perhaps its most famous statistic is the fact that on a hot summer day the bridge is a metre longer than on a frosty day in winter *(see also p93).*

24 Edinburgh Zoo

Over 1,000 animals, from mammals to amphibians, reptiles to birds, are kept in some 80 acres of sloping parkland. Many are rare species with important breeding programmes underway, but perhaps the most famous creatures are the penguins which parade outside their enclosure every lunchtime (Mar–Oct). Activities and events such as animal handling, talks, touch tables, exhibitions and trails run throughout the year.

D3 *Three miles W of Edinburgh city centre on A8.*

P WC ⛊ ✕ ⛫ E AV ⊼ 𝄃 ⊞ ££

🕐 Apr–Sept, daily 9am–6pm. Nov–Feb, 9am–4.30pm. Oct & Mar, daily, 9am–5pm.

Tel 0131 334 9171 www.edinburghzoo.org.uk

25 Georgian House

Robert Adam designed this stylish Georgian town house as part of Charlotte Square, built at the end of the eighteenth century as part of the city of Edinburgh's New Town. A number of opulent rooms contain silver, china, paintings and furniture reflective of the era.

U3 *Charlotte Square, off west end of Princes Street, Edinburgh city centre.*

⛫ AV ⚹ ⊞ ££

🕐 Mar & Nov, daily, 11am–3pm. Apr–Jun & Sep–Oct, 10am–5pm. July–Aug, 10am–7pm. Last admission 30 mins before closing.

Tel 0131 226 3318 www.nts.org.uk

Greyfriars Bobby, Edinburgh

26 Gladstone's Land 👻 🏰

This six-storey building is an excellent example of a seventeenth century tenement built in the overcrowded Old Town area of Edinburgh. It contains furnished rooms typical of the era and beautiful painted ceilings.

W2 *In the Lawnmarket, at the castle end of the Royal Mile, Edinburgh city centre.*

♿ 🏛 ££
⊕ Apr–Oct, daily, 10am–5pm; Sun, 2–5pm. July–Aug, 10am–7pm.
Tel 0131 226 5856   www.nts.org.uk

27 Glenkinchie Distillery 🥃

A working distillery featuring an exhibition, guided tour and tastings.

F2 *At Peastonbank, turn S off A6093 at Pencaitland.*

🅿 WC ♿ 🏛 E AV 🍴 🧗 🎫 ££
⊕ Easter–Oct, Mon–Sat, 10am–4pm (last tour); Sun, 12 noon–4pm. Restricted hours in winter; telephone for details.
Tel 01875 342004   www.malts.com

28 Granton Centre 🏛

The major store for the National Museums of Scotland where important conservation work is carried out, preparing thousands of objects for display at NMS museums. The centre also plays a vital role in saving scientific evidence for research.

D3 *West Granton Road, Edinburgh.*

🅿 WC £
⊕ Every Tue; visits must be booked a day in advance.
Tel 0131 247 4470
www.nms.ac.uk

29 Greyfriars Bobby ★

A bronze statue of Greyfriars Bobby, stands opposite Greyfriars Kirk. The Skye terrier famously sat by his master's grave in the churchyard for 14 years until his own death in 1872. He was given the Freedom of the City and his engraved collar and feeding bowl can be seen at the Museum of Edinburgh (see page 78). John Gray's grave lies just inside the entrance to the kirkyard and the little dog is buried nearby.

W2 *Greyfriars Place, George IV Bridge, S of Edinburgh city centre.*

Free
⊕ Open access.

30 Greyfriars Kirk

Very little remains of the original 17th-century church building, but it was there in 1638 that the congregation and Scots noblemen gathered to sign the National Covenant. Visitors can see an original copy of the Covenant on display in the church, and tour the Kirkyard, which is full of fascinating 17th- and 18th-century graves and monuments.

W2 *Greyfriars Place, off George IV Bridge, S of Edinburgh city centre.*

♿ 🏛 E AV Free
⊕ Easter–Oct, Mon–Fri, 10.30am–4.30pm; Sat, 10.30am–2.30pm. Nov–Mar, Thur, 1.30–3.30pm only.
Tel 0131 226 5429
www.greyfriarskirk.com

31 Gullane Golf Course

Established in 1882, Gullane has been an important centre for the game of golf. Gullane No 1, the principle of the three courses, has been a venue for many important championships in its long history.

G4 *On A198, 16 miles E of Edinburgh.*

P WC ⅃ X ⌂ E

⊕ Booking essential.

Tel 01620 842255
www.gullanegolfclub.co.uk

32 Holyrood Park

This huge open area in the heart of Edinburgh contains many sites of historic interest, including a prehistoric farmstead, the remains of St Anthony's Chapel and a number of holy wells, the most interesting of which is St Margaret's Well, a fifteenth century Gothic construction. Visitors can also make use of various walks past one of three lochs, and scale Arthur's Seat, part of an old volcano offering stunning views across the city and beyond. Holyrood Lodge Information Centre houses an exhibition, and a ranger service provides a number of services.

Z2 *E of Edinburgh city centre and SE of Holyrood Palace, on Queen's Drive.*

P E 🚶 Free

⊕ Open access. Visitor Centre: Mon–Thur, 10am–4pm; Fri, 10am–3.30pm.

Tel 0131 652 8150
www.historic-scotland.gov.uk

33 Hopetoun House

Home of the Marquis of Linlithgow, Hopetoun House is situated in extensive parkland by the Firth of Forth, with views of the famous bridges and the Fife coast. The original building was extended in the early eighteenth century by William Adam. Contents include fine furniture, paintings, tapestries and ceramics.

C4 *South Queensferry, twelve miles NW of Edinburgh city centre.*

P WC X ⌂ E 🚶 🚶 E ££

⊕ Apr–Sept, daily, 10am–5.30pm. Last entry 4.30pm.

Tel 0131 331 2451
www.hopetounhouse.com

34 House of the Binns

Situated in extensive parkland, this seventeenth century house has been the home of the Dalyell family for nearly 400 years. Visitors can see impressive moulded plaster ceilings along with a collection of furnishings, china and portraits.

B3 *Linlithgow, fifteen miles W of Edinburgh on A904.*

P WC ⅃ 🚶 🚶 ££

⊕ Jun–Sept, daily except Friday, 2–5pm.

Tel 01506 834255
www.nts.org.uk

35 Inchcolm Abbey

These well preserved ruins of an Augustinian monastery are located on the island of Inchcolm in the Firth of Forth, and include an octagonal chapter house and cloister of the thirteenth/fourteenth centuries. Island wildlife includes seals, dolphins, puffins and various other sea and shore birds. Access is via the *Maid of the Forth* ferry, which takes passengers under the famous Forth Rail Bridge.

D4 *Inchcolm, Firth of Firth. Ferry service from Hawes Pier, South Queensferry, and Town Pier, North Queensferry.*

WC ⅃ ⌂ E 🚶 ££

⊕ Apr–Sept, weather permitting.

Abbey: Tel 01383 823332
www.historic-scotland.gov.uk
Cruises: Tel 0131 331 4857
www.maidoftheforth.co.uk

36 Inveresk Lodge Garden

Shrubs, old roses and herbaceous beds form this beautiful terraced garden, which also contains an aviary, tree ferns and exotics. The hill part of the garden provides views of the Pentlands.

E3 *Inveresk, on A6124, S of Musselburgh.*

⅃ 🚶 £

⊕ All year, daily, 10am–6pm or dusk if earlier. House not open.

Tel 01721 722502
www.nts.org.uk

John Knox House, Edinburgh

37 John Knox House

A medieval house associated with John Knox, Scotland's religious reformer, although it is uncertain whether he actually lived here. An exhibition portrays his life and work, along with information on goldsmith James Mossman, also connected to the house. Original features include a magnificent painted ceiling.

X3 *High Street, Edinburgh city centre.*

WC & ✕ ⌂ E AV £ £

🕑 Closed for refurbishment due to re-open summer 2005. Telephone for details.

Tel 0131 556 9579

38 John Muir's Birthplace

John Muir, a pioneering conservationist in North America, was born on the top floor of this house in 1838, and lived here as a child before moving abroad. The flat is decorated and furnished in the style of the era.

J3 *High Street, Dunbar town centre.*

WC & ⌂ E AV Free

🕑 Apr–Oct, Mon–Sat, 10am–5pm; Sun, 1–5pm. Nov–Mar, closed Mon–Tue.

Tel 01620 828203 www.jmbt.org.uk

39 John Muir Country Park

Parkland set in a scenic position on the coast, with miles of open country to explore.

J4 *Near Dunbar, on the coast, off A1.*

P WC & 🌾 🧍 Free

🕑 Open access.

Tel 01620 827318

40 Kinneil Museum

As well as housing local history exhibits, the building also acts as an interpretive centre for Kinneil Estate.

B4 *Bo'ness, on S shore of the Firth of Forth, W of Edinburgh on A904.*

P WC ⌂ E AV ⌖ Free

🕑 All year round, Mon–Sat, 12.30–4pm.

Tel 01506 778530 www.falkirk.gov.uk

41 Lauriston Castle

Lauriston began life as a 1590s tower house, and was later extended in the early nineteenth century. Successive private owners enjoyed its enviable location by the Firth of Forth, until the estate was finally left in trust to the nation. Guided tours highlight furniture, paintings, tapestries and porcelain, all in classic Edwardian style. Events run from Easter to December.

D3 *Cramond Road South, NW of Edinburgh city centre.*

P WC & E 🍴 🚌 🚶 ££

🕐 Apr–Oct, Sat–Thur, 11am–1pm & 2–5pm.
Nov–Mar, weekends, 2–4pm.
Last admission 40 minutes before closing.

Tel 0131 336 2060   www.cac.org.uk

42 Lennoxlove House

Dating from the fourteenth century and home to the Duke of Hamilton, Lennoxlove contains fine furniture, paintings and Mary, Queen of Scots memorabilia including a Death Mask and silver casket.

G3 *Two miles S of Haddington, off B6368/9.*

P WC & 🍴 🚶 🔲 ££

🕐 Easter–Oct, Wed, Thur & Sun, 11.30am–3pm.
Times subject to change.
Groups at anytime by prior arrangement.

Tel 01620 823720   www.lennoxlove.org

43 Linlithgow Canal Centre

Visitors can take boat trips along the Union Canal to the Avon Aqueduct or through the town of Linlithgow. A museum contains photographs and canal artefacts.

B3 *Manse Road Basin, Linlithgow; follow signs.*

P WC & 🍴 E AV 🍴 ££

🕐 Museum (free): Easter–Oct, weekends, 2–5pm.
Jul & Aug, daily, 2–5pm. Trips: Easter–Oct,
weekends, from 2pm. Jul–Aug, daily from 2pm.

Tel 01506 671215   www.lucs.org.uk

44 Linlithgow Palace 🏰

Built in the fifteenth century, Linlithgow has many connections with royalty; it was the birthplace of James V (the coat of arms pictured above show the four orders of chivalry to which he belonged) and Mary, Queen of Scots and Bonnie Prince Charlie spent the night here in 1745. These impressive ruins are set in parkland by Linlithgow Loch.

B3 *Linlithgow, off the M9 at J3 northbound; J4 southbound.*

P WC 🔔 E 🍴 £

🕐 Apr–Sept, daily, 9.30am–6.30pm.
Oct–Mar, daily, 9.30am–4.30pm.

Tel 01506 842896
www.historic-scotland.gov.uk

Detail from Linlithgow Palace

45 Linlithgow Story 🏛

A museum telling the story of Linlithgow, past and present, set in an eighteenth century town house with a large, peaceful garden.

B3 *High Street, near town centre, W of Linlithgow Cross.*

WC 🔔 E AV 🍴 £

🕐 Easter–Oct, 10am–5pm; Sun, 1–4pm.

Tel 01506 670677   www.linlithgowstory.org.uk

46 Malleny Garden

A walled garden with a large collection of old-fashioned roses and fine herbaceous borders. Special features include four 400-year-old clipped yew trees, a herb garden and the National Bonsai Collection for Scotland.

C2 *Balerno, off the A70, six miles W of Edinburgh city centre.*

P WC & £

🕐 All year, daily, 10am–6pm or dusk if earlier.

Tel 0131 449 2283   www.nts.org.uk

47 Midlothian Snowsports Centre

An artificial ski centre with two main slopes, two nursery slopes and a jump slope, all floodlit throughout winter. Ski and snowboard instruction and equipment are provided. Also available is a downhill mountain bike trail, and chairlift which is open to sightseers.

D2 *On A702, half a mile off Edinburgh City bypass at Lothianburn Junction.*

P WC 🍴 🚌 🚶 🔲 ££

🕐 Sept–Apr, Sun, 9.30am–7pm, Mon–Sat & May–Aug,
Mon–Fri, 9.30am–9pm; Sat–Sun, 9.30am–7pm.

Tel 0131 445 4433   www.midlothian.gov.uk

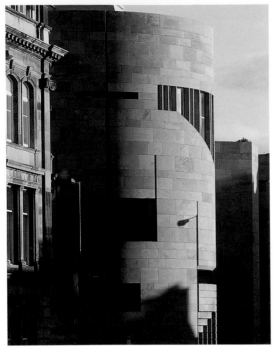

Museum of Scotland, Edinburgh

48 Museum of Childhood 🏛

A museum looking at the history of childhood, with displays of toys and games from all over the world, from dolls to teddy bears, train sets to tricycles. Temporary exhibitions and events are also organised for visitors.

X2 *High Street, Edinburgh city centre.*

  ⟋ 🏛 E AV ⌷ Free

🕑 Mon–Sat, 10am–5pm.
Jul & Aug, also Sun, 12 noon–5pm.

Tel 0131 529 4142 www.cac.org.uk

49 Museum of Edinburgh 🏛

This museum looks at the history of Edinburgh, and along with occasional exhibitions, it contains silver, ceramics and a floor dedicated to Edinburgh-born Earl Haig, soldier and founder of the British Legion.

Y3 *The Canongate, Edinburgh city centre.*

WC 🏛 E Free

🕑 All year round, Mon–Sat, 10am–5pm
(during the festival open Sun, 2–5pm).

Tel 0131 529 4143 www.cac.org.uk

50 Museum of Flight 🏛

Two massive hangars, part of a Second World War airfield, house Scotland's national aviation collection, including a variety of aeroplanes, rockets and memorabilia. Among the exhibits are the huge single-seater Lightning, Blue Streak rocket and a 100-year-old hang glider The Hawk. New for 2005, *The Concorde Experience.*

G3 *East Fortune Airfield, on B1347, NE of Haddington.*

P WC ⟋ 🍵 🏛 E ⌷ ⋇ 🖾 £

🕑 Apr–Oct, daily, 10am–5pm.
Nov–Mar, telephone for details.

Tel 01620 880308 www.nms.ac.uk/flight

51 Museum of Scotland 🏛

A museum devoted to the history of Scotland, including its land, people and their achievements. A series of galleries take visitors from Scotland's geological beginnings through to the twentieth century.

W2 *Chambers Street, Edinburgh city centre.*

WC ⟋ 🍵 ✕ 🏛 E AV ⌷ ⋇ 🖾 Free

🕑 Mon–Sat, 10am–5pm; Tue, 10am–8pm;
Sun, 12 noon–5pm.

Tel 0131 247 4422 www.nms.ac.uk/mos

52 Myreton Motor Museum 🏛

Houses a range of vehicles dating from 1896, including cars, motor cycles, bicycles, military vehicles and interesting ephemera.

G4 *Off A198, three miles from Aberlady.*

P WC ££

🕑 Apr–Oct, daily, 11am–4pm.
Nov–Mar, Sat–Sun, 11am–3pm.

Tel 01875 870288

53 National Flag Heritage Centre 🏛

This occupies a lectern doocot built in 1583 by George Hepburn, father of Sir John Hepburn, the founder and first colonel of the Royal Scots. An audio-visual dramatisation tells the story of the St Andrew's Cross, Scotland's national flag, believed to have originated in a battle fought near Athelstaneford.

G3 *Twenty miles E of Edinburgh on A1, turning off at B1347.*

WC AV ⋇ 👫 Free

🕑 Apr–Oct, daily, 10am–6pm.

Tel 01368 863239

EDINBURGH NEW TOWN

Fletcher of Saltoun, the Scottish patriot, wrote in 1698 that 'the bad situation of Edinburgh, has been one great occasion of the poverty and uncleanliness in which the greater part of the people of Scotland live'. This was a strong element in the drive to create a New Town. The city fathers ran a competition, and the winner was an unknown architect, James Craig, whose symmetrical grid iron plan was adopted thereafter. The axis and highest point was George Street, balanced to the north by Queen Street, facing gardens, and to the south by Princes Street, likewise open on one side to gardens. St Andrew's Square balanced Charlotte Square. Lesser streets with smaller properties – Rose Street matching Thistle Street, complete with service lanes – were also in the plan, which was mostly built before the end of the eighteenth century.

Other developments followed on to the north in the accepted New Town idiom of colonnaded, symmetrical facades – palace-fronted in the case of the north side of Charlotte Square – sometimes overlooking leafy private but communal gardens. Early New Town main-door properties even had entrance halls designed to accommodate the long handles of sedan chairs.

54 National Gallery of Scotland

Home to Scotland's greatest collection of European paintings and sculpture from the Renaissance to Post-Impressionism. Included amongst the some 20,000 items are fine examples of Italian and Netherlandish drawings, and a collection of Scottish art featuring Ramsay, Raeburn, McTaggart and Wilkie plus many others.

W3 *Centre of Edinburgh on the Mound, off Princes Street.*

WC & ⊞ E ⊞ Free

☉ Daily, 10am–5pm; Thur until 7pm. Extended opening during the Festival. Closed 25 & 26 Dec.

Tel 0131 624 6200   www.natgalscot.ac.uk

55 National War Museum

The National War Museum, (formerly the Scottish United Services Museum), explores the Scottish experience of war and military service over the last 400 years. It also reveals the extent to which war and military service have influenced Scotland's history, its sense of identity and reputation abroad.

V2 *Within Edinburgh Castle, top of the Royal Mile, city centre.*

P WC & ♥ ⊞ ⚹ ⊞ ££

☉ Apr–Oct, daily, 9.45am–5.30pm. Nov–Mar, closes 4.45pm.

Tel 0131 225 7534   www.nms.ac.uk

56 Nelson Monument ★

Erected in the early nineteenth century, this telescopic-shaped tower honours Admiral Nelson's victory and death at the battle of Trafalgar. A time ball, added in 1852, is lowered every day as the one o'clock gun is fired from Edinburgh Castle. Visitors can climb to the top of this 100 ft tower and enjoy views across the city.

X3 *East end of Edinburgh city centre, on Calton Hill.*

P ⊞ E ⚹ £

☉ Apr–Sept, Mon, 1–6pm; Tue–Sat, 10am–6pm. Oct–Mar, Mon–Sat, 10am–3pm.

Tel 0131 556 2716   www.cac.org.uk

57 Newhailes

A late 17th-century palladian house with 18th-century additions and interiors. The house contains a collection of paintings, including portraits by Sir John Medina and Allan Ramsay. Guided tours only - booking advised.

E3 *Off A6095 Newhailes Road, Musselburgh.*

P WC & ⊞ ⚹ ⊞ £££

☉ House & Visitor centre: Apr–Sept, Thur–Mon, 12–5pm; Oct, Sat–Sun, 12–5pm. Grounds: All year, 10am–6pm.

Tel 0131 653 5599   www.nts.org.uk

Palace of Holyroodhouse, Edinburgh

58 Newhaven Heritage Centre 🏛

A local history museum telling the story of
Newhaven, once a busy fishing village set on the
Firth of Forth, and the people who lived there.

D3 *Newhaven Harbour, N of city centre.*

🅿 ♿ ⛪ E AV Free
🕐 All year round, daily, 12 noon–4.45pm.
Tel 0131 551 4165   www.cac.org.uk

59 No. 28 Charlotte Square 🏛

Designed by Robert Adam, Charlotte Square
is one of the finest Georgian squares in Britain.
No. 28 is now the head office of the National
Trust for Scotland, and contains a typical 1820's
drawing room with Regency furniture and
a collection of twentieth century paintings.

U3 *Edinburgh city centre, off west end
of Princes Street.*

♿ ♨ ✕ ⛪ Free
🕐 Mid Jan–24 Dec, Mon–Sat, 9.30am–5pm.
Tel 0131 243 9300   www.nts.org.uk

60 North Berwick Golf Course 🏌

Founded in 1832, North Berwick Golf Club
is one of Scotland's oldest; players encounter
a number of blind shots, ridges across fairways
and walls on this ancient links. Although private,
visitors can play at a reasonable fee.

G4 *Off A198, E of Edinburgh.*

WC ♿ ✕ ⛪
🕐 Booking advisable.
Tel 01620 892135

61 Our Dynamic Earth ★

Our Dynamic Earth tells the story of our
planet using the latest technology. Visitors
travel back in time to witness the Big Bang
and the formation of the earth, and go on
to experience volcanoes, earthquakes, glaciers,
polar ice and a tropical rainstorm.

Y2 *Holyrood Road, Edinburgh, next to the Palace
of Holyroodhouse.*

🅿 WC ♿ ✕ ⛪ E AV ☀ ⛺ 🚌 £££
🕐 Apr–Oct, daily, 10am–6pm.
    Nov–Mar, Wed–Sun, 10am–5pm.
    Last entry 80 minutes before closing.
Tel 0131 550 7800   www.dynamicearth.co.uk

62 Palace of Holyroodhouse 🏰 ⚜

Situated at the foot of Arthur's Seat and
in the pleasant surroundings of Queen's Park,
the palace is the official residence of Her Majesty
the Queen in Scotland. Visitors can see an
impressive array of furnishings, plasterwork
ceilings and tapestries in the palace's State
Apartments and a collection of Stewart relics.

The remains of Holyrood Abbey, located within the grounds, date back to the twelfth and thirteenth centuries. The Queen's Gallery, opened in 2002, exhibits fine art from the Royal Collection.

Z3 *At the E end of the Royal Mile, Edinburgh city centre.*

WC & ⛪ 🎫 £££

🕐 Apr–Oct, 9.30am–5.15pm (last admission). Nov–Mar, 9.30am–3.45pm (last admission). Times subject to change at short notice.

Tel 0131 556 7371
www.the-royal-collection.org.uk

63 People's Story

Located in the Canongate Tolbooth, the museum recounts the story of the people of Edinburgh from the end of the eighteenth century onwards. A series of reconstructions from the city's past are accompanied by sights, sounds and smells.

Y3 *Next to Canongate Church, near the foot of the Royal Mile.*

WC & ⛪ E AV Free

🕐 All year round, Mon–Sat, 10am–5pm; Festival hours, Sun, 2–5pm.

Tel 0131 529 4057   www.cac.org.uk

64 Polkemmet Country Park

A former private estate with the River Almond flowing through mixed woodlands. Facilities include a golf course and driving range, barbecue site, play area, walks, and a ranger service.

A2 *On N side of B7066, between Whitburn and Harthill; signposted from J4 & J5 of M8.*

P WC & 🍴 ✕ 🎍 👫 Free

🕐 Park open at all times. Facilities: summer 7am–9pm; winter Mon–Fri, 10am–6pm; weekends, 9am–4.30pm.

Tel 01501 743905   www.beecraigs.com

65 Preston Mill and Phantassie Doocot

Visitors can see the water wheel and grain milling machinery in action at this eighteenth century mill, which is set in a scenic spot beside a millpond inhabited by ducks and geese.

H3 *East Linton, off the A1, 23 miles E of Edinburgh.*

P & ⛪ E 🎍 👫 £

🕐 Apr–Sept, Thur–Mon, 12 noon–5pm;

Tel 01620 860426
www.nts.org.uk

66 Prestongrange Museum

This museum, based at a former colliery, tells the story of local industries and the people who worked in them. Visitors can see a Cornish Beam Engine which once pumped water from the mine, and ride on colliery locomotives on specific 'steam days'. Also on site is an exhibition on stars, planets and space exploration, and the story of the local pottery industry.

F3 *Fifteen miles E of Edinburgh on B1348 by Prestonpans.*

P WC & 🍴 ⛪ E 🎍 ☀ 👫 Free

🕐 End Mar–Oct, daily, 11am–4pm.

Tel 0131 653 2904
www.prestongrangemuseum.org

67 Queensferry Museum

A museum portraying the history of Queensferry, with views across the Forth to the two bridges. An exhibition describes the building of the bridges, the development of the Queensferry Passage and the expansion of the former royal burgh – previously known as the 'Queen's Ferry' – named in honour of Queen Margaret (1046–1093).

C3 *Off A90, 12 miles W of Edinburgh.*

E ☀ Free

🕐 Open all year, Mon, Thur, Fri & Sat, 10am–1pm & 2.15–5pm; Sun, 12 noon–4.30pm. Last admission 30 min before closing.

Tel 0131 331 5545   www.cac.org.uk

68 Roslin Glen Country Park

The glen, set along the North Esk river, is a haven for wildlife including kingfishers, the daubenton bat, roe deer and great spotted woodpeckers. Other features include old gunpowder mills, Roslin Castle and views of Rosslyn Chapel.

E2 *On B7026 S of Edinburgh.*

P 🎍 ☀ 👫 Free

🕐 Apr–Sept, daily, 8am–8pm. Oct–Mar, daily, 8am–5pm.

Tel 01875 821990

THE ROYAL MILE AND OLD TOWN, EDINBURGH

In the shadow of the rock on which Edinburgh Castle was founded, the town of Edinburgh grew up. Long ages before, an eastward grinding glacier had rounded both sides of the castle crag, creating a tail of material which sloped down to the east. The Old Town spread down this ramp, with the castle as its head and the chain of streets as a backbone which became known as the Royal Mile. From the Royal Mile closes (alleyways) lead off like ribs from the backbone, these narrow ways hemmed in by tall tenements or 'lands'.

Defining the extent of the early settlement, the first town wall was built around 1450 and was known as the King's Wall. The Flodden Wall (1514 onwards) took in a much larger area, crossing today's Royal Mile at the Netherbow then running by Drummond Street, through the site of the Royal Museum of Scotland. The best preserved portion of the later Telfers Wall (1623 onwards) survives by the Vennel, on the south side of the Grassmarket. Eventually, closely confined on its windy ridge, the increasingly insanitary and overcrowded Old Town was ready for expansion by the mid-18th century.

69 Rosslyn Chapel ♣

This unique chapel was built in 1446 by William St. Clair, Prince of Orkney, and stands on the edge of the wooded Esk Valley. Conforming neither to the architecture or fashions of its time, the chapel retains an aura of mystery. The interior is heavy with sculptures and intricate carvings of Biblical stories plus the famous Apprentice Pillar, and there are many references to the Knights Templar and Freemasonry.

E2 *Roslin village, six miles S of Edinburgh off A701 at Straiton Juntion.*

🅿 ♿ ♿ ☕ ⛪ E ☀ ♟ ⌨ ££

⏰ Mon–Sat, 10am–5pm; Sun, 12 noon–4.45pm.

Tel 0131 440 2159   www.rosslynchapel.org.uk

70 Royal Botanic Gardens Edinburgh ❀

Seventy acres of gardens containing glasshouses, a rock garden, Chinese garden and herbaceous border, along with views of the city skyline and a programme of events, exhibitions and activities.

D3 *Inverleith Row, one mile N of city centre.*

♿ ♿ ♿ ✗ ⛪ E ☀ ♟ ⌨ Free

⏰ All year round, daily, 10am. Closes: Mar & Oct, 6pm; Apr–Sept, 7pm; Nov–Feb, 4pm.

Tel 0131 552 7171   www.rbge.org.uk

71 Royal Museum 🏛

This museum houses outstanding collections reflecting the diversity of life on earth and the ingenuity of human kind. The Victorian building is distinguished by a glass-topped roof which floods the main hall with natural light.

W2 *Chambers Street, Edinburgh city centre.*

♿ ♿ ♿ ⛪ E ⌨ Free

⏰ Mon–Sat, 10am–5pm; Tue open until 8pm; Sun, 12 noon–5pm.

Tel 0131 247 4219   www.nms.ac.uk/royal

72 Royal Observatory Visitor Centre 🏛

Includes hands-on exhibits, computer gallery, exhibition on the history of the Royal Observatory and Astronomy in Edinburgh and the second largest telescope in Scotland. There are also special events and workshops during school holidays, winter lectures, public observing (Oct–Mar) and astronomy classes.

D3 *Leave City Bypass at Straiton, follow A701 to lights at W Mains Road, turn left and follow signs.*

P WC ⛪ E ✳ ⚔ 🎫 ££

🕐 All year, Fri only, 7–9pm.
   Check website for details.

Tel 0131 668 8405   www.roe.ac.uk

73 Royal Yacht Britannia   ★

The Royal Yacht Britannia, launched at Clydebank in 1953, served the Royal Family for over forty years, and travelled over a million miles. Now berthed at Leith, visitors can take an audio tour of five decks, and discover what life was like for the Royal family and crew on board. On show is the royal dining room, sitting room and sun lounge on the Verandah deck, along with the bridge and engine room. As well as the vessel itself, visitors can tour the visitor centre which houses an audio-visual presentation, the royal barge, reconstructed wheelhouse and an exhibition of photographs featuring the Royal family on the Britannia.

D3 *Signposted through Leith, NW end of Edinburgh; a dedicated bus runs from Waverley Bridge, beside Waverley train station.*

P WC ♿ ⛪ E AV ✳ 🎫 £££

🕐 Nov–Feb, daily, 10am–3.30pm (last admission).
   Mar–Oct, 9.30am–4.30pm (last admission).

Tel 0131 555 5566
www.royalyachtbritannia.co.uk

74 Scotch Whisky Heritage Centre   🏛

Visitors can discover the secrets of whisky making via a special 'barrel ride' and commentary; malts, grain and blends are explained, and there are free tastings for adults.

W2 *Top of Royal Mile, adjacent to Edinburgh Castle.*

WC ♿ 🍴 ⛪ AV 🎫 £££

🕐 Summer, daily, 9.30am–5.30pm.
   Winter, 10am–5pm. Closed 25 Dec.

Tel 0131 220 0441   www.whisky-heritage.co.uk

75 Scott Monument   ★

When writer Sir Walter Scott died in 1832, a competition was launched welcoming designs for a suitable memorial. The winner was George Meikle Kemp, and his imposing 200 ft monument was erected in the city centre between 1840 and 1846. Features include carvings of Scott's literary characters and a statue of the writer himself made from marble. Visitors can still climb the 287 steps to the top and admire panoramic views over Edinburgh.

W3 *East Princes Street, Edinburgh city centre.*

✳ £

🕐 Apr–Sept, Mon–Sat, 9am–6pm; Sun, 10am–6pm.
   Oct-Mar, Mon–Sat, 9am–3pm; Sun, 10am–3pm.

Tel 0131 529 4068/3993   www.cac.org.uk

76 Scottish Mining Museum   🏛

A mining museum which describes the highs and lows of an industry that was once the backbone in Scotland. Set inside the restored Lady Victoria Colliery, visitors can see, hear and feel the many different elements that made up this dangerous and sometimes deadly working environment.

E2 *Newtongrange, off A7.*

P WC ♿ 🍴 ✕ ⛪ E AV 🪑 ✳ 🎫 ££

🕐 Feb–Oct, daily, 10am–5pm.
   Nov–Jan, daily, 10am–4pm.

Tel 0131 663 7519
www.scottishminingmuseum.com

77 Scottish National Gallery of Modern Art

The gallery is set in a neo-classical building and contains major works by Vuillard, Matisse, Kirchner, Picasso, Magritte, Dali and Ernst. Also housed here is a collection of 20th century Scottish art by Charles Rennie Mackintosh, the Colourists and members of the Edinburgh School such as Gillies, Redpath, MacTaggart and Philipson. The surrounding grounds provide a setting for sculptures by Henry Moore, Barbara Hepworth and Anthony Caro.

D3 *Belford Road, in the W end of Edinburgh.*

P WC & ⛾ ⌘ E ☀ ⊞ Free

⊕ All year round, daily, 10am–5pm; Thur closes 7pm. Closed Christmas. Extended Festival opening.

Tel 0131 624 6200   www.natgalscot.ac.uk

78 Scottish National Portrait Gallery

The visual history of Scotland is told through portraits of the figures who shaped it, including royals and rebels, poets and philosophers, heroes and villains. The collection features work by Scottish artists along with English, European and American masters such as Van Dyck, Gainsborough and Rodin. Sculptures, miniatures, coins, medallions, drawings and watercolours are also housed here along with the National Photograph Collection. Charge is made for some exhibitions.

W3 *E end of Queen Street, Edinburgh city centre.*

WC & ⛾ ⌘ E ⊞ Free

⊕ Daily, 10am–5pm; Thur, closes 7pm. Closed Christmas. Extended Festival opening.

Tel 0131 624 6200   www.natgalscot.ac.uk

79 Scottish Parliament ★

Visitors can see Parliament in action in the new Scottish Parliament building opened in 2004. View the Debating Chamber from the public galleries, visit an exhibition that explains how Parliament works. Guided tours available (charges apply).

Y3 *Holyrood, at the foot of the Royal Mile, Edinburgh city centre.*

WC & ⛾ ⌘ E ⊞ Free

⊕ Business days (normally Tues–Thur), all year, 9am–7pm. Non-business days (normally Mon & Fri and every weekday when in recess), Apr–Oct, 10am–9pm. Nov–Mar, 10am–4pm.

Tel 0131 348 5200   www.scottishparliament.uk

80 Scottish Seabird Centre ★

The centre looks towards the islands in the Firth of Forth off North Berwick which act as a haven for over 150,000 nesting seabirds. The Bass Rock alone attracts 100,000 gannets every year, while the Isle of May is home to a breeding seal colony. Visitors can zoom in on gannets, puffins and various other shore and seabirds via live interactive cameras, and see close up images of seal pups throughout the winter season.

G4 *Harbour front, North Berwick; signposted from Edinburgh on A1.*

P WC & ⛾ ✕ ⌘ C AV 🚌 ☀ 🧍 ⊞ ££

⊕ All year round, summer, 10am–6pm. Winter, 10am–4pm; weekends, closes 5.30pm.

Tel 01620 890202   www.seabird.org

81 Seton Collegiate Church

Visitors can see the remains of this fifteenth century church, which includes an impressive vaulted chancel and apse.

F3 *One mile SE of Cockenzie off the A198.*

P E ⌘ £

⊕ Apr–Sept, daily, 9.30am–6.30pm.

Tel 01875 813334   www.historic-scotland.gov.uk

82 St Giles' Cathedral

Evidence suggests that a church stood on this site as far back as the ninth century, but the current building was erected in the fourteenth and fifteenth centuries. External features include its unique crown spire, an integral part of the city's skyline for the last 500 years. Inside, visitors can see memorials to many great Scots such as Stevenson and Burns, modern and traditional stained glass windows and Lorimer's early twentieth century Thistle Chapel.

W2 *Parliament Square, on the Royal Mile, Edinburgh city centre.*

WC ⛾ ⌘ ⊞ Free

⊕ May–Sept, Mon–Fri, 9am–7pm; Sat, 9am–5pm. Oct–Apr, Mon–Sat, 9am–5pm; All year Sun, 1–5pm.

Tel 0131 225 9442   www.stgiles.net

83 St Mary's Episcopal Cathedral ✝

This Victorian Gothic cathedral by George Gilbert Scott is the largest ecclesiastical building to be built in Scotland since the Reformation. Features include the seventeenth century Old Coates House and the Song School famous for its restored mural painted by Phoebe Anna Traquair.

D3 *Palmerston Place, W end of Edinburgh city centre.*

[WC] & 🏛 Free

🕐 Mon–Fri, 7.30am–6pm; Sat, 7.30am–5pm; Sun, 8am–5pm.

Tel 0131 225 6293   www.cathedral.net

84 Tantallon Castle

Set dramatically on cliffs edging the Firth of Forth, Tantallon Castle has suffered a turbulent history. It was originally built in the fourteenth century, and featured huge 50 ft walls with an imposing set of towers. Much fought over, it was strengthened during the sixteenth century, but eventually set into ruins by General Monk and his followers in 1651.

H4 *Three miles E of North Berwick off the A198.*

[P] [WC] & 🏛 E ☙ £

🕐 Apr–Sept, daily, 9.30am–6.30pm. Oct–Mar, Sat–Wed, 9.30am–4.30pm

Tel 01620 892727   www.historic-scotland.gov.uk

85 Tartan Weaving Mill and Exhibition

A working mill offering visitors the chance to learn about the making of tartan and try their hand at weaving.

W2 *East end of the Royal Mile, Edinburgh city centre.*

[WC] & 🥤 ✕ 🏛 E [AV] 🎫 ££

🕐 Apr–Oct, Mon–Sat, 9am–6.30pm; Sun, 10am–6.30pm. Nov–Mar, closes at 5.30pm.

Tel 0131 226 1555
www.tartanweavingmill.co.uk

86 Torphichen Preceptory

A thirteenth century church erected by the Knights of St John of Jerusalem (or Knights Hospitaller), and altered over the following two hundred years. Remains include a tower and transepts.

A3 *Torphichen, on B792 off A706.*

[P] [WC] E £

🕐 Apr–Sept, Sat 11am–5pm; Sun & bank holidays, 2–5pm.

Tel 01506 654142   www.historic-scotland.gov.uk

87 Tron Old Town Information & Visitor Attraction ★

Inside the Tron Kirk is the Old Town Information centre along with a section of the lost street of Marlin's Wynd, demolished in 1635 to make way for the new church and only discovered in 1974.

X2 *Tron Kirk, Royal Mile, Edinburgh city centre.*

& 🏛 E Free

🕐 All year. Apr–Oct, daily, 10am–5pm. Nov–Mar, daily, 12 noon–4pm.

Tel 0131 225 8408

88 Vogrie Country Park

A country park featuring seven miles of woodland walks, some of which follow the River Tyne and its rich grasslands, plus an adventure play area, sculptures and a garden centre.

F2 *Take A68 through Dalkeith, and turn off on B6372 before Pathhead. Continue through Dewarton Park on left.*

[P] [WC] & 🎋 ☙ 🏃 Free

🕐 Dawn–dusk.

Tel 01875 821990

89 Water of Leith

The Water of Leith is a narrow river which runs from the Pentland Hills into Balerno in the south west of Edinburgh, through the heart of the city, eventually emptying into the Firth of Forth at Leith. Walkers can follow the stream via a number of scenic pathways, while a family visitor centre provides information on wildlife, history and the effect of floods and droughts.

D3 *Visitor centre: SW of city centre, Lanark Road, Slateford.*

[P] [WC] & 🏛 E [AV] 🎋 ☙ 🏃 £

🕐 Walkways: open access. Visitor Centre: Apr–Sept, daily, 10am–4pm. Oct–Mar, Wed–Sun, 10am–4pm.

Tel 0131 455 7367
www.waterofleith.edin.org

90 Writers' Museum

Scotland's three great writers, Scott, Stevenson and Burns, are honoured in the historic seventeeth century Lady Stair's House with a display of portraits, artefacts and manuscripts. Other writers feature in a programme of changing exhibitions.

W2 *Below Edinburgh Castle on the Royal Mile.*

[WC] 🏛 E Free

🕐 All year round, Mon–Sat, 10am–5pm; Festival hours Sun, 2–5pm.

Tel 0131 529 4901   www.cac.org.uk

St Andrews Cathedral and town from the air

KINGDOM OF FIFE

Fife's setting between two Firths has always given it a sense of somewhere different. The 'Kingdom' part is a reference to its status long ago as an independent Pictish chiefdom. Fife is quintessential Lowland Scotland, even down to the low rainfall and high sunshine records of the eastern portion (in contrast to, say, the West Highlands) and, again, in the east in particular, has a well-to-do air, with quiet little communities such as Ceres or Falkland with their red-roofed cottages tucked into the farming landscape. Ceres is also noted for the portrait of rural life in the Fife Folk Museum, while Falkland is dominated by the renaissance frontage of Falkland Palace, a former hunting lodge of the Stewart monarchs.

Another notable characteristic of Fife is that the further east visitors travel, the further they are from any sign of heavy industry, or from any kind of scarring from the industrial revolution. In contrast, West Fife towns are associated with commerce and industry, so that a visit to Dunfermline will include not just its Andrew Carnegie connections, but also the story of its association with damask linen, for example. Similarly, Kincardine means coal-mining, Burntisland aluminium processing and Kirkcaldy is associated with linoleum.

One of the most interesting parts of west Fife is the extraordinary little town of Culross (see p95). With the other towns in the area developed their industries in the eighteenth and nineteenth centuries, this place slipped behind in the race and entered the twentieth century with many seventeenth and eighteenth century domestic buildings intact. This attracted the attention of the National Trust for Scotland. Today, preserved and restored houses with their the red pantiles, as well as the cobbled streets and mercat cross make Culross feel like a film set (which it has been in the past) and it remains as a unique survivor on the shores of the Forth estuary.

Away in the east, the spires of St Andrews are a reminder of a town with many themes. One is its former role as Scotland's ecclesiastical capital. (Its ruined cathedral was once the largest church in Scotland). Then there is its academic life as an important university town. But mingling with the chattering students in the streets, there are also the golfing widows, perhaps intent upon the town's upmarket shops. St Andrews is also the spiritual home of Scottish golf. This mixing of visitors, golfers and academia in a town with handsome buildings and a long history all makes St Andrews one of the most characterful of Scottish towns.

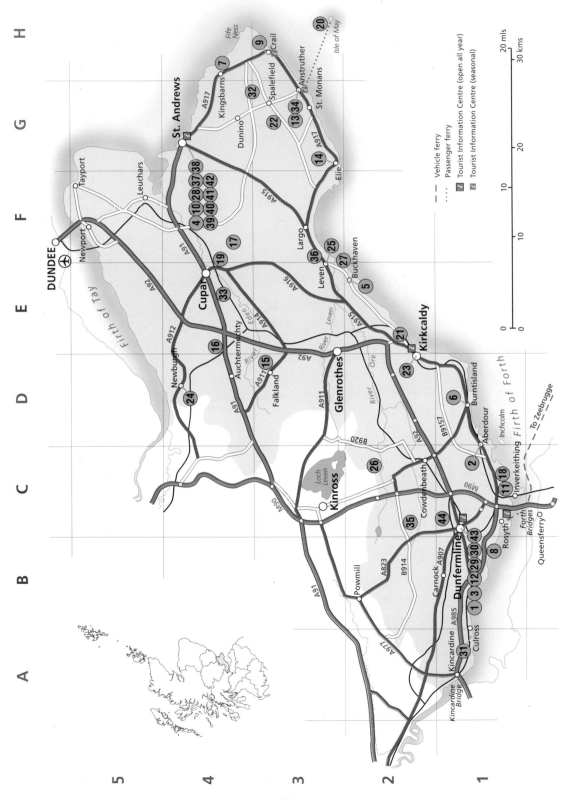

A map of Fife, Scotland, showing towns including Dundee, St. Andrews, Cupar, Glenrothes, Kirkcaldy, Kinross, Dunfermline, and coastal locations. Key features include the Firth of Tay, Firth of Forth, Loch Leven, and numerous roads.

Key:

- - - Vehicle ferry

···· Passenger ferry

Tourist Information Centre (open all year)

Tourist Information Centre (seasonal)

Scale: 0 — 10 — 20 mls / 0 — 30 kms

VISITOR INFORMATION

MAIN TOURIST INFORMATION CENTRE

St Andrews
70 Market Street KY16 9NU
Tel: 01334 472021
Web: www.standrews.com/fife
E-mail: standrewstic@kftb.ossian.net
Open: all year round

YEAR ROUND TOURIST INFORMATION CENTRES

Kirkcaldy
19 Whytescauseway
Kirkcaldy KY1 1XF
Tel: 01592 267775
Open: all year round

Forth Bridges
c/o Queensferry Lodge Hotel
North Queensferry KY11 1HP
Tel: 01383 417759
Open: all year round

Dunfermline
1 High Street
Dunfermline KY12 7DL
Tel: 01383 720999
Open: All year round

SEASONAL TOURIST INFORMATION CENTRES

Anstruther
Tel: 01333 311073
Open: Apr–Sept

Crail
Tel: 01333 450869
Open: Apr–Sept

ADDITIONAL INFORMATION

GENERAL TRAVEL INFORMATION
Traveline Scotland
Tel: 0870 608 2608
Provides timetable information for all public transport in Scotland and the rest of Great Britain.

TRAINS

First ScotRail
Caledonian Chambers
87 Union Street
Glasgow
G1 3TA
Tel: Fares & Train Times: 08457 484950
Telesales: 08457 550033
Customer Relations: 0845 601 5929
Web: www.firstscotrail.co.uk
E-mail: scotrail.enquiries
@firstgroup.com

COACH

Scottish Citylink Coaches Limited
Buchanan Bus Station
Killermont Street
Glasgow
G2 3NP
Tel: 08705 505050
Web: www.citylink.co.uk
E-mail: info@citylink.co.uk
Routes: Fife–Aberdeen
Fife–Dundee
Fife–Edinburgh
Fife–Glasgow
Fife–Inverness
Fife–Perth

BUS

Stagecoach in Fife
Esplanade
Kirkcaldy KY1 1SP
Tel: 01592 261461
Web: www.stagecoachbus.com
E-mail: customerservices
@stagecoachbus.com
Routes: operates an extensive bus
network throughout Fife
Fife–Dundee
Fife–Edinburgh
Fife–Glasgow
Fife–Perth

St Andrew's Park & Ride
During the summer months a free
park & ride service operates into
St Andrews town centre from
the Petherum Bridge Car Park

CAR HIRE

Enterprise Rent-A-Car
Dunfermline
Tel: 01383 723333
Web: www.enterprise.com

Good News Car Hire
Kirkcaldy
Tel: 01592 592592
Web: www.goodnewsselfdrive.com
E-mail: operations
@goodnewsselfdrive.com

Practical Car & Van Rental
Lochgelly
Tel: 01592 654999

TAXIS

A A Cabs, Kirkcaldy
Tel: 01592 644000

Carnegie Radio Taxis
Dunfermline
Tel: 01383 623456

Dunfermline Taxi Rank
Dunfermline
Tel: 01383 732257

Golf City Taxis, St Andrews
Tel: 01334 477788

Jay's Taxis, St Andrews
Tel: 01334 476622

1   Abbot House Heritage Centre

A varied museum located in Abbot House, once the administrative headquarters of the first Benedictine abbey in Scotland. Exhibitions look at the area's history through the ages, including local connections with Robert the Bruce and William Wallace.

C1   *Off the High Street, on the edges of Pittencrieff Park, Dunfermline.*

🅿 🆆 ♿ 🍴 ⛪ E 🆎 🎫 £

☺ All year round, daily, 10am–5pm (last admission 4.15pm). Disabled access ground floor only.

Tel 01383 733266   www.abbothouse.co.uk

2   Aberdour Castle

This thirteenth century castle features terraced gardens, a dovecot and views over the Forth.

D1   *Aberdour, on A921, three miles W of Burntisland.*

🅿 🆆 ♿ 🍴 ⛪ 🎪 🌿 🎫 £

☺ Apr–Sept, daily, 9.30am–6.30pm. Oct–Mar, 9.30am–4.30pm. Closed Thur & Fri.

Tel 01383 860516   www.historic-scotland.gov.uk

3   Andrew Carnegie Birthplace Museum

The birthplace cottage and museum tell the extraordinary rags-to-riches story of Dunfermline's most eminent son and millionaire benefactor, Andrew Carnegie. Weaving demonstrations are held on the first Friday of each month, and there are guided walks during the summer.

C1   *Moodie Street, Dunfermline town centre.*

🅿 🆆 ♿ ⛪ E £

☺ Apr–Oct, Mon–Sat, 11am–5pm; Sun, 2–5pm.

Tel 01383 724302   www.carnegiebirthplace.com

4   British Golf Museum

Traces the 500-year history of golf, both in Britain and abroad.

G4   *By the 1st tee on the Old Course, behind the R&A Club House St Andrews.*

🅿 🆆 ♿ ⛪ E 🆎 🌿 🎫 ££

☺ Apr–Oct, Mon–Sat, 9.30am–5.30pm; Sun, 10am–5pm. Nov & Mar, Mon–Sat, 10am–4pm. Dec–Feb, Mon–Sat, 11am–3pm.

Tel 01334 460046   britishgolfmuseum.co.uk

5   Buckhaven Museum

A museum devoted to the history of Buckhaven, with particular emphasis on the fishing industry. Locally made stained glass windows are well worth seeing along with an exhibition of 1920s domestic objects.

E2   *College Street, Buckhaven, eight miles E of Kirkcaldy.*

🆆 ⛪ E Free

☺ Tue, 10am–1pm & 2–5pm; Thur, 10am–1pm, 2–5pm & 5.30–7pm; Fri, 2–5pm; Sat, 10am–12.30pm.

Tel 01592 412860

6   Burntisland Edwardian Fair Museum

Housed at the library, exhibits include reproduction Edwardian fairground items and information on the history of Burntisland.

D1   *High Street, Burntisland, on A921.*

🆆 E Free

☺ Mon–Sat, 10am–1pm & 2–5pm. Tue & Thur, closes at 7pm.

Tel 01592 412860

7   Cambo Estate Gardens

A Victorian walled garden designed around the Cambo burn with willow, waterfall and bridges. The productive garden supplies the mansion house (not open to the public) with flowers, fruit and vegetables, while seventy acres of woodland walks follow the burn to the sea.

H4   *On A917, one mile S of Kingsbarns.*

🅿 🆆 🚶 £

☺ Daily, 10am–dusk.

Tel 01333 450054   www.camboestate.com

8   Charlestown Workshops ★

These workshops are devoted to preserving Scotland's traditional masonry buildings using traditional building crafts. Visitors can learn about building with stone and lime, and of the lime cycle.

B1   *Charlestown, off A985 between Cairneyhill and Rosyth.*

🅿 🆆 ♿ E 🚶 🎫 £

☺ Mar–Nov, Tue–Thur, 9.30am–4.30pm; Fri, 9.30am–1.30pm.

Tel 01383 872722   www.scotlime.org

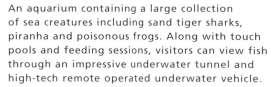

Dunfermline Palace

9 Crail Museum and Heritage Centre

Provides an insight into the past life of this ancient Royal Burgh, including its seafaring tradition and 200-year-old golf club.

H3 *Centre of Crail, adjacent to Tolbooth; on A917, four miles NE of Anstruther.*

🅿 ♿ 🏛 E Free

🕐 Apr & May, weekends, 2–5pm.
Easter, 10am-1pm & 2-5pm. Jun–Sept, Mon–Sat, 10am-1pm & 2-5pm; Sun, 2–5pm.

Tel 01333 450869

10 Crawfords Arts Centre

A visual arts centre with a varied programme of regularly changing arts and crafts exhibitions.

G4 *North Street, St. Andrews, opposite the police station.*

♿ 🏛 E Free

🕐 All year round, Mon–Sat, 10am–5pm; Sun, 2–5pm.

Tel 01334 474610
www.crawfordarts.free-online.co.uk

11 Deep Sea World

An aquarium containing a large collection of sea creatures including sand tiger sharks, piranha and poisonous frogs. Along with touch pools and feeding sessions, visitors can view fish through an impressive underwater tunnel and high-tech remote operated underwater vehicle.

C1 *North Queensferry; take J1 off M90 and follow signs.*

🅿 🚻 ♿ ☕ 🏛 E AV 🎋 ♿ £££

🕐 Apr–Aug, daily, 10am–6pm. Sept–Mar, Mon–Fri, 10am–5pm; Sat & Sun, 10am–6pm.

Tel 01383 411880   www.deepseaworld.com

12 Dunfermline Palace and Abbey

The site marks the remains of an eleventh century Benedicitine abbey founded by Queen Margaret; the foundations of her church are beneath the nave of the current twelfth century building. Robert the Bruce was buried in the choir area where the parish church now stands. The Royal Palace, adjacent to the Abbey, was converted from the monastery guesthouse; this was the birthplace of Charles I.

C1 *St. Margaret Street, Dunfermline, off the A907.*

🏛 E £

🕐 Apr–Sept, daily, 9.30am–6.30pm.
Oct–Mar, Mon–Sat, 9.30am–4.30pm (closed Thur afternoons and Fri); Sun, 2–4.30pm.

Tel 01383 739026   www.historic-scotland.gov.uk

13 East Neuk Outdoors

A centre for outdoor activities including abseiling, canoeing, putting, and archery.

G3 *Cellardyke Park, Anstruther on A917.*

🅿 🚻 🏛 🎋 ⛷ £££

🕐 Apr–Sept, daily, 10am–5pm.
Rest of year by arrangement.

Tel 01333 311929   www.eastneukoutdoors.co.uk

14 Elie Watersports

Offers equipment hire and instruction on watersports such as windsurfing, dinghies, canoes, water-skiing and inflatable rides.

G3 *By Elie harbour, S of St Andrews off A917.*

🅿 🚻 🏛 ♿ ££

🕐 Easter–late Sept, daily, 10am–6pm.
Other times by arrangement.

Tel 01333 330962   www.eliewatersports.com

FIFE COASTAL VILLAGES

Facing south on to a glittering sea and looking across the Firth of Forth to East Lothian, Fife's East Neuk villages show Dutch influence in their architecture, with their crow stepped gables and red-pantiled roofs. These are, in turn, reminders of the long established trading links across the North Sea in centuries gone by. In Crail (above), the easternmost of the East Neuk communities, the handsome tolbooth houses an ancient bell cast in Holland in 1520. Crail is also noted for its highly picturesque harbour.

Next along this bare coast, going west, is Anstruther, with more of a holiday resort air and with the Scottish Fisheries Museum conspicuous on the waterfront. Pittenweem, with its active fishing harbour, continues the colourful theme of whitewashed walls and red roofs. Take a narrow alleyway away from the front to find the curious cave or rock-cut cell (the 'weem' part of the town name, from Gaelic uaime, cave) associated with St Fillan, a sixth century hermit and saint who lived here.

The shrine of another holy man, St Moineinn, is said to be the origin of St Monans, the next fishing village. (A well associated with the saint was used to wash the local fishers' gear.) The parish church overlooking the sea-edge was originally founded in 1362. As well as fishing, St Monans was formerly also involved in salt pans, and a preserved windmill close by was used for pumping. Finally, in this East Neuk string of villages is the town of Elie (the former burgh of Elie and Earls ferry) where its old harbour and bay are popular with leisure craft and windsurfers.

15 Falkland Palace and Garden

Built on the site of earlier castle and palace buildings, Falkland Palace (sixteenth century) acted as a country base for the Stewart kings and queens, including Mary, Queen of Scots. Highlights include the chapel, and King's Bedchamber, along with portraits of the Stewarts and seventeenth century tapestry wall hangings. The garden contains herbaceous borders, shrubs and herbs, and there are displays mounted at the Town Hall and Royal Tennis Court, the oldest in Britain still in use.

D3 *On A912, ten miles from M90 J8.*

P & ⊞ E £££

⊕ Palace, garden and Town Hall: Mar–Oct, Mon–Sat, 10am–6pm; Sun, 1–5.30pm.
Last admission 1 hour before closing.

Tel 01337 857397   www.nts.org.uk

16 Fife Animal Park

Over 150 animals are kept in the park, which also has two play areas, a trampoline and a handling room.

E4 *Off the A91, eight miles N of Glenrothes.*

P & ⛟ ✕ ⊞ ⌂ ⚘ ⊞ ££

⊕ Apr–Oct, daily, 10am–5pm.

Tel 01337 831830

17 Fife Folk Museum

A museum devoted to the history of everyday rural life in the area. Visitors can see a weaver's cottage, costumes, toys, examples of Fife pottery, craftsmen's tools and a collection of patchwork, samplers and lace.

F4 *High Street, Ceres, on B939, eight miles W of St. Andrews.*

🅿 ⊞ £

🕐 Easter weekend, May–Oct, daily, 11.30am–4.30pm.

Tel 01334 828180

18 Forth Bridges Exhibition

Drawings, models, artefacts and a video tell the history of the unique road and rail bridges spanning the Firth of Forth; visitors can admire views towards the bridges and across to the opposite shoreline. *(See also p73)*

C1 *Queensferry Lodge Hotel, N of Inverkeithing; on B981 off A90.*

🅿 wc ♿ ♥ ✕ ⊞ E AV ⚶ 🖾 Free

🕐 Mon–Sat, 10am–5pm; Sun, 11am–4pm.
Jun–Mid Sept, daily, 9.30am–5.30pm.

Tel 01383 417759   www.forthbridges.org.uk

19 Hill of Tarvit

Renowned Scottish architect Sir Robert Lorimer built this mansionhouse in 1906 for a Dundee industrialist whose furniture collection is on view along with fine paintings by Raeburn and Ramsay and various Dutch artists, Flemish tapestries and Chinese porcelain. The formal terraced gardens and grounds contain one of the longest mixed borders in the country and several plants of horticultural interest.

F4 *Two miles S of Cupar off the A916.*

🅿 wc ♿ ♥ ⊞ 🖾 ⚶ 🏃 £££

🕐 House: Apr–Sept, daily, 1–5pm.
1st weekend in Oct, Sat & Sun, 1–5pm.
(last admission 4.15pm). Garden and grounds: all year round, daily, 9.30am–sunset.

Tel 01334 653127   www.nts.org.uk

20 Isle of May Nature Reserve

The Isle of May – also known as the Island of Lost Souls – is located in the mouth of the Firth of Forth. Waymarked paths around the island guide visitors to areas of interest, while numerous species of wildlife including seals,

puffins, terns and guillemots can be observed from viewing points. Boats available from Anstruther Tel 01333 310103.

H3 *Five miles E of Anstruther.*

wc ⚶ 🏃 Free

🕐 Daily, Apr–Sept. Weather dependant.

Tel 01334 654038   www.snh.org.uk

21 John McDouall Stuart Museum

The house marks the birthplace of John McDowall Stuart, the first European explorer to make a return journey across Australia in 1861–2. Displays describe his journeys, the Australian wilderness and the Aborigines who made a life there.

E2 *Rectory Lane, Dysart, two miles NE of Kirkcaldy on A915.*

E Free

🕐 Jun–Aug, daily, 2–5pm.

Tel 01592 412860

22 Kellie Castle

Kellie Castle, dating from the fourteenth century, was restored in the late nineteenth century, and contains beautiful plaster ceilings and painted panelling, a mural by Phoebe Anna Traquair and a selection of fine furniture. The Victorian garden features old-fashioned roses and herbaceous plants.

G3 *Three miles NW of Pittenweem on B9171.*

🅿 wc ♿ ♥ ⊞ AV 🛋 £££

🕐 Castle: Easter & May–Sept, daily, 1–5pm.
Garden and grounds: all year round, daily, 9.30am–sunset.

Tel 01333 720271   www.nts.org.uk

23 Kirkcaldy Museum and Art Gallery

Set in the War Memorial Gardens, the gallery houses an excellent collection of eighteenth to twentieth century Scottish paintings, including works by Peploe and McTaggart. The museum tells the story of the social, industrial and natural history of the district, with a changing exhibition programme.

D2 *Centre of Kirkcaldy, beside railway station.*

🅿 wc ♿ ♥ ⊞ E 🖾 Free

🕐 Mon–Sat, 10.30am–5pm; Sun, 2–5pm.

Tel 01592 412860

St Andrews Golf Courses from the air

24 Laing Museum

A museum focussing on Newburgh's social, maritime and industrial history.

D4 *High Street, Newburgh.*

E 🌿 💷 Free

🕐 Apr–Sept, daily, 12 noon–5pm.

Tel 01337 883017

25 Letham Glen

An ecologically important area consisting of a picturesque glen with nature trails throughout.

E3 *On the A915 at Leven near Buckhaven.*

🅿 🚻 ♿ 🚶‍♂️

🕐 Open access.

Tel 01333 429231

26 Lochore Meadows Country Park

Lochore Meadows is one of the best examples of landscape renewal in the UK. Visitors can go fishing, golfing, horse riding, use the children's play area, take advantage of the many watersports or enjoy the footpaths and open spaces.

C2 *Leave M90 at A92; signposted from Lochgelly.*

 🅿 🚻 ♿ ♥ E 🪑 🌿 🚶‍♂️

🕐 April–Sept, centre, 9am–5pm;
   outdoor centre, 8am–8.30pm.
   Winter, 9am–5pm.

Tel 01592 414300

27 Methil Heritage Centre

A centre devoted to the history of Methil and the surrounding area; also runs a number of temporary exhibitions.

E3 *High Street, Lower Methil.*

🚻 ♿ ♥ E Free

🕐 All year round, Tue–Thur, 11am–4.30pm;
   Sat, 1–4.30pm.

Tel 01333 422100   www.methilheritage.co.uk

28 Old Course, St Andrews Golf Course

Golf has been played on the Old Course at St Andrews for more than 400 years. The Old Course is classic seaside links; the fairways are wide with little elevation and interrupted at intervals by huge double greens. Handicap requirement to play – 24 for men, 36 for women.

G4 *Off A91, near St Andrews town centre.*

🅿 🚻 ♿ ✗ 🏛 💷

Pittenweem from the air

⊕ Booking essential, see website for details.

Tel 01334 466666   www.standrews.org.uk

29 Pittencrieff House Museum 🏛

This seventeenth century private mansion was converted to a public building in 1911; fine period features include a plaster ceiling designed by Robert Lorimer. Exhibitions change every six weeks.

C1 *In Pittencrieff Park, west side of Dunfermline; parking off A994.*

🅿 ♿ ⊞ E AV ⛱ 🌿 Free

⊕ Apr–Sept, daily, 11am–5pm.
   Oct–Mar, daily, 11am–4pm.

Tel 01383 313838   www.fifedirect.org

30 Pittencrieff Park 🌳

Pittencrieff Park, gifted to the townsfolk of Dunfermline by Andrew Carnegie, provides a number of facilities including play areas, animal centre, greenhouses and walks.

C1 *Top of the High Street, Dunfermline town centre.*

🅿 WC ♿ ✕ 👫

⊕ Park and glass houses: all year round, daily, daylight hours.

Tel 01383 726313 (ranger); 739272 (pavilion)

31 Royal Burgh of Culross 🍴 🏰 🏛

Visitors can relive the domestic life of the fifteenth and sixteenth centuries, and wander round the old buildings and cobbled streets of this royal burgh, situated on the shores of the Forth. The refurbished palace, dating from 1597, houses a collection of pottery and furniture, while the garden is typical of the seventeenth century, with popular vegetables, herbs and perennials of the era. The town house and study are open to the public, and other restored houses can be viewed from the outside.

A1 *Off the A985, 12 miles W of Forth Road Bridge.*

🅿 WC ♿ 🐶 ⊞ E AV ££

⊕ Palace, Study & Town House: Easter Fri–Sept, daily, 12 noon–5pm.
   Garden all year, 10am–6pm or sunset if earlier.

Tel 01383 880359   www.nts.org.uk

32 Scotland's Secret Bunker

A farmhouse conceals the entrance to this labyrinth, built 100 feet below ground and encased in 15 feet of reinforced concrete, where central government and military commanders would have run the country had the UK entered a nuclear war. Features include two cinemas, operations, RAF and Royal Observer Corps centre and sleeping quarters.

G4 *On B940, five miles W of Crail.*

P WC ☕ ⌂ E AV ♿ ££

🕐 Apr–Oct, daily, 10am–5pm.

Tel 01333 310301   www.secretbunker.co.uk

33 Scottish Deer Centre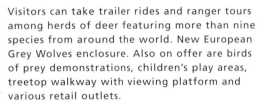

Visitors can take trailer rides and ranger tours among herds of deer featuring more than nine species from around the world. New European Grey Wolves enclosure. Also on offer are birds of prey demonstrations, children's play areas, treetop walkway with viewing platform and various retail outlets.

E4 *On A91, three miles W of Cupar.*

P WC ♿ ☕ ✕ ⌂ E ⌐ ☀ 👥 ♿ ££

🕐 Summer, daily, 10am–6pm.
   Winter, 10am–5pm.

Tel 01337 810391

34 Scottish Fisheries Museum

A museum tracing the history of the Scottish fishing industry, with full-size and model boats on show, along with equipment, a fisherman's cottage and a collection of paintings and photographs.

G3 *Harbourhead, Anstruther, on A917.*

P WC ♿ ☕ ⌂ E AV ££

🕐 Apr–Sept, Mon–Sat, 10am–5.30pm;
   Sun, 10am–5pm. Oct–Mar, Mon–Sat,
   10am–4.30pm; Sun, 12 noon–4.30pm.
   Last admission 1 hour before closing.

Tel 01333 310628
www.scotfishmuseum.org

35 Scottish Vintage Bus Museum

Houses a number of buses dating from the 1920s, along with a steam railway collection.

C2 *From the M90 N bound, exit at J4 and follow signs for Commerce Park.*

P WC ♿ ☕ ⌂ E AV ⌐ £

🕐 Easter–Sept, Sun, 1–5pm.
   Third weekend in August is annual
   open weekend.

Tel 01383 623380
www.fifeattractions.com

36 Silverburn Estate

Along with gardens and woodland walks featuring a variety of wildlife, visitors can visit the nature centre and learn about the conservation work of the estate, or visit the childrens play area.

F3 *On A915, one mile E of Leven.*

P WC ♿ ⌐ ☀ 👥 Free

🕐 Estate: open access, all year.

Tel 01333 427568

37 St Andrews Aquarium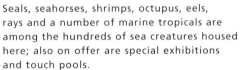

Seals, seahorses, shrimps, octopus, eels, rays and a number of marine tropicals are among the hundreds of sea creatures housed here; also on offer are special exhibitions and touch pools.

G4 *The Scores, St Andrews, off A91.*

P WC ✕ ⌂ E ⌐ ☀ ♿ ££

🕐 Apr–Oct, daily, 10am–6pm.
   Please telephone for winter opening hours.

Tel 01334 474786
www.standrewsaquarium.co.uk

38 St Andrews Botanic Garden

Included in these eighteen acres of landscaped gardens are trees, shrubs, bulb and herbaceous borders, ponds and waterfalls, and glassshouses containing a variety of exotic plants.

G4 *The Canongate, St Andrews, off the A915 to Largo.*

P WC ♿ ☕ ⌐ 👥 £

🕐 Oct–Apr, daily, 10am–4pm.
   May–Sept, 10am–7pm

Tel 01334 476452/477178
www.st-andrews-botanic.org

39 St Andrews Castle

These castle ruins, dating from the thirteenth century, mark the remains of the main residence of the bishops and archbishops of St Andrews – the focal point of the church in medieval Scotland. Visitors can still see the bottle dungeon, and unique mines tunnelled during a siege in 1546.

G4 *St Andrews sea front, off North Street.*

📠 E 🏛 ⚭ ££

🕐 Apr–Sept, daily, 9.30am–6.30pm.
Oct–Mar, daily, 9.30am–4.30pm

Tel 01334 477196   www.historic-scotland.gov.uk

40 St Andrews Cathedral
and St Rule's Tower

The dramatic ruins of the largest cathedral in Scotland, plus various adjoining out-buildings; a museum contains an interesting collection of sculptures and relics found on the site. St Rule's Tower, located nearby, is part of a twelfth century Augustinian church. Visitors can climb to the top and enjoy views of the surrounding area.

G4 *St Andrews sea front at the head of North Street.*

🏛 E ⚭ £

🕐 Apr–Sept, daily, 9.30am–6.30pm. Oct–Mar, daily, 9.30am–4.30pm.

Tel 01334 472563   www.historic-scotland.gov.uk

41 St Andrews Museum

A local history museum telling the story of St Andrews and the surrounding area. A gallery houses temporary exhibitions, often on a local theme.

G4 *Kinburn Park, N end of Market Street.*

🅿 📠 ⚭ 🍴 🏛 E Free

🕐 Apr–Sept, daily, 10am–5pm.
Oct–Mar, 10.30am–4pm.

Tel 01334 412933

42 St Andrews Preservation
Trust Museum and Gardens

A sixteenth century house containing a wealth of material on the history of the town and its people. There are reconstructions of old interiors including a chemist shop, grocer's and dentist's workshop, along with old photographs, many depicting the local fishing community. A walled garden houses rare plants and exhibitions.

G4 *North Street, near the Cathedral, St. Andrews.*

🏛 E Free

🕐 May–Sept & St Andrew's Week, 2–5pm.
Check website or call for details of exhibitions.

Tel 01334 477629
www.standrewspreservationtrust.co.uk

43 St Margaret's Cave

This atmospheric cave, lying eighty-four steps below a town centre car park, was where Margaret, Queen of Scotland, went to meditate and pray.

C1 *Chalmers Street car park, off A994, Dunfermline.*

🅿 🏛 E Free

🕐 Apr–Sept, daily, 11am–4pm.

Tel 01383 313838

44 Townhill Country Park ♣

Footpaths take walkers round Town Loch and through Townhill Wood, a mixed woodland with a variety of wildlife.

C1 *Two miles N of Dunfermline.*

🅿 ⚭ 🎋 ⚭ 🏇 Free

🕐 All year round, daily, daylight hours.

Tel 01383 725596

Inveraray Castle from the air

ARGYLL & THE ISLES, LOCH LOMOND, STIRLING AND TROSSACHS

The first tourists in the modern sense arrived in Scotland before the end of the eighteenth century. This was at the dawning of the Romantic Age, when, as a reaction to the order and desire to tame which had characterised the neo-classicists, a poetic 'cult of the picturesque' had begun to develop, along with a taste for untamed and wild landscape.

Naturally, in the pre-railway age, these first tourists venturing into the Highlands could not travel far on the poor roads. So they were content with the first picturesque sites (and sights) they encountered: hence the fame of the Trossachs and Loch Lomond, soon after to be followed by Oban and the islands and sea lochs of the west, for those with a taste for sea voyages.

Today, the area still attracts plenty of visitors, and the scenic qualities remain intact. Mild south-westerlies bring their moisture laden but mostly gentle winds to the long sea lochs of the west. It is this interplay of vivid green hillslope with sea-weed-fringed shore which is so much of an Argyll characteristic – as are the so-called Atlantic woodlands, the lush green broadleaved trees, especially oak, with their mossy trunks growing through honeysuckle and fern. Other parts of this area also have their own personality: the drowned valleys of Knapdale and the long Kintyre peninsula offers ever-changing views of Islay and Jura; while, further east, the high green hills of Breadalbane, around Crianlarich, are wild places with their base-rich rocks sheltering rare Arctic-alpine plants.

The Lowland edge, too, has its own appeal, especially the Ochil Hills, east of the gateway town of Stirling. Geographically below the Highland line, these rounded hills whose steep scarp faces define the edge of the Forth valley, have a surprisingly wild air. Swift running waters carve deeply through the scarp. These formerly powered the mills of the Hillfoots towns, the small textile communities that grew up below the slopes.

In fact, the essence of this area straddling the Highland line is its Highland and Lowland contrasts. Even today, only the least romantic of travellers could fail to have some anticipation as the Highland line is crossed and the trees close in by the white waters of the Pass of Leny above Callander; or to have some sense of entering another country – even if only hopping across the Firth on the ferry which leaves the urban sprawl of Clydeside for the woods and lochs of Cowal.

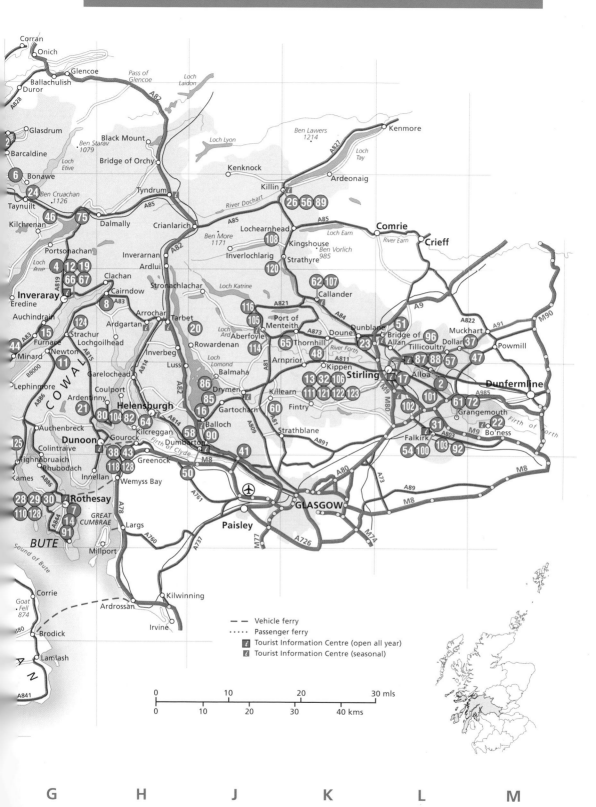

VISITOR INFORMATION

MAIN TOURIST INFORMATION CENTRES

Dunoon
7 Alexandra Parade
Dunoon PA23 8AB
Tel: 08707 200 629
Web:
www.visitscottishheartlands.org
E-mail: info
@dunoon.visitscotland.com
Open: all year round

Oban
Argyll Square
Oban PA34 4AN
Tel: 08707 200 630
Web:
www.visitscottishheartlands.org
E-mail:info
@oban.visitscotland.com
Open: all year round

Royal Burgh of Stirling
Castle Esplanade
Stirling FK8 1EH
Tel: 08707 200 622
Web:
www.visitscottishheartlands.org
E-mail: info
@rbsvc.visitscotland.com
Open: all year round

YEAR ROUND TOURIST INFORMATION CENTRES

Alva
Mill Trail Visitor Centre
West Stirling Street
Alva FK12 5EN
Tel: 8707 200 605
E-mail:
info@alva.visitscotland.com

Dumbarton
Milton, A82 Northbound
Dumbarton G82 2TZ
Tel: 08707 200 612
E-mail:
info@milton.visitscotland.com

Islay
The Square
Bowmore
Islay PA43 7JP
Tel: 08707 200 617
E-mail:
info@islay.visitscotland.com

Campbeltown
MacKinnon House
The Pier
Campbeltown PH28 6EF
Tel: 08707 200 609
E-mail:
info@campbelltown.visitscotland.com

Falkirk
2/4 Glebe Street
Falkirk
FK1 1HX
Tel: 08707 200 614
E-mail:
info@falkirk.visitscotland.com

Rothesay
Isle of Bute Discovery Centre
Victoria Street
Rothesay PA20 0AT
Tel: 08707 200 619
E-mail:
info@rothesay.visitscotland.com

Craignure
The Pier
Isle of Mull PA65 6AY
Tel: 08707 200 610
E-mail:
info@mull.visitscotland.com

Inveraray
Front Street
Inveraray PA32 8UY
Tel: 08707 200 616
E-mail:
info@inverary.visitscotland.com

Stirling
41 Dumbarton Road
Stirling FK8 2QQ
Tel: 08707 200 620
E-mail:
info@stirlingtic@aillst.osian.net

SEASONAL TOURIST INFORMATION CENTRES

Aberfoyle
Tel: 08707 200 604
E-mail: info@aberfoyle.visitscotland.com
Open: Apr–Oct & weekends only Nov–Mar

Helensburgh
Tel: 08707 200 615
E-mail: info@helensburgh.visitscotland.com
Open: Apr–Oct

Ardgartan
Tel: 08707 200 606
E-mail: info@ardgarten.visitscotland.com
Open: Apr–Oct

Killin
Tel: 08707 200 627
E-mail: info@killin.visitscotland.com
Open: Mar–Oct & weekends only during Feb

Balloch
Tel: 08707 200 607
E-mail: info@balloch.visitscotland.com
Open: Apr–Oct

Lochgilphead
Tel: 08707 200 618
E-mail: info@lochgilphead.visitscotland.com
Open: Apr–Oct

Balloch
National Park Gateway Centre
Tel: 08707 200 631
E-mail: info@lochlomond.visitscotland.com
Open: Apr–Oct

Pirnhall
Stirling M9/M80, Junction 9
Tel: 08707 200 621
E-mail: info@pirnhall.visitscotland.com
Open: Apr–Oct

Bo'ness
Tel: 08707 200 608
E-mail: info@boness.visitscotland.com
Open: Apr–Sept

Tarbert (Loch Fyne)
Tel: 08707 200 624
E-mail: info@tarbert.visitscotland.com
Open: Apr–Oct

Callander
Tel: 08707 200 628
E-mail: info@callander.visitscotland.com
Open: Mar–Dec & weekends only Jan–Feb

Tarbet (Loch Lomond)
Tel: 08707 200 623
E-mail: info@tarbet.visitscotland.com
Open: Apr–Oct

Drymen Library
Tel: 08707 200 611
E-mail: info@drymen.visitscotland.com
Open: May–Sept

Tobermory
Tel: 08707 200 625
E-mail: info@tobermory.visitscotland.com
Open: Apr–Oct

Dunblane
Tel: 08707 200 613
E-mail: info@dunblane.visitscotland.com
Open: May–Sept

Tyndrum
Tel: 08707 200 626
E-mail: info@tyndrum.visitscotland.com
Open: Apr–Oct. Weekends only Nov–Mar

ADDITIONAL INFORMATION

GENERAL TRAVEL INFORMATION

Traveline Scotland
Tel: 0870 608 2608
Provides timetable information for all public transport in Scotland and the rest of Great Britain.

AIR TRAVEL

Campbeltown Airport
Highlands & Islands Airports Limited
Civil Air Terminal
Moss Road
Campbeltown PA28 6NU
Tel: 01586 552571
Web: www.hial.co.uk/campbeltown-airport.html
E-mail: hial@hial.co.uk

Isle of Islay Airport
Highlands & Islands Airports Limited
Glenegadale PA42 7AS
Tel: 01496 302022
Web: www.hial.co.uk/islay-airport.html
E-mail: hial@hial.co.uk

Isle of Tiree Airport
Highlands & Islands Airports Limited
The Reef
Crossapol PA77 4YN
Tel: 01879 220456
Web: www.hial.co.uk/tiree-airport.html
E-mail: hial@hial.co.uk

Airlines

British Airways PLC (operated by Loganair)
Civil Air Terminal
Moss Road
Campbeltown PA28 6NU
Tel: British Airways central reservations: 08457 733377
Web: www.britishairways.com
Route: Glasgow–Campbeltown

British Airways PLC (operated by Loganair)
Isle of Islay Airport
Glenegadale PA42 7AS
Tel: British Airways central reservations: 08457 733377
Web: www.britishairways.com
Route: Glasgow–Islay

British Airways PLC (operated by Loganair)
The Reef
Crossapol PA77 4YN
Tel: British Airways central reservations: 08457 733377
Web: www.britishairways.com
Route: Glasgow–Tiree

TRAINS

First ScotRail
Caledonian Chambers
87 Union Street
Glasgow G1 3TA
Tel: Fares & Train Times: 08457 484950
Telesales: 08457 550033
Customer Relations: 0845 601 5929
Web: www.firstscotrail.co.uk
E-mail: scotrail.enquiries@firstgroup.com

COACHES

Bowmans Coaches Mull Limited
Craignure, Isle of Mull PA65 6BA
Tel: 01631 563221
Web: www.bowmanstours.co.uk
E-mail: bowmanstours@supanet.com
Routes: Craignure–Fionnphort
Craignure–Tobermory

Ian Morrison Coaches
9 Array Road, Tobermory
Isle of Mull PA75 6PS
Tel: 01688 302220
Route: Tobermory–Dervaig–Calgary

Mull Shuttle
13 Breadalbane Street,
Tobermory PA75 6PD
Tel: 01688 302345 www.mullshuttle.com
Route: Craignure–Tobermory

Scottish Citylink Coaches Limited
Buchanan Bus Station
Killermont Street, Glasgow G2 3NP
Tel: 08705 505050
Web: www.citylink.co.uk
E-mail: info@citylink.co.uk
Routes: Campbeltown–Glasgow
Campbeltown–Inverness
Oban–Glasgow

BUS

Oban & District Buses Limited
Glengallan Road
Oban PA34 4HH
Tel: 01631 570500
Web: www.westcoastmotors.co.uk
E-mail: enquiries@westcoastmotors.co.uk
Routes: operates local bus services throughout North Argyll

West Coast Motor Service Co.
Benmhor
Campbeltown PA28 6DN
Tel: 01586 552319
Web: www.westcoastmotors.co.uk
E-mail: enquiries@westcoastmotors.co.uk
Routes: operates local and long distance bus services throughout South & Mid Argyll

FERRIES

Caledonian MacBrayne Limited
The Ferry Terminal
Gourock PA19 1QP
Tel: Enquiries: 01475 650100
Vehicle Reservations: 08705 650000
Brochure Hotline: 01475 650288
Web: www.calmac.co.uk
Route: Oban–Castlebay–Lochboisdale

Inter island ferries

Argyll & Bute Council
Kilbowie House
Gallanach Road
Oban PA34 4PF
Tel: 01631 562125
Web: www.argyll-bute.gov.uk
Routes: Cuan–Luing
Easdale–Easdale Island
Port Appin–Lismore

Argyll & Bute Council
Kilmory
Lochgilphead PA31 8RT
Tel: 01546 602233
Web: www.argyll-bute.gov.uk
Route: Islay–Jura

Caledonian MacBrayne Limited
The Ferry Terminal
Gourock
PA19 1QP
Tel: Enquiries: 01475 650100
Vehicle Reservations: 08705 650000
Brochure Hotline: 01475 650288
Web: www.calmac.co.uk
Routes: Colintraive–Rhubodach (Bute)
Dunoon–Gourock
Fionnphort (Mull)–Iona
Kennacraig (Kintyre)–Port Ellen (Islay)
Kennacraig (Kintyre)–Port Askaig (Islay)
Lochaline–Fishnish (Mull)
Oban–Coll–Tiree
Oban–Colonsay
Oban–Craignure (Mull)
Oban–Lismore
Port Askaig (Islay)–Colonsay
Rothesay (Bute)–Wemyss Bay
Tarbert (Kintyre)–Portavadie (Bute)
Tayinloan (Kintyre)–Gigha
Tobermory (Mull)–Kilchoan

Clyde Marine Limited
Victoria Harbour
Greenock PA15 1HW
Tel: 01475 721281
Web: www.clyde-marine.co.uk
E-mail: enquiries@clyde-marine.co.uk
Route: Gourock–Kilcreggan–Helensburgh

Duncan MacEachen
The Ferry
Isle of Kerrera
Oban PA34 3SX
Tel: 01631 563665
E-mail: kerreraferry@hotmail.com
Route: Gallanach–Isle of Kerrera

Western Ferries (Clyde) Limited
Hunter's Quay
Dunoon
Argyll PA23 8HJ
Tel: 01369 704452
Web: www.westernferriesclyde.co.uk
E-mail: enquiries@western-ferries.co.uk
Route: Dunoon (Hunter's Quay)–Gourock (McInroy's Point)

Inter-island passenger only ferries

Gordon Grant Marine
Achavaich
Isle of Iona PA76 4HQ
Tel: 01681 700338

Web: www.staffatours.com
E-mail: fingal@staffatours.com
Routes: Fionnphort–Staffa
Iona–Staffa

Staffa Boat Trips
David Kirkpatrick
Tigh na Traigh
Isle of Iona PA76 6SJ
Tel: 01681 700358
Web: www.staffatrips.f9.co.uk
E-mail: dk@staffatrips.f9.co.uk
Routes: Fionnphort–Staffa
Iona–Staffa

Turus Mara
Penmore Mill
Isle of Mull PA75 6QS
Tel: 01688 400297
Web: www.turusmara.com
E-mail: info@turusmara.com
Route: Ulva Ferry–Staffa–Treshnish Isles

CAR HIRE

Arnold Clark Car Rental, Helensburgh
Tel: 01436 678081
Web: www.arnoldclark.co.uk

Arnold Clark Hire Drive, Stirling
Tel: 01786 478686
Web: www.arnoldclark.co.uk

Burnbank Garage, Campbeltown
Tel: 01586 552772
E-mail: sales@burnbankcars.2u.co.uk

County Garage, Dunoon
Tel: 01369 703199
Web: www.countygarage.co.uk
E-mail: info@countygarage.co.uk

Enterprise Rent-A-Car, Greenock
Tel: 01475 721444
Web: www.enterprise.com

Enterprise Rent-A-Car, Stirling
Tel: 01786 479100
Web: www.enterprise.com

Flit Self Drive, Oban
Tel: 01631 566553
E-mail: flit@freeuk.com

Ford Rent-A-Car, Stirling
Tel: 01786 445445
E-mail: carhire019@macraeanddick.co.uk

Ian Grieve, Stirling
Tel: 01786 811234
Web: www.iangrieve.co.uk
E-mail: ian.grieve@dial.pipex.com

TAXIS

A&S Radio Taxis, Dunoon
Tel: 01369 705606

Clydebank T.O.A. Radio Taxis, Clydebank
Tel: 0141 941 1101

Drymen Taxi Service, Drymen
Tel: 01360 660077

Leven & District Taxis, Alexandria
Tel: 01389 754884

1 Achamore Gardens, Gigha

Over 50 acres of beautiful rare and exotic plants, rhododendrons and azaleas. There's also a walled garden with herbaceous border and greenhouses containing tender and unusual plants.

E3 *Ferries to Isle of Gigha from Tayinloan; gardens 1.5 mile walk from pier.*

🅿 ᵂᶜ 🚶 £

🕐 Dawn–dusk, all year round.

Tel 01583 505254   www.isle-of-gigha.co.uk

2 Alloa Tower

A fully restored and furnished medieval tower house containing a dungeon, first floor indoor well, original oak roof and collection of family portraits.

L5 *Off A907, close to Alloa town centre.*

🅿 ♿ � ££

🕐 Apr–Oct, daily, 1–5pm.

Tel 01259 211701   www.nts.org.uk

3 An Tobar

Art Centre and Gallery based in a renovated Victorian school which plays host to local artists and touring groups.

D8 *Argyll Street, overlooking Tobermory Bay, Isle of Mull.*

🅿 ᵂᶜ ♿ ☕ 🏛 E 🌿 ♿ Free

🕐 Oct–Dec & Mar–June, Tue–Sat, 10am–4pm. July–Sep, Mon–Sat, 10am–5pm; Sun, 1–4pm.

Tel 01688 302211
www.antobar.co.uk

4 Arctic Penguin Maritime Museum

The Arctic Penguin, a three-masted schooner, houses a collection of Clyde maritime displays, memorabilia, archive film and hands-on activities. There are also daily trips in the summer aboard a working puffer.

G6 *Inveraray Pier, Loch Fyne.*

🅿 🏛 E ᴬⱽ ♿ ££

🕐 Apr–Sept, daily, 10am–6pm. Oct–Mar, 10am–5pm.

Tel 01499 302213 (for museum and puffer)

5 Ardbeg Distillery

Learn the workings of a distillery via a tour, and try a dram of Ardbeg single malt whisky.

D3 *SE side of Islay, three miles from Port Ellen.*

🅿 ᵂᶜ ♿ ✕ 🏛 E 🪑 ♿ £

🕐 All year round, Mon–Fri, 10am–4pm. Jun–Aug, daily, 10am–5pm. Advisable to book tours in advance.

Tel 01496 302244   www.ardbeg.com

6 Ardchattan Priory and Garden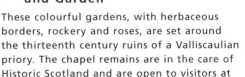

These colourful gardens, with herbaceous borders, rockery and roses, are set around the thirteenth century ruins of a Valliscaulian priory. The chapel remains are in the care of Historic Scotland and are open to visitors at the same time as the gardens.

G7 *By Loch Etive, off the A828, seven miles NE of Oban.*

ᵂᶜ ♿ 🌿 £

🕐 Apr–Oct, daily, 9am–6pm.

Tel 01631 750274   www.historic-scotland.gov.uk

7 Ardencraig Gardens

A walled garden with fuchsias, pot plants and a water garden. It serves as a propogation and show garden, supplying all of Rothesay's bedding displays.

G4 *E of Rothesay on A844.*

🅿 ᵂᶜ Free

🕐 May–Sept, Mon–Fri, 10am–4.30pm; weekends, 1–4.30pm.

Tel 01700 504644

8 Ardkinglas Woodland Garden

This 25 acre garden contains a collection of rhododendrons and conifers, plus a 'champion tree trail' (the tallest or broadest of their species within the UK) with a massive conifer, silver fir and a 200 ft tall grand fir.

H6 *Cairndow, at the head of Loch Fyne, on A83.*

P WC ☕ ✕ ⊞ ⌂ ☀ ☗ £

☀ All year round, daylight hours.

Tel 01499 600263   www.ardkinglas.com

9 Ardmaddy Castle Gardens

Ardmaddy rises above its formal walled garden and woodlands on one side with views of the islands on the other side. Dwarf box hedges surround a mixture of vegetables, cane fruit and herbaceous perennials. Walks through shrubs and trees lead to water gardens and bluebell woods, which contain rhododendrons more than half a century old.

F7 *Thirteen miles S of Oban off B844 at Easdale.*

P WC & ⊞ ⌂ ☀ ☗ £

☀ All year round, daily, 9am–sunset.

Tel 01852 300353

10 Arduaine Garden

This garden contains a selection of plants and trees, many of which are rare and unusual, also offers a spectacular coastal viewpoint.

F6 *Off A816, behind Loch Melfort Hotel, between Oban and Lochgilphead.*

P WC & ☀ ☗ ££

☀ Reception Centre: Apr–Sep, daily, 9.30am–4.30pm. Garden: All year, daily, 9.30am–sunset.

Tel 01852 200366   www.nts.org.uk

11 Argyll Forest Park

Argyll Forest Park was established in 1935, and covers a vast area round the Cowal Peninsula, running by Loch Fyne and Loch Long. Along with walking a number of marked trails, visitors can fish, horse ride, cycle, camp, picnic and simply enjoy the views and beautiful scenery.

G5 *Stretches across the Cowal area of Argyll; approx. one hour's drive from Glasgow.*

P WC ⌂ ☀ ☗ Free

☀ Open access.

Tel 01877 382383
www.forestry.gov.uk/argyllforestpark

12 Argyll Wildlife Park

The park is set in 55 acres of ground around Loch Fyne, with animals roaming free in their natural habitat. Visitors can see wildcats, badgers, red and silver foxes, fallow deer, wild goats, monkeys, owls, buzzards, racoons, along with many other species.

G6 *On A82, Glasgow–Tarbet road.*

P WC & ☕ ⊞ ⌂ ☗ ££

☀ Apr–Oct, 10am–5pm, daily.

Tel 01499 302264

13 Argyll's Lodging

This fine example of a seventeenth century townhouse contains a number of restored rooms in a style reflective of the era.

L5 *Near Stirling Castle on Castle Wynd.*

WC & ⊞ E AV ☀ ☗ ⊡ ££

☀ Apr–Sept, daily, 9.30am–6.30pm (last admission 5.15pm). Oct–Mar, daily, 9.30am–5.30pm (last admission 4.45pm).

Tel 01786 431319   www.historic-scotland.gov.uk

14 Ascog Hall Fernery and Garden

A restored sunken Victorian fern house containing a collection of ferns, many from sub-tropical parts of the world. A survivor from the original collection is reputed to be 100 years old. Restored gardens feature paths running through flower covered banks and beds.

G4 *Three miles SE of Rothesay, Bute, on A844.*

P ☗ £

☀ Easter–Oct, Wed–Sun, 10am–5pm.

Tel 01700 504555
www.ascoghallfernery.co.uk

15 Auchindrain Township Open Air Museum

An original and historic Highland township which has been restored, furnished and equipped to offer visitors a glimpse of a Highlander's lifestyle in a past age.

G6 *Six miles SE of Inveraray on A83.*

🅿 📶 ♿ E ☼ 🏕 ⛷ ££

🕓 Daily, Apr–Sept, 10am–5pm.

Tel 01499 500235

16 Balloch Castle Country Park

Two hundred acres of varied countryside with a visitor centre, facilities and ranger service and gateway to Loch Lomond National Park.

J5 *S end of Loch Lomond on A811, off A82.*

🅿 📶 ♿ ☼ ⛷ 🎫 Free

🕓 Country Park: all year, daily.
   Visitor Centre: Easter–Oct, daily, 10am.
   Closing times vary, please check.

Tel 01389 722600
www.lochlomond-trossachs.org

17 Bannockburn Battlefield

The site of King Robert the Bruce's victory against Edward II's army in 1314, marking the greatest single step in Scotland's battle for independence. A statue of King Robert the Bruce stands beside the Borestone, by tradition his command post for the battle, while a heritage centre contains an exhibition and heraldic banners.

L5 *On A872, two miles S of Stirling.*

🅿 📶 ♿ ☕ ♿ E AV 🏕 🎫 ££

🕓 Site: all year round, daily. Heritage Centre, shop and cafe: Apr–Oct, 10am–5.30pm. Feb–Mar, Nov–24 Dec, 10.30am–4pm.

Tel 01786 812664   www.nts.org.uk

18 Barnluasgan Visitor Centre

Situated on the edge of Knapdale Forest, the centre contains information about the area which is ideal for walking, cycling and watching the wildlife. This National Scenic Area also contains sites of historical and archaeological interest.

F5 *Near Achnamara. Follow B841 towards Crinan, then B8025 Bellanoch/Tayvallich road.*

🅿 🏕 ⛷ Free

🕓 All year round, daylight hours.

Tel 01546 602518   www.forestry.gov.uk

19 Bell Tower of All Saints Episcopal Church

Visitors can climb to the top of this 126 ft tower and enjoy stunning views across Loch Fyne and beyond. Also of interest are the bells which, at a total weight of nearly eight tons, makes them the second heaviest ring of ten bells in the world.

G6 *Centre of Inverary, on A831/A819, by Loch Fyne.*

E ☼ £

🕓 May–Sept, daily, 10am–1pm & 2–5pm.

Tel 01499 302259

20 Ben Lomond

Ben Lomond (3,193 ft) is the most southerly of Scotland's Munros; the path winding up from Rowardennan, by Loch Lomond, leads to the summit, offering panoramic views.

J6 *Rowardennan, on B837, off A811, on E shores of Loch Lomond.*

🅿 📶 ☼ ⛷ Free

🕓 Open access.

Tel 01360 870224   www.nts.org.uk

21 Benmore Botanic Garden

Benmore houses a collection of conifers, flowering trees, rhododendrons and shrubs, along with an avenue of giant redwoods, some of which are over 40 m tall. Various

trails lead to viewpoints overlooking
the Eachaig Valley and Holy Loch.

G5 *On A815, seven miles N of Dunoon.*

P WC & ♿ ✕ ⌂ ⌷ ☼ ♿ ⊞ ££

🕐 Mar & Oct, daily, 10am–5pm. Apr–Sept,
10am–6pm. Other times by arrangement.

Tel 01369 706261   www.rbge.org.uk

---

22 Blackness Castle

This castle was constructed in the fifteenth
century, and later fortified before
becoming an ammunition depot; it was
finally restored as a building of historic
significance in the 1920s.

M5 *Four miles N of Linlithgow, on the Firth of Forth,
off the A904.*

P WC ♿ ⌂ ⌷ £

🕐 Apr–Sept, daily, 9.30am–6.30pm.
Oct–Mar, Sat Wed, 9.30am–4.30pm

Tel 01506 834807
www.historic-scotland.gov.uk

---

23 Blair Drummond Safari and Adventure Park

Visitors can drive amongst lions,
tigers, bears, camels, antelopes and many
other wild animals, and see donkeys, llamas,
wallabies, otters, penguins etc., at a pet's farm.
Other activities include sea lion shows,
adventure playgrounds and a boat trip
to chimp island.

K6 *Turn off M9 at J10 to A85 Doune road.*

P WC & ♿ ✕ ⌂ ☼ ⌷ ♿ ⊞ £££

🕐 Apr–Sept, daily, 10am–5.30pm
(last admission 4.30pm).

Tel 01786 841456   www.blairdrummond.com

---

24 Bonawe Iron Furnace

Bonawe, the most complete charcoal fuelled
ironworks in Britain, was established in the
eighteenth century. Visitors can learn how
iron was made via various displays.

G7 *Between the S shores of Loch Etive and Taynuilt,
off the A85.*

P WC & E ⌷ £

🕐 Apr–Sept, daily, 9.30am–6.30pm.

Tel 01866 822432   www.historic-scotland.gov.uk

---

25 Bowmore Distillery

Established in 1779, Bowmore is the oldest
distillery on Islay, and still uses traditional
methods and equipment to produce its single
malt whisky.

C4 *Off A846, on shores of Loch Indaal,
Bowmore, Islay.*

P WC & ⌂ E AV ⊞ £

🕐 All year round, Mon–Fri, 9am–5pm.
Summer tours: 10am, 11am, 2pm, 3pm. Sat, 10am
Winter tours: Mon–Fri, 10am, 2pm.
Other times can be arranged.

Tel 01496 810441   www.morrisonbowmore.co.uk

---

26 Breadalbane Folklore Centre 🏛

St Fillans Mill, with its restored waterwheel, is
the venue for this museum which looks at local
myths and legends, natural history and the clans.

K7 *Killin, by Falls of Dochart, on A827,
SW tip of Loch Tay.*

⌂ E AV ☼ ⊞ £

🕐 Mar–May & Oct, 10am–5pm.
Jun & Sept, 10am–6pm.
Jul & Aug, 9.30am–6.30pm.

Tel 01567 820254

---

27 Bunnahabhain Distillery

Set in a secluded bay at the north end of Islay,
this distillery produces Bunnahabhain Malt and
Black Bottle, a blend of all seven Islay Malts.

D4 *Three miles N of A846, turning off between
Kellis and Port Askaig.*

P WC ⌂ ☼ ⊞ Free

🕐 Apr–Oct, Mon–Fri, tours at 10am, 12.45pm,
2pm & 3.15pm. Nov–Mar by appointment only.
Shop: 9.30am–4pm.

Tel 01496 840646   www.burnstewartdistillers.com

---

28 Bute Discovery Centre 🏛

The centre is housed in the restored
Grade A listed Winter Garden, an elegant
1920s domed building made of glass and iron.
An interactive exhibition and film tell visitors
about Rothesay and the Isle of Bute.

G4 *Victoria Street, by the sea front, Rothesay.*

WC & ✕ ⌂ E AV ☼ ⊞ Free

🕐 All year round, daily;
please telephone to check times.

Tel 01700 502151

THE ISLE OF BUTE

The Clyde estuary island of Bute sits only a little adrift from the peninsula of Cowal, separated by the narrows of the famously scenic Kyles of Bute. Lying within easy reach by water of the bustling Clydeside conurbation, the island's main town of Rothesay grew round its sheltering bay and soon developed as a holiday resort. The atmosphere of the town in its Victorian heyday, when a network of steamers brought the workers from the city for their annual holiday, is captured in the Bute Museum in Rothesay.

However, the Victorian origins of Rothesay are even plain to any visitor who explores the seafront. The magnificently restored Victorian toilets, especially the gents of 1899, are a working monument in brass, copper marble and clear-sided cisterns, and a minor tourist attraction in themselves, along with the restored Winter Garden, with its cinema and visitor centre.

Another major attraction on the island is Mount Stuart House, a magnificent Victorian Gothic pile. Though the island has plenty of places to visit, its appeal lies in its peaceful, rural air. It offers pleasant walks and sandy bays, as well as a slightly wilder landscape at the north end of the island; like Arran, it is split by the Highland Boundary Fault. The most serene place of all is St Blane's Chapel, which sits in a sheltered bowl, shaded by tall trees. This twelfth century ruined chapel marks an even earlier Celtic monastic site.

29 Bute Museum 🏛

Exhibits show the natural history, geology and archaeology of the island, while a children's area includes an aquarium and display of island wildlife.

G4 *Stuart Street, Rothesay, behind the castle.*

🚻 ♿ ⛫ E £

🕐 Apr–Sept, Mon–Sat, 10.30am–4.30pm; Sun 2.30–4.30pm. Oct–Mar, Tue–Sat, 2.30–4.30pm.

Tel 01700 505067

30 Bute Sailing School ⚓

Provides sailing courses, day sails and cruises to Islay distilleries, St Kilda and Ireland.

G4 *Battery Place, Rothesay.*

🅿 🚻 ♿ ££

🕐 Mar–Nov, 9am–5pm. Course times vary.

Tel 01700 504881   www.butesail.clara.net

31 Callendar House 🏰

The history of Callendar House stretches back for some 900 years. Visitors can see a working Georgian kitchen, with actors in appropriate dress carrying out chores and kitchen duties typical of the 1820s. Also of interest are exhibitions devoted to William Forbes' Falkirk and the story of the house, along with two other galleries containing displays of varying themes.

L5 *Callendar Park, one mile E of Falkirk town centre.*

P WC & ♥ ⌂ E AV ⌐ ⚒ ⊞ £

⊕ All year round, Mon–Sat, 10am–5pm.
Apr–Sept, also Sun, 2–5pm. Last admission 4pm.

Tel 01324 503770
www.falkirkmuseums.demon.co.uk

32 Cambuskenneth Abbey

A tower and foundations remain of what was
once a house of the Augustinian canons. Robert
Bruce's Parliament was held here in 1326, and
James III and his queen buried on the site during
the following century.

L5 *Off A907, one mile E of Stirling.*

Free

⊕ Keys available locally at these times:
Apr–Sept, daily, 9.30am–6.30pm.
View from the exterior only.

Tel 0131 668 8800   www.historic-scotland.gov.uk

33 Campbeltown Heritage Centre

This centre displays information and artefacts
showing the history of Kintyre and its people;
it also runs a programme of events and
demonstrations. Exhibits include a working
model of the former Campbeltown/Machrihanish

light railway and three historical murals by local
artist Pat Nugent.

E2 *On B843 Southend/Machrihanish road,
off Campbeltown Main Street.*

P WC & ♥ ⌂ E AV ⌐ £

⊕ Apr–Oct, Mon–Sat, 11am–4.30pm; Sun, 2–4.30pm.

Tel 01586 553173

34 Caol Ila Distillery

Situated in a scenic cove overlooking the
Sound of Islay and Isle of Jura; provides tours
and a dram of single malt.

D4 *By Port Askaig, E side of Islay on A846.*

P WC ⌂ E ⚘ ⊞ £

⊕ All year round. Tours by appointment only.

Tel 01496 840207

35 Carnasserie Castle

This sixteenth century tower house was
built for John Carswell, a Protestant Bishop
of the Isles who went on to translate the first
book printed in Gaelic.

F6 *Off A816, two miles N of Kilmartin.*

Free

⊕ Open access.

Tel 0131 668 8800   www.historic-scotland.gov.uk

Campbeltown, Kintyre

36 Carradale Network Heritage Centre

This centre features artefacts from farming, fishing and forestry, Carradale's three main industries. Activities for visitors and locals of all ages are organised during the summer.

F3 *Carradale, 16 miles N of Campbeltown on B842.*

P WC ♿ ☕ ⌂ E AV 🚻 🚶 Free

🕐 Easter–mid Oct, Mon–Sat, 10.30am–4.30pm; Sun, 12 noon–4.30pm. Times may vary.

Tel 01583 431278

37 Castle Campbell

Also known as Castle Gloom, Castle Campbell once acted as a stronghold for the Campbells. Features of interest include a well preserved tower dating from the fifteenth century, splendid views across the Forth Valley, plus woodland walks round Dollar Glen.

M6 *At the head of Dollar Glen, ten miles E of Stirling, off the A91. Car parks at bottom, middle and top of the glen.*

P WC ☕ ⌂ 🚻 🚶 🚼 ££

🕐 Apr–Sept, daily, 9.30am–6.30pm (last admission 6pm). Oct–Mar, Sat–Wed, 9.30am–4.30pm (last admission 4pm).

Tel 01259 742408   www.historic-scotland.gov.uk

38 Castle House Museum

Once the house of the Provost of Glasgow, this villa now houses a museum telling the story of Dunoon and district through various displays. Four rooms portray life in the Victorian era.

H5 *Opposite Dunoon Pier.*

P WC ♿ ⌂ E AV 🚻 🚼 🚶 £

🕐 Easter–Oct, Mon–Sat, 10.30am–4.30pm; Sun, 2–4.30pm.

Tel 01369 701422
www.castlehousemuseum.org.uk

39 Castle Stalker

This striking fourteenth/fifteenth century castle, seat of the Stewarts of Appin, is set on an island in Loch Linnhe, near Appin. Made up of three storeys with a prison below, it is best seen on the approach road to Appin A828.

F8 *On A828 Oban/Fort William road, near Appin.*

🚼 Free

🕐 Visits by appointment only; please telephone for details.

Tel 01631 730234   www.castlestalker.com

Castle Stalker, Appin, Argyll

COLL

In early times plundered by Vikings, Coll, like its neighbour Tiree, was later a stronghold of the Macleans of Duart. Less fertile also than Tiree, Coll's characteristic landscape feature is weathered rock in hummocks breaking through heather and grassland in the eastern portion. Dunes and machair prevail along the west side. Some of these dunes along with grazings and hay meadows, as well as heather moor are in the care of the Royal Society for the Protection of Birds. The speciality on the reserve is the corncrake, a ground-nesting bird in sharp decline because of modern farming practices elsewhere.

40 Castle Sween

Located on the tranquil shores of Loch Sween, this castle is one of the oldest in Scotland. The remains date back to the eleventh or twelfth century, with additions built over the next few hundred years.

E5 *Off B8025, on the SE shore of Loch Sween.*

 Free

⊕ Open access.

Tel 0131 668 8800   www.historic-scotland.gov.uk

41 Clydebank Museum

Situated beside the shipyard where many of the famous liners of the Clyde were built, the museum houses various artefacts relating to life in Clydebank and to it's shipbuilding and engineering industries. Also of interest is a large collection of sewing machines and an exhibition on the Clydebank Blitz.

J4 *At Town Hall, Dumbarton Road, Clydebank.*

🅿 ⓦ ♿ 🏛 E AV 🏃 Free

⊕ Mon, Wed, Thur & Fri, 2–4.30pm; Tue & Sat, 10am–4.30pm. Group bookings by appointment.

Tel 01389 738702

42 Colonsay House Garden

The woodland garden contains unusual trees and shrubs, plus a large collection of rhododendrons, while the more formal walled gardens produce colourful arrays of flowers in season.

D5 *Isle of Colonsay; ferries depart from Oban, Sun, Wed & Fri, or from Kennacraig on Wed. Transport available from pier to garden.*

🍴 🏛 🏃 £

⊕ Woodland garden: all year round. Walled garden: Easter–Sept, Wed & Fri afternoon only.

Tel 01951 200211   www.colonsay.org.uk

43 Cowal Bird Garden

A number of exotic birds such as macaws, parrots and rheas are kept here, along with a collection of pigs, donkeys, guinea pigs, chipmunks and rabbits. Facilities include a dry sledge run, play area and nature trail.

H5 *Sandbank Road, one mile N of Dunoon on A855.*

🅿 ⓦ ♿ 🏛 🍴 🏃 ££

⊕ Easter–Oct, daily, 10.30am–6pm (last entry 5pm).

Tel 01369 707999

COLONSAY AND ORONSAY

So many modern travellers speak well of Colonsay that it seem to have become a kind of yardstick for Hebridean charm. Only 8 miles (13km) long, visitors can walk everywhere and enjoy the relaxed pace of life dictated by the ferry times. The island has a landscape of rock and moorland, as well as good examples of Atlantic woodlands – natural oak and hazel, dwarfed and contorted by the sea-winds. There is further habitat diversity by way of farmlands, sandy bays, tidal flats and coastal crags, much of this enjoyed by the local bird speciality, the chough, the red-beaked crow which attracts lots of birdwatchers.

As well as exploring the coast and visiting Kiloran Gardens, there is also an attractive walk to the island of Oronsay, though the trip across the open sands is only possible at low tide. Oronsay is noted for its ruined medieval priory, especially the magnificently carved Oronsay Cross, a fifteenth century work notable as one of the last achievements of the Iona school of carving.

44 Crarae Gardens

Stretching across a scenic glen, Crarae contains a host of unusual trees and shrubs, with various walks through deciduous woodland.

G6 *On A83, 11 miles S of Inveraray.*

P WC & ♥ E ㅠ ☀ ☆ ⊞ ££

⊕ Garden: Open all year, daily, 9.30am–sunset. Visitor Centre: Apr–Sep, daily, 10am–5pm.

Tel 01546 886388/614   www.nts.org.uk

45 Crinan Canal ★

The Crinan Canal stretches from the picturesque village of Crinan to Ardrishaig and connects Loch Fyne to the Atlantic, thus cutting out the long sea journey round the Mull of Kintyre. There are pleasant walks along the banks of the canal,

particularly from the Crinan end, where walkers can enjoy views over the Sound of Jura.

F5 *Runs for nine miles from Crinan off B841/B8025, to Ardrishaig on A83, on NW banks of Loch Fyne.*

☀ ☆ Free

⊕ Open access.

British Waterways: Tel 01546 603210

46 Cruachan: The Hollow ★ Mountain

Visitors are taken by bus through a tunnel into the centre of Ben Cruachan, where a huge man-made cavern contains a working power station. Interactives describe the workings of electricity and its production at Cruachan, the site of the world's first reversible pumped storage scheme.

G7 *Eighteen miles E of Oban on A85.*

P WC ☕ ♿ E ⌂ ☀ ££
⊕ Easter–Nov, daily, 9.30am–5pm.
 Aug, 9.30am–6pm. Guided tours every 30 minutes.
Tel 01866 822618
www.visitcruachan.co.uk

47 Dollar Museum

Looks at the history of Dollar and the surrounding area, and features a fine collection of photographs; also houses temporary exhibitions.

L6 *High Street, Dollar, off A91.*

P WC ♿ ♿ E AV Free
⊕ Apr–Dec, Sat, 11am–1pm & 2–4.30pm.
 Sun, 2–4.30pm. Other times by arrangement.
Tel 01259 742895 www.dollarweb.co.uk

48 Doune Castle

A well preserved courtyard castle built for the Regent Albany in the fourteenth century.

K6 *Doune, off the A820.*

P ♿ E ⌂ £
⊕ Apr–Sept, daily, 9.30am–6.30pm.
 Oct–Mar, Sat–Wed, 9.30am–4.30pm.
Tel 01786 841742
www.historic-scotland.gov.uk

49 Duart Castle ♜

Duart Castle, the ancient home of the Chief of Clan Maclean, stands on a clifftop overlooking the Sound of Mull. Visitors can see the fourteenth century keep, dungeons and state rooms, and learn the history of both Duart and the Maclean families over the last 600 years. A ferry runs from Oban to the castle, weather permitting.

E7 *E side of the Isle of Mull, off A849 between Craignure and Lochdon.*

P WC ☕ ♿ E ⌂ ☀ 🐾 🖼 ££

⊕ Apr, Sun–Thur, 11am–4pm.
 May–mid Oct, daily, 10.30am–5.30pm.
Tel 01680 812309 www.duartcastle.com

50 Dumbarton Castle

The castle remains lie on Dumbarton Rock, a volcanic rock measuring around 250 ft in height which divides into two summits.

J5 *Dumbarton on the A82.*

P WC ☕ ♿ E £ ☀
⊕ Apr–Sept, daily 9.30am–6.30pm.
 Oct–Mar, Sat–Wed, 9.30am–4.30pm.
Tel 01389 732167
www.historic-scotland.gov.uk

51 Dunblane Cathedral

This fine thirteenth century church with Romanesque tower was restored by Sir Rowand Anderson and Sir Robert Lorimer over 100 years ago. Internal features of note include the organ, stained glass windows and choir stalls.

L6 *Dunblane, just off the B8033.*

Free
⊕ All year round.
Tel 01786 823388 www.historic-scotland.gov.uk

52 Dunstaffnage Castle and Chapel

Ruins of a thirteenth century castle, including two remaining towers; architecturally, the chapel is particularly impressive.

F7 *By Dunbeg off the A85, three miles N of Oban.*

P WC ♿ ♿ £
⊕ Apr–Sept, daily, 9.30am–6.30pm.
 Oct–Mar, Sat–Wed, 9.30am–4.30pm.
Tel 01631 562465 www.historic-scotland.gov.uk

53 Easdale Islands Folk Museum 🏛

A pictorial collection portraying the domestic
and industrial history of the Easdale area.
A walk round the island reveals sea-filled slate
quarries devastated by the great storm of 1881.

E7 *Eight miles S of Oban on A816, turning off on
B844 towards Easdale. Short ferry trip to museum.*

WC ☕ E ⚒ 🏃 £

🕐 Apr–mid Oct, daily,
    10.30am–5.30pm.

Tel 01852 300370 www.slate.co.uk

54 Falkirk Wheel ★

The world's first rotating boat lift, designed to
connect the Forth & Clyde and Union Canals which
run between Edinburgh and Glasgow. It is a huge
structure, able to lift boats from one canal to
another. Visitors can witness the wheel in motion
from 'trip' boats or from the visitor centre.

L5 *On the outskirts of Falkirk, off A803 or M9 at J6.*

P WC ♿ ☕ 🏛 E ⚒ 🖼 ££

🕐 Visitor Centre: Apr–Nov, daily, 9am–6pm.
    Nov–Mar, 9am–5pm. Last admission 30 mins
    before closing. Boat trips from 9.30am–5pm.
    Booking recommended.

Tel 01324 619888 www.thefalkirkwheel.co.uk

55 Finlaggan 🏛

Finlaggan, Islay was the home of the MacDonald
chiefs from the twelfth to sixteenth centuries.
Relics of the occupation include carved
graveslabs, the head of a decorated stone cross,
and prehistoric crannogs (man-made islets)
which are situated on the nearby island of
Eilean Mhuireill. Information is available
at an interpretative centre.

D4 *One mile off A846, Ballygrant/Port Askaig road.*

🕐 Please telephone to confirm times.

Tel 01496 810629 www.islay.com

56 Falls of Dochart 📷

Dramatic waterfalls run through the
village of Killin as the River Dochart
flows towards Loch Tay. An eighteenth
century bridge over the falls provides an
excellent viewpoint.

K7 *Killin, on A827, at SW end of Loch Tay.*

P Free

🕐 Open access.

Tel 01567 820254

GIGHA

At only around six miles long by a couple
of miles wide, Gigha lies close to the
Kintyre mainland in a favoured spot which
gives the place its own temperate
microclimate. Frosts are uncommon, a fact
appreciated by the camellias growing in
profuse thickets below the sheltering trees
of Achamore Gardens, in the policies (Scots
for grounds) of the island's 'big house'.
Rhododendrons and azaleas make these
gardens well worth a visit. Ancient sites
with cairns and standing stones are another
feature of Gigha worth exploring.

57 Gartmorn Dam Country 🌳 🐦
Park and Local Nature Reserve

Gartmorn Dam was built in the eighteenth
century and is Scotland's oldest man-made
reservoir. There are opportunities for walking,
cycling, birdwatching orienteering and fishing.

L5 *One mile NE of Alloa, in Sauchie.*

P WC ♿ 🏛 E 🪑 ⚒ 🏃 Free

🕐 Visitor centre: Apr–Sept, daily, 8.30am–8.30pm.
    Oct–Mar, weekends, 1–4pm.
    Dam and park: daily, till dusk.

Tel 01259 214319

58 Geilston Garden 🌷 ❀

Set around a seventeenth century house,
Geilston features a fruit and vegetable garden,
walled garden with glasshouses and a burn
which runs through the wooded glen.

J5 *On A814, at west end of Cardross,
18 miles N of Glasgow.*

P WC ⚒ 🏃 ££

🕐 April–Oct, daily, 9.30am–5pm.

Tel 01389 841867 www.nts.org.uk

59 Glenbarr Abbey Visitor Centre

This eighteenth century Laird's house contains a collection of china, uniforms, patchwork, plus gloves worn by Mary, Queen of Scots. Glenbarr is also the centre for the Macalister clan.

E3 *On A83, twelve miles N of Campbeltown.*

P WC ☕ ♿ E ⊓ 👫 ⊞ £

⏲ Easter–mid Oct, daily (closed Tue), 10am–5pm.

Tel 01583 421247

www.visitscottishheartlands.org

60 Glengoyne Distillery

Visitors can tour this 150-year-old distillery and learn the secrets behind malting, mashing, fermentation and distillation, before sampling the end product, Glengoyne single malt whisky.

J5 *On A81, three miles N of Strathblane.*

P WC ♿ ♿ E AV ⊓ 🍴 👫 ⊞ ££

⏲ All year, daily, 10am–4pm;
   Sun, 12 noon–4pm. Tours every hour.

Tel 01360 550254

www.glengoynedistillery.co.uk

61 Grangemouth Museum

Looks at the social and industrial history of the town from the eighteenth century onwards.

L5 *Bo'ness Road, Grangemouth town centre.*

WC ♿ E Free

⏲ All year round, Mon–Sat, 12.30–5pm.

Tel 01324 504699

62 Hamilton Toy Collection

A family toy museum containing a range of exhibits such as dolls and accessories, trains, teddy bears, soldiers, puppets, cars and books.

K6 *Main Street, Callander.*

♿ E £

⏲ Easter–Oct, daily except Mon, 12 noon–4.30pm.

Tel 01877 330004

63 Hebridean Whale and Dolphin Trust

The trust works to research and conserve whales and dolphins found in Hebridean waters. A discovery centre contains displays and interactives, some of which are aimed at children.

D8 *Main Street, Tobermory, Mull.*

♿ E AV ⊞ Free / Whale-watching £££

⏲ Jun–Sept, Mon–Fri, 10am–6pm; weekends, 10am–5pm. Oct–Mar, Mon–Fri, 11am–4pm.

Tel 01688 302620   www.hwdt.org

Whale-watching Tel 01688 400223

64 Hill House

The Hill House is Mackintosh's domestic masterpiece. Most of the original furniture and fittings are still in place including designs by Margaret Macdonald Mackintosh. As well as Mackintosh's interiors, there are several small exhibitions of modern domestic design. The gardens command views over the Clyde.

H5 *Upper Colquhoun Street, Helensburgh.*

P ☕ ♿ E 🍴 👫 ⊞ £££

⏲ Apr–Oct, daily, 1.30–5.30pm.

Tel 01436 673900   www.nts.org.uk

65 Inchmahome Priory

This thirteenth century Augustinian monastery is set in a scenic location on an island in the Lake of Menteith. Visitors can sail across during the summer; the crossing lasts under ten minutes.

K6 *On an island in the Lake of Menteith. Reached by ferry from Port of Menteith, four miles E of Aberfoyle, off the A81.*

P WC ♿ ⊓ ££

⏲ Apr–Sept, daily, 9.30am–6.30pm.

Tel 01877 385294

www.historic-scotland.gov.uk

IONA

The small island of Iona is a place of excursion, almost of pilgrimage, for thousands of visitors every year. They make the journey on the single-track road across the Ross of Mull, then take the short ferry crossing. The island's restored abbey, reached via the ruined nunnery, is their goal. Having achieved it, they return to Mull.

The Irish monk Columba chose this place as a monastery in 563AD and as a base for his mission to convert the northern tribes of Picts. He was successful in this and Iona became the burial place of Scottish kings until the 11th century. The island also has a history of atrocities committed by Viking raiders. (Martyr's Bay near the pier is so called because on one raid alone 68 monks were slain.) There is, however, another Iona. It can be glimpsed from the top of Dun I, the tiny hill from which the whole island can be surveyed. It is from here that the quality of light shines out – the watercolour tints of white sand shining through emerald waves, the patterns of rocks and breakers and the long whaleback of Mull filling the horizon. This is an island to explore on foot, to discover the tiny bays and the butterfly-haunted machair. Many have commented on the curious sparkle of the light which makes this other Iona very beguiling. It is a place of great enchantment with an appeal beyond any religious significance.

66 Inveraray Castle

This eighteenth century castle is built on the site of a much earlier construction, and is home to the Duke and Duchess of Argyll, the senior branch of Clan Campbell. Contents include fine furniture and artwork, tapestries and a collection of armoury.

G6 *On A83, on outskirts of Inveraray.*

🅿 🚾 🍴 🏛 🏕 🧗 ££

🕐 Apr, May & Oct, Mon–Thur, 10am–5.45pm; Sun, 1–5.45pm. Jun–Sept, Mon–Sat, 10am–5.45pm; Sun, 1–5.45pm. Last admission at 5pm.

Tel 01499 302203   www.inveraray-castle.com

67 Inveraray Jail

A look at life in a nineteenth century prison and court room, with costumed actors/actresses taking the roles of wardens and prisoners. Visitors can see an airing yard and trials, and compare an old prison with an 1848 building, a model prison of its day.

G6 *In centre of Inveraray, on A83.*

🚾 🏛 E 🚭 ££

🕐 Apr–Oct, 9.30am–6pm (last admission 5pm). Nov–Mar, 10am–5pm (last admission 4pm).

Tel 01499 302381   www.inverarayjail.co.uk

68 Iona Abbey and Nunnery

St Columba founded Iona Abbey in the year 563, and the island has since been a place of pilgrimage for Christians from all over the world. Visitors can admire the restored abbey and monastic buildings which now contain an important collection of medieval carved stones. Also of interest are the graves of Scottish, Norweigan, Irish and French kings who were buried in the nearby graveyard, and ruins of a thirteenth century nunnery.

ISLAY

With more a sense of a working community than some other Hebridean islands, Islay is busy with distilling and farming. The cultivated part of the island lies mainly in the western half. The Royal Society for the Protection of Birds has an important reserve around Loch Gruinart, where spectacular views of barnacle and white-fronted geese can be enjoyed. (In summer it is noted for corncrakes). Seals often haul out on to the long sandy beaches by the head of the loch. In addition to its famous whiskies with their peaty, seaweedy tang, its association with the Lords of the Isles and its wildlife spectacle, Islay is also noted for the early Christian cross known as the Kildalton Cross, by the mediaeval church of the same name. The Kildalton Cross is a ringed cross dating from the second half of the eighth century and, carved from a single piece of a rock called epidiorite, is still in a remarkable complete state.

C7   *Isle of Iona, on SW tip of Mull.*

WC ⌂ E AV ⊓ ⊞ ££

☺ All year round, daily, times dependent on ferries.

Tel 01681 700512   www.historic-scotland.gov.uk

69 Iona Heritage Centre

An exhibition portraying life on the island of Iona over the last two hundred years.

C7   *Isle of Iona, half a mile from ferry terminal.*

◗ ⌂ E £

☺ Apr–Oct, Mon–Sat, 10.30am–4.30pm.

Tel 01681 700576

70 Islay Wildlife Information Centre   ★

Visitor centre with displays and photographs of Islay's natural history, a pond and sea life aquaria, children's room and hands-on activities and experiments. Also available is an extensive library and records of local wildlife.

C4   *Port Charlotte, beneath SYHA Hostel.*

WC ♿ ⌂ £

☺ Easter–Oct, Sun–Fri, 10am–3pm.
   Jul & Aug, daily, 10am–5pm.

Tel 01496 850288

www.islaywildlife.freeserve.co.uk

71 Isle of Ulva Heritage Centre

An information centre focusing on the Isle of Ulva, plus a restored croft house with thatched roof.

D8   *Ulva Ferry, off W side of Mull.*

P WC ◗ ⊓ ⚒ ⚐ ££

☺ Easter–Oct, Mon–Fri, 9am–5pm.
   Jun–Aug, also open Sun.

Tel 01688 500241

JURA

Jura, with its lonely, empty air, is famous for its statistic that deer outnumber people by around twenty to one. Aside from the wild reaches of quartzite strewn moorland dominated by the Paps of Jura, the island has one road, one hotel, one distillery and is mostly several large sporting estates. It is possible to go by public road most of the length of the east coast, but beyond the house at Lealt the tarmac stops and the road is not passable in an ordinary vehicle. Further on lies Barnhill, the house where George Orwell wrote his futuristic novel *1984*. Beyond that, and accessible only on foot is the view to the spectacular tide-race of the Corryvreckan.

72 Jupiter Urban Wildlife Centre

Once a disused railway yard near the centre of municipal Grangemouth, Jupiter Urban Wildlife Centre – at 10 acres, Scotland's biggest wildlife garden – is an oasis consisting of plantlife, woodlands and ponds that attract and provide shelter for a number of wildlife species.

L5   *Off A905, near Grangemouth town centre.*

P WC ᕦ ᴦ ᝅ Free

⏰ All year, Mon–Fri, 10am–5pm.

Tel 01324 494974
www.swt.org.uk

73 Jura House Walled Garden ✽

An organic walled garden containing a number of unusual plants and shrubs.

D4   *Ardfin, southern tip of Jura, off A846.*

P WC ᕦ ᴦ ᝅ ᝅ £

⏰ All year round, daily, 9am–5pm.

Tel 01496 820315

74 Keills Chapel and Cross

The chapel contains grave slabs and a collection of early medieval sculpture, the best example of which is Keills Cross.

E5   *Off B8025, SW of Tayvallich.*

Free

⏰ Open access.

Tel 0131 668 8800   www.historic-scotland.gov.uk

75 Kilchurn Castle

These picturesque castle ruins, dating from the fifteenth century, are set on a peninsula in Loch Awe. The remains contain the first purpose built barracks in Scotland. A steamer regularly ferries passengers over to the castle; the crossing lasts approx. ten minues.

G7   *Steamer leaves from Loch Awe Pier, one mile W of Dalmally off A85.*

ᝅ ££

⏰ Easter–Sept,
dependent on ferry timetable and weather; please telephone for details.

Ferry company: Tel 01866 833333
www.historic-scotland.gov.uk

76 Kildalton Cross

This high cross, measuring 2.6 m in height, bears intricate biblical carvings and dates from the late eighth/early ninth centuries. Made of a single chunk of epidiorite, it is very well preserved and lies in a churchyard beside the ruins of a chapel and a number of medieval carved grave-slabs.

D3   *NE of Ardbeg, off A846, SE tip of Islay.*

Free

⏰ Open access.

Tel 0131 668 8830   www.historic-scotland.gov.uk

77 Kilmartin House Museum

A museum housing artefacts, reconstructions and interactive displays relating to the some 150 prehistoric sites to be found within a six-mile radius of Kilmartin village *(see p121)*.

F6   *On A816, eight miles N of Lochgilphead.*

P WC ᕦ ᴥ ᚛ E AV ᴦ ᝅ ᝅ ££

⏰ Mar–Oct, daily, 10am–5.30pm.
Nov–Feb, Fri–Mon, 10am–3pm.

Tel 01546 510278   www.kilmartin.org

KILMARTIN AND DUNADD

Perhaps nowhere else on mainland Scotland can be seen such a concentration of prehistoric sites and evidence of former cultures than the remains in Kilmartin Glen. Amongst the very early surviving monuments, dating from the second millennium BC, are the linear cemetery of burial cairns centred on Nether Largie South. Also notable are the ritual monuments such as Temple Wood Circles, again from the second millennium BC and earlier. (In fact, radiocarbon dating indicates that one of the two here is one of the very earliest in Scotland.) The standing stones here are also decorated with the mysterious cup and ring markings, Bronze Age art whose symbolic meaning is much debated. They appear as pecked out small central depression surrounded by rings or spirals. There are other displays of these markings in the area. One of the most extensive sites in Scotland, for example, is north of Cairnbaan at Achnabreck. From a later date, there are fine medieval carved crosses at Kilmartin Church, with ancient grave slabs nearby. Further south, the distinctive profile of the rocky outcrop known as Dunadd looks out over the level marshlands of the Moss or Moine Mhor. An ancient causeway leads up to this high place on the plain, and a steep path goes to the top of the hill. Around 500AD, this was an important stronghold, of the first Scots kingdom of Dalriada, (after the Scots had arrived from Ireland). There are traces of walling and defensive structures and also other signs of occupation on the rocky summit in the form of carvings on the smooth rock. These comprise of a carved figure of a boar, an outline of a footprint and a hollowed out basin. There are also lines of ogam writing, the ancient script of Irish origin. Though hard to work out from casual observation how this site must have looked when occupied – excavation has found signs of extensive metalworking, for example – the setting on the long moss, surrounded by wooded hills, is certainly atmospheric.
(See also Kilmartin House Museum, p 120)

Historic Scotland care for some twelve ancient sites in the Kilmartin Glen area. The main ones (as mentioned above) are: Cairnbaan Cup and Ring Marks, at the A816/B841 junction; Dunadd Fort, off the A816, two miles S of Kilmartin; Kilmartin Sculptured Stones, Kilmartin village at the churchyard, on the A816; Nether Largie Cairns, off the A816, between Nether Largie and Kilmartin; Temple Wood Stone Circles, off the A816, SW of Netherlargie. Open access to all of these sites, all year round. For further information contact Historic Scotland: Tel 0131 668 8800 www.historic-scotland.gov.uk

78 Kilmory Knap Chapel & Macmillan's Cross

This isolated medieval chapel houses a number of grave slabs and a collection of medieval carved stones, including Macmillan's Cross.

E4 *Between Loch Sween and Loch Caolisport, Knapdale off B8024 or B8025.*

Free

⏲ Open access.

Tel 0131 668 8800   www.historic-scotland.gov.uk

79 Kilmory Woodland Park

Herbaceous borders, ferns, alpines and rhododendrons form part of this park which also offers nature trails, bird watching, woodland walks, archaeological sites and family events throughout the year.

F5 *Two miles NE of Lochgilphead on A83.*

P ⋔ ⚘ ⅄ Free

⏲ All year round, daily, 9am–6pm.

Tel 01546 602127

80 Kilmun (St Munn's) Church

Situated on the shores of the Holy Loch, this church is built on the site of St Munn's tenth century settlement, and is the burial place of the Dukes of Argyll and Elizabeth Blackwell, the first female doctor. Other features include a fifteenth century tower, water driven organ, stained glass and ancient graveyard.

H5 *Turn off A815 on to A880; drive for one mile to Kilmun.*

P ⓦⓒ ☕ ⚏ ⚘ Free

⏲ Apr–Sept, Tue & Thur, 1.30–4.30pm all other times by appointment.

Tel 01369 840342

81 Lagavulin Distillery

Visitors can book a guided tour of this distillery, and enjoy beautiful views towards Lagavulin Bay and the ruins of Dunyveg Castle.

D3 *S tip of Islay, three miles E of Port Ellen on A846.*

P ⓦⓒ ⓰ ⚏ ⚘ ☒ ££

⏲ Tours, Mon–Fri, by appointment only, please telephone for details (cost of the tour is redeemable against a bottle of whisky).

Tel 01496 302400

82 Linn Botanic Gardens

A garden with water features, herbaceous borders, rockery and cliff garden, containing a huge number of exotic plants.

H5 *Cove, by Helensburgh, on B833.*

ⓦⓒ £

⏲ Gardens: All year, daily, dawn to dusk.

Tel 01436 842242

83 Loch Fyne Miniature Railway

Offers trips on a replica of the 4472 Flying Scotsman, beside the banks of Loch Fyne.

F5 *Front green, Ardrishaig, two miles SW of Lochgilphead on A83.*

P ⓦⓒ £

⏲ Apr–Sept, weekends, 11am–6pm; also Bank and local holidays.

Tel 01546 602918

84 Loch Gruinart RSPB Nature Reserve

This reserve attracts a variety of resident and visiting birds including hen harriers, corncrakes, geese, ducks and waders. Bird hides provide views across the loch, and guided walks are organised once a week.

C4 *Loch Gruinart, N side of Islay, off A847 on B8017.*

P ⓦⓒ ⅃ E ⒶⓋ ⋔ ⚘ ⅄ Free

⏲ Reserve: open at all times.
   Visitor centre: Apr–Oct, daily, 10am–5pm.
   Nov–Mar, closes at 4pm.

Tel 01496 850505   www.rspb.org.uk

85 Loch Lomond Shores

Forming a gateway for Loch Lomond and the Trossachs National Park, the Drumkinnon Tower features exhibitions, film shows and viewing galleries over Loch Lomond, as well as shopping and dining. The adjacent National Park Gateway Centre contains an information centre and is staffed by Park Rangers offering advice on the range of activities available throughout the national park.

J5 *Off the A82 at Balloch, S shore of Loch Lomond.*

P ⓦⓒ ⅃ ☕ ✕ E ⒶⓋ ⋔ ⚘ ⅄ ☒ ££

⏲ Open all year, daily, 10am-6pm.
   Closed 25 Dec. Entry charge for Tower and films.

Tel 01389 722406

www.lochlomondshores.com

LOCH LOMOND

One of the most interesting points on the journey by train on the West Highland line is when the tidal waters of Loch Long are left behind for the fresh water of Loch Lomond. The north-bound train snakes through the woodlands high above Loch Long on the left, then gathers speed on its descent through Arrochar and Tarbet station. Only a minute or two's travel time separates views west to Loch Long from views east over Loch Lomond, Scotland's largest loch by surface area.

Though both lochs are fjord-like, long, narrow and fill deep-gouged glacial trenches, Loch Lomond is a freshwater loch because the southward-moving glacier, part of a great ice-sheet trundling off Rannoch Moor to the north, also dumped a load of gavels and glacial debris at today's Balloch, making a dam and leaving Loch Lomond only 27ft (8m) above sea level.

It was the work of this glacier, a mere 10,000 years ago, which created the 'bonnie banks', famed in song. The tough Highland rocks hemmed in its southward progress, creating the long narrow loch of today. The Highland Boundary Fault, which runs diagonally through the loch at Balmaha, marks a change to softer rock type, allowing the glacier of old to spread out and hence today's Loch Lomond to spill up to the gentler fields of the Lowland edge around Gartocharn. (See this from the top of Duncryne Hill, behind Gartocharn.) The southern end is also where most of the islands are. Some are inhabited, with one, Inchcailloch, a national nature reserve with important oakwoods.

Loch Lomond's proximity to the populated Lowlands now means meeting the leisure needs of recreational users of all kinds – from waterskiers and boating enthusiasts to anglers and birdwatchers. See page 262 for feature on Loch Lomond & Trossachs National Park.

86 Lomond Adventure

Situated on the scenic west banks of Loch Lomond, Lomond Adventure offers tuition in a number of water sports including canoeing, kayaking, sailing and waterskiing, along with equipment hire.

J5 *Balmaha, W shore of Loch Lomond, off A811.*

P WC ⚘ ££

⊕ All year round.

Tel 01360 870218

87 Menstrie Castle

The birthplace of Sir William Alexander, poet, scholar and courtier, who founded the Plantation of Nova Scotia; an exhibition describes how he set out to establish a Scottish colony in Canada.

L6 *Menstrie, off A91, five miles NE of Stirling.*

&. E Free

⊕ Easter Sunday & May–Sept, Wed & Sun, 2–5pm.

Tel 01259 211701   www.nts.org.uk

Mount Stuart

88 Mill Trail Visitor Centre 🏛

Describes traditional weaving, spinning and knitting processes, and compares them to the workings of a modern mill.

L6 *Eight miles E of Stirling at Alva, on A91.*

🅿 ♿ ⚿ ☕ ♨ E 💷 Free

🕑 Jul–Aug, daily, 9am–5pm. Sept–Jun, 10am–5pm.

Tel 01259 769696

89 Moirlanich Longhouse 🎭 🏰

A traditional furnished nineteenth century cruck frame cottage and byre. A nearby building houses a selection of clothes found in the Longhouse, and relates the building's history and restoration.

K7 *One mile NW of Killin, off A827, Glen Lochay Road.*

🅿 ♿ E £

🕑 Easter Sunday & May–Sept, Wed & Sun only, 2–5pm.

Tel 01567 820988 www.nts.org.uk

90 Motoring Heritage Centre 🏛

Argyll Motor Works, set in an impressive Edwardian building, was at one time Europe's largest car factory. It now houses a shopping complex and motor museum with examples of Scottish cars, archive film and information regarding Scottish motor racing heroes.

J5 *Adjacent to Loch Lomond Outlet Shopping Centre, off A811, turning right at Balloch roundabout.*

🅿 ♿ ⚿ ☕ ✕ ♨ 💷 E 📺 £

🕑 All year, daily, 9.30am–5.30pm. Sun, 11am–5pm.

Tel 01389 607862 www.motoringheritage.co.uk

91 Mount Stuart 🏰 ❋

This Victorian Gothic house was built by the third Marquess of Bute and his architect Sir Robert Rowand Anderson. Highlights include an art collection of old masters, depictions of British royalty and family portraits, plus a horoscope room and marble staircase. Three-hundred acres of landscape and woodland contain rare plants, rock and kitchen gardens and a Limetree Avenue leading to the coast. There is also a play area, ranger service with guided island walks and a plant centre.

G4 *Five miles S of Rothesay, Bute, off A844.*

🅿 ♿ ⚿ ☕ ✕ ♨ E 📺 🎪 ☘ 🚶 🎫 £££

🕑 May–Sept, daily (closed Tue & Thur).
   Gardens: 10am–6pm. House: 11am–5pm.
   Please telephone to confirm times.

Tel 01700 503877 www.mountstuart.com

92 Muiravonside Country Park ♣

A country park containing woodland walks, children's farm and play areas, along with a range of wildlife habitats. A ranger service provides summer events such as badger watching and guided walks.

L5 *Signposted from J4 off the M9.*

🅿 ♿ ⚿ E 🎪 ☘ 🚶 Free

🕑 Park: all year round. Centre: summer, Mon–Fri, 9.30am–5pm; weekends, 10.30am–6pm. Winter, weekends only, 10am–4pm.

Tel 01506 845311

93 Mull Museum 🏛

Contains historical artefacts and information relating to the Isle of Mull from it's geological beginnings to the present day. Topics covered include shipwrecks around the coast, crofting, farming and the effects of war on island life.

D8 *Tobermory Main Street, overlooking the pier.*

E £

🕑 Easter–mid Oct, Mon–Fri, 10am–4pm; Sat, 10am–1pm.

Tel 01688 302493

94 Mull Rail 🚂

A miniature steam or diesel hauled train takes visitors on a 20 minute coastal journey from Craignure to Torosay Castle *(see p133)*.

E7 *Old Pier Station near Craignure ferry terminal, off A849, E side of Mull.*

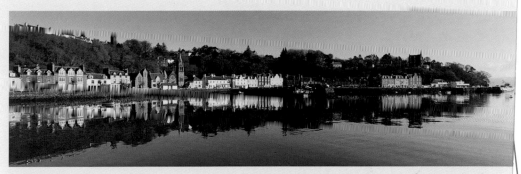

MULL

This is a large Hebridean island which saw voluntary emigration because of a growing population in the early nineteenth century before enforced clearances took further toll. The prevailing island colours are green and grey – the rock type and fertile soil allow pasture rather than heather to flourish in so many parts of the island.

The lava flows from ancient volcanoes give Mull its distinctive and impressive landscapes. The hard rock from which much of the island is made reaches its highest point in all of Britain on Ben More, which at 966m (3168 ft) is the only Munro on the Scottish islands (apart from Skye). This rock has also built high seacliffs and stepped terraces, most noticeable on the Ardmeanach peninsula on the west coast. This is a real wilderness area, some of it in the care of the National Trust for Scotland, notably the Burg, a cliff-face in which can be seen a 50 million year old fossil tree. Equally spectacular coastline can be found on the south coast at Carsaig, where the Carsaig Arches are tunnelled rock formations, accessible only at low tide.

Mull is also noted as one of the places to see sea eagles, re-introduced as part of a conservation plan. In such wild coastlines otters are also reasonably common. Aside from the wilderness experience which Mull offers, the largest centre on the island is the small town of Tobermory (above), originally founded as a fishing station.

🅿 ⛪ ♿ ££

🕑 Easter–Oct, daily, 11am–5pm.
A connecting ferry runs from Oban to Craignure; joint ferry/rail tickets are available from Calmac, Oban.

Railway: Tel 01680 812494   www.mullrail.co.uk
Ferry: Tel 01631 566688   www.calmac.co.uk

---

95 Museum of Islay Life 🏛

Located in an old church, this museum describes life on Islay through a series of artefacts, archives and photographs.

C4 *At the entrance to Port Charlotte, Islay.*

🅿 ♿ ⛪ E £

🕑 Easter–end Oct, Mon–Sat, 10am–5pm; Sun, 2–5pm.
Tel 01496 850358

---

96 National Wallace Monument ★

Built as a tribute to Sir William Wallace, who won the Battle of Stirling Bridge against the English in 1297, this 220 ft tower, with 246 steps, dominates the surrounding countryside, and gives superb views as far as the Forth Bridges to the east and Ben Lomond in the west. The monument was completed in 1869, with the Hall of Heroes, featuring other great Scots sculpted in marble, added later.

L6 *Three miles NE of Stirling.*

🅿 ♿ ☕ ⛪ E ♿ 🧗 ♿ ££

🕑 Dates and times vary;
please telephone for details.
Tel 01786 472140

---

97 Oban Distillery Visitor Centre 🍾

Visitors can learn about the production of malt whisky, along with the history of Oban via an exhibition and audio-visual show.

F7 *Stafford Street, Oban town centre.*

♿ ⛪ E AV ♿ ££

🕑 All year round, Mon–Fri, 9.30am–5pm.
Jul–Sept, open until 8.30pm; Sat, 9.30am–5pm.
Sun, 12 noon–5pm.
Last tour leaves one hour before closing.
Tel 01631 572004

Part island gateway and ferry port, part traditional holiday resort, Oban has the advantage of a natural harbour sheltered by the island of Kerrera. The town's role as a route-centre and transit point was confirmed by the arrival of the railway to the western seaboard in 1880. Tourists remain important to the town and the ferries are still the lifeblood of the islands, so that Oban retains its bustling air. Unlike at Fort William, the western seaboard's other major tourist centre, the railway was forbidden to approach the town along the seafront, so that Oban's breezy promenade is very much a part of the experience of the town. From here, the little pleasure cruises depart, to look for seals or circumnavigate an island or two.

There is a good range of attractions for the visitor, and evening entertainments of a traditional kind, as well as walks to viewpoints such as Pulpit Hill, overlooking Oban Bay, and to McCaig's Tower or Folly. This coliseum-like monument dominates the town skyline and commemorates a well-to-do local banker. He intended it both as a family memorial and as a means of creating more local employment in its building.

98 Oban Rare Breeds Farm Park

A collection of rare farm animals including sheep, goats, pigs, poultry and cattle.

F7 *Two miles NE of Oban.*

P WC & ● ⊞ ⊓ ☼ 槼 £££

⏲ Apr–Oct, 10am–6pm.
Nov–Dec, weekends, 11am–4pm.

Tel 01631 770608/604
www.oban-rarebreeds.com

99 Old Byre Heritage Centre

The history of Mull is portrayed through a number of tableaux, exhibits and a short film show.

D8 *Dervaig, on B8073 in the NW of Mull.*

P WC ● ⊞ E AV £ ££

⏲ Apr–Oct, daily, 10.30am–6.30pm.

Tel 01688 400229

100 Park Gallery

Visual arts and crafts gallery situated in the grounds of Callendar Park. It runs a rolling programme of exhibitions and contemporary arts and crafts by local, national and international artists and makers.

L5 *Callendar Park, Falkirk.*

P ● E ⊓ Free

⏲ Oct–Mar, Mon–Sat, 10am–4pm.
Apr–Sept, Mon–Sat, 10am–5pm, also Sun, 2–4pm.

Tel 01324 503789

101 Pineapple

An eccentric eighteenth century garden folly built in the shape of a pineapple.

L5 *Seven miles SE of Stirling on A905, near Dunmore.*

P ⊼ Free

⊕ Grounds: all year round, daily, 9.30am–sunset.

Tel 01324 831137   www.nts.org.uk

102 Plean Country Park

A country estate formed from the grounds of Plean Country House, with woodland walks, parkland, picnic areas, orienteering course and special routes for the disabled.

L5 *On the A9 between Stirling and Falkirk, on the outskirts of Plean village.*

P WC ⅋ ⊼ ☀ ⋔ Free

⊕ Dawn–dusk.

Tel 01786 442541   www.stirling.gov.uk

103 Polmonthill Ski Centre

Tutors for all levels of experience are on hand at these artificial and short starter slopes.

L5 *Off A803, SE of Falkirk.*

P WC ⊼ ££

⊕ All year round, Mon–Fri, 9am–9.30pm; Sat, 9am–5pm. Nov–Easter, Sun, 10am–3pm.

Tel 01324 503835

104 Quadmania

Specialists in quad-biking adventure trekking across farmland, forests and mountains. Additional pursuits include clay-pigeon shooting, watersports, archery, climbing and gorge walking.

H5 *Blairmore, on W bank of Loch Long; nine miles N of Dunoon on B833.*

⊕ All year round, daily, 9am–dusk.

Tel 01369 810246
www.quadmaniascotland.co.uk

105 Queen Elizabeth Forest Park and Visitor Centre

A forest park running from Loch Lomondside to the uplands of the Trossachs, with walks, drives, cycle routes, picnic areas and viewpoints.

J6 *On A821, one mile N of Aberfoyle.*

P WC ☕ ⌂ E ⊼ ☀ ⋔ £

⊕ Centre: Apr–June, Sept & Oct, daily, 10am–5pm. Jul–Aug, daily 10am–6pm. Nov–Dec, daily, 11am–4pm. Jan–Feb, Sat & Sun, 11am–4pm. (weather permitting). Forest drive: Apr–Sept.

Tel 01877 382258

106 Regimental Museum of the Argyll and Sutherland Highlanders

The Regimental Museum traces the history of the 91st Argyllshire Highlanders and the 93rd Sutherland Highlanders, who amalgamated in 1881. On display are uniforms, weapons, pictures, medals, colours, pipe banners and a collection of Regimental silver.

L5 *Within Stirling Castle, top of Castle Wynd. Entry to the museum is free, but visitors pay to enter the castle.*

P WC ☕ ⌂ £ ££

⊕ Easter–Sept, Mon–Sat, 10am–5.45pm; Sun, 11am–4.45pm. Oct–Easter, daily, 10am–4.15pm.

Tel 01786 475165   www.argylls.co.uk

107 Rob Roy and Trossachs Visitor Centre

A centre devoted to the history of seventeenth century Scottish outlaw Rob Roy MacGregor, with an exhibition, recreated farmhouse and film.

K6 *Ancaster Square, Callander, off A84.*

P WC ⅋ ⌂ E AV £ £

⊕ Mar–May & Sept–Dec, daily, 10am–5pm. Jun–Aug, daily, 10am–6pm. Jan–Feb, limited hours. Times may vary. Last entry for exhibition 45 mins before closing.

Tel 01877 330342

108 Rob Roy's Grave

The burial place of Rob Roy MacGregor (who died in 1734), his wife Mary and four sons.

J7 *Balquhidder churchyard, two miles W of Kingshouse, off A84.*

Free

⊕ Open access.

109 Ross of Mull Historical Centre

A heritage centre focussing on the geology, wildlife, genealogy and social history of the Ross of Mull. Organised events during the summer include ceilidhs, and historical presentations.

D7 *Adjacent to community centre, Bunessan on A849, Ross of Mull.*

P E £

⊕ Apr–Oct, Mon–Fri, 10am–1pm & 2–4pm. Weekends by appointment.

Tel 01681 700659   www.lineone.net/-romhc

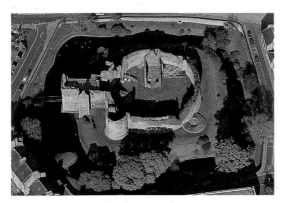

110 Rothesay Castle

This thirteenth century circular castle, with sixteenth century additions, was popular with the Stewart kings.

G4 *Centre of Rothesay, Bute.*

WC E AV £

⊕ Apr–Sept, daily, 9.30am–6.30pm. Oct–Mar, Sat–Wed, 9.30am–4.30pm.

Tel 01700 502691
www.historic-scotland.gov.uk

111 Royal Burgh of Stirling Visitor Centre

Looks at the colourful history of this royal burgh via an audio-visual show and sound and light exhibition.

L5 *Castle Esplanade, Stirling.*

P & 🏛 E AV ♿ Free

⊕ All year round, daily, from 9.30am (closing times vary).

Tel 01786 462517/479901

112 Scottish Sealife and Marine Sanctuary

Provides an interactive experience with native marine life, including starfish, stingrays, octopuses and seals. There are daily talks and feeding demonstrations, while an active seal rescue and rehabilitation programme means seal pups are often on view prior to their release in the wild. New Otter exhibition.

F8 *On A828, ten miles N of Oban.*

P WC & ♿ ✕ 🏛 E 🏕 ☀ 🐾 ♿ £££

⊕ Mid Feb–Nov, daily, 10am–5pm; closes 6pm during the summer. Telephone for winter opening times. Last admission 1 hour before closing.

Tel 01631 720386   www.sealsanctuary.co.uk

113 Scottish Slate Islands Heritage Trust Centre

A collection of photographs, models and pictures portray life around the Slate islands over the last 200 years.

F7 *Ellenabeich, S of Oban on A816, turning off to B844.*

& E £

⊕ Apr–Oct, 10.30am–5.30pm.

Tel 01852 300449
www.slate.org.uk

114 Scottish Wool Centre ★

Visitors can learn the story of Scottish wool via a live presentation, try spinning and weaving, and see sheepdog demonstrations during the summer months.

J6 *·Off Main Street, Aberfoyle.*

P WC & ♿ 🏛 ♿ £

⊕ May–Sept, Mon–Fri, 9.30am–5.30pm; weekends, 9.30am–6pm. Oct–Apr, 10am–5pm.

Tel 01877 382850

115 Skipness Castle and Chapel

A castle and chapel dating from between the thirteenth–sixteenth centuries; the chapel contains various grave slabs, and is situated at Skipness Point overlooking the Isles of Arran and Bute.

F4 *On B8001, E coast of Kintyre.*

P ☀ Free

⊕ Open access.

Tel 0131 668 8800   www.historic-scotland.gov.uk

Staffa

116 SS Sir Walter Scott ★

This Victorian steamship takes passengers
on an eight-mile cruise on Loch Katrine, from
Trossachs Pier to Stronachlachar, via various
sites of historic interest.

J6   *Loch Katrine Complex on A821,
eight miles W of Callander.*

🅿 WC ♿ ☕ 🏛 AV 🎋 ⛏ 🏃 🎫 £££

⏰ Complex: daily, 9am–5pm.
  Sailing: daily, Apr–Oct;
  times vary – telephone for details and bookings.

Tel 01877 376316   www.scottishwater.co.uk

117 St Columba Centre 🅱 🏛

Visitors can learn how St Columba and his
fellow-monks established and ran a monastery
on the island of Iona from the year 563.

C7   *Fionnphort, on A849 on W coast of Mull.*

🅿 ♿ 🏛 E AV 🎫 Free

⏰ Easter–Sept, daily, 11am–5pm.
  Other times by prior arrangement
  with Iona Abbey.

Tel 01681 700640   www.historic-scotland.gov.uk

118 St John's Church ✚

An 'A' listed Victorian building in
French Gothic style featuring a manual
pipe organ (1895), stained glass by Stephen
Adam and Gordon Webster, a Lauder
Memorial window and Normandy Gothic
spired tower.

H5   *Argyll/Hanover Street, Dunoon.*

🅿 WC ☕ E Free

⏰ Jun–Sept, Mon–Fri, 10am–12 noon.
  Sunday services: 10.15am; 6.30pm on last
  Sunday of the month.

Tel 01369 830639

119 Staffa 👺 🐾

A tiny uninhabited island featuring
stunning columnar rock formations
formed from the cooling of volcanic lava.
Fingal's Cave is the most famous of the
formations, but others include the Wishing
Chair, Causeway, Colonnade and
Clamshell Cave.

C7   *Seven miles W of Mull; six miles NE of Iona.*

⛏ £££

⏰ Sailings: Easter to Oct,
  weather conditions permitting.

NTS: Tel 01631 570000   www.nts.org.uk
Cruise operators: Tel 01681 700338/700358
(both sail from Iona and Fionnphort);
01688 400297 (sails from Ulva Ferry, Mull)
www.turusmara.com

STIRLING CASTLE

In early times, Stirling Castle guarded the lowest bridging point of the River Forth. With the Ochil Hills above and the Campsies below it was natural that routes between Highland Lowland would pass close by the rocky crag on which the fortress still stands. Besides, the carselands to the west were treacherous marshlands until they were drained from the eighteenth century onwards.

This important strategic location also became the royal court of the Stewart monarchy and major buildings still to be seen today were constructed by them. Beyond the gatehouse complex with its defensive ditches and batteries, the now restored Great Hall was completed for King James III around 1503. The Palace by King James V, dates from around 1538-42 and is noted for its exterior Renaissance decoration in the French style, which includes a variety of ornately worked figures. King James VI, in turn, was responsible for the Chapel Royal in 1594. The castle's fortunes changed greatly after the removal of the Scottish court to London in 1603. Thereafter the castle had a prolonged military occupation – which continues today. However, aside from the historic interest, an important element in the castle visit is simply the view from the ramparts. In the east, this extends down the Forth valley, the cradle of the industrial revolution in this part of Scotland, right down to the tip of one of the cantilevers of the Forth Bridge. In the other direction, the panorama is, in contrast, thoroughly Highland. Ben Chonzie beyond Crieff can be seen to the north-west, with the Trossachs hills westwards and, a little further off, the Arrochar Alps usually plainly visible.

120 Standing Waves Leisure

Canoeing and kayaking lessons, courses and equipment hire for beginners and more advanced paddlers.

K7 *Forestry Cabin, Main Street, Strathyre; on A84, N of Callander.*

P WC & 环 林 ⊞ £££

⊕ Apr–Oct, daily, 10am–dusk.
Other times by arrangement.

Tel 01877 384361   www.standingwaves.co.uk

121 Stirling Castle

Set dramatically above Stirling on a rock outcrop, and with a number of fascinating architectural features, this is one of Scotland's finest castles. (For further text above).

L5 *Top of Castle Wynd, centre of Stirling.*

P WC & 🍴 ⊞ E ⚹ £££

⊕ All year round, daily, 9.30am–6pm.
Oct–Mar, daily, 9.30am–5pm.

Tel 01786 450000   www.historic-scotland.gov.uk

TIREE

Tiree is so flat that it is sometimes known by a Gaelic name meaning 'the land below the waves'. Its barley was once used for whisky distilling and was a source of supply for the Lords of the Isles. Later, it was the scene of an unpleasant episode in 1885 when the then owner, the Duke of Argyll, sent a force of police and marines to evict its crofting population. The marines were sympathetic, however, and the matter settled in the crofters favour by the passing of the Crofters Act the following year.

Tiree has a greater proportion of good grazing land than Coll. Its prevailing colour is bright green, its landscape bathed in – statistically speaking – long sunshine hours, as there are no hills to catch the rain clouds. Wind is an ever present factor, hence the thick walls and low profile of the older houses and the reputation of the islands for good surfing. With its machair, dazzling beaches and wide skies, Tiree has more of the ambience of the Western Isles, rather than that of Mull, its nearest neighbour.

122 Stirling Old Town Jail 🏛

Looks at life in a nineteenth century jail, with living history performances, original cells, audio tour, exhibitions and roof top views.

L5 *St John Street in Stirling's old town; follow signs for Stirling Castle.*

P WC ♿ ☀ 🎫 ££

⏲ Dates and times vary; please telephone for details.

Tel 01786 450050

123 Stirling Smith Art Gallery and Museum 🏛

The Stirling Smith is home to some remarkable pieces such as the oldest dating curling stone, ancient tartans and the world's oldest football.

L5 *From J10 on M9, follow signs for Stirling Castle.*

On Dumbarton Road, 200 yards from Tourist Office.

P WC ♿ ☕ 🎫 E Free

⏲ Tue–Sat, 10.30am–5pm; Sun 2–5pm.

Tel 01786 471917
www.smithartgallery.demon.co.uk

124 Strachur Smiddy Museum and Craft Shop 🏛

A Highland smiddy, dating from the eighteenth century, restored to working order, with implements, photographs and artefacts on display, plus occasional demonstrations.

G6 *Strachur, 18 miles N of Dunoon on A815.*

P WC ♿ 🎫 AV £

⏲ Easter–Sept, daily, 1-4pm. Other times by appointment.

Tel 01369 860565

THE TROSSACHS

The Trossachs became the byword for Scottish scenery very early. A promotional brochure from the North British Railway in 1914 stated that 'To the tourist who undertakes the journey no surfeit of laudation is possible, for in the Trossachs the superlative reigns absolute'. Few other pieces of Scottish scenery have had so much praise heaped upon them over the years.

Their fame even predates Sir Water Scott's *Lady of the Lake*, the best-selling verse narrative of 1810 which peopled the Trossachs' landscapes with romantic figures. The Wordsworths were here by 1803, having heard of the beauties from even earlier published works.

Some writers confine the location of the Trossachs to the narrow defile which links Loch Achray with Loch Katrine. In Scott's day, this was a winding pathway overhung with trees. Today it leads down to the main car park and pier form where the steamboat, the Sir Walter Scott *(see p129)*, has given views of Loch Katrine's shores for generations of tourists. The widest definition of the Trossachs takes the area west to the shores of Loch Lomond and up as far as Balquhidder, a fine Highland glen associated with local folk-hero Rob Roy MacGregor *(see Rob Roy and Trossachs Visitor Centre and Rob Roy's Grave p127)*.

The standard Trossachs excursion goes by the Duke's Road (or Duke's Pass) from Aberfoyle. This goes up and over the Highland line, passing a superb viewpoint across the rolling waves of forestry from which Ben Venue and Ben Ledi emerge like islands from a dark green sea. The area combines a wild air with remarkable accessibility – virtually every loch in the area, for example, can be seen and reached by car. Best of all, in spite of their popularity, the Trossachs, even today, at least give the impression of somewhere unspoilt, with just a hint of the grandeur which attracted the early Romantics.

(See also Breadalbane Folklore Centre p109; Falls of Dochart p116; Hamilton Toy Collection p117; Inchmahome Priory p117, Queen Elizabeth Forest Park and Visitor Centre p127, Scottish Wool Centre p128)

125 Tighnabruaich Sailing School ⵗ

Sailing and windsurfing taught in coastal sheltered waters around the Kyles of Bute, with all instructors RYA qualified. Courses run for five days or weekends.

G4   *Follow A8003 S to Tighnabruaich.*

⌂ ⎕ £££

☉ Season runs from May–Sept.

Tel 01700 811717   www.tssargyll.co.uk

126 Tobermory Distillery   🍶

Offers guided tours of Mull's only distillery, showing the processes involved in whisky production.

D8   *Tobermory, Isle of Mull.*

P ⌂ AV ⎕ £

☉ Easter–Oct, Mon–Fri, 10am–5pm.
   Other times by appointment.

Tel 01688 302647
www.burnstewartdistillers.com

127 Torosay Castle and   🏰 ❋
Gardens

Set in twelve acres of gardens, this Victorian family home contains a collection of portraits, family scrapbooks and memorabilia. The terraced formal garden features limestone figures sculpted by Antonia Bonazza, and contrasts with a less formal woodland area and pool. Also of interest are a variety of rhododendrons, alpines, walled and rock gardens, and an oriental garden with impressive sea views *(see also p124).*

E7   *Two miles SE of Craignure on A849.*

P WC ⌂ ☕ ⌂ E ⏚ ⚘ ⚘ ⎕ ££

☉ House: April–October, 10.30am–5pm.
   Other times by arrangement.
   Gardens: all year round, 9am–dusk.

Tel 01680 812421   www.torosay.com

128 Waverley Paddle Steamer   ★

The *Waverley*, the last sea-going paddle steamer in the world, cruises round the waters of the Firth of Clyde, including stop-offs at Dunoon and Rothesay on the Isle of Bute.

G4 / H5   *Cruises depart from Dunoon and Rothesay.*

P WC ✕ ££

☉ Timetable runs from Easter–Oct, depending on weather conditions.

Tel 0141 243 2224
www.waverleyexcursions.co.uk

Ben Cruachan and Loch Etive, Argyll

Glen Lyon

Loch Tay and Ardtalnaig

PERTHSHIRE

The old county of Perthshire still revolves round Perth as a busy town serving a mostly rural but comparatively affluent hinterland (hence the description of Perthshire as 'Scotland's Hampshire'). Stand, for example, on the top of the Knock Hill, a worthwhile woodland walk from Crieff town centre, and the view to the south across Strathearn, towards the northen slopes of the Ochils, takes in a wide prospect of grainfields and wooded field-edges, with a well-kept prosperous appearance. Turn to face the north-west and the woodlands of the Highland edge run up to the high green hills.

Crieff is just one of the Highland edge resorts, such as Dunkeld, Aberfeldy and Pitlochry, which flourish with one foot in the Highlands, yet without the remoteness of places further north. Thanks partly to the improving lairds of the area's grand estates, Perthshire is also strongly associated with trees and boasts some national records. In the churchyard in Fortingall grows, it is said, the oldest living thing in Europe – a 3000 year old yew. By the main road between Perth and Blairgowrie, at Meikleour is the tallest beech hedge in the world, at around 30m (100ft) *(see p138)*. A pleasing walk by the River Bran in the sheltering woods by the River Bran near Dunkeld reveals one of the tallest trees in Scotland – a Douglas fir around the 60m (200ft) mark.

But not unexpectedly for an area stretching into the Highlands, there is a wilder side to this comfortable county. East-west running glens hold scenic lochs such as Loch Tay and Lochs Tummel and Rannoch, allowing a choice of circular tours. Glen Lyon is typical upland Perthshire, one of the longest glens in Scotland, with the classic u-shaped glacial profile, with some farming along the river-flats, then steep-sided slopes for sheep grazing. There is a hydro-electric dam at the head of the glen – also typical in the area – and the glen has its share of high mountains. On the north side extensive plateau offers cross-country and ski touring in winter, especially around Carn Mairg. Close by to the south is Ben Lawers, the summit of a grand massif which is the most extensive and highest in the southern Highlands *(see p138)*. But even here the impression is of greenness, with the slopes offering more of interest to botanists than to rock climbers.

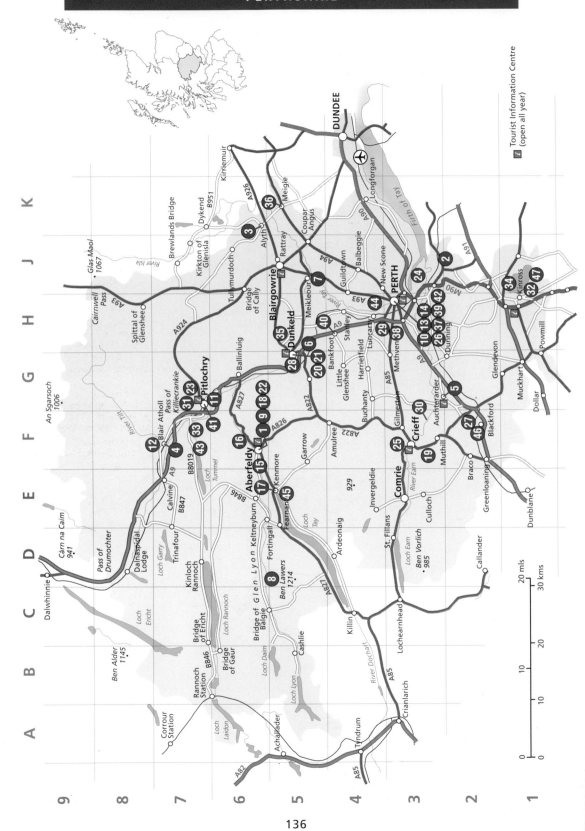

Tourist Information Centre
(open all year)

VISITOR INFORMATION

MAIN TOURIST INFORMATION CENTRE

Perth
Lower City Mills
West Mill Street
Perth PH1 5QP
Tel: 01738 450600
Web: www.perthshire.co.uk
E-mail: perthtic@perthshire.co.uk
Open: all year round

YEAR ROUND TOURIST INFORMATION CENTRES

Aberfeldy
The Square
Aberfeldy PH15 2DD
Tel: 01887 820276
E-mail:
aberfeldytic@perthshire.co.uk

Auchterarder
90 High Street
Auchterarder PH3 1BJ
Tel: 01764 663450
E-mail:
auchterardertic@perthshire.co.uk

Blairgowrie
26 Wellmeadow
Blairgowrie PH10 6AS
Tel: 01250 872960
E-mail:
blairgowrietic@perthshire.co.uk

Crieff
High Street
Crieff PH7 3HU
Tel: 01764 652578
E-mail: criefftic@perthshire.co.uk

Dunkeld
The Cross
Dunkeld PH8 0AN
Tel: 01350 727688
E-mail:
dunkeldtic@perthshire.co.uk

Kinross
Service Area, Junction 6, M90
Kinross KY13 7NQ
Tel: 01577 863680
E-mail:
kinrosstic@perthshire.co.uk

Pitlochry
22 Atholl Road
Pitlochry PH16 5BX
Tel: 01796 472215/472751
E-mail:
pitlochrytic@perthshire.co.uk

ADDITIONAL INFORMATION

GENERAL TRAVEL INFORMATION
Traveline Scotland
Tel: 0870 608 2608
Provides timetable information for all public transport in Scotland and the rest of Great Britain.

TRAINS
First Scotrail
Caledonian Chambers
87 Union Street
Glasgow G1 3TA
Tel: Fares & Train Times:
08457 484950
Telesales: 08457 550033
Customer Relations:
0845 601 5929
Web: www.firstscotrail.co.uk
E-mail: scotrail.enquiries@
firstgroup.com

COACH
Scottish Citylink Coaches
Limited
Buchanan Bus Station
Killermont Street
Glasgow G2 3NP
Tel: 08705 505050

Web: www.citylink.co.uk
E-mail: info@citylink.co.uk
*Routes: Perth–Aberdeen
Perth–Edinburgh
Perth–Glasgow
Perth–Dundee
Perth–Inverness*

BUS
Stagecoach Perth
Dunkeld Road
Perth PH1 5TW
Tel: 01738 629339
Web: www.stagecoachbus.com
E-mail:
customerservices@ssne.co.uk
*Routes: operates an extensive
bus network throughout
Perthshire
Perth–Dundee
Perth–Stirling*

CAR HIRE
Oakburn Self Drive,
Pitlochry
Tel: 01796 472080
Web:www.pitlochry-
scotland.co.uk
E-mail:
ian@oakburn.clara.co.uk

Struan Rental,
Perth
Tel: 01738 445566
E-mail: rental@struan.co.uk

Dollar Fifty Car Rental,
Perth
Tel: 01738 633677
Web: www.thrifty.co.uk
E-mail:
thrifty.perth@thrifty.co.uk

TAXIS
Blairgowrie Taxis
Tel: 01250 872116

Scotia Cabs,
Blairgowrie
Tel: 01250 874444

SR Taxis,
Pitlochry
Tel: 01796 473931

Strathearn Taxis,
Crieff
Tel: 01764 652516

1 Aberfeldy Watermill 🏛

This restored nineteenth century mill now houses an Art Gallery, music and bookshop.

F6 *Mill Street, Aberfeldy, on A826/A827.*

🅿 🚾 ♿ ☕ 🎁 E ⛱ Free

🕐 All year, Mon–Sat, 9am–5pm; Sun, 12 noon–5pm.

Tel 01887 822896

www.aberfeldywatermill.com

2 Abernethy Round Tower ⊛ 🏰

Dating from the eleventh century, this narrow tower is one of only two Irish-style round towers left in Scotland, the other being Brechin Cathedral Round Tower *(see p150).* Measuring 74 ft in height, it was originally used as a look-out and offers good views of the surrounding area.

J2 *Centre of Abernethy on A913.*

⚘ Free

🕐 Apr–Sept, daily, 9.30am–6.30pm.

Tel 0131 668 8800

www.historic-scotland.gov.uk

3 Alyth Museum 🏛

A folk museum focussing on local social and farming history.

K6 *Alyth town centre on the B952, five miles E of Blairgowrie.*

🅿 E Free

🕐 May–Sept, Wed–Sun, 1–5pm.

Tel 01738 632488

www.pkc.gov.uk/ah/alyth_museum

4 Atholl Country Life Museum 🏛

This museum gives an insight into the country life and social history of the people of Atholl. Many aspects of farming, wildlife, school, road, rail and postal communications are explored. Features include the original Trinafour Post Office and shop and an authentic nineteenth century kitchen.

F7 *Blair Atholl, near entrance to Blair Castle.*

🅿 🚾 ♿ ☕ 🎁 ⛱ £

🕐 June–Sept, daily, 1.30pm–5pm.
July–Aug, Mon–Fri, from 10am.

Tel 01796 481232   www.heartlander.scotland.net

5 Auchterarder Heritage 🏛

An exhibition devoted to the history of the town and surrounding area.

G3 *Off A9, Auchterarder town centre, opposite the Town Hall.*

E Free

🕐 Apr–Oct, Mon–Sat, 9.30am–5pm. Jul–Aug, closes at 6pm; Sun, 11am–4pm. Oct–Apr, call for details.

Tel 01764 663450

6 Beatrix Potter Exhibition and Garden 🏛 ❉

An exhibition focusing on writer and illustrator Beatrix Potter, and her friendship with the local postman and naturalist who encouraged her interest in natural history. She spent many childhood holidays in the Birnam area and is thought to have written *The Tale of Peter Rabbit* on one of her visits. Potter's garden and favourite woodland walks are also open to the public.

H5 *Birnam, one mile S of Dunkeld, on A9.*

🚾 ♿ ☕ 🎁 E AV ⛱ 👫 ♿ £

🕐 All year, daily, 10am–5pm.
Oct–Mar, Sun, 11am–5pm

Tel 01350 727674   www.birnaminstitute.com

7 Beech Hedge

Planted in 1746, this amazing hedge is the tallest in the world, measuring approx. 30 metres high and 550 metres in length.

J5 *On the A93, five miles S of Blairgowrie.*

Free

🕐 Open access.

Tel 01250 87 2960

8 Ben Lawers ♟ 🐦

Ben Lawers stands by Loch Tay, and at 3,980 ft, is Perthshire's highest mountain. As wells as attracting various species of birds such as the curlew, raven and red grouse, the mountain is renowned for its unusual array of Arctic-Alpine plants growing in its rich calcareous soil. A nature trail and visitor centre are situated at the base.

D5 *Six miles NE of Killin, off A827.*

🅿 ♿ 🎁 AV ⚘ 👫 £

🕐 Open access. Visitor centre: May–Sept, daily, 10.30am–5pm; sometimes closed between 1–2pm.

Tel 01567 820988   www.nts.org.uk

Blair Castle

9 Birks of Aberfeldy

Footpaths take walkers through woodland consisting of birch trees and some oak, ash and elm, to a bridge above the Falls of Moness, offering views down into the Moness Gorge. The birch trees in particular turn beautiful colours in autumn.

F6 *Path begins at the centre of Aberfeldy on A826/A827.*

P ⊼ ⅏ ⅍ Free

⊕ Open access.

Tel 01887 820276

10 Black Watch Museum

On display at this museum are a range of weapons, medals, paintings and artefacts relating to the 200-year history of the Black Watch, Scotland's oldest Highland regiment.

H3 *Balhousie Castle in Hay Street, Perth city centre.*

P WC ⛪ Free

⊕ May–Sept, Mon–Sat,10am–4.30pm
(closed last Sat in June).
Oct–Apr, Mon–Fri, 10am–3.30pm
(closed Dec 23–Jan 6)

Tel 0131 310 8530   www.theblackwatch.co.uk

11 Blair Athol Distillery

Blair Athol is one of the oldest working distilleries in Scotland, and takes its water from the Allt Dour; tours end with a dram.

G6 *Half a mile S of Pitlochry, off A9.*

⊕ Easter–Sept, Mon–Sat, 9.30am–5pm.
Jun–Sept, Sun, 12 noon–5pm. Jan–Easter,
Nov & Dec, Mon–Fri, 10.30am–4pm.
Oct, 10am–4pm. Last tour 1 hour before closing.

Tel 01796 482003

12 Blair Castle

Blair Castle has been the traditional home of the Earls and Dukes of Atholl from 1269. Visitors have access to 30 furnished rooms which contain furniture, paintings, arms and armour, china, lace and embroidery. Facilities in the grounds include the Hercules Garden, deer park and children's play area; a ranger service arranges walks and events during the summer.

F7 *Blair Atholl, off A9, seven miles NW of Pitlochry.*

P WC ♿ ☕ ✗ ⛪ E ⊼ ⅏ ⅍ ⊞ £££

⊕ Apr–Oct, daily, open 9.30am
(last admission to castle, 4.30pm).
Nov–Mar, limited opening;
please telephone for details.

Tel 01796 481207   www.blair-castle.co.uk

13 Branklyn Garden

A small but impressive garden containing rhododendrons, alpines, herbaceous and peat-garden plants.

H3 *On A85 Dundee Road, SE side of Perth city centre.*

P WC & 冊 AV ££

⊕ Apr–Oct, daily, 10am–5pm.

Tel 01738 625535

www.nts.org.uk

14 Caithness Glass Visitor Centre ★

Visitors can see glass paperweights being made by skilled craftsmen through viewing galleries.

H3 *N side of Perth city centre on the A9, off Inveralmond Roundabout.*

P WC & ✕ 冊 AV Free

⊕ Mar–Nov, Mon–Sat, 9am–5pm; Sun, 10am–5pm.
Dec–Feb, Mon–Sat, 9am–5pm; Sun, 12 noon–5pm.

Tel 01738 492320   www.caithnessglass.co.uk

15 Castle Menzies

The sixteenth century castle was the seat of the Chiefs of Clan Menzies for over 400 years, and was restored by the Clan Society. Rich in history, Bonnie Prince Charlie rested there on his way to Culloden in 1746. Architecturally, it is an interesting example of the transition between earlier rugged fortress and later mansion house.

F6 *Weem, two miles NW of Aberfeldy, on B846.*

P WC & ☕ 冊 ⯭ 兵 ££

⊕ Apr–mid Oct, Mon–Sat, 10.30am–5pm; Sun, 2–5pm. Last entry 4.30pm.

Tel 01887 820982   www.menzies.org

16 Cluny House Gardens

Cluny is a woodland garden set in the Strathtay valley, growing mainly Himalayan and North American plants. Highlights include primulas, meconopsis, trilliums, lillies, rhododendrons plus various mature trees and shrubs.

F6 *Four miles NE of Aberfeldy; cross Wade's Bridge on B847, turn right at Ailean Chraggan Hotel, and left after three miles, following signs.*

P 兵 ⯭ ⯭ £

⊕ Mar–Oct, daily, 10am–6pm.

Tel 01887 820795

17 Croft Na Caber

Offers a range of watersports and other outdoor activities, plus cruises on Loch Tay.

E5 *Kenmore, on the A827, five miles W of Aberfeldy.*

P WC ☕ ✕ ⯭ ⯭ ££

⊕ All year round, daily, 9am–5pm.
Closed mid Dec–mid Jan.

Tel 01887 830588

18 Dewar's World of Whisky   ★

A visitor centre focussing on Dewar's whisky, with various interactives, a giant video wall, trivia quiz and a 'nosing and tasting bar'. Also on offer is a tour of Aberfeldy Distillery which produces a single malt whisky using traditional methods.

F6 *On the edge of Aberfeldy, on A827.*

P WC & ☕ 冊 E AV 兵 ⯭ 兵 ⯭ ££

⊕ Apr–Oct, Mon–Sat, 10am–6pm; Sun, 12 noon–4pm.
Nov–Mar, Mon–Sat, 10am–4pm
(last admission one hour before closing).

Tel 01887 822010

www.dewarsworldofwhisky.com

19 Drummond Castle Gardens

The gardens were initially laid out in the early seventeenth century by John Drummond, 2nd Earl of Perth, and renewed in the 1950's by Phyllis Astor, Countess of Ancaster. With their ancient yew hedges and copper beech trees, these remain some of Scotland's finest formal gardens.

F3 *Two miles S of Crieff on A822.*

P WC 冊 ⯭ ££

⊕ May–Oct, daily, 2–6pm. Open Easter weekend.

Tel 01764 681257

20 Dunkeld Cathedral

These picturesque ruins are set on the banks of the Tay, surrounded by tranquil lawns. The fifteenth century tower and nave of the cathedral are cared for by Historic Scotland, while the choir area acts as the parish church; of particular note are two Pictish slabs and the tomb of the Wolf of Badenoch.

G5 *Cathedral Street, centre of Dunkeld, on the banks of the River Tay.*

兵 Free

⊕ All year round, daily;
please telephone to check times.

Tel 0131 668 8800   www.historic-scotland.gov.uk

21 Dunkeld

A number of Dunkeld's eighteenth century terraced houses have been restored by the National Trust for Scotland and turned into homes for local people. Although they can only be viewed from the exterior, their whitewashed walls along Cathedral Street and around the square area give the village a unique atmosphere. The Tourist Information Centre runs a video on Dunkeld.

G5 *Fifteen miles N of Perth off A9.*

P ᵂᶜ ♿ ♥ ✕ 🏛 AV 🎋 👥 💷 Free

🕐 Open access.

Tel 01350 727460   www.nts.org.uk

22 Dunolly Adventure Outdoors

Activities for all ages including river rafting, high ropes challenge cable ascent, archery and biking.

F6 *W side of Aberfeldy next to River Tay.*

P 🏛 👥 ££

🕐 Daily, 8.30am–5.30pm.

Tel 01887 820298
www.dunollyadventures.co.uk

23 Edradour Distillery

Visitors can take a free tour and sample Edradour Single Malt Whisky at Scotland's smallest distillery.

G7 *On A924, three miles N of Pitlochry.*

P ᵂᶜ ♿ 🏛 E AV 💷 Free

🕐 Mar–Oct, Mon–Sat, 9.30am–5pm;
Sun, 12 noon–4pm.
Nov–mid Dec, Mon–Sat, 9.30–4pm. Jan & Feb,
Mon–Sat, 10am–4pm; Sun, 11.30am–5pm.

Tel 01796 472095   www.edradour.co.uk

24 Elcho Castle

This imposing sixteenth century fortified mansion, set on the banks of the Tay, features projecting towers and original protective iron grilles round the windows.

J3 *Five miles N of Bridge of Earn off the A912.*

🎋 £

🕐 Apr–Nov, daily, 9.30am–6.30pm.

Tel 01738 639998   www.historic-scotland.gov.uk

25 Famous Grouse Experience at Glenturret Distillery

Glenturret, Scotland's oldest Highland malt distillery, was established in 1775, and dates back to 1717. Visitors can see a state of the art interactive show, 'The Flight of the Grouse' and learn how the *Famous Grouse* whisky is produced and sample the final product.

F3 *Off A85, two miles N of Crieff.*

P ᵂᶜ ♿ ✕ 🏛 E AV 🎋 👥 💷 ££

🕐 Jan–Dec, daily, 9am–6pm; (last tour 4.30pm).
Jul–Aug, daily, 9am–6.30pm (last tour 5.30pm).

Tel 01764 656565   www.famousgrouse.com

26 Fergusson Gallery

A gallery devoted to the work of Scottish colourist painter Fergusson (1874–1961), containing a collection of his paintings, drawings, photographs, sculptures and related archive material. A changing programme of six exhibitions are run throughout the year.

H3 *Marshall Place, beside River Tay, Perth city centre.*

ᵂᶜ ♿ 🏛 E Free

🕐 Telephone or check website for opening times.

Tel 01738 441944
www.pkc.gov.uk/ah/fergussongallery

27 Gleneagles Golf Course

The King's Course was officially opened in 1919 and the first professional tournament played a year later. After the hotel was completed in 1923, Gleneagles' reputation began to grow, and many important events have since been played here including the Bell's Scottish Open, McDonald's WPGA Championship of Europe and the PGA Cup matches.

F2 *The M9 becomes the A9, continue for 11 miles.*

P ♿ ✕ 🏛 💷

🕐 May–Jun, daily, 8am–dusk. Jul–Aug, 7.30am–dusk.
Sept–Oct, 7.30am–dusk. Nov–Apr, 8am–dusk.

Tel 01764 694469   www.gleneagles.co.uk

28 Hermitage

Beautiful river walks lead through a mix of conifer and deciduous woodland, and pass by Britain's tallest tree, a Douglas Fir which measures 212 ft. Ossian's Hall, a restored eighteenth century folly, looks down into the River Braan.

G5 *Two miles W of Dunkeld off A9.*

P 👥 ≋ £

🕐 All year round, daily, daylight hours.

Tel 01350 728641/01796 473233
www.nts.org.uk

Killiecrankie

🕐 Mar–Oct, Mon–Sat, 10am–12.45pm & 2–4.45pm; Sun, 2–4pm. Closed Thurs. Nov–Feb, by appointment.
Tel 01764 652819
www.strathearn.com/p1/innerpeffray

31 Killiecrankie

The River Garry runs through this dramatic gorge, with deciduous woodland cloaking the steep banks on either side. Of historic interest is Soldier's Leap, where a soldier jumped from one bank to the other in an effort to escape capture during the Battle of Killiecrankie in 1689. Displays in the visitor centre look at the history and wildlife of the area, and a camera set in the woods sends pictures of nesting birds.

G7 *Three miles N of Pitlochry on B8079.*

🅿 ♿ ☕ ⛩ E ⛺ 👣 **Free**
🕐 Site: all year round, daily.
Visitor Centre: Apr–Oct, daily.
Tel 01796 473233
www.nts.org.uk

29 Huntingtower Castle

These two well-preserved fifteenth/sixteenth century towers were later connected by a simple three-storey range. The eastern tower has retained impressive painted ceilings.

H4 *Two miles W of Perth, off the A85.*

🅿 ⛩ ⛺ £
🕐 Apr–Sept, daily, 9.30am–6.30pm.
Oct–Mar, Sat–Wed, 9.30am–4.30pm.
Tel 01738 627231
www.historic-scotland.gov.uk

32 Kinross House Gardens

These formal gardens were designed by Sir William Bruce, Surveyor-General to Charles II and architect of Kinross House. They contain roses, herbaceous borders, trees and topiary and overlook Loch Leven and Castle Island where Mary, Queen of Scots was imprisoned.

H1 *Kinross; follow signposts.*

🅿 ♿ ⛺ £
🕐 Apr–Sept, daily, 10am–7pm.
Tel 01577 862900   www.kinrosshouse.com

30 Innerpeffray Library

The oldest existing library in Scotland founded by Lord Madderty in 1680, is situated on the north bank of the River Earn adjacent to St Mary's Chapel. Guided tours of the library and chapel can be arranged.

F3 *on B8062, Crieff to Auchertarder road 5 miles SE of Crieff.*

33 Linn of Tummel

A series of woodland paths run along the banks of the Rivers Tummel and Garry to the Linn where the two rivers meet, creating a series of dramatic rapids.

F7 *Three miles NW of Pitlochry on B8019.*

🅿 ⛺ 👣 **Free**
🕐 All year round, daily, daylight hours.
Tel 01796 473233/01350 728641
www.nts.org.uk

34 Loch Leven Castle

Mary, Queen of Scots was imprisoned on this island with its imposing fourteenth/fifteenth century tower for nearly a year, before finally escaping in 1568. A short boat trip transports visitors across to the island.

J1 *On an island in Loch Leven, accessible by boat from Kingate Park, Kinross.*

P WC 🚻 ⛱ ££

🕐 Apr–Sept, daily, 9.30am–6.30pm, in conjunction with ferry timetable.

Tel 07778 040483   www.historic-scotland.gov.uk

35 Loch of the Lowes Visitor Centre

An observation hide provides views of an osprey nest in breeding season, along with a variety of waterfowl and woodland birds. The visitor centre contains displays on local wildlife. Limited wheelchair access.

H5 *Two miles N of Dunkeld, off A923.*

P WC ♿ 🚻 E ♨ £

🕐 Apr–Sept, daily, 10am–5pm.

Tel 01350 727337

36 Meigle Museum

An impressive collection of sculptured monuments from the Pictish period.

K5 *Meigle, on A94.*

WC ♿ 🚻 E ♨ £

🕐 Apr–Sept, daily, 9.30am–6pm.

Tel 01828 640612
www.historic-scotland.gov.uk

37 Noah's Ark ★

An indoor adventure play area featuring three separate areas for up to three years, under fives and five to twelves, plus family indoor karting.

H3 *Old Gallows Road, Western Edge, Perth.*

P WC ♿ ☕ ✕ ⛱ ♨ ££

🕐 Playbarn: daily, 10.30am–6.30pm. Karts and Bowling: weekends, 10.30am–6.30pm; Mon–Fri, seasonal opening hours; please telephone to confirm times.

Tel 01738 445568   www.noahs-ark.co.uk

38 Perth Mart Visitor Centre ★

A number of farm animals such as sheep, goats, cattle and horses are on display, along with information on Scotland's agriculture, past and present.

H3 *Two miles W of Perth, on A85.*

P WC ✕ 🚻 ⛱ ♨ £

🕐 All year round, daily, 10am–5pm.

Tel 01738 474170

39 Perth Museum and Art Gallery

One of Britian's oldest museums with collections of art, local history, archaeology and natural history, plus a programme of changing exhibitions.

H3 *George Street, Perth city centre, adjacent to Perth Bridge.*

P WC ♿ 🚻 E Free

🕐 All year round, Mon–Sat, 10–5pm.

Tel 01738 632488
www.pkc.gov.uk/ah/perth_museum

Queen's View

40 Perthshire Visitor Centre ★

Along with a retail and play area is the *Macbeth Experience*, a multi-media exhibition telling the real history of Macbeth who ruled Scotland nearly 1,000 years ago.

H4 *Bankfoot, on B867 off A9, eight miles N of Perth.*

🅿 ♿ ✕ ☕ 🏛 E AV 💷 £

🕐 Easter–Sept, daily, 9am–8pm. Oct–Mar, 9am–7pm.

Tel 01738 787696   www.macbeth.co.uk

41 Pitlochry Visitor Centre ★ and Dam

Salmon can be seen ascending the fish ladder through a special viewing chamber, and an audio-visual presentation describes the fish's journey after passing through the dam. An exhibition looks at the spread of hydro generation schemes through Scotland.

G7 *By the waterfront, Pitlochry, off A9/A924.*

🅿 🏛 E AV 💷 £

🕐 Apr–Oct, daily, 10.30am–5.30pm.

Tel 01796 473152   www.scottish-southern.co.uk

42 Quarrymill Woodland Park 🌳

A country park with trails running through a wooded valley, scenic picnic areas and viewpoints.

H3 *Half a mile from Perth city centre on A93.*

🅿 ♿ ☕ 🏛 ⛱ ✲ 🚶 Free

🕐 Visitor centre and tearoom: May–Sept, daily, 10am–4.30pm. Walks and picnic area: all year round.

Tel 01738 633890

43 Queen's View

The view across Loch Tummel to Schiehallion is one of the most famous in Scotland. Queen Victoria took tea here in 1866, but the viewpoint actually commemorates Queen Isabella, wife of Robert the Bruce. A nearby visitor centre tells the story of the people and forests of Highland Perthshire and acts as an information centre for the surrounding Tay Forest Park.

F7 *Six miles W of Pitlochry on B8019.*

🅿 ♿ ☕ 🏛 E AV ⛱ ✲ 🚶 💷 £

🕐 Apr–Oct, daily, 10am–6pm.

Tel 01350 727284

Scone Palace

44 Scone Palace

Scone Palace has been the family home of the Earls of Mansfield for 400 years. It was the crowning site of the Kings of Scotland, and has played host to the Old Pretender, his son Bonnie Prince Charlie, Queen Victoria and Prince Albert among others; a replica Stone of Destiny is on display. Visitors can see a collection of porcelain and bedhangings worked on by Mary, Queen of Scots, while the grounds contain a David Douglas trail, mature pinetum and adventure playground.

H4 *Two miles N of Perth on A93.*

P WC ♥ ✕ ✿ E ⊼ 㣙 ⊞ £££

🕓 Palace: Easter–Oct, 9.30am–5.30pm (last admission 5pm).
Grounds: close 6pm.
Winter: By arrangement.

Tel 01738 552300   www.scone-palace.co.uk

45 Scottish Crannog Centre

A crannog was an ancient timber homestead built in water to protect habitats from potential invasion. The centre comprises of a recreated crannog on the shores of Loch Tay, where traces of these dwellings have been uncovered. Guided tours are provided along with exhibits, video and demonstrations of ancient crafts.

E5 *Six miles W of Aberfeldy, off the A827 by Kenmore.*

P WC ♿ ✿ E AV 㣙 ⊞ ££

🕓 Mid Mar–Oct, daily, 10am–5.30pm.
Nov, daily, 10am–4pm,
(last entry one hour before closing).

Tel 01887 830583   www.crannog.co.uk

46 Tullibardine Distillery

Nestling at the foot of the Ochil Hills, this new visitor centre opened in 2004, allows visitors to learn about malt whisky production and sample the end product.

F2 *On the A9 at Blackford, between Perth and Stirling.*

P WC ♥ ♿ ✿ ✕ ⊞ £

🕓 All year, Mon–Sat, 8am–6pm, Sun, 10am–6pm.

Tel 01764 682252   www.tullibardine.com

47 Vane Farm Nature Reserve

An RSPB visitor and educational centre with nature trails and hides, set in a mixture of wet grassland, woodland and a heather-clad hill. The centre contains an observation room with displays and telescopes to view a huge variety of birds in season (binoculars are available for hire). Events are organised throughout the year.

J1 *On the S shore of Loch Leven, on the B9097, two miles E of J5 on M90.*

P WC ♿ ♥ ✿ ⊼ 㣙 㣙 ⊞ £

🕓 Daily, 10am–5pm. Reserve: open at all times.

Tel 01577 862355   www.rspb.org.uk

ANGUS AND CITY OF DUNDEE

Angus falls neatly into three separate landscape experiences. Firstly, there is the seacoast. This is at its finest between Arbroath and Montrose, with red rock cliffs and coves, the quaintly picturesque former fishing village of Auchmithie and the long sandy reaches of Lunan Bay. The second element lies between mountain and sea with only the rise of the Sidlaw Hills behind Dundee to interrupt its simplicity. This is the long vale of Strathmore, through which the main lines of communication run north to the red earth of the Mearns. A rich farming landscape noted for potatoes and soft fruits, as well as the usual barley, rape and cattle, is serviced by towns such as Brechin and Forfar.

The third part changes the personality of Angus completely. From Strathmore, the long wall of the Grampians seem impenetrable, with big domed hills stretching back to a blue horizon. But roads, then tracks and paths as ancient rights of way, run far into these silent places. Each glen has its own character: Glen Esk, known to Queen Victoria on her excursions from Balmoral; delightful Prosen with its silent woodlands and tales of polar heroism – curiously, this is where Captain Scott and Dr Wilson planned their last South Pole expedition; then there is Clova with plant rarities – some say Britain's rarest plant grows here – and high level routes across the plateau of the Mounth to Deeside; finally, Isla where rugged cliffs and screes also hold great botanical interest. The Angus Glens are a world apart, with half-hidden Kirriemuir as their gateway.

In a sense, the city of Dundee has the Angus mountains as its playground. This city was formerly associated with the three activities of jute processing, journalism and jam-making. The jute heritage is all but consigned to museums now – of which the Verdant Works, a converted mill, gives an excellent portrait (see p157). Publishing still thrives, while the hinterland of Dundee still grows soft fruits in abundance. (It is the largest soft-fruit growing area in the EU.)

Dundee itself has left behind its old image as a grim industrial centre, and has a thriving cultural life, thanks to focal points such as the Dundee Contemporary Arts Centre. Dundee Science Centre is a magnet for children. The flagship – almost literally – of Discovery Point with the polar vessel RRS Discovery and its theme of Antarctic expeditions with their Dundee links (see p153), lends further interest to this changing city.

Edzell Castle and Garden

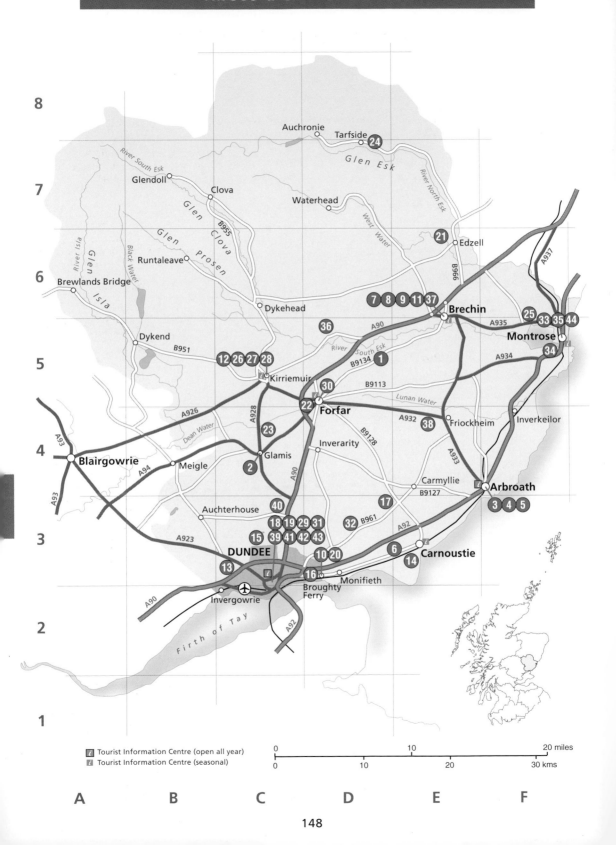

Auchronie
Tarfside ⓩ④
Glen Esk
River South Esk
Glendoll
Clova
Waterhead
River North Esk
West Water
㉑
Edzell
A937
Runtaleave
Brewlands Bridge
River Isla
Glen Isla
Black Water
Glen Clova
Glen Prosen
B955
Dykehead
B966
⑦ ⑧ ⑨ ⑪ ㊲
Brechin
㊱
A90
A935
㉕ ㉝ ㉟ ㊹
Montrose
Dykend
B951
River South Esk
B9134
①
A934
㉞
⑫ ㉖ ㉗ ㉘
Kirriemuir
㉚
B9113
Lunan Water
A926
A928
㉒ Forfar
Inverkeilor
Dean Water
㉓
A932
㊳ Friockheim
Blairgowrie
A94
Meigle
②
Glamis
Inverarity
B9128
A90
A933
Carmyllie
Auchterhouse
⑰
B9127
Arbroath
A93
A923
㊵
⑱ ⑲ ㉙ ㉛
㉜ B961
A92
③ ④ ⑤
⑮ ㊴ ㊶ ㊷ ㊸
⑥
DUNDEE
⑩ ⑳
⑭ Carnoustie
⑬
⑯
Monifieth
A90
Invergowrie
Broughty Ferry
A92
Firth of Tay

ℹ Tourist Information Centre (open all year)
ℹ Tourist Information Centre (seasonal)

0 ——— 10 ——— 20 miles
0 — 10 — 20 — 30 kms

8
7
6
5
4
3
2
1

A   B   C   D   E   F

VISITOR INFORMATION

MAIN TOURIST INFORMATION CENTRE

Dundee
21 Castle Street
Dundee DD1 3AA
Tel: 01382 527527
Web: www.angusanddundee.co.uk
E-mail: enquiries@angusanddundee.co.uk
Open: all year round

YEAR ROUND TOURIST INFORMATION CENTRE

Arbroath
Market Place
Arbroath DD11 1HR
Tel: 01241 872609
Web: www.angusanddundee.co.uk
E-mail: enquiries@angusanddundee.co.uk
Open: all year round

Brechin
Tel: 01356 623050
E-mail:
enquiries@angusanddundee.co.uk
Open: Apr–Sept

SEASONAL TOURIST INFORMATION CENTRES

Forfar
Tel: 01307 467876
E-mail:
enquiries@angusanddundee.co.uk
Open: Apr–Sept

Kirriemuir
Tel: 01575 574097
E-mail:
enquiries@angusanddundee.co.uk
Open: Apr–Sept

Carnoustie
Tel: 01241 852258
E-mail:
enquiries@angusanddundee.co.uk
Open: Apr–Sept

Montrose
Tel: 01674 672000
E-mail:
enquiries@angusanddundee.co.uk
Open: Apr–Sept

ADDITIONAL INFORMATION

GENERAL TRAVEL INFORMATION
Traveline Scotland
Tel: 0870 608 2608
Provides timetable information for all public transport in Scotland and the rest of Great Britain.

AIR TRAVEL
Dundee Airport
Riverside Drive
Dundee DD2 1DH
Tel: 01382 643242
Web: www.dundeecity.gov.uk/airport/main.html
E-mail:
david.johnston@dundeecity.gov.uk

Airline
ScotAirways
Cambridge Airport
Newmarket Road
Cambridge CB5 8RT
Tel: 0870 606 0707
Web: www.scotairways.com
Route: Dundee–London City

TRAINS
First ScotRail
Caledonian Chambers
87 Union Street
Glasgow G1 3TA
Tel: Fares & Train Times:
08457 484950
Telesales:
08457 550033
Customer Relations:
0845 601 5929
Web: www.firstscotrail.co.uk
E-mail: scotrail.enquiries@firstgroup.com

COACH
Scottish Citylink Coaches Limited
Buchanan Bus Station
Killermont Street
Glasgow G1 3NP
Tel: 08705 505050
Web: www.citylink.co.uk
E-mail: info@citylink.co.uk
*Routes: Dundee–Edinburgh
Dundee–Glasgow
Dundee–Perth*

BUS
Strathtay Scottish Omnibuses Limited
Seagate Bus Station
Dundee DD1 2HR
Tel: 01382 228345
E-mail: gdivine@strathtaybuses.com
*Routes: operates an extensive bus
network throughout Angus & Dundee*

G&N Wishart
Station Road
Friockheim DD11 4FF
Tel: 01241 828747
E-mail: gnwishart@fsnet.co.uk
*Routes: operates a number of buses in
the Brechin and Arbroath areas*

CAR HIRE
Arnold Clark Car Rental, Dundee
Tel: 01382 225382
Web: arnoldclark.co.uk

Economy Car & Van Rental, Dundee
Tel: 01382 400200

Hertz Rent-A-Car, Dundee
Tel: 01382 223711
Web: www.hertz.co.uk

National Car Rental, Dundee
Tel: 01382 224037
Web: www.nationalcar.com

TAXIS
Broughty Ferry Taxis, Broughty Ferry
Tel: 01382 477255

Discovery Taxi Services, Broughty Ferry
Tel: 01382 732111

Dundee Taxi Cab Company Limited,
Dundee
Tel: 01382 203020

Mitchell's Taxis (Dundee) Limited,
Dundee
Tel: 01382 623623

Tay Taxis, Dundee
Tel: 01382 450450

1 Aberlemno Sculptured Stones

An important set of Pictish stones consisting of a seventh-century symbol stone and two cross slabs, one of which measures around 3 m and is intricately decorated. A fourth stone, a carved cross slab, is located in the nearby churchyard.

D5 *Aberlemno, six miles NE of Forfar on B9134.*

Free

⊘ Open access, but covered during winter.

Tel 0131 668 8800   www.historic-scotland.gov.uk

2 Angus Folk Museum

Six 18th-century cottages house artefacts and remnants, providing a glimpse of how country people lived and worked. An exhibition, *Life on the Land*, is located in the adjacent farm steading.

C4 *Off the A94, five miles NW of Forfar.*

P ⱳ ㄴ ££

⊘ Apr–Jun & Sept, Fri–Tue, 12 noon–5pm; Sun, 1–5pm. Jul–Aug, daily, 11am–5pm. Sun, 1–5pm. Last admission 4.30pm

Tel 01307 840288   www.nts.org.uk

3 Arbroath Abbey

Established in 1178 by William the Lion, this historic abbey is closely linked with the Declaration of Arbroath of 1320 professing Scotland's independence from England. The surviving ruins of this former Tironensian monastery include sections of the abbey church and some domestic buildings.

F4 *Just off the A92, in the centre of Arbroath.*

㐀 E £

⊘ Apr–Sept, daily, 9.30am–6.30pm. Oct–Mar, daily, 9.30am–4.30pm;

Tel 01241 878756
www.historic-scotland.gov.uk

4 Arbroath Art Gallery

Two galleries contain works from Angus Council's permanent collection along with temporary exhibitions featuring the work of local artists and groups.

F4 *Above the public library, Arbroath town centre.*

ⱳ Free

⊘ Mon & Wed, 9.30am–8pm; Tue, 10am–6pm; Thur, 9.30am–6pm; Fri & Sat, 9.30am–5pm.

Tel 01241 872248
www.angus.gov.uk/history.htm

5 Arbroath Signal Tower Museum

The Regency Signal Tower complex was built in 1813 as the shore station for the Bell Rock Lighthouse which lies on a sunken reef about eleven miles from Arbroath. The museum gives a history of the lighthouse, along with Arbroath's textile and engineering industries, civic history and a recreated 1950s classroom and Victorian Lighthouse Keeper's parlour.

F4 *Ladyloan, Arbroath, near the harbour area.*

P ⱳ 㐀 E Free

⊘ All year round, Mon–Sat, 10am–5pm. Jul & Aug, Sun, 2–5pm.

Tel 01241 875598   www.angus.gov.uk/history.htm

6 Barry Mill

This water-powered meal mill was built in 1814 on a site used since 1539. A working mill until 1982, it is still in good order, and visitors can see corn being ground and the turning waterwheel.

E3 *Two miles W of Carnoustie, between A92 and A930.*

P ⱳ ㄴ 🎋 ££

⊘ Apr–Sept, Thur–Mon, 12 noon–5pm; Sun, 1–5pm.

Tel 01241 856761   www.nts.org.uk

7 Brechin Castle Centre

This 62 acre country park offers walks, an ornamental lake and a farm containing a variety of Scottish domestic species, pets corner and displays.

E6 *Off A90 at Brechin junction, 25 miles N of Dundee.*

P ⱳ ㄴ 🍴 㐀 🎋 ££

⊘ Summer, Mon–Sat, 9am–5pm; Sun 10am–6pm. Winter, Mon–Sat, 9am–5pm; Sun, 10am–5pm.

Tel 01356 626813
www.brechincastlecentre.co.uk

8 Brechin Cathedral Round Tower

Erected in the eleventh century, with later additions, Brechin is one of two surviving towers of its type in Scotland *(see Abernethy Round Tower, p138)*. Visitors can view the tower, complete with impressive carved doorway, from the outside. The church adjacent, contains a worthwhile collection of carved stones.

Broughty Ferry Castle Museum

E6 *Off the A933, Brechin town centre.*

Free

⊕ Open access (viewing from outside only).

Tel 0131 668 8800   www.historic-scotland.gov.uk

---

9 Brechin Museum

Tells the history of the town, with displays of local archeology, the once thriving textile and whisky industries, early pistols and an exhibition by local printmaker and artist David Waterson.

E6 *Brechin Town House, High Street, town centre.*

WC Free

⊕ Mon–Tue & Thur–Sat, 10am–5pm.
Wed, 10am–1pm.

Tel 01356 625536
www.angus.gov.uk/history.htm

---

10 Broughty Ferry Castle Museum

A fifteenth century fort at the mouth of the Tay estuary containing displays on the life and times of Broughty Ferry and seashore life. Also on offer is a military gallery and a changing programme of events, activities and displays. The castle is in the care of Historic Scotland, and the exhibition run by Dundee City Council.

D3 *Four miles E of Dundee city centre, off the A930, in Broughty Ferry.*

P WC 🍵 🏛 E AV ☀ Free

⊕ Apr–Sept, Mon–Sat, 10am–4pm; Sun, 12.30–4pm.
Oct–Mar, Tue–Sat, 10am–4pm; Sun, 12.30–4pm.

Tel 01382 436916   www.dundeecity.gov.uk

---

11 Caledonian Railway (Brechin) Ltd

A nostalgic steam-hauled journey from the historic city of Brechin to Bridge of Dun. Period engines, carriages and stations transport visitors back in time.

E6 *At the Brechin turnoff on the A90 Dundee/Aberdeen road.*

P WC ♿ 🍵 🏛 E 🪑 ☀ 👥 ££

⊕ Late May–mid Sept & Dec, Sun only.

Tel 01356 622992
www.caledonianrailway.co.uk

The Tay Bridges, Firth of Tay and the city of Dundee

12 Camera Obscura

This Camera Obscura was presented
to Kirriemuir by writer J M Barrie,
along with a cricket pavilion on Kirrie Hill.
Views of the surrounding area can be seen
on a large screen.

C5 *Kirriemuir, off A90/A926,
six miles NW of Forfar.*

🅿 ⊓ ⚒ ££

🕐 Apr–Sept, daily, 12 noon–5pm, last viewing
4.40pm. (dependent on weather).

Tel 01575 572646   www.nts.org.uk

13 Camperdown Country Park

Visitors can enjoy an 18-hole golf course,
woodland walks, pitch and putt and a
boating pond. The park also houses a
wildlife centre with over 80 species.

C3 *On A923, three miles N of Dundee.*

🅿 🚾 ♿ 🏛 ⊓ 🚶 ££

🕐 Mar–Sept, daily, 10am–4.30pm.
Oct–Feb, daily, 10am–3.30pm.

Tel 01382 431818/431811   www.dundeecity.gov.uk

14 Carnoustie Golf Course

Allan Robertson – the first of the great early
professional players – is credited with having laid
out the first formal holes at Carnoustie around

150 years ago, but golf has been played here
for centuries before that. The challenge on this
historic links course is its ever-changing nature –
no more than two holes consecutively run in the
same direction.

E3 *On A92, follow signposts for Carnoustie.*

🅿 🚾 ♿ ✕ 🏛 🅿

🕐 Booking essential.

Tel 01241 853789
www.carnoustiegolflinks.co.uk

15 Clatto Country Park

Situated on the outskirts of Dundee,
the parkland encompasses 24 acres of water.
Visitors can make use of woodland walks, a
visitor centre and play area, plus watersports
during summer months.

C3 *Off A972, near Camperdown Country Park.*

🅿 🚾 ♿ 🏛 ⊓ 🚶 Free

🕐 Apr–Sept, Mon–Tue, 9am–9pm;
Wed–Sun, 9am–5pm.

Tel 01382 436505   www.dundeecity.gov.uk

16 Claypotts Castle

Remarkably intact, this castle was built in the
sixteenth century by John Strachan. It possesses a
number of distinct architectural features and was
occupied until the nineteeth century.

Discovery Point and RRS Discovery, Dundee

D3 *South of the A92, near Broughty Ferry.*

£

🕐 Limited opening times;
please telephone to confirm.

Tel 01786 431324   www.historic-scotland.gov.uk

---

17 Crombie Country Park 🌳

The 250 acres of parkland includes
Crombie loch – originally a Victorian reservoir –
and extensive conifer woodland. For outdoor
enthusiasts the park offers trails, a ranger
service, guided walks and a wildlife hide.

D3 *Signposted from A92 to the B961,
three miles NW of Muirdrum.*

🅿 🚾 ♿ E 🎋 ☀ 🚶 Free

🕐 May–Aug, daily, 9am–9pm.
Sept–Apr, daily, 9am–dusk.

Tel 01241 860360

---

18 Discovery Point and
RRS Discovery 🏛

Home to Captain Scott's famous Royal Research
Ship Discovery. Launched in 1901, she ventured
deep into the unknown waters of Antarctica
and secured her place in the heroic age of polar
exploration. Visitors can see interactive and
multimedia galleries, original polar exploration
equipment and view the decks and restored
Captain's Bridge.

C3 *Opposite Dundee Railway Station on Riverside
Drive, by the Tay.*

🅿 🚾 ♿ 💬 ✗ 🎋 E 🅰 ☀ ♿ £££

🕐 Apr–Oct, Mon–Sat, 10am–6pm; Sun, 11am–6pm.
Nov–Mar, Mon–Sat, 10am–5pm; Sun, 11am–5pm.
Last admission 1 hour before closing.

Tel 01382 201245
www.rrsdiscovery.com

---

19 Dundee Contemporary Arts 🏛

Facilities include two galleries, cinema, print
studio, changing exhibitions and workshops.

C3 *Nethergate, Dundee city centre.*

🅿 🚾 ♿ 🎋 💬 ✗ E 🅰 ☀ ♿ Free

🕐 Galleries: Tue–Sat, 10.30am–5.30pm; Thur
closes 8pm; Sun, 12 noon–5.30pm. Cafe: Mon–Sat,
10.30am–midnight; Sun from 12 noon.

Tel 01382 909900   www.dca.org.uk

Glamis Castle

20 Eduardo Alessandro Studios 🏛

A large, independent gallery showcasing paintings, ceramics, sculpture and jewellery by Scottish contemporary artists.

D3 *Gray Street, near Broughty Ferry waterfront, three miles E of Dundee city centre on A930.*

🅿 🚻 ♿ ☕ ✗ 🏛 E 🅰 Free

🕐 Mon–Sat, 9.30am–5.30pm.
Winter closing time may vary.

Tel 01382 737011   www.eastudios.com

21 Edzell Castle and Garden 🅱 🏰 ❊

The impressive grounds comprise of a sixteenth-century courthouse mansion adjoined to a late medieval round tower house. Later additions were made to the gardens in 1604, including a summerhouse and walled garden.

E6 *At Edzell, off the B966, six miles N of Brechin.*

🅿 🚻 ♿ 🏛 E 🅰 £

🕐 Apr–Sept, daily, 9.30am–6.30pm.
Oct–Mar, Sat–Wed, 9.30am–4.30pm.
Last entry 30 minutes before closing.

Tel 01356 648631   www.historic-scotland.gov.uk

22 Forfar Loch Country Park ♣

The parkland covers an area of 93 acres with Forfar Loch a predominant feature of the landscape. The ranger service organises a number of events throughout the year including guided walks.

D5 *Off the A94, W of Forfar town centre.*

🅿 🚻 ♿ ☕ E 🅰 ☀ 🏃 Free

🕐 Park & Loch: all year round, daily, dawn–dusk.
Visitor Centre: Apr–Oct, daily, 1–4pm.
Nov–Mar, daily, 2–4pm.

Tel 01307 461118

23 Glamis Castle 🏰 ❊

Built in red sandstone and set in extensive parkland, Glamis Castle is the family home of the Earls of Strathmore and Kinghorne, childhood home of H M Queen Elizabeth the Queen Mother and birthplace of H R H The Princess Margaret. Rooms open to visitors include the Queen Mother's Bedroom and Sitting Room, and the Chapel with its beautifully decorated panels. The grounds contain a nature trail, pinetum of Douglas Firs and hardwood trees, walled and Italian gardens.

C4 *Six miles S of Kirriemuir on A94.*

🅿 ♿ ⬤ ✕ ⬛ E ⊓ ♞ 🔲 £££

🕐 Mar–Oct, daily, 10am–6pm, last admission 4.30pm.
Nov–Dec, 11am–4pm, last admission 3pm.

Tel 01307 840393
www.glamis-castle.co.uk

---

24 Glenesk Folk Museum

Set in Glenesk, the most north easterly glen in
Angus, this museum displays a wide range of
local archives and artefacts depicting how the
community lived and worked over the last
century. Themed rooms include a kitchen,
costume room, music room and children's room.

D7 *Nine miles NW of A90 up Glenesk.*

🅿 ♿ ⬤ ⬛ 🔲 £

🕐 Easter–end Jun, weekends, 12 noon–6pm.
Daily from Jul–mid Oct.

Tel 01356 670254

---

25 House of Dun 🎭 🏰 ✿

William Adam designed this fine Georgian house
in 1730 for David Erskine, Lord Dun. Contents
include family portraits, furniture, porcelain,
royal artefacts and needlework, along with
beautiful plasterwork. Outdoors, visitors can
explore a number of wooded walks and a walled
garden, restored in a Victorian style with plants
chosen to reflect the era.

F5 *Three miles W of Montrose on A935.*

🅿 ♿ ⬤ ⬛ E 🔳 ⊓ ⚘ ♞ 🔲 £££

🕐 House: Apr, Jun & Sept, Wed–Sun, 12.30–5pm.
Jul & Aug, daily, 11.30am–5.30pm.
Last admission 45 mins before closing.
Open Bank Holidays, Fri–Mon.

Tel 01674 810264   www.nts.org.uk

---

26 J M Barrie's Birthplace 🎭 🏰

Novelist and dramatist J M Barrie, creator of
Peter Pan, was born here in 1860. An exhibition
with audio presentation contains memorabilia,
stage costumes, miniature stage sets and the
original Wendy house, while the garden houses
a living willow crocodile.

C5 *Brechin Road, Kirriemuir.*

♿ ⬤ ⬛ 🔳 ⊓ ££

🕐 Apr–Jun & Sept, Sat–Wed, 12–5pm; Sun, 1–5pm.
Jul–Aug, daily, 11am–5pm; Sun, 1–5pm.
Last entry 4.30pm. Open Bank Holidays, Fri–Mon.

Tel 01575 572646   www.nts.org.uk

---

27 Kirriemuir Aviation Museum 🏛

The museum houses a private collection of World
War Two memorabilia, including radar sets,
wireless and transmitters for aircraft, uniforms
and medals.

C5 *Bellies Brae, Kirriemuir, off the A926/A928.*

Free

🕐 Apr–Sept, Mon–Thur & Sat, 10am–5pm; Fri & Sun
11am–5pm. Other times by arrangement.

Tel 01575 573233

---

28 Kirriemuir – Gateway to the 🏛 Glens Museum

Situated in The Town House, Kirriemuir's oldest
building, the museum recounts the social and
political history of the town – from the Romans
to the present day. Colourful displays and
detailed models bring Kirriemuir's past to life.

C5 *Kirriemuir town centre, five miles off A90.*

♿ ♿ ⬛ E 🔳 ⚘ Free

🕐 Mon–Sat, 10am–5pm; Thur 1–5pm.
Jul–Aug, closed Thur.

Tel 01575 575479   www.angus.gov.uk/history.htm

---

29 McManus Galleries 🏛

This gothic building houses a collection of fine and
decorative art, plus award-winning displays of local
history, archaeology, wildlife and the environment.
Highlights include works by MacTaggart, James
McIntosh Patrick, Millais and Rossetti.

C3 *Albert Square, Dundee city centre.*

♿ ♿ ⬤ ⬛ E Free

🕐 Mon–Sat, 10.30am–5pm; Thur til 7pm;
Sun, 12.30–4pm.
Closed from Oct 05–07 for major re-furbishment.

Tel 01382 432350   www.dundeecity.gov.uk

---

30 Meffan Museum and 🏛 Art Gallery

The museum depicts Forfar's history, which
includes a witch burning tableau, an interactive
guide to a collection of Pictish Stones and
a cobbled vennel complete with a series of
quaint shops. The two art galleries host
a number of changing exhibitions from
contemporary Scottish artists.

D5 *In the centre of Forfar, three miles from the A90.*

♿ ♿ 🔳 E 🔲 Free

🕐 Mon–Sat, 10am–5pm.

Tel 01307 464123   www.angus.gov.uk/history.htm

31 Mills Observatory

Mills Observatory, the UK's only full-time public observatory runs a changing programme of activities, events and displays. Visitors can view stars and planets through a Victorian telescope and looks at safe images of the sun on sunny days. An artificial night sky shows constellations and planets.

C3 *Balgay Park, one mile W of Dundee city centre.*

P WC ⛪ E AV ☙ ⛄ Free

⊕ Apr–Sept, Tue–Fri, 11am–5pm; weekends, 12.30–4pm. Oct–Mar, Mon–Fri, 4–10pm; weekends, 12.30–4pm.

Tel 01382 435967   www.dundeecity.gov.uk/mills

32 Monikie Country Park

Situated on a network of reservoirs, the park offers a range of water sports and woodland walks.

D3 *Signposted off the A92.*

P WC ♿ ⛱ ⛄ £

⊕ Summer, daily, 9am–9pm. Winter, daily, 9am–dusk.

Tel 01382 370202   www.monikie.org.uk

33 Montrose Air Station Heritage Centre

Wartime artefacts, pictures and memorabilia are housed in the old wartime RAF Montrose HQ, and tell the story of the aerodrome from 1913. Aircraft and vehicles are on occasional display, along with an old RAF Leuchars control van, Bofors gun, wartime pillbox and Anderson shelter. Annual events include a military vehicle rally and Airfield Extravaganza.

F5 *Waldron Road, N side of Montrose on A92.*

P WC ⛪ E £

⊕ Apr–Sept, Mon–Sat, 10am–4pm; Sun, 12 noon–4pm. Nov–Mar, Sun only, 12 noon–4pm.

Tel 01674 678222   www.rafmontrose.org.uk

34 Montrose Basin Wildlife Centre

Montrose Basin, an enclosed estuary of the South Esk river, provides a rich feeding ground for thousands of resident and migrant birds. A wildlife centre allows visitors to view the area through telescopes, binoculars and television cameras. Also available are various interactive displays.

F5 *On A92, one mile S of Montrose.*

P WC ♿ ⛪ E AV ⊠ ⛱ ☙ ⛄ £

⊕ Apr–Oct, daily, 10.30am–5pm. Nov–Mar, daily, 10.30am–4pm.

Tel 01674 676336   www.montrosebasin.org.uk

35 Montrose Museum and Art Gallery

Purpose-built in 1841, the museum looks at the history of Montrose from prehistoric times, including the maritime and natural history of the area. Among the exhibits are Pictish stones, Montrose silver and pottery, Napoleonic items, paintings by local artists and sculptures by William Lamb.

F5 *Panmure Place, E of town centre.*

P WC ⛪ E Free

⊕ Mon–Sat, 10am–5pm.

Tel 01674 673232   www.angus.gov.uk

36 Mountains Animal Sanctuary ★

This sanctuary, set in countryside surroundings, is home to over 170 rescued horses, ponies and donkeys. Features include guided tours and an adoption scheme. New Visitor Centre opened in July 2004.

D5 *Turn off A90 at Finavon Hotel, following signs to Glenogil.*

P WC ♿ ⛪ ⛱ ☙ Free

⊕ Apr–Oct, daily, 2–4.30pm. Nov–Mar, Fri–Mon, 2–4.30pm.

Tel 01356 650258

37 Pictavia Visitor Centre

The Picts, known as the 'painted people', lived in Scotland from the third century, but very little is known about them. This exhibition provides an insight into the lives of these mysterious people in Angus.

E6 *Off A90, at Brechin junction, 25 miles N of Dundee.*

P WC ♿ ☕ ⛪ E ⛱ ☙ ⛄ ⊠ ££

⊕ Apr–Sept, Mon–Sat, 9.30am–5.30pm; Sun, 10.30am–5.30pm. Oct–Mar, Sat, 9am–5pm; Sun, 10am–5pm.

Tel 01356 626241   www.pictavia.org.uk

38 Pitmuies Gardens and Grounds ❀

Set in the grounds of an eighteenth century house and courtyard, these walled gardens lead down towards a river walk past an unusual turreted dovecote and Gothic wash-house. Semi-formal gardens feature old and new roses and borders containing delphiniums and herbacious perennials.

E4 *Seven miles E of Forfar on A932.*

P WC 🚻 🏕 £

⊕ Easter–Oct, daily, 10am–5pm.

Tel 01241 828245

39 Sensation Dundee 🏛

Containing over 65 interactive exhibits, this science centre is designed to raise awareness of our senses: sight, sound, touch, smell and taste. Through a series of hands-on activities, visitors are encouraged to understand what is happening in the world around us.

C3 *Greenmarket, Dundee city centre.*

WC ♿ ☕ 🏕 E AV 🅿 £££

⊕ All year round, daily, from 10am.

Tel 01382 228800   www.sensation.org.uk

40 Tealing Dovecot and Earth House 🏕

An elegant dovecot of the late 16th century standing in a modern farmyard. A short walk leads to the remains of an earth house, or souterrain, of Iron Age date. Re-used stones with Bronze Age rock carvings can be seen in its walls.

C3 *Close to the village of Balgray 5miles N of Dundee off the A90.*

P Free

⊕ Open access.

Tel 0131 668 8800
www.historic-scotland.gov.uk

41 Unicorn (HM Frigate) 🏛

Launched in 1824, the *Unicorn* is the oldest British-built ship afloat, and a fine example of a wooden warship. It now houses a naval museum with changing maritime displays and exhibitions.

C3 *Victoria Dock, beside Tay Road Bridge, Dundee.*

P WC 🏕 E AV ££

⊕ Apr–Oct, daily, 10am–5pm.
  Nov–Mar, daily (closed Mon & Tue),
  Wed–Fri, 12 noon–4pm; Sat–Sun, 10am–4pm.

Tel 01382 200900   www.frigateunicorn.org

42 University of Dundee Botanic Garden

A garden sloping towards the River Tay, featuring conifers, broad-leaved trees and shrubs, tropical and temperate glasshouses, and water and herb gardens.

C3 *Riverside Drive, three miles W of Dundee city centre.*

P WC ♿ 🏕 ☕ £

⊕ Daily, Mar–Oct, 10am–4.30pm.
  Nov–Feb, 10am–3.30pm.

Tel 01382 647190
www.dundeebotanicgarden.co.uk

43 Verdant Works 🏛

During its peak, the jute industry employed 50,000 people in the city of Dundee. Verdant Works, a working jute mill, takes visitors on a tour of the trade, from its beginnings in the Indian sub-continent to the end product. A range of displays include film shows, hands-on exhibits, interactives and historic machinery.

C3 *West Henderson Wynd, NW of Dundee city centre.*

P WC ♿ ☕ 🏕 E AV 🅿 ££

⊕ Apr–Oct, Mon–Sat, 10am–6pm;
  Sun, 11am–6pm.
  Nov–Mar, Wed–Sat, 10.30am–4pm; Sun, 11am–4pm.

Tel 01382 225282   www.verdantworks.com

44 William Lamb Sculpture Studio 🏛

Studio displaying sculptures, carvings, etchings and watercolours by William Lamb. Included in the display are sculptures of the heads of Princess' Elizabeth and Margaret, commissioned by the Queen Mother in 1932.

F5 *Panmure Place, Montrose town centre.*

WC 🏕 E 🚻 Free

⊕ July–Mid Sept, Mon–Sun, 2–5pm.

Tel 01674 673232   www.angus.gov.uk/history

Stonehaven Harbour

Cruden Bay Golf Course

ABERDEEN AND GRAMPIAN

Some curious confusion of identity surrounds this area. It has the best-known Highland Games in Scotland at Braemar, yet is the heartland of the Lowland Scots tongue. It lies north of the Highland line, yet the farming of the rolling Buchan plain is essentially Lowland practice.

Scenically, it is a cross-section. Ben Macdui, as the second highest mountain in Scotland, is typical of the tundra wilderness of the Cairngorm plateau on the eastern side. Then the terrain leads down by a series of shelves to lesser heights. Rivers such as the Dee, Don and Spey, lead away from the central massif and are typified by upland woods of birch and pine. Below the eastern Cairngorms, the natural or semi natural pinewoods are typically seen around Glen Derry, with the birch at its finest on the national nature reserve of Dinnet, east of Ballater.

Similarly, marginal upland farming gradually gives way to the agriculture of the heavy clays of the lowland plains, an entirely different rural world with its own heritage of speech and song. Like other parts of Lowland Scotland, the rolling farmlands of Buchan in the far north-east knuckle, or Formartine, north of Aberdeen, reveal an entirely man-made landscape, built from the toil of generations of men of the land. They broke in the moor (called moss locally) and the heathery scrub which is its natural cover, to create productive ground.

As any coastal walker will recognise, their farming work stopped at the cliff edge (sometimes perilously near the edge). There are impressive cliffs by Stonehaven or – even more dramatic – the Moray Firth coast between Fraserburgh and Macduff – unspoilt and sometimes near vertical havens for wildlife. Spectacular seabird colonies, puffins in plenty and even Scotland's only mainland gannet colony (at Troup Head), can be seen here. Beaches too are a north-east speciality, with miles of sand stretching between, say, Aberdeen and Newburgh, Peterhead and Fraserburgh and around Lossiemouth. These beaches, backed by old grey dunes, are places of endless horizontals and a forgotten air, especially at places such as Rattray Head, north of Peterhead. Near Rattray too is the Loch of Strathbeg, Scotland's largest land-locked lagoon, an internationally important wintering place for grey geese. All this scenic variety lies within easy reach of Aberdeen, sparkling with its silver granite when the sun shines, busy with its role as oil capital of Europe but still functioning as an overgrown market town for its rural hinterland.

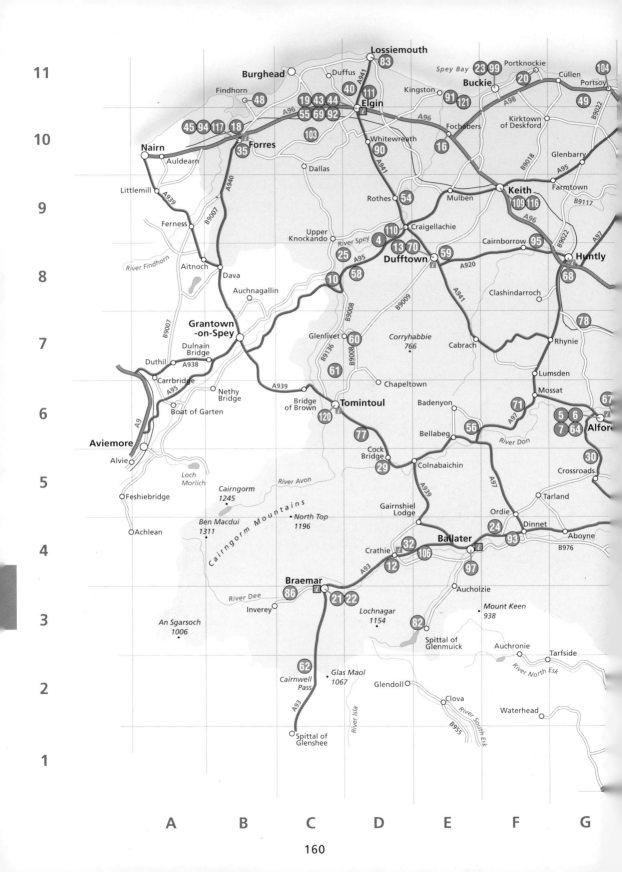

Banff
15 28
Macduff
33
98
Rosehearty
Pennan
Kinnaird Head
107
51 74
Fraserburgh
39 84
B9031
Gardenstown
New Aberdour
B9092
Rathen
85
St. Combs
B9025
Peatknowe
A947
A98
96
New Byth
New Pitsligo
A981
Strichen
Rattray Head
A90
57
B9024
Turriff
36
Darra
A950
Mintlaw
Inverugie
A952
Peterhead
River Deveron
B9001
Aucharnie
88
New Deer
3
Longside
8 100
Badenscoth
Cot-town
52
Fyvie
B9170
A952
Boddam
Buchan Ness
Methlick
A948
Kinknockie
St. Katherines
66
Hilton
A90
Colpy
Ellon
Toll of Birness
Cruden Bay
101
A96
A920
119
A920
50
9
Pitcaple
80
Oldmeldrum
Pitmedden
Newburgh
17
102
Whiterashes
26
Inverurie
Newmachar
Keig
Kintore
Balmedie
79
Monymusk
11
Pitcaple
B933
27
Sauchen
76
Dyce
1 2 42 63 73 75
A944
Tornaveen
53
Elrick
81 87 105 108 112 114
Echt
34
ABERDEEN
Girdle Ness
Torphins
A980
Peterculter
72 37
38
Banchory
31
115
B9077
Portlethen
14
Dee
Lochtin
Netherley
Strachan
A957
Rickarton
Mowtie
118
Bridge of Dye
Stonehaven
B974
41
Auchenblae
46
B967
A97
65
ettercairn
Inverbervie
B966
B9120
47
B974
Laurencekirk
89
A937
B9120
Johnshaven
dzell
St. Cyrus
113
rechin
Montrose

To Kirkwall and Lerwick

— — — Vehicle ferry
🛈 Tourist Information Centre (open all year)
🛈 Tourist Information Centre (seasonal)

0   10   20   30 mls
0   10   20   30   40 kms

H   J   K   L   M   N

VISITOR INFORMATION

MAIN TOURIST INFORMATION CENTRE

Aberdeen
23 Union Street
AB11 5BP
Tel: 01224 288828
Web: www.aberdeen-grampian.com
E-mail: info@agtb.org
Open: all year round

YEAR ROUND TOURIST INFORMATION CENTRES

Ballater
The Old Royal Station
Station Square
Ballater AB35 5QB
Tel: 013397 55306
E-mail: info@agtb.org
Open: Open all year

Elgin
17 High Street
Elgin IV30 1EG
Tel: 01343 542666
E-mail: info@agtb.org
Open: all year round

Braemar
The Mews, Mar Road
Braemar AB35 5YL
Tel: 013397 41600
E-mail: info@agtb.org
Open: Open all year

Inverurie
18 High Street
Inverurie AB51 3XQ
Tel: 01467 625800
E-mail: info@agtb.org
Open: all year round

SEASONAL TOURIST INFORMATION CENTRES

Alford
Tel: 019755 62052
E-mail: info@agtb.org
Open: Easter–Oct

Forres
Tel: 01309 672938
E-mail: info@agtb.org
Open: Apr–Oct

Banchory
Tel: 01330 822000
E-mail: info@agtb.org
Open: Apr–Oct

Fraserburgh
Tel: 01346 518315
E-mail: info@agtb.org
Open: Apr–Oct

Banff
Tel: 01261 812419
E-mail: info@agtb.org
Open: Apr–Sept

Huntly
Tel: 01466 792255
E-mail: info@agtb.org
Open: Apr–Oct

Crathie
Tel: 013397 42414
E-mail: info@agtb.org
Open: Apr–Nov

Stonehaven
Tel: 01569 762806
E-mail: info@agtb.org
Open: Apr–Oct

Dufftown
Tel: 01340 820501
E-mail: info@agtb.org
Open: Apr–Oct

Tomintoul
Tel: 01807 580285
E-mail: info@agtb.org
Open: Apr–Oct

ADDITIONAL INFORMATION
GENERAL TRAVEL INFORMATION
Traveline Scotland
Tel: 0870 608 2608
Provides timetable information for all public transport in Scotland and the rest of Great Britain.

AIR TRAVEL
Aberdeen Airport
BAA Aberdeen
Aberdeen Airport
Dyce
Aberdeen AB21 7DU
Tel: 01224 722331
Web: www.baa.co.uk/main/airports/aberdeen

TRAINS
First ScotRail
Caledonian Chambers
87 Union Street
Glasgow G1 3TA
Tel: Fares & Train Times: 08457 484950
Telesales: 08457 550033
Customer Relations: 0845 601 5929
Web: www.firstscotrail.co.uk
E-mail: scotrail.enquiries@firstgroup.com

COACH
Scottish Citylink Coaches Limited
Buchanan Bus Station
Killermont Street
Glasgow G2 3NP
Tel: 08705 505050
Web: www.citylink.co.uk
E-mail: info@citylink.co.uk
Routes: Aberdeen–Edinburgh
Aberdeen–Glasgow

BUS
First
395 King Street
Aberdeen AB24 5RP
Tel: 01224 650065
Web: www.firstaberdeen.co.uk
Routes: operates an extensive network
in the city of Aberdeen

Stagecoach Bluebird
Guild Street
Aberdeen AB11 6GR
Tel: 01224 212266
Web: www.stagecoachbus.com
E-mail: customer.care@bluebirdbuses.co.uk
Routes: operates an extensive network throughout
Aberdeenshire

FERRIES
Northlink Ferries
Northlink Orkney and Shetland Ferries Ltd
The New Harbour Building
Ferry Road
Stromness KW16 3BH
Tel: 01856 851144
Web: www.northlinkferries.co.uk
E-mail: info@northlinkferries.co.uk
Routes: Aberdeen–Lerwick
Aberdeen–Orkney–Lerwick

CAR HIRE
Aberdeen 4x4 Self Drive, Aberdeen
Tel: 01224 790858
Web: www.aberdeen4x4.co.uk
E-mail: info@aberdeen4x4.co.uk

Arnold Clark Car Rental, Aberdeen
Tel: 01224 249159
Web: www.arnoldclark.co.uk

Arnold Clark Hire Drive, Elgin
Tel: 01343 547688
Web: www.arnoldclark.co.uk

Budget Rent A Car, Aberdeen Airport
Tel: 01224 771777
Web: www.budget.co.uk

G&L Marshall, Huntly
Tel: 01466 792594
Web: www.glmarshall.co.uk
E-mail: marshallgl@talk21.com

Glenvarigill Co Limited, Aberdeen
Tel: 01224 826300
Web: www.peugeot.co.uk/glenvarigill
E-mail: glenvarigill@dealers.peugeot.co.uk

Vauxhall Car & Van Rental, Aberdeen
Tel: 01224 853610
E-mail: belmont_vauxhall_rental@hotmail.com

TAXIS
Ballater Taxis, Ballater
Tel: 013397 55548

Central Taxis, Aberdeen
01224 898989

City Rainbow, Aberdeen
Tel: 01224 494949

Computer Cars, Aberdeen
Tel: 01224 353535

ABERDEEN

In spite of excellent communication links with the south, Scotland's third city is sometimes perceived as a long way north, even by the central belt of Scotland. Consequently, it has an air of going its own way, of self-containment partly brought about by the wealth the last three decades of oil development has brought it. Formerly, the city also had a role as large summer holiday resort, and, even today, much of its recreation revolves around the leisure centres, from permanent fun fair to a choice of eating places, all along its windy promenade.

The granite of downtown Aberdeen lends it one of Scotland's most distinctive cityscapes. The university's Marischal College is, for example, the second largest granite building in the world, and on its facade manages to turn the tough and unyielding granite into decorative silvery icing. The city's art gallery even features granite columns of different colours from different sources as well as the more predictable attractions of, for example, an excellent watercolour collection. Belying its northern latitude, Aberdeen has also specialised in flower displays over the years, with sheets of spring bulbs in public spaces all over town. It is a noted rose growing centre and, it is said, has the largest covered glasshouse in Europe, at the Winter Gardens in the Duthie Park.

1 Aberdeen Art Gallery 🏛

This gallery houses a fine collection of decorative arts and paintings, particularly from the nineteenth and twentieth century, including works by Lavery, Guthrie, Spencer and Bacon. It also runs a programme of special exhibitions, talks and events.

L5 *Schoolhill, Aberdeen city centre.*

WC ♿ 🍽 ⛪ E ♿ Free

🕐 Mon–Sat, 10am–5pm; Sun, 2–5pm.

Tel 01224 523700

www.aberdeencity.gov.uk

2 Aberdeen Maritime Museum 🏛

A museum focusing on the history of the North Sea, with multi-media displays and exhibitions on the offshore oil industry, shipbuilding, fishing and clipper ships. Part of the museum is located in Provost Ross's House, the third oldest house in Aberdeen, which is owned by the National Trust for Scotland.

L5 *Shiprow, Aberdeen city centre.*

WC ♿ 🍽 ⛪ E AV ♨ ♿ Free

🕐 Mon–Sat, 10am–5pm; Sun, 12 noon–3pm.

Tel 01224 337700   www.aberdeencity.gov.uk

3 Aberdeenshire Farming Museum

Situated in Aden Country Park, the museum depicts the history of farming in the Aberdeenshire area. Visitors can explore the semi-circular Home Farm steading and learn the story of Aden Estate.

L9 *Off the A952, near Mintlaw.*

P & ☕ ⊞ E **AV** ⊟ ⅍ Free

⏰ Apr & Oct, School holidays & weekends, 12 noon–4pm. May–Sept, daily, 11am–4.30pm.

Tel 01771 622906

www.aberdeenshire.gov.uk/heritage/

4 Aberlour Distillery

Visitors embark on an in-depth guided tour of the distillery, learning of the whisky making process ending at the warehouse where they can sample several different whiskies. Tours last approximately 90 minutes and are by appointment only.

D9 *Off the A95, at Charlestown of Aberlour.*

P **WC** & ⊞ 🅳 £££

⏰ Tours: end Mar–end Oct, Mon–Sat, 10.30am & 2pm. Sun, 11.30am & 3pm.

Tel 01340 881249   www.aberlour.com

5 Alford Heritage Centre

Provides an insight into the lives of the people of Donside and rural north east Scotland. Themed displays include a schoolroom, farm steading, kitchen and shops plus vintage tractors and implements. One room is dedicated to local poet Charles Murray.

G6 *Centre of Alford, opposite police station.*

P **WC** & ⊞ E £

⏰ Apr–Oct, Mon–Sat, 10am–5pm; Sun, 1–5pm

Tel 019755 62906

6 Alford Ski Centre

All year round skiing and snowboarding on a dry slope, with instruction and equipment hire.

G6 *Centre of Alford, 25 miles W of Aberdeen on A944.*

P **WC** & 🅳 £££

⏰ Apr–Sept, Sun, 1.30–3pm. Oct–Mar, weekends, 1.30–3pm; Fri, 6.30–8.30pm.

Tel 019755 63024

7 Alford Valley Railway

Scotland's first 2'-0" narrow gauge passenger railway runs from Alford Station to Haughton Country Park. The thirty-minute round trip runs through Alford Golf Course along a section of General Wades Military Road and into a wooded section.

G6 *Twenty-five miles W of Aberdeen on A944.*

⏰ Apr, May & Sept, weekends. Jun, Jul–Aug, daily, 1–4.30pm. Coaches/parties can be booked anytime.

Tel 019755 62045

8 Arbuthnot Museum

Arbuthnot is one of Aberdeenshire's oldest museums, housing a wealth of Peterhead's maritime history, a large coin collection and Inuit artefacts.

N9 *Peterhead town centre off A950/A952.*

⊞ E Free

⏰ All year round, Mon–Tue & Thur–Sat, 11.30am–1pm & 2–4.30pm; Wed, 11am–1pm.

Tel 01771 622906

www.aberdeenshire.gov.uk/heritage/

9 Archaeolink Prehistory Park

Transports visitors back in time to learn about the lives of our ancestors 6000 years ago. In and outdoor attractions include computer simulations, galleries, a film presentation, sandpit dig and reconstructions of an Iron Age Farm and a Stone Age settlement.

H7 *Oyne village, eight miles NW of Inverurie.*

P **WC** & ✕ ⊞ E **AV** ⊟ ⅍ 🅳 ££

⏰ Apr–Oct, daily, 10am–5pm. Nov–Mar, 11am–4pm.

Tel 01464 851500   www.archaeolink.co.uk

10 Ballindalloch Castle

Ballindalloch, the home of the Macpherson-Grants, has been lived in continuously by the family since 1546. Visitors can see a number of elegant rooms, along with rock and rose gardens, an observation beehive and electric trains.

C8 *Fourteen miles NE of Grantown-on-Spey on A95.*

P **WC** & ☕ ⊞ **AV** ⊟ ⅍ 🅳 £££

⏰ Easter–Sept, Sun–Fri, 10.30am–5pm. Last admission 4.45pm.

Tel 01807 500206

www.ballindallochcastle.co.uk

Balmoral Castle

11 Balmedie Country Park ♣

Located on a sandy beach with dunes and linksland, visitors to this country park can enjoy a range of outdoor activities; a ranger service offers guided walks.

L6 *Off the A90, N of Aberdeen.*

🅿 🆆🅲 ♿ ⛺ 🥾 £

🕐 All year round, daily.
Visitor Centre, please telephone for details.

Tel 01358 742396

12 Balmoral Castle 🏰 ✲

Since Prince Albert bought the estate in 1852, Balmoral has been the official Highland residence of the Royal Family. The original castle was too small for royal needs, and demolished in favour of a new building which was constructed from local granite. Inside visitors can see an exhibition of paintings, tartans and a selection of royal items. The extensive grounds, which lead through woodland and along the river, are open to the public and can be seen via a series of paths, ranger-led walks (Wed only) or on one of the Balmoral Stalking Ponies. The garden contains a glasshouse, conservatory, water and kitchen areas.

D4 *Off A93, eight miles W of Ballater.*

🅿 🆆🅲 ♿ ☕ 🏛 E ⛺ 🥾 🎫 £££

🕐 Apr–July, daily, 10am–5pm (last admission 4pm).

Tel 01339 742534 www.balmoralcastle.com

13 Balvenie Castle 🅱 🏰

Balvenie started life in the thirteenth century as a modest quadrangular construction, but was later turned into a more stylish residence by John Stewart, 4th Earl of Atholl, who added a large round tower and various Rennaissance features.

E8 *Dufftown, on the A941.*

🅿 🆆🅲 ♿ 🏛 ⛺ £

🕐 Apr–Sept, daily, 9.30am–6.30pm.

Tel 01340 820121 www.historic-scotland.gov.uk

14 Banchory Museum

Houses a number of exhibits including collections of nineteenth century tartans and royal commemorative china. Visitors can also learn about the natural history of Deeside.

H4 *On the A93, Banchory town centre.*

⌂ E Free

🕐 May–June & Sept, Mon–Sat, 11am–1pm
& 2–4.30pm. July–Aug, Mon–Sat, 11am–1pm
& 2–4.30pm; Sun, 2–4.30pm.
Please telephone prior to visit for
Apr & Oct times

Tel 01771 622906
www.aberdeenshire.gov.uk/heritage/

15 Banff Museum

Founded in 1828, Banff is one of the oldest museums in Scotland, containing an assortment of artefacts and relics including Banff silver, an electrotype copy of the Deskford Carnyx, and the natural history and geology of the local area.

H11 *Off A97/A98, Banff town centre, above the library.*

🅿 ⌂ E Free

🕐 Jun–Sept, Mon–Sat, 2pm–4.30pm.

Tel 01261 815704
www.aberdeenshire.gov.uk/heritage/

16 Baxters Highland Village

A visitor centre with information on how food producers Baxters started their business, a shop museum, tours and occasional culinary demonstrations and tastings.

E10 *One mile W of Fochabers on A96.*

🅿 ♿ & ♨ ✕ ⌂ .E AV 🎋 ☀ 🚶 ☒ Free

🕐 Apr–24 Dec, daily, 9am–5.30pm.
Jan–Feb, 10am–5pm.

Tel 01343 820666   www.baxters.com

17 Bennachie Centre

This environmental interpretation centre, with interactive and multi-media displays and exhibitions, acts as a start point for a number of walks. Various ranger events are held throughout the year.

J7 *Essons car park, Chapel of Garioch, off A96, NW of Inverurie.*

🅿 ♿ & E AV 🎋 ☀ 🚶 Free

🕐 Apr–Sept, 10am–5pm. Oct–Mar, 9.30am–4pm.

Tel 01467 681470

18 Benromach Distillery

Visitors can tour this newly revived family owned distillery and enjoy a dram in the Malt Whisky Centre, formally the Drier House.

B10 *On N side of Forres bypass; leave at sign marked 'Waterford' and follow road over level-crossing.*

🅿 ♿ & ⌂ E AV 🎋 ☒ £

🕐 Apr–Oct, Mon–Fri, 10am–4pm. May–Sept, Mon–Sat, 9.30am–5pm. July–Aug, Sun, 12 noon–4pm. Last tour 1 hour before closing.

Tel 01309 675968   www.benromach.com

19 Biblical Garden

This 3 acre garden contains every species of plant cited in the bible plus life-size sculptures which portray a number of well-known parables.The garden's central path, modelled on a Celtic cross, is an impressive feature.

D10 *King Street, Elgin, adjacent to the Cathedral.*

♿ Free

🕐 May–Sept, daily, 10am–7pm.

www.moray.gov.uk

20 Bow Fiddle Rock

An unusual quartzite offshore stack, supposed to resemble a musical instrument.

F11 *Portknockie, on A942 E of Buckie.*

☀ Free

🕐 Open access.

21 Braemar Castle

An I-shaped castle, built in 1628 by the Earl of Mar, and now owned by the Farquharsons. Visitors can see a number of rooms containing fine furniture, paintings and curios including the world's largest cairngorm and a collection of Canadian Indian objects.

C3 *Half a mile N of Braemar on A93.*

🅿 ♿ ⌂ 🎋 ☀ 🚶 ££

🕐 Apr–Oct, 10am–6pm; closed Fri except for Jul & Aug (last entry 5.30pm).

Tel 013397 41219   www.braemarcastle.co.uk

22 Braemar Highland Heritage Centre

The centre's audio-visual show recounts the story of Braemar, the Highland Games and Braemar Gathering, along with Balmoral, the Cairngorms and the River Dee. See feature on page 177.

C3 *In the centre of Braemar, opposite the Fife Arms Hotel.*

P WC ♿ 🏛 E AV 🎦 Free

🕐 All year round, daily, 9am–5pm.

Tel 01339 741944

23 Buckie Drifter

A maritime heritage centre telling the story of herring fishing in the North Sea, with a re-created 1920s quayside complete with fishing boat and an RNLI lifeboat which was on station at Anstruther from 1965–1990.

F11 *Buckie harbour area, on A942, off A98.*

P WC ♿ ☕ ✕ 🏛 E AV £

🕐 Apr–Oct, Mon–Sat, 10am–5pm;
Sun, 12 noon–5pm.

Tel 01542 834646   www.moray.org/bdrifter

24 Cambus O'May Forest Walks ⛷

Four routes of varying distance run through woodland, including one specifically designed for wheelchair users. Offers views across Deeside from various points.

F4 *Off N side of A93 between Ballater and Dinnet.*

P ♿ 🍴 🌿 👫 Free

🕐 Open access.

www.forestry.gov.uk

25 Cardhu Distillery

Licensed since 1824, visitors can tour this historic distillery; the admission charge is redeemable against a bottle of whisky.

C8 *Off the B9102, 17 miles NE of Grantown-on-Spey.*

P WC 🏛 🍴 🎦 ££

🕐 Easter–Sept, Mon–Fri, 10am–5pm;
July–Sept, Sun, 12 noon–5pm.
Oct–Easter: Tours at 11am, 1 & 2pm.
Last tour one hour before closing.

Tel 01340 872555

26 Carnegie Inverurie Museum 🏛

Devoted to the history of Aberdeenshire, the museum contains a variety of archeological artefacts such as flint arrowheads, bronze swords and Pictish carved stones. Visitors can also learn about the Beaker folk and the local transportation network.

J6 *Off A96, Inverurie town centre.*

🏛 E Free

🕐 All year round; Mon & Wed–Fri, 2–4.30pm;
Sat, 10am–1pm & 2–4pm.

Tel 01771 622906

www.aberdeenshire.gov.uk/heritage/

Castle Fraser

CAIRNGORMS (EAST)

The eastern approaches to the Cairngorms, the undulating dissected plateau which represents the highest continuous stretch of tundra-land in Scotland, usually start from some point in Royal Deeside. The eastern outliers include Lochnagar, whose 'steep frowning glories', celebrated in Lord Byron's poem, comprise a spectacularly blue corrie loch surrounded by a horseshoe of dizzying cliffs split by gullies. It is a long day's hillwalk from Glen Muick. Ben Avon, with its curious granite tors visible from the main road near Braemar, and Beinn a' Bhuird both exhibit the special characteristics of the area – high table-land and long slopes on one side, spectacular cliffs and wild corries on the other.

Other eastern approach routes start from Inverey and the Linn of Dee. For example, a very long day's walking could include Ben Macdui via Glen Derry and Loch Etchacan, the highest major water-body in Britain. At 1309m (4296ft) Ben Macdui is also the second-highest point in Britain and a good place to sample the sheer scale of the boulder-fields and late season snowfields. Portions of both the east and west Cairngorms have national nature reserve status. The Cairngorms National Park was formerly established in 2003. See feature on page 263.

27 Castle Fraser

This z-plan castle was begun in 1575 by the sixth laird, Michael Fraser, and completed in 1636. Contents include many Fraser family portraits, including one Raeburn, plus eighteenth and nineteenth century carpets, curtains and bed hangings. The walled ornamental garden contains shrubs, fruit, vegetables and flowers.

J6 *Off A944, four miles N of Dunecht.*

P WC ☕ ⛪ ⛷ 👥 ♿ £££

⊕ Castle: Apr–Jun & Sep, 12 noon–5pm.
  Closed Fri & Mon.
  Jul–Aug, daily, 11am–5pm.
  Last admission 45 mins before closing.
  Grounds: all year round, daily.

Tel 01330 833463   www.nts.org.uk

Corgarff Castle

28 Colleonard Sculpture Garden and Gallery

An unusual collection of sculptures in wood and stone, set in a picturesque 6 acre garden.

H11 *On the edges of Banff, on the A97.*

P & E Free

By appointment only (winter).
Apr–Oct, daily, 10am–5pm.

Tel 01261 818284

29 Corgarff Castle

Originally a sixteenth century tower house, Corgarff suffered a series of raids and attacks, but has been rebuilt and restored to its present complete state. Surrounded by an unusual star-shaped wall, drivers are given a good view of the castle as they drive from the Lecht towards the A939 junction. It was used for military purposes including a barracks (1748) and centre for controlling illicit whisky smuggling (1827–1831).

D5 *On A939, eight miles W of Strathdon.*

P 🏛 E ££

Apr–Sept, daily, 9.30am–6.30pm.
Oct–Mar, Sat & Sun only, 9.30am–4.30pm.

Tel 01975 651460   www.historic-scotland.gov.uk

30 Craigievar Castle

A well-proportioned Baronial castle built during the seventeenth century, with towers, turrets, cupolas and corbelling dominating the upper half. Among the contents are family portraits and fine furniture.

G5 *Six miles S of Alford on A980.*

P 🚶 ££

Castle: Apr–Sept, Fri–Tue, 12 noon–5.30pm (last admission 4.45pm).
Grounds: all year round, daily, 9.30am–sunset.

Tel 01339 883635   www.nts.org.uk

31 Crathes Castle

This splendid sixteenth century tower house contains family portraits, furniture and original painted ceilings. Also of note are the gardens where visitors can admire topiary dating from 1702, yew hedges and trails, plus a walled garden with herbaceous borders.

J4 *On A93, three miles E of Banchory.*

P WC & ✕ 🏛 🚻 ☀ 🚶 £££

Apr–Sept, daily, 10am–5.30pm.
Oct, daily, 10am–4.30pm (last admission 45 minutes before closing).

Tel 01330 844525   www.nts.org.uk

Crovie

32 Crathie Church ✟

With Balmoral close by, the Royal Family regularly attend Crathie for the Sunday morning service. The foundation stone of the building was laid in 1893 by Queen Victoria, and the church opened in 1895. Inside are memorial busts, plaques and stained glass windows which commemorate royalty, ministers and local people.

D4 *On the A93, Aberdeen/Braemar road, near Balmoral Castle.*

🅿 ⛪ E ♨ Free

🕐 Apr–Oct, Mon–Sat, 9.30am–5pm; Sun, 12.45–5pm.

Tel 013397 42344

33 Crovie ★

Crovie is a picturesque village set below cliffs, looking on to the North Sea. It has the narrowest space between shore and cliff of any Scottish village.

K11 *Off the B9031, one mile E of Gardenstown.*

Free

🕐 Open access.

Tel 01346 518315   www.agtb.org

34 Cullerlie Farm Park & Heritage Centre 🏛

This privately owned collection of farming and housing memorabilia is situated in a converted traditional steading. The farm holds a collection of domestic animal species including ducks, geese and lambs and rare breeds of sheep, goats, pigs and horses.

J5 *Off the B9125, 12 miles W of Aberdeen.*

🅿 🚻 ♿ ☕ ⛪ E 🪑 👫 £

🕐 Apr–Oct, daily, 10am–5.30pm.
Nov–Mar, by appointment only.

Tel 01330 860549

35 Dallas Dhu Historic Distillery ⊕ ♨

Visitors can see the traditional processes involved in whisky production at this nineteenth century former working distillery. There is also an audio-visual presentation and the chance to sample a dram.

B10 *Off the A940, one mile S of Forres.*

🅿 🚻 ♿ ⛪ E AV 🪑 👫 ⊞ ££

🕐 Apr–Sept, daily, 9.30am–6.30pm.
Oct–Mar, Sat–Wed, 9.30am–4.30pm.

Tel 01309 676548   www.historic-scotland.gov.uk

36 Delgatie Castle 🏰

Notable features in this eleventh century tower house include painted ceilings, a turnpike stair (reputedly one of the widest in Scotland) and a baby's four-poster bed, along with displays of paintings, Victorian clothes and armour. Mary, Queen of Scots stayed here for three days after the Battle of Corrinchie. Disabled facilities for tearoom only.

J9 *Turn E off A947, one mile N of Turriff.*

🅿 🚻 ♿ ☕ 👫 ££

🕐 Apr–mid Oct, daily, 10am–5pm.
Mid Oct–Mar, Fri–Sun, 10am–4pm.

Tel 01888 563479   www.delgatiecastle.com

37 Doonies Farm

This 219 acres farm centre contains a number of rare breeds. Visitors are encouraged to explore and learn about the animals, including Shetland ponies, Clydesdale horses, chickens, sheep and pigs.

L5 *Off A956, on the old coast road, S of Aberdeen.*

🅿 ♿ ⬥ ⛱ ⚒ £

🕐 Summer, daily, 10am–6.30pm.
  Winter, daily, 10am–3.30pm.

Tel 01224 875879

38 Drum Castle

The oldest intact building under the care of the National Trust for Scotland, Drum Castle has a thirteenth century tower with adjoining mansion and extensions. The Irvine family owned the property for over 600 years, and visitors can see a collection of memorabilia, portraits and furniture. The grounds contain historic roses, a pond garden and woodland.

J4 *Off A93, ten miles SW of Aberdeen.*

🅿 ♿ ⬥ ⛱ ⚒ £££

🕐 Apr–May & Sep, daily, 12.30–5.30pm. Jun–Aug, daily, 10am–5.30pm (last admission 4.45pm). Grounds: all year daily, 9.30am–sunset.

Tel 01330 811204   www.drum-castle.org.uk

39 Duff House

Duff House was designed by William Adam and built between 1735–40 for William Duff of Braco, 1st Earl of Fife. Restored and re-opened in 1995 as a country house gallery, it contains fine pictures (including works by El Greco, Boucher, Allan Ramsay and Henry Raeburn), furniture and is now an important cultural centre for Banffshire providing concerts, lectures, workshops and outdoor events.

H10 *One mile S of Banff, on A947.*

🅿 ♿ ⬥ ⛱ E AV ⚒ ££

🕐 Apr–Oct, daily, 11am–5pm.
  Nov–Mar, Telephone for details.

Tel 01261 818181   www.duffhouse.com

Elgin Cathedral

40 Duffus Castle

The fourteenth century ruins of a motte and bailey castle, and seat of the Moray family. The large stone keep stands on a mound (now subsiding), giving good views of the surrounding countryside.

D11   *On B9012, five miles NW of Elgin.*

🅿 ⚘ Free

🕐 Open access.

Tel 01667 460232   www.historic-scotland.gov.uk

41 Dunnottar Castle

Spectacular ruined clifftop castle reflecting much of Scotland's tragic history. St Ninian, William Wallace, Mary, Queen of Scots and the Marquis of Montrose have all appeared on its dramatic stage. Famously a small garrison held out against Cromwell's army for eight months and saved the Scottish crown jewels.

K3   *Exit A92 1.5 miles east of Stonhaven.*

🅿 ⛨ ⚘ ££

🕐 Easter–end Oct, Mon–Sat, 9am–6pm; Sun, 2–5pm.
End Oct–Easter, Fri–Mon, 10.30am–dusk.

Tel 01330 860223   www.dunechtestates.co.uk

42 Duthie Park Winter Gardens ❀

The winter gardens set in 2 acres of ground are now reputed to be one of the largest covered gardens in Europe and are listed in the top 20 free visitor attractions in Scotland.

L5   *Close to Riverside Drive, Aberdeen.*

🅿 ⛨ ♿ ✕ 🏛 ♞ ⊞ Free

🕐 From 9.30am daily.

Tel 01224 585310   www.aberdeencity.gov.uk

43 Elgin Cathedral

This thirteenth century cathedral was considered to be one of Scotland's most beautiful. It was greatly reconstructed after a fire and raid by the Wolf of Badenoch in 1390; the restored octagonal chapter house, choir, presbytery, east gable and a Pictish cross slab are the most notable features.

D10   *Elgin on the A96.*

♿ 🏛 E £

🕐 Apr–Sept, daily, 9.30am–6.30pm.
Oct–Mar, closed, Thur and Fri.

Tel 01343 547171   www.historic-scotland.gov.uk

44 Elgin Museum

Looks at local and social history, and contains a collection of fossils and Pictish stones. Also runs a number of activities, lectures and workshops.

D10   *Signposted through Elgin; E end of High Street.*

⛨ ♿ 🏛 E £

🕐 Apr–Oct, Mon–Fri, 10am–5pm; Sat, 11am–4pm;
Nov–Mar, by appointment.

Tel 01343 543675   www.elginmuseum.org.uk

45 Falconer Museum

A museum devoted to the history of Forres and its people, with displays of advertising memorabilia, archaeological items and a tribute to Roy Williamson of The Corries.

B10   *Tolbooth Street, off the High Street, Forres, off A96/A940.*

⛨ ♿ 🏛 E AV Free

🕐 Apr–Oct, Mon–Sat, 10am–5pm.
Nov–Mar, Mon–Thur, 11am–12.30pm & 1–3.30pm.

Tel 01309 673701   www.moray.org/museums/

46 Fasque

Situated in extensive grounds, this Victorian stately home was owned by the Gladstone family – William Ewart Gladstone became Prime Minister for the first time in 1868. The house contains a collection of artefacts relating to Gladstone while the grounds house a deer park.

H2   *Off the B974, N of Fettercairn.*

🅿 ⛨ ♿ 🏛 E ££

🕐 Open for coach and guided tours (10+ groups).
Must be pre-booked.

Tel 01561 340569

47 Fettercairn Distillery 🥃

Fettercairn, nestling at the foot of the Cairngorms, was established in 1824 and is one of Scotland's oldest distilleries. Visitors can take a free guided tour and learn the processes involved in producing Old Fettercairn Single Malt Scotch Whisky; a tasting is provided.

H2   *Five miles N of A90 on B974.*

🅿 ⛨ ♿ 🏛 AV ⊞ Free

🕐 May–Sept, Mon–Sat, 10am–2.30pm,
last tour 2pm.

Tel 01561 340205.

Forvie National Nature Reserve

48 Findhorn Village Heritage Centre & Ice House 🏛

Describes the social and natural history, and ecology of this tranquil village.

B11 *Findhorn, on B9011, four miles N of Forres.*

🚾 ♿ E Free

🕐 May & Sept, weekends, 2–5pm.
Jun–Aug, daily, 2–5pm.

Tel 01309 690659

49 Fordyce Joiner's Workshop and Visitor Centre 🏛

The visitor centre illustrates the significance of the rural carpenter to local communities in the last 150 years. Early tools and workshop machinery are on display, and craftsmen can be seen working with wood.

G11 *Fordyce, four miles SW of Portsoy.*

🅿 🚾 ♿ E 🆎 🚶 Free

🕐 Apr–Oct, Thur–Mon, 10am–8pm.
Nov–Mar, Fri–Mon, 1–6pm.

Tel 01771 622906
www.aberdeenshire.gov.uk/heritage/

50 Forvie National Nature Reserve 🐦

Forvie is one of the UK's largest mobile sand dune systems. The combination of coastal heath, sea cliffs and the Ythan estuary attract a rich diversity of birdlife including, terns, eider ducks, geese and waders during the winter months.

M7 *Off A975, 12 miles N of Aberdeen.*

🅿 🚾 ♿ E 🆎 🚶 Free

🕐 Visitor Centre: daily, Apr–Oct, 9am–5pm.
Otherwise, by request.
Restrictions to tern breeding area, Apr–Aug.

Tel 01358 751330   www.snh.org.uk

51 Fraserburgh Heritage Centre 🏛

Traces the history of Fraserburgh through various artefacts and hands-on exhibits. Among the topics covered are the fishing industry, railway, Marconi experiments and fashion designer Bill Gibb. Children can play on a fishing boat and tap out their own messages in morse code in the Marconi Hut.

L11 *Adjacent to Scotland's Lighthouse Museum at Kinnaird Head, Fraserburgh, off A92/A98.*

🅿 📶 ♿ ♨ E 📺 📧 £

🕐 Apr–Oct, Mon–Sat, 11am–5pm; Sun, 1–5pm.

Tel 01346 512888

www.fraserburghheritage.com

52 Fyvie Castle   ♛ 🏰 ❀

Fyvie was once a royal stronghold, with the oldest part dating back to the thirteenth century. Interesting features include a fine wheel stair, panelling and plaster ceilings, along with portraits, tapestries and armoury. The grounds contain a walled garden, ice house, bird hide and lochside walks.

J8 *Off A947, eight miles SE of Turriff.*

🅿 ♿ ☕ ♨ 🍴 🚶 £££

🕐 Castle: Apr–Jun & Sept, Sat–Wed, 12 noon–5pm. Jun–Aug, daily, 11am–5pm. Last admission 45 mins before closing. Grounds: all year round, daily.

Tel 01651 891266   www.nts.org.uk

53 Garlogie Mill Power House Museum   🏛

Situated in Garlogie Mill, the museum depicts the early days of the Industrial Revolution in Scotland. Visitors will encounter the rare beam engine, which powered the woollen mill and see at first-hand the scale of power house machinery.

J5 *On the B9119, 11 miles W of Aberdeen.*

🅿 📶 ♿ E 📺 🍴 Free

🕐 Times may vary. Telephone for details.

Tel 01771 622906

www.aberdeenshire.gov.uk/heritage/

54 Glen Grant Distillery   🍾 ❀

Founded in 1840, Glen Grant offers a tour of the distillery, exhibition, dram and access to 20 acres of beautiful restored Victorian gardens. Admission to the distillery and garden is redeemable against a bottle of whisky in the adjoining shop.

D9 *On the A941, 10 miles S of Elgin.*

🅿 📶 ♿ ♨ E 📺 🚶 📧 Free

🕐 Apr–Oct, Mon–Sat, 10am–4pm; Sun, 12.30–4pm.

Tel 01340 832118 www.chivas.com

55 Glen Moray Distillery   🍾

Guided tours by distillery workers offer an interesting insight into the production of this classic single malt whisky. Scenic setting by the River Lossie.

D10 *W side of Elgin, off A96.*

🅿 📶 ♨ 📧 £

🕐 Mon–Fri, 9am–5pm. June–mid Sept, also Sat, 10am–4pm.

Tel 01343 542577   www.glenmoray.com

56 Glenbuchat Castle   🅗 🏰

This imposing sixteenth century z-plan tower house was occupied by John Gordon and Helen Carnegie, both renowned Jacobites. Although now without a roof, the castle is in a well preserved state, and sits in a scenic position above the River Don.

E6 *On A97, six miles W of Kildrummy.*

🅿 Free

🕐 Open access.

Tel 01466 793191   www.historic-scotland.gov.uk

57 Glendronach Distillery

Visitors can learn about traditional processes at this nineteenth century distillery, and taste the fifteen-year-old single malt.

H9 *Off A97 on B9001, six miles N of Huntly.*

P ⓦ ♿ 🏛 AV 🔭 ⓔ Free

🕐 Mon–Fri, 9am–4pm.
   Tours: 10am & 2pm, (these may be restricted due to essential work in summer 2005).

Tel 01466 730245

58 Glenfarclas Distillery

Visitors can tour this independent working distillery, founded in 1836, and enjoy a dram of whisky in the Ships Room.

D8 *Off A95, SW of Aberlour.*

P ⓦ 🏛 🔭 ⓔ ££

🕐 Apr–Sept, Mon–Fri, 10am–5pm.
   July–Aug, Sat, 10am–4pm.
   Oct–Mar, Mon–Fri, 10am–4pm
   (last tour one hour before closing).

Tel 01807 500245   www.glenfarclas.co.uk

59 Glenfiddich Distillery

Established in 1887, the whisky made in Glenfiddich distillery is distilled, matured and bottled on site. Following an audio-visual introduction, visitors are taken on a guided tour.

E8 *On the A941, 0.3 miles N of Dufftown.*

P ⓦ ♿ 🏛 E AV 🔭 ⓔ Free

🕐 All year round; Mon–Fri, 9.30am–4.30pm.
   Easter–mid Oct, Sat, 9.30am–4.30pm;
   Sun, 12 noon–4.30pm.

Tel 01340 820373   www.glenfiddich.com

60 Glenlivet Distillery

Glenlivet was founded in 1824 by George Smith, and was one of the first to be granted a licence to legally distil whisky. Guided tours and tastings are provided, along with an interactive exhibition.

D7 *Ten miles N of Tomintoul on B9008.*

P ⓦ ♿ 🍴 🏛 E AV 🔭 ⓔ Free

🕐 Apr–Oct, Mon–Sat, 10am–4pm; Sun, 12.30–4pm.

Tel 01340 821720   www.theglenlivet.com

61 Glenlivet Estate

A large Highland estate encompassing over 90 square miles of hills, glens and forests in the foothills of the Cairngorms. Visitors can use over 100 miles of trails for walking, mountain biking, horse riding and skiing. Maps, guides and other leaflets are available. A ranger service operates from the Estate Information Centre in Tomintoul, which houses a variety of displays and information.

C7 *Fourteen miles SE of Grantown-on-Spey on the A939.*

P ⓦ ♿ E AV 🔭 ⛷ 🚶 Free

🕐 Open access.

Tel 01807 580283
www.crownestate.co.uk/glenlivet

62 Glenshee Ski Centre

Located at some 2,200 ft above sea level, and with over 25 miles of downhill runs, Glenshee is undoubtedly Scotland's largest ski resort. A large network of ski lifts provide access to 38 runs spread across three valleys and four mountains; the runs include ten green, 13 blue, 13 red and two black, the longest being the Glas Maeol, at 1.25 m. All abilities are catered for, and facilities include ski and snowboard instruction and equipment hire.

C2 *On A93, nine miles S of Braemar.*

P ⓦ ♿ 🛍 ✕ 🏛 ⛷ £££ ⓔ

🕐 Dec–Apr, daily, 8.30am–5pm.
   Call for summer opening.

Tel 013397 41320   www.ski-glenshee.co.uk

63 Gordon Highlanders Museum

Tells the story of the Gordon Highlanders, one of the country's most famous regiments. The exhibition includes interactive displays, reconstructions, a handling area and collection of Victoria Crosses.

L5 *Viewfield Road, W end of Aberdeen; signposted from Anderson Drive/Queen's Road roundabout.*

P ⓦ ♿ 🛍 🏛 E AV ⓔ £

🕐 Apr–Oct, Tue–Sat, 10.30am–4.30pm;
   Sun, 1.30–4.30pm. Nov–Mar, appointment only.

Tel 01224 311200   www.gordonhighlands.com

HIGHLAND GAMES

The popular explanation of Highland Games suggests that chieftains of the clans of old who needed bodyguards would hold trials of strength and skill to find the strongest or nimblest men for their court. This is why many of the feats of strength involve everyday material found in the Highlands – such as tree-trunks (cabers) or water-worn boulders (for putting the shot). Similarly, eager for prestige, these same chieftains would hold auditions for dancers and pipers.

Tests of strength and musical skill combine to form the modern recipe for Highland Games. Promoting Gatherings, thereby giving members a chance to dress up in Highland costume, was also the role of various Highland and Celtic Societies. These arose at the beginning of the nineteenth century when the Highlands were 'rehabilitated' and no longer seen as an uncivilised place and hotbed of rebellion.

The most famous Highland Games is the Braemar Gathering, held annually in September. A direct descendant of the gatherings of old, this meeting was established as early as 1800, and became associated with royalty in 1848, when it was first attended by Queen Victoria.

64 Grampian Transport Museum

A collection of 200 road and railway vehicles including the Craigievar Express, a nineteenth century steam tricycle and the Cruden Bay Tramcar. Numerous events are staged throughout the season.

G6 *Centre of Alford, 25 miles W of Aberdeen on A944.*

🅿 WC ♿ 🍴 ♿ E AV 🍴 ££
⊕ Apr–Sept, daily, 10am–5pm. Oct, closes at 4pm.
Tel 019755 62292   www.gtm.org.uk

65 Grassic Gibbon Centre

A centre with exhibition and video dedicated to Scottish novelist Lewis Grassic Gibbon, author of the trilogy *A Scots Quair*.

J2 *Arbuthnott on B967, between Fordoun (A94) and Inverbervie (A92).*

🅿 WC ♿ 🍴 ✕ ♿ E AV ☀ 🍴 🕴 £ £
⊕ Apr–Oct, daily, 10am–4.30pm.
Tel 01561 361668   www.grassicgibbon.com

66 Haddo House

This eighteenth century house, designed by William Adam and containing fine furniture and paintings, has been the home of the Gordon family for 400 years. Lying adjacent to the estate is Haddo Country Park, with its lakes, walks and wildlife.

K8 *Off B999, four miles N of Pitmedden.*

🅿 WC ♿ 🍴 ♿ E 🕴 £££
⊕ House: Easter weekend, May–Jun & Sept,.
   Sat & Sun only, 11am–4.30pm.
   Jul–Aug, daily, 11am-4.30pm.
   Garden & Country park: all year round, daily,
   9.30am–sunset.
Tel 01651 851440   www.nts.org.uk

Kildrummy Castle

67 Haughton Country Park ♣

An extensive park and woodland with wild flower meadow and river, ideally situated for walks and picnics. The park also offers a ranger service, putting green and interpretative centre, with local information.

G6 *Off the A944, on the outskirts of Alford.*

P WC ♿ ⛱ ⚐ £

🕐 All year round, daily, daylight hours.

68 Huntly Castle ♿ 🏰

An impressive set of ruins made up of an original twelfth century motte and a palace block which dates from the sixteenth century. Notable features include fine architectural and heraldic details.

G8 *Huntly, off A96.*

P WC ♿ 🏛 E ⚐ ££

🕐 Apr–Sept, daily, 9.30am–6.30pm.
   Oct–Mar, closed Thur and Fri.

Tel 01466 793191   www.historic-scotland.gov.uk

69 Johnstons Cashmere Visitor Centre 🏛

A tour and audio-visual presentation describe how cashmere items are produced, and an exhibition tells the story of cashmere intertwined with Johnstons' 200 years history.

D10 *On the banks of the River Lossie, Elgin, opposite the Cathedral.*

P WC ♿ ✕ 🏛 E AV ⚐ 🏷 Free

🕐 Mon–Sat, 9am–5.30pm; from Easter, Sun, 11am–5pm. Jul & Aug, Mon–Fri, open until 6pm.

Tel 01343 554099   www.johnstonscashmere.com

70 Keith & Dufftown Railway

Passengers on this heritage railway can enjoy some of Banffshire's charming scenery on the journey between Dufftown and the market town of Keith.

E8 *Dufftown Station, on A941.*

P WC ☕ 🏛 E AV ⚐ 🏷 ££

🕐 Please telephone for timetable details.

Tel 01340 821181   www.keith-dufftown.org.uk

71 Kildrummy Castle and Garden

This water and alpine shrub garden lies beside the ruins of Kildrummy Castle. The garden is adorned with a variety of plants such as azaleas and rhododendrons; the vibrant colours are at their most impressive between September and October.

F6 *On A97, ten miles W of Alford.*

P WC & ♥ ♿ AV ⩋ ☀ ⚇ £

⊕ Apr–Oct, daily, 9.30am–6pm.

Tel 01975 571331   www.historic-scotland.gov.uk

72 Kincorth Hill Local Nature Reserve

An important local nature reserve, Kincorth Hill is an area of extensive heathland, gorse scrub and woodlands, and is home to a wide variety of wildlife. Visitors can enjoy panoramic views across Aberdeen from Peterhead to Deeside.

L5 *Between the A956 & A92 S of Aberdeen city centre.*

P Free

⊕ Open access. Limited parking.

Tel 01224 272137

73 King's College Chapel

Notable features in this fifteenth century collegiate chapel include fine late-medieval wood carving on the ceiling, stall and the oak screen which separates the nave and choir.

L5 *Off King Street, Aberdeen city centre.*

& ♥ ♿ E AV ⩋ Free

⊕ All year round, Mon–Fri, 9am–4.30pm.

Tel 01224 272137

74 Kinnaird Head Castle Lighthouse and Museum

The museum tells the history of lighthouses via audio-visual presentations and interactives plus an exhibition of lenses and equipment. Visitors are given a guided tour of Kinnaird Head Castle Lighthouse, a sixteenth century castle with lighthouse addition (1787), the first to be built by the Northern Lighthouse Board.

L11 *Kinnaird Head, Fraserburgh, off A92/A98.*

P WC & ♥ ♿ E AV ⩋ ☀ ⚇ ⊞ ££

⊕ Apr–Oct, Mon–Sat, 10am–5pm; Sun, 12 noon–5pm.
July–Aug, Mon–Sat, 10am–6pm; Sun, 11am–6pm.
Nov–Mar, Mon–Sat, 10am–4pm; Sun, 12 noon–4pm.

Tel 01346 511022   www.lighthousemuseum.co.uk

75 Kirk of St Nicholas

Aberdeen's original parish church possesses a 48-bell carillion, one of the largest in Scotland. Interior features include twentieth-century stained glass windows, notable medieval and seventeenth century woodwork and medieval effigies.

L5 *Union Street, Aberdeen city centre.*

WC & ♿ Free

⊕ May–Sept, Mon–Fri, 12 noon–4pm; Sat, 1–3pm.
Oct–Mar, Mon–Fri, 10am–1pm.

Tel 01224 643494

76 Kirkhill Forest Walks

A working forest offering waymarked walks, orienteering, horse and cycle trials, sculptures plus views from the top of Tyrebagger Hill.

K6 *N of the A96 between the Dyce and Blackburn roundabouts.*

P ☀ ⚇

⊕ Open access.

Tel 01330 844537   www.forestry.gov.uk

Kinnaird Head Lighthouse

Leith Hall

77 Lecht 2090 Ski and Multi Activity Centre

More compact than Glenshee, the region's other ski centre, the Lecht is nonetheless a popular area for winter sports. A number of chairlifts and tows take skiiers on to one of twenty slopes, consisting of seven green, seven blue, five red and one black. A special race piste features timing and rapid slalom poles. Also available are a number of snowboarding runs, dedicated tubing areas and a dry ski/snowboarding slope, plus tuition and equipment hire. Summer activities include karting, tubing, quad bikes and chairlift rides.

D6 *On the A939, between Cockbridge and Tomintoul.*

P WC ☕ ⊞ ☀ ££

⏱ Summer activities: Jun–Oct, daily, 8.30am–5.30pm. Winter: Dec–Apr, daily, 8.30am–5.30pm.

Tel 01975 651440   www.lecht.co.uk

78 Leith Hall and Garden

Leith Hall is at the centre of an estate and was home to the Leith family from 1650. Contents include items belonging to successive lairds and a military exhibition, while the gardens feature primulas, alpines, herbacious borders, a bird hide and nature trails.

G7 *On B9002, one mile W of Kennethmont.*

P WC ♿ ☕ E ⊞ ☀ ⚇ £££

⏱ House: Easter, Fri–Mon, 12 noon–5pm. May–Sept, Fri–Tue, 12 noon–5pm. Garden and grounds: all year round, daily, 9.30am–dusk.

Tel 01464 831216   www.nts.org.uk

79 Little Treasures

A museum housing a collection of doll's houses, miniatures, dolls and toys.

J6 *On B993, three miles S of Inverurie.*

P WC ♿ ⊞ E ⊞ ⊞ £

⏱ Jul–Aug, daily, 10am–5pm. Jan–June & Sept–Nov, Fri–Mon, 10am–5pm; Sun, 1–5pm. Dec, Mon–Sat, 10am–5pm; Sun, 1–5pm.

Tel 01467 642332   www.littletreasures.uk.com

80 Loanhead Stone Circle

A fine example of a ring cairn surrounded by a recumbent stone circle; a burial area lies nearby.

J7 *Off A96, five miles NW of Inverurie, near Daviot.*

P Free

⏱ Open access.

Tel 01466 793191   www.historic-scotland.gov.uk

81 Lochinch Visitor Centre ★

A visitor centre focusing on the surrounding area which is home to an assortment of wildlife and waterfowl (particularly in winter), Highland cattle and sheep.

L5 *Redmoss Road, Aberdeen, off A90.*

🅿 🆆🅲 ♿ E 🆅 🌲 ⛷ 🚶 Free

🕐 Opening times vary; please telephone prior to visit.

Tel 01224 897400   www.aberdeencity.gov.uk

82 Loch Muick and Lochnagar Wildlife Reserve

The reserve was established in 1974 between the Balmoral Estate and Scottish Wildlife Trust. Lochnagar is classified as a Special Protection Area for upland birds, with large numbers of breeding dotterel.

E3 *Off B976, ten miles SW of Ballater.*

🅿 ♿ E 🌲 ⛷ 🚶 Free

🕐 Apr–Oct, daily, 9am–dusk; please telephone to confirm times prior to visit. A charge is made for parking.

Tel 013397 55059   www.balmoralestate.com

83 Lossiemouth Fisheries and Community Museum 🏛

Looks at the history of Lossiemouth, with particular emphasis on the local fishing industry. James Ramsay Macdonald, Britain's first Labour Prime Minister was born in Lossiemouth, and visitors can see a reconstruction of his study.

D11 *Pitgaveny Street, Lossiemouth, on A941.*

E £

🕐 Easter–Oct, Mon–Sat, 10.30am–5pm.

Tel 01343 813772

84 Macduff Marine Aquarium 🐟

Focuses on sea life of the Moray Firth, with a living community of wolf fish, conger eels, lobsters, cod and small sharks, along with a splash tank, ray pool, rock pool displays and touch pools. Talks, video presentations and feeding shows run through the week.

H11 *E of the harbour, Macduff, on A98.*

🅿 🆆🅲 ♿ E 🆅 🌲 ⛷ 🎦 ££

🕐 All year round, daily, 10am–5pm.

Tel 01261 833369   www.marine-aquarium.com

85 Maggie's Hoosie 🏛

An ancient fisher cottage restored and furnished with original artefacts depicting the family home and lifestyle of the fishing community in north east Scotland.

M11 *Shore Street, Inverallochy, five miles SE of Fraserburgh on B9107.*

🅿 🆅 ⛷ 🚶 £

🕐 Telephone for details.

Tel 01346 514761   www.brown-mcrae.co.uk

86 Mar Lodge Estate 🐾

An extensive conservation area in the Cairngorms, which takes in four of the five highest mountains in the UK, upper parts of the River Dee and native Caledonian pine forests. Many areas are Sites of Special Scientific Interest and National Scenic Areas, and contain a variety of wild/birdlife.

C3 *Five miles W of Braemar, off A93.*

🅿 🚶 ⛷ Free

🕐 Estate: all year round, daily, daylight hours. Lodge and ballroom: special open days; contact estate office for details.

Tel 013397 41433   www.nts.org.uk

87 Marischal Museum 🏛

A museum holding Pictish stones, Egyptian mummies and various other objects from around the world.

L5 *Marischal College, Aberdeen city centre.*

E Free

🕐 Mon–Fri, 10am–5pm; Sun, 2–5pm.

Tel 01224 274301
www.abdn.ac.uk/marischal-museum

88 Maud Railway Museum 🏛

Located in the former Maud Railway Station, the museum takes a reminiscent look at the days of steam trains with memorabilia and nostalgic sound effects.

L9 *On the B9106, W of Mintlaw at Maud.*

🅿 E 🚶 Free

🕐 Telephone for details.

Tel 01771 622906
www.aberdeenshire.gov.uk/heritage/

89 Mill of Benholm

A traditional water-powered meal mill in working order, set beside paddocks and ancient woodlands.

K2 *Off A92 Aberdeen/Dundee road, 13 miles S of Stonehaven.*

P ⓦ ⓐ E ⌂ 👪 £

⏰ Please telephone for details.

Tel 01561 361969

90 Millbuies Country Park ♣

Surrounded by extensive parkland, visitors can enjoy a range of outdoor activities including lochside walks and nature trails. Fishing boats are available for hire during the summer months.

D10 *On the A941, S of Elgin.*

P ⓦ ⓐ ⌂ 👪 Free

⏰ All year round, daily, 8am–dusk.

Tel 01343 860234

91 Moray Firth Wildlife Centre

An exhibition devoted to the dolphins of the Moray Firth and other wildlife. There are good views of the coast and opportunities to see dolphins, osprey, seals, otters and coastal birdlife.

E11 *Spey Bay, five miles N of Fochabers on B9014, off A96.*

P ⓦ ⓐ 🍴 🏛 E AV ⌂ 💕 👪 🎫 £

⏰ Apr–Oct, daily, 10.30am–5pm; please telephone for winter hours.

Tel 01343 820339 www.mfwc.co.uk

92 Moray Motor Museum

Situated in a converted mill building, the museum contains a wide-ranging collection of cars and motor cycles.

D10 *Near Elgin town centre, off A96/A941.*

P ⓦ ⓐ £

⏰ Easter–Oct, daily, 11am–5pm.

Tel 01343 544933

93 Muir of Dinnet Nature Reserve 🦆

A nature reserve with visitor centre containing information on the surrounding area. It is an ideal location for walkers and wildlife enthusiasts.

F4 *On A93, four miles W of Aboyne.*

P ⓦ ⓐ E AV 💕 👪 Free

⏰ Reserve: all year round.
Visitor Centre: Easter–late Oct, Wed–Mon, 9am–5.30pm.
Times may vary, telephone for details.

Tel 013398 810222 www.snh.gov.uk

94 Nelson Tower ★

The most northerly built monument to Nelson in the country, it was funded largely by public subscription and opened in 1812. It offers fine views of Forres, Findhorn, the Black Isle and the mountains of the north west. A flag flies on the top of the tower to indicate it is open.

B10 *A short walk up Cluny Hill, above Forres; follow signposts from Grant Park.*

🏛 💕 👪 Free

⏰ May–Sept, Tue–Sun, 2–4pm. Telephone to confirm.

Tel 01309 673701 www.moray.org/museums/

95 North East Falconry Visitor Centre

Four flying demonstrations take place every day, with Master Falconers describing the skills and talents of various birds of prey. Falcons, owls and eagles are permanently on display, and red deer can be viewed from the cafe.

F8 *Off A920/A96, three miles NW of Huntly.*

P ⓦ ⓐ 🍴 🏛 ⌂ 🎫 ££

⏰ Mar–Oct, daily, 10.30am–5.30pm.
Displays: 11am, 12.45pm, 2.30pm & 4.15pm.

Tel 01466 760328 www.huntly-falconry.co.uk

96 Northfield Farm Museum

Houses a collection of farming equipment including tractors, household items, tools and a smiddy engineers workshop.

K10 *Off the A98, 10 miles SW of Fraserburgh.*

P ⓦ ⓐ ⌂ E £

⏰ May–Sept, daily, 11am–5.30pm.

Tel 01771 653504

97 Old Royal Station

This beautifully restored Victorian railway station houses an exhibition on its historic connection with royalty. Visitors can also see Queen Victoria's waiting room.

Picardy Symbol Stone

E4 *Station Square, Ballater, on A93.*

♿ ⌂ E [AV] 📷 Free

⊕ Times vary according to season;
please telephone to confirm hours.

Tel 013397 55306

98 Pennan ★

Reached by a steep and twisting road, Pennan
is set round an attractive bay under cliffs, with
only a road separating the houses from the sea.
The film *Local Hero* was filmed here in 1983.

K11 *Off B9031, W of Fraserburgh.*

Free

⊕ Open access.

Tel 01346 518315   www.agtb.org

99 Peter Anson Gallery 🏛

Features watercolour paintings from a collection
of over 700 works by the renowned maritime
artist and historian.

F11 *The Library, Cluny Place, Buckie town centre.*

⌂ E £

⊕ Mon-Fri, 10am-6pm; Sat, 10am-12 noon.

Tel 01309 673701   www.moray.org/museum/

100 Peterhead Maritime 🏛
Heritage

Visitors can learn about Peterhead's maritime
past and present through a series of interactive
and audio-visual displays.

N9 *Off the A952, on the S side of Peterhead.*

P [WC] ♿ 📷 ✕ ⌂ E [AV] 🛋 📷 £

⊕ Telephone for details.

Tel 01771 622906

101 Picardy Symbol Stone Ⓑ 🏛

Thought to date from the seventh century,
this stone is one of the oldest symbol stones
in Scotland.

H7 *Off A96 towards Raes of Insch,
eight miles SE of Huntly.*

Free

⊕ Open access.

Tel 01466 793191   www.historic-scotland.gov.uk

102 Pitmedden Garden and ⚘ ⚘ 🏛
Museum of Farming Life

Situated on a large estate, this enclosed
seventeenth century garden comprises
of plants, herbaceous borders, fountains,
sundials and a herb garden. Visitors can
enjoy woodland trails, a wildlife garden,
ponds and a farming museum.

K7 *On the A920, 14 miles N of Aberdeen.*

P [WC] ♿ 📷 ⌂ E 🛋 🐾 📷 ££

⊕ Grounds: All year round.
Museum: May-Sept, daily, 10am-5.30pm.

Tel 01651 842352   www.nts.org.uk

103 Pluscarden Abbey ✟

Pluscarden Abbey was founded in 1230
by Alexander II for Valliscaulian monks,
burned in 1390 by the Wolf of Badenoch,
became Benedictine in 1454 and fell into lay
hands after the Reformation. In 1948 it was
re-founded from Prinknash Abbey, and the
medieval buildings restored. The monks
welcome visitors to witness daily Gregorian
chants and view the fine modern stained glass.

C10 *Between Forres and Elgin, signposted from
the A96 and B9010.*

P [WC] ♿ ⌂ E 📷 Free

⊕ All year round, daily, 9am-5pm.

Tel 01343 890257   www.pluscardenabbey.org

ROYAL DEESIDE

As early as 1847, Queen Victoria had developed a love of Scotland and what it represented in her attempts to escape court politics in Windsor and the other cares of office. Victoria and Albert in that year had a very wet holiday in the west but the drier climate on the eastern side of the Cairngorms was reported by her own doctor. They acquired the lease of the Balmoral estate in the next year, later buying it, so that by 1855 a new castle at Balmoral was complete *(see p166)*.

The hills, pinewoods and rushing river reminded Albert of his native Germany. The Queen was equally beguiled. She wrote in her diary that 'All seemed to breathe freedom and peace, and to make one forget the world and all its sad turmoils.' As for the valley of the River Dee, its future was secure as a royal playground and neighbouring landowners and their staff wholeheartedly adopted the tartan, the Highland balls and gatherings which has been in the past so unkindly described as Balmorality.

Had the valley of the River Dee not had its royal connections, it would still have been an area of high landscape value. From Aberdeen – the Deeside gateway – to Banchory, there are castles and fine woodlands; from Banchory

Balmoral Castle and River Dee

westwards via Aboyne and Ballater, the hills gradually increase in size, so that beyond Ballater, the long profile of Lochnagar is conspicuous on the south-west horizon. The finest section is west of Braemar, up to the public road end near the Linn of Dee. There are fine prospects of the eastern Cairngorms and some relic natural pinewoods.

104 Portsoy Harbour ★

Dating from 1692, the harbour is thought to be the earliest on the Moray Firth. Along with restored warehousing and merchants' houses, the area has retained an authentic period atmosphere.

G11 *On A98, between Cullen and Banff.*

☼ ♐ Free

🕓 Open access.

105 Provost Skene's House 🏛

Dating from 1545, Provost Skene's House contains a series of period room settings recalling the elegant furniture of earlier times. Visitors can also see a series of religious paintings and changing fashions along with displays of local interest, coins and archaeology.

L5 *Guestrow, Aberdeen city centre.*

🚻 ♐ E Free

🕓 Mon–Sat, 10am–5pm; Sun 1–4pm.

Tel 01224 641086   www.aberdeencity.gov.uk

106 Royal Lochnagar Distillery 🏃

Tours are given at this, the most local distillery to Balmoral since Queen Victoria's time. An admission charge includes a discount voucher redeemable towards the purchase of whisky in the shop.

E4 *Leave A93 at Crathie and head S on B976 for half a mile.*

🅿 🚻 ♿ ⊞ AV ⊞ ££

🕓 Oct–Apr, Mon–Fri, 11am–4pm.
May–Sept, Mon–Sat, 10am–5pm;
Sun 12 noon–4pm.
(last tour one hour before closing).

Tel 013397 42700

107 Sandhaven Meal Mill

Visitors can tour this nineteenth-century meal mill and see how oatmeal used to be ground.

L11 *On the B9031, W of Fraserburgh.*

P WC & E Free

⊕ Telephone for opening times.

Tel 01771 622906
www.aberdeenshire.gov.uk/heritage/

108 Satrosphere

A hands-on science and discovery centre which gives visitors the chance to explore heat, light and sound, and learn the principles of technology and the magic of space. Shows, exhibits, events and workshops are suitable for all ages.

L5 *Constitution Street, by Aberdeen beach.*

P WC & ☕ ⌂ E 🎫 ££

⊕ Daily, 10am–5pm.

Tel 01224 640340   www.satrosphere.net

109 Scottish Tartans Museum

Along with over 700 tartans, visitors can discover their heritage using a computerised database which contains a number of family tartans.

F9 *Keith town centre, off A95/A96.*

WC & £

⊕ Apr–Nov, Mon–Sat, 11am–3pm.
Extended opening hours, Jul–Aug.

Tel 01542 888419   www.keithcommunity.co.uk

110 Speyside Cooperage Visitor Centre ★

Visitors can learn about the ancient craft of cask making and the significance of casks throughout the ages. Skilled coopers and apprentices, situated in the workshops, repair oak casks and visitors are encouraged to participate using the demonstration cask.

D9 *On the A941, S of Craigellachie.*

P WC & ☕ ⌂ E 🎫 ££

⊕ All year round, Mon–Fri, 9.30am–4.30pm.

Tel 01340 871108   www.speysidecooperage.com

111 Spynie Palace

Spynie Palace was the residence of the bishop's of Moray from the fourteenth century to 1686. Features include a tower built by Bishop David Stewart which gives views across Spynie Loch and the surrounding area.

D11 *Two miles N of Elgin off the A941.*

P WC & ⌂ 🎫 £

⊕ Summer, daily, 9.30am–6.30pm.
Winter, Sat & Sun, 9.30am–4.30pm.

Tel 01343 546358   www.historic-scotland.gov.uk

Spynie Palace

112   St Andrew's Cathedral   ✠

Opened in 1817, the original building was designed as a chapel to seat 1200 people, and became a cathedral in 1914. Internal features, such as the choir screen and the bishop's throne, are later additions.

L5   *King Street, Aberdeen city centre.*

♿ ☕ ♨ E 🅰 Free

🕑 Cathedral: May–Sept, Tue–Fri, 11am–4pm.
  Tearoom: Fri, 10am–12 noon.

Tel 01224 640119
www.aberdeen.anglican.org/Cathedral.htm

113   St Cyrus   🦆

The sand dunes and cliffs of St Cyrus are an ideal venue for walkers of all abilities. The reserve's fertile soil provides optimum conditions for a variety of plants and insects, including butterflies and several species of moth.

J1   *On A92, six miles N of Montrose.*

P 🚾 ♿ E 🥾 🧗 Free

🕑 Visitor Centre: daily, Apr–Oct, Thur–Mon.
  Restrictions to bird breeding area, Apr–Aug.

Tel 01674 830736   www.snh.org.uk

114   St Machar's Cathedral   ✠

Situated on an ancient site of worship, the present building dates from 1350. The mainly fifteenth century cathedral with twin-towered west front has a Renaissance heraldic ceiling depicting the notable sovereigns of Europe and ecclesiastical households of Scotland.

L5   *Off St Machar Drive, N side of Aberdeen.*

🚾 ♿ ♨ E Free

🕑 All year round, daily, 9am–5pm.

Tel 01224 485988   www.stmachar.com

115   Storybook Glen   ★

Popular nursery rhymes and fairytales, both old and new, are brought to life in this extensive children's theme park. Models of well-loved fictional characters and fantasy buildings are scattered amongst the trees, flowers and waterfalls of these scenic gardens.

K4   *Off the B9077, SW of Aberdeen.*

P 🚾 ♿ ☕ ✕ ♨ 🧗 ♿ ££

🕑 All year, daily, 10am–6pm. Weather permitting.

Tel 01224 732941
www.storybookglenaberdeen.co.uk

116   Strathisla Distillery   🍶

Strathisla was founded in 1786, and is home to the Chivas Regal, a blended Scotch whisky. Visitors can take a self-guided tour and try a tutored nosing of various whiskies.

F9   *Seafield Avenue, Keith, on the A96; signposted through the town.*

P 🚾 ♿ ♨ E ♿ ££

🕑 Apr–Oct, Mon–Sat, 10am–4pm; Sun, 12.30–4pm.

Tel 01542 783044   www.chivas.com

Tolquhon Castle

117 Sueno's Stone

Sueno's Stone, standing 20 ft in height, and dating from the ninth/tenth century, is one of the must stunning sculptured monuments in the country. Several carved panels depict scenes from a bloody Pictish battle.

B10 *Off A96, on E side of Forres.*

🅿 Free

🕘 Open access (enclosed in a protective glass case).

Tel 01667 460232 www.historic-scotland.gov.uk

118 Tolbooth Museum

The museum is located in Stonehaven's oldest building – the Earl Marischal's sixteenth century storehouse – which served as the County Tolbooth of Kincardineshire from 1600–1767. Visitors can learn about Stonehaven's links with the sea and why Episcopal priests were imprisoned here in 1748.

K3 *Stonehaven town centre.*

🅿 ✕ ♨ E ⚓ 👫 Free

🕘 May-Oct, Wed–Mon, 1.30pm–4.30pm.

Tel 01771 622906
www.aberdeenshire.gov.uk/heritage/

119 Tolquhon Castle

This fifteenth century tower with its adjoining mansion and decorated gatehouse was built by the Forbes family and is one of the few castles in the area built round a courtyard.

K7 *Tarves churchyard, on A920, 15 miles N of Aberdeen.*

🅿 ⓦⓒ ♿ ⛱ £

🕘 Apr–Sept, daily, 9.30am–6.30pm.
Oct–Mar, weekends only, 9.30am–4.30pm.

Tel 01651 851286 www.historic-scotland.gov.uk

120 Tomintoul Museum and Visitor Centre

Situated in one of the highest villages in Britain, the museum features displays on local history and wildlife, and an old-fashioned Highland kitchen.

C6 *Tomintoul Square, on A939.*

🅿 ♨ E £

🕘 End Mar–May, Mon–Fri, 9.30am–12 noon & 2–4pm.
Jun–Aug, Mon–Sat, 9.30am–12 noon & 2–4.30pm.
Sept, Mon–Sat, 9.30am–12 noon & 2–4pm.
Oct, Mon–Fri, 9.30am–12 noon & 2–4pm.

Tel 01309 673701 www.moray.org/museums/

121 Tugnet Ice House

An unusual building with vaulted brick ceiling, which was once used by the salmon industry to store river ice. The adjacent Moray Firth Wildlife Centre *(see p182)* looks after visitor interests at Tugnet, and provides various facilities.

E11 *Spey Bay, five miles N of A96/A98 junction on B9104.*

🅿 Free

🕘 Apr–Oct, daily, 1–5pm.
Jul–Aug, closes 7pm.

Tel 01343 820339

Loch an Eilein, Rothiemurchus, Strathspey

Loch Hourn, Lochaber

THE HIGHLANDS OF SCOTLAND

All of the180 miles between, say, Duncansby Head at the Caithness tip of Scotland and Ardnamurchan Point on the westernmost extremity are in the Highlands, yet are far from uniform in scenery. The Highlands are large enough to have their own distinct regions, so that, for instance, the Caithness light and landscape is very different from the Hebridean ambience of the Small Isles.

It is these extremes and contrasts of landscape that draw visitors – and a new wave of residents as well – to this marginal land on the edge of the Europe which some ecologists have unfairly described as a wet desert. The Highland story is one of the gradual demise of a native population which, with its clan system, represented a different kind of society to the rest of the UK. The struggle of these clans' descendants to wrest a living from the unforgiving land in the changed world of the nineteenth century adds its own poignant layer to the tale. This, too, is written into the Highland landscape. In places in the west, the low sun still picks out the long parallel ridges of the old lazy beds or cultivation strips. Likewise, many a hillwalker has stumbled over tumbled walls high in some grassy upland – the ruins of the shielings or shelters used by the locals when their cattle were on the high summer pastures.

In contrast to the sense of emptiness and abandonment in some of the western glens, the eastern Highland seaboard shares aspects with other stretches of the east coast. Nairn, on the inner Moray Firth, is a golfing resort which prospered with the arrival of the railway. Handsome little Dornoch in Sutherland is likewise associated with the essentially Lowland pastime of golf and is sometimes referred to as the 'St Andrews of the Highlands'. Cromarty, on the Black Isle, is often cited as a good example of an old Scots burgh, bypassed by time. On the other hand, Inverness, as the Highland capital, is thriving, expanding and suitably proud of its new city status.

These east-side communities do not fit in with many visitors' conception of the Highlands. Instead, they are drawn to the rocky ramparts of Glen Coe, the birchwoods and waterfalls of Glen Affric on the spine of Scotland, the terraces of sandstone which build the Torridon mountains – or a thousand other prospects which change with the seasons and as the light turns through each day. Cult of the picturesque or not – the Highlands have landscapes to stir the heart.

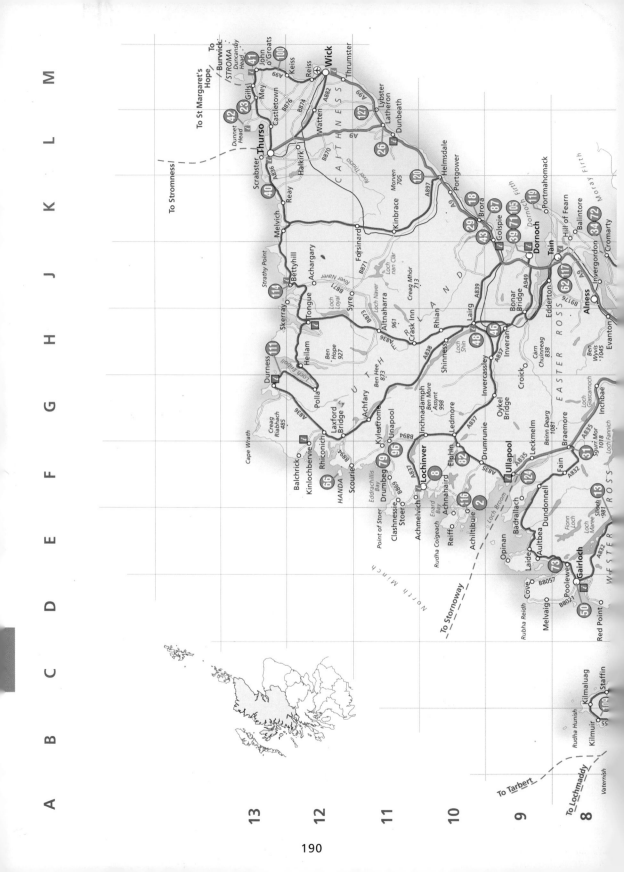

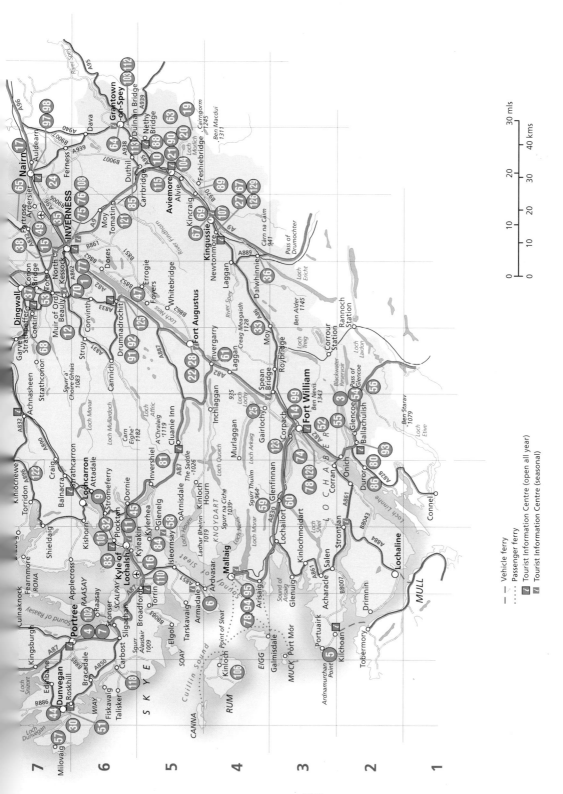

— — Vehicle ferry

······ Passenger ferry

Tourist Information Centre (open all year)

Tourist Information Centre (seasonal)

VISITOR INFORMATION

MAIN TOURIST INFORMATION CENTRE

Inverness
Castle Wynd
Inverness IV2 3BJ
Tel: 01463 234353
Web: www.visithighlands.com
E-mail: inverness@host.co.uk
Open: all year round

YEAR ROUND TOURIST INFORMATION CENTRES
Contact Telephone number: 0845 22 55 121   E-mail: info@visitscotland.com

Achnasheen
The Studio, Achnasheen
Ross-shire IV22 2EE

Golspie
Fountain Road, Golspie
Sutherland KW10 6TH

Aviemore
Grampian Road, Aviemore
Inverness-shire PH22 1PP

Kilchoan
Pier Road, Kilchoan
Acharacle, Argyll PH36 4LJ

Ballachulish
Albert Road, Ballachulish
Argyll PA39 4JR

Kinlochbervie
Harbour Office
The Pier, Kinlochbervie

Broadford
The Car Park, Broadford
Isle of Skye IV49 9AB

Nairn
The Library, 68 High Street
Nairn IV12 4AU

Cluanie
The Cluanie Inn, Cluanie
Inverness-shire IV3 6YW

Nethy Bridge
Nethy Bridge Stores, Nethy Bridge
Inverness-shire PH25 3DA

Dornoch
The Square, Dornoch
Sutherland IV25 3SD

Newtonmore
Main Street, Newtonmore
Inverness-shire PH20 1DA

Drumnadrochit
The Car Park, Drumnadrochit
Inverness-shire IV63 6TX

Plockton
Post Office, Rhu Cottage
Plockton, Ross-shire IV52 8TL

Dunbeath
The Old School, Dunbeath
Caithness KW6 6ED

Portree
Bayfield House, Bayfield Road
Portree, Isle of Skye IV51 9EL

Dunvegan
2 Lochside, Dunvegan
Isle of Skye IV55 8WB

Strathcarron
Strathcarron Station
Strathcarron IV54 8YR

Durness
Durine, Durness
Sutherland IV27 4PN

Strathpeffer
The Square, Strathpeffer
Ross-shire IV14 9DW

Fort William
Cameron Square, Fort William
Inverness-shire PH33 6AJ

Tongue
Gordon Skene Grocers & General Merchants
Tongue, Sutherland IV27 4XF

Gairloch
Achtercairn, Gairloch
Inverness-shire IV22 2DN

Ullapool
Argyle Street, Ullapool
Ross-shire IV26 2UB

SEASONAL TOURIST INFORMATION CENTRES

Beauly
The Square
Beauly
Inverness-shire
IV4 7BX

Bettyhill
Clachan
Bettyhill
Sutherland
KW14 7SS

Daviot Wood
Picnic Area
Daviot Wood
By Inverness
IV1 2ER

Dunnet Head
Dunnet Head Educational Trust
Dunnet Head
Caithness
KW14 8YE

Fort Augustus
Car Park
Fort Augustus
Inverness-shire
PH32 4DD

Glenelg
Glenelg Candles
Glenelg
Ross-shire
IV40 8LA

Grantown on Spey
54 High Street
Grantown on Spey
PH26 3EH

John O'Groats
County Road
John O'Groats
Caithness
KW1 4YR

Kingussie
Highland Folk Museum
Kingussie
Inverness-shire
PH21 1JG

Kyle of Lochalsh
Car Park
Kyle of Lochalsh
Ross-shire
IV40 8AQ

Lairg
Ferrycroft Centre
Lairg
Sutherland
IV27 4AZ

Lochinver
Assynt Visitor Centre
Main Street
Lochinver
Sutherland
IV27 4LX

Mallaig
The Pier
Mallaig
Inverness-shire
PH41 4SQ

North Kessock
Picnic Site
North Kessock
Ross-shire
IV1 3UB

Spean Bridge
Kingdom of Scotland
Spean Bridge
By Fort William
PH34 4EP

Strontian
Acharacle
Argyll
PH36 4HZ

Tain
Tain Through Time
Tower Street, Tain
Ross-shire
IV19 1DY

Thurso
Riverside
Thurso
Caithness
KW14 8BU

Wick
Norseman Hotel
Riverside, Wick
Caithness
KW1 4NL

ADDITIONAL INFORMATION

GENERAL TRAVEL INFORMATION
Traveline Scotland
Tel: 0870 608 2608
Provides timetable information for all public transport in Scotland and the rest of Great Britain.

AIR TRAVEL

Inverness Airport
Terminal Building
Highlands & Islands Airports Limited
Head Office
Inverness Airport
Inverness IV2 7JB
Tel: 01667 464000
Web: www.hial.co.uk/
inverness-airport.html
E-mail: hial@hial.co.uk

Wick Airport
Highlands & Islands Airports Limited
Wick
Caithness KW1 4QP
Tel: 01955 602215
Web: www.hial.co.uk/wick-airport.html
E-mail: hial@hial.co.uk

TRAINS

First ScotRail
Caledonian Chambers
87 Union Street
Glasgow G1 3TA
Tel: Fares & Train Times: 08457 484950
Telesales: 08457 550033
Customer Relations: 0845 601 5929
Web: www.firstscotrail.co.uk
E-mail: scotrail.enquiries@firstgroup.com

COACH

Scottish Citylink Coaches Limited
Buchanan Bus Station
Killermont Street
Glasgow G2 3NP
Tel: 08705 505050
Web: www.citylink.co.uk
E-mail: info@citylink.co.uk
Routes: Inverness–Campbeltown
Inverness–Edinburgh
Inverness–Glasgow
Inverness–Isle of Skye
Inverness–Thurso–Scrabster
Inverness–Ullapool
Isle of Skye–Edinburgh
Isle of Skye–Glasgow

FERRIES

Caledonian MacBrayne
Head Office
The Ferry Terminal
Gourock PA19 1QP
Tel: Enquiries: 01475 650100
Vehicle Reservations: 08705 650000
Brochure Hotline: 01475 650288

Routes: Mallaig–Armadale
Mallaig–Eigg–Muck–Rum–Canna
Sconser–Raasay

Glenelg Kylerhea Car Ferry
Corriehallie
Inverinate
Kyle IV40 8HD
Tel: 01599 511302
Web: www.skyeferry.co.uk
E-mail: roddy@skyeferry.co.uk
Route: Glenelg–Isle of Skye

BUS

Highland Country Buses Limited
Head Office
1 Seafield Road
Inverness IV1 1TN
Tel: 01463 710555
Web: www.rapsons.co.uk
E-mail: info@rapsons.co.uk
Routes: operates an extensive network
throughout The Highlands

Stagecoach Inverness
Head Office
Guild Street
Aberdeen AB11 6GR
Tel: Ticket Information: 0870 608 2608
Other Enquiries: 01463 239292
Web: www.stagecoachbus.com
E-mail:
customer.care@bluebirdbuses.co.uk
Routes: operates an extensive network
throughout The Highlands

CAR HIRE

Aberdeen 4x4 Self Drive, Inverness
Tel: 01463 871083
Web: www.aberdeen4x4.co.uk
E-mail: info@aberdeen4x4.co.uk

Autovision Car & Van Rental, Inverness
Tel: 01463 234311
Web: www.autovision.co.uk
E-mail: rental@autovision.freeserve.co.uk

Easydrive Car & Van Rental, Fort William
Tel: 01397 701616
Web: www.easydrivescotland.co.uk
E-mail: rossco@easydrive.fsnet.co.uk

Ewan Macrae Limited, Portree, Skye
Tel: 01478 612554
E-mail: ewanmacraemotors@aol.com

Hawco Volkswagen Rental, Inverness
Tel: 01463 236111
Web:
www.hawcoinverness.volkswagen.co.uk
E-mail:
central.control@volkswagen.co.uk

Macdonalds Self-Drive, Aviemore
Tel: 01479 811444

Hawco, Fort William
Tel: 01397 700900
Web:
www.hawcofortwilliam.volkswagen.co.uk

Practical Car Rental, Fort William
Tel: 01397 772404

Ross Rentals, Strathcarron
Tel: 01520 722205
E-mail: rossrentals@yahoo.co.uk

Sharps Reliable Wrecks, Inverness
Tel: 01463 236684
Web: www.sharpsreliablewrecks.co.uk
E-mail:
enquiries@sharpsreliablewrecks.co.uk

Skye Car Rental, Isle of Skye
Tel: 01471 822225
Web: www.skye-car-rental.com
E-mail: info@skye-car-rental.com

TAXIS

Al's Taxis, Fort William
Tel: 01397 702545

A2B Taxis, Portree
Tel: 01478 613456

Bremners of Aviemore
Tel: 01479 812322

Gus's Taxis & Minibus Hire, Portree
Tel: 01478 613000

Mackays, Dornoch
Tel: 01862 810162

Moray Taxis, Nairn
Tel: 01667 455552

Nairn Taxis, Nairn
Tel: 01667 453342

Central Highland Taxis, Inverness
Tel: 01463 222222

Tartan Taxis, Inverness
Tel: 01463 233033

Sutherlands Taxi, Minibus & Coach Hire,
Invergarry
Tel: 01809 501222

'The Three Sisters', Glencoe

1 Abriachan Gardens ❖

The gardens stand above Loch Ness, and feature native oak, hazel and birch, along with walled beds of plants from around the world, giving colour and interest all year.

H6 *On the A82, nine miles W of Inverness.*

🅿 🛋 ⚴ 🚶 £

🕐 Daily, Feb–Apr & Oct, 9am–5pm.
May–Sept, 9am–7pm.

Tel 01463 861232

2 Achiltibuie Hydroponicum ❖

An unusual purpose-built indoor garden which grows a range of tropical plants, exotic fruit and vegetables, and flowers using soil-less methods.

E10 *23 miles NW of Ullapool, off A835.*

🅿 🅆🅒 ♿ ✗ ☕ 🛋 ⚴ 🎫 ££

🕐 Easter–Sept, daily, 10am–6pm.
Oct, Mon–Fri, 11.30am–3.30pm.

Tel 01854 622202   www.thehydroponicum.com

3 Aluminium Story Visitor ★ 🏛
Centre

A number of audio-visual exhibits and a video describe how aluminium has been produced in Kinlochleven for over eighty years, and tell the story of the people who have worked there.

F2 *Off B863, near Kinlochleven.*

🅿 🅆🅒 ♿ E 🆅 🛋 Free

🕐 Apr–Oct, Mon–Fri, 10am–1pm & 2–5pm.
Nov–Mar, Mon, 10am–12 noon & 2–5pm;
Tue–Thur, 10am–1pm & 2–5pm; Fri, 10am–1pm.

Tel 01855 831663

4 An Tuireann Arts Centre 🏛

A centre for visual arts and crafts with work by local and national artists.

C6 *Struan Road, Portree, Skye.*

🅿 🅆🅒 ♿ ☕ ☕ E 🛋 🎫 Free

🕐 Apr–Oct, Mon–Sat, 10am–5pm.
Nov–Mar, Tue–Sat, 10am–5pm.

Tel 01478 613306   www.antuireann.org.uk

5 Ardnamurchan Point 🏛
Lighthouse

This 36 m working lighthouse stands at the most westerly point of the British mainland, offering fine views across to the Hebrides and Small Isles. Features include an exhibition, engine room, fog horn and keepers' cottages.

Loch Assynt, Sutherland

C3 *Ardnamurchan Point, off B8007.*

🅆🅒 ☕ E 🆅 ⚴ 🚶 £

🕐 Apr–Oct, daily; please telephone to confirm times.

Tel 01972 510210

6 Armadale Castle Gardens 🏛 ❖ 🏰
and Museum of the Isles

Run by the Clan Donald Lands Trust, the estate contains the ruins of Armadale Castle and a museum devoted to the history of the Highlands with artefacts, paintings, weapons and crafts. The gardens, however, are the main attraction, and date back as far as the seventeenth century. Set in the Gulf Stream, they contain a range of trees, shrubs and flowers, and provide paths through formal terraces and woodland.

D5 *Sixteen miles S of Broadford on A851, Skye. A ferry runs from Mallaig.*

🅿 🅆🅒 ♿ ☕ ✗ ☕ E 🆅 ⚴ 🛋 🚶 🎫 ££

🕐 Apr–Oct, daily, 9.30am–5pm.

Tel 01471 844305   www.clandonald.com

7 Aros Experience 🏛

A large visitor centre with displays, a cinema and traditional music concerts. Exhibition themes include the history of Skye, sea eagles and herons, both with nest live-cams, while featured outdoors are forest walks and a children's play area.

C6 *Viewfield Road, on A87, S of Portree, Skye.*

🅿 🅆🅒 ♿ ☕ ✗ ☕ E 🆅 🛋 ⚴ 🚶 🎫 ££

🕐 Exhibition: all year round, daily, 9am–6pm
(last entry 5.15pm).
Open late for films and shows.

Tel 01478 613649   www.aros.co.uk

8 Assynt Visitor Centre ★ 🏛

Visitor centre includes informative displays on the history, culture and natural environment of the area. Models of crafts, a sea cliff and undersea scene. Live TV link to nesting Herons. Countryside Ranger base.

F10 *Main Street, Lochinver on the A837.*

🅿 ♿ ♿ 🍽 ⚘ E ♨ Free

🕐 May–Sept, Mon–Sat, 10.30am–5.30pm;
Sun, 10am–4pm.
Disabled facilities ground floor only.

Tel 01571 844330

9 Attadale Gardens ✿

These formal gardens and woodlands were set up at the end of the nineteenth century, and feature rhododendrons, azaleas plus a host of unusual trees and shrubs, waterfalls and a sunken garden. Numerous paths lead through the garden and across the hills above the shores of Loch Carron.

E6 *On A890 between Strathcarron and South Strome.*

🅿 ♿ ♿ ⚘ 🚶 £

🕐 Apr–Oct, Mon–Sat, 10am–5.30pm.

Tel 01520 722217 www.attadale.com

10 Auchgourish Nursery Garden ✿

Contains a winter garden with large rockery, Japanese garden, Himalayan and Chinese areas and a range of unusual plants.

K5 *On B970, eight miles N of Aviemore.*

🅿 🚶 ££

🕐 Apr–Oct, daily, 10am–5pm.
Nov–Mar, daily, 11am–3pm. Subject to weather.

Tel 01479 831464
www.auchgourishgardens.com

11 Balmacara Estate and 🐾 🐾 ✿
Lochalsh Woodland Garden

Balmacara estate takes in a variety of landscapes and features a number of walks with views towards Skye. The woodland garden, on the shores of Loch Alsh, contains an array of native and exotic plants and trees, with collections of rhododendrons, ferns, bamboo and fuchsia.

D6 *Off A87, by Kyle of Lochalsh.*

🅿 ♿ E 🚏 ⚘ 🚶 £

🕐 Estate: all year round.
Garden: all year round, daily, 9am–sunset.

Tel 01599 566325 www.nts.org.uk

12 Beauly Priory 🏛 ✠

The remains of a thirteenth century Valliscaulian priory, with sixteenth century additions.

H7 *Beauly, on the A862.*

🅿 £

🕐 Mid Jun–Sept, daily, 9.30am–6.30pm.

Tel 01667 460232 www.historic-scotland.gov.uk

13 Beinn Eighe National 🐾 🐦
Nature Reserve

Situated amongst remnants of ancient Caledonian pinewood, Beinn Eighe reserve, looking onto Loch Maree, is surrounded by impressive mountain scenery. It's also home to a diversity of wildlife, including golden eagles, red deer and pine martens. The upland areas of the reserve sustain healthy populations of arctic-alpine plants. Walks for all abilities.

E8 *Off A832, two miles NW of Kinlochewe.*

🅿 ♿ ♿ 🏛 E 🅰🆅 🚏 ⚘ 🚶 Free

🕐 Visitor Centre: Easter–End Oct, daily, 10am–5pm.
Reserve: all year round.

Tel 01445 760254 www.snh.org.uk

14 Ben Nevis Distillery 🍾

Founded in 1825, Ben Nevis is one of the oldest licensed distilleries in Scotland. Along with a tour and tasting, visitors can see an audio-visual presentation.

F3 *Two miles N of Fort William on the A82.*

🅿 ♿ ♿ 🍽 🏛 E 🅰🆅 ♨ £

🕐 Easter–Oct, Mon–Fri, 9am–5pm; Sat, 10am–4pm.
Jul & Aug, closes 6pm; also Sun, 12 noon–4pm.
Oct–Easter, by arrangement.

Tel 01397 700200 www.bennevis.co.uk

BEN NEVIS

Scotland's highest mountain, at 1344 m (4409 ft) is all the more remarkable as its summit, as the crow flies, is only a little over 6 km (four miles) from the sea. It dominates views to the south-east on the approach to Fort William down the Great Glen. 'The Ben' is most often climbed from the path from Achintee Farm, reached from Bridge of Nevis. Time to the summit by a fit walker is likely to be 3½ hours. The stony desert which is the summit plateau gives way to a line of cliffs on the north side, from which deep gullies bite deeply into the summit area. (Take special care in mist.)

Between 1883 and 1904 Ben Nevis was the site of a meteorological observatory. Its ruins can still be seen. During that time, the records show that the summit mean annual rainfall was 399 cm (157 inches) and its mean monthly temperature ½°F below freezing! Thus the top of Ben Nevis is only for fit and well clad walkers and mountaineers.

15 Black Isle Wildlife and Country Park

Animals on site include goats, sheep, llamas, deer, cattle, pigs and rabbits, along with ducks, geese and swans.

J7 *Over the Kessock Bridge, N of Inverness; head NE off A9 towards Munlochy.*

P WC ♿ ☕ ⌂ ⛱ ♿ ££

⏰ Apr–Oct, daily, 10am–5pm.

Tel 01463 731656

16 Bright Water Visitor Centre

A centre telling the story of local landscapes, people and traditions. Daily trips to the wildlife haven on the island of Eilean Ban take visitors to the Stevenson Lighthouse, wildlife hide, sensory garden and Gavin Maxwell Museum (author of *Ring of Bright Water*).

D6 *Kyleakin Pier, at end of Skye Bridge, on A87.*

♿ ⌂ E AV ☀ ⚇ ♿ £

⏰ Apr–Oct, Mon–Sat, 9am–6pm. Times may vary.

Tel 01599 530040   www.eileanban.org

17 Brodie Castle

The family house of the Brodies for over 700 years, Brodie Castle contains unusual plaster ceilings, an art collection, furniture, porcelain and a Victorian kitchen. Visitors can make use of the grounds with woodland walks and an adventure playground and see an impressive display of daffodils in the spring.

K7 *Off A96 between Forres and Nairn.*

P WC ♿ ☕ ⌂ E ⛱ ⚇ ££

⏰ Apr, Jul–Aug, daily, 12 noon–4pm.
    May–Jun & Sept, Sun–Thur, 12 noon–4pm.
    Grounds all year 9.30am–sunset.

Tel 01309 641371   www.nts.org.uk

18 Brora Heritage Centre 🏛

A heritage centre reflecting Brora's past production of coal, bricks, tiles, textiles, malt whisky and salt from the sea. An archaeology exhibition reveals the world of Celtic farmers in Strathbrora, from brochs to township, and a hands-on display contains historical photographs, local artefacts and genealogy. Children can make use of a dinosaur play area.

K10 *Signposted from centre of Brora.*

P WC ♿ ⛪ E AV 🍴 ☕ 🧗 Free

🕐 May–Sept, Mon–Sat, 10.30am–5.30pm.

Tel 01408 622024;

Oct–Apr 01408 633033

CAIRNGORMS

The Cairngorms from the north, that is, from Strathspey, present a long wall of high tops, backlit for much of the day. The trough of the Lairig Ghru, the hill pass joining Speyside with Deeside, is usually conspicuous as the largest gash in this dissected plateau. The Lairig also defines the western Cairngorms, the massif of Braeriach and Cairn Toul, which lie apart from Cairn Gorm proper.

The northern corries, with their steep and rocky headwalls, hold good quantities of snow, hence the development of skiing on Cairn Gorm and the opening of Scotland's only mountain railway *(see p200)*. This takes visitors high on to the fragile environment of the tundra of the summit plateau. However, the deep-sunk Loch Avon, beyond Cairn Gorm itself and one of the most spectacular glacial trenches of the area, retains something of the atmosphere of a hidden mountain fastness.

Aside from the high ground, the edge of the Cairngorms has extensive natural or semi-natural pinewoods – the remnants of the original Caledonian pine forest. Good places to sample the atmosphere of the ancient woods include Abernethy and Rothiemurchus *(see p218)*. The old trees, spaced quite widely apart, and with a distinctive 'understorey' of juniper, blaeberry and heather, are home to a number of Highland bird specialities such as crested tit, crossbill and the (sadly declining) capercaillie. See page 263 for feature on the Cairngorms National Park.

CAITHNESS AND SUTHERLAND

Nowhere else in Scotland is quite like Caithness and Sutherland. Drive from the route-centre of Lairg, say, towards Tongue and, out beyond the geometric blocks of conifer which pattern the bare heath, distant profiles of peaks stand out, grey and blue in the distance. This feeling of openness and rolling space, with far northern hills such as Ben Klibreck or Ben Loyal seeming to change their shape completely as the roads run round them, is typical of the far north. Caithness in particular refines this openness further, notably in the flow country. Here the wet moorland with interlaced lochs supports its own specialised flora and fauna, as well as providing nesting habitat for spectacular bird life such as hen harrier, merlin and short-eared owl. The RSPB reserve at Forsinard (also reachable by train) makes a good starting point for discovering this unique environment.

Further west, the peaks near the seaboard are among the most distinctive anywhere in Scotland. Arkle and Foinaven, with their tumbling quartzite screes, overlook the sugar-loaf shape of Suilven behind Lochinver. This can only be climbed after a long walk-in over an endless table of rocky moorland by the River Kirkaig, Here in the west, notably at Inverpolly, there is a good chance of glimpsing the elusive pine marten, while otters are also comparatively common. Botanists, in particular, enjoy the limestone outcrops around Inchnadamph and the slopes of grey screes of Ben More Assynt, home to a range of uncommon Arctic-alpine species.

19 Cairngorm Mountain Experience

A winter skiing and snowboarding venue, comprising of eight green runs, eight blue, eight red and two black; equipment hire and tuition are available. Other attractions include various walks, one of which is suitable for the disabled, and a centre set 1097 m (3600 ft) above sea level, accessible by a mountain railway.

K5 *SE of Aviemore on ski road, past Loch Morlich.*

P WC ♿ 🍴 ✕ 🚽 E AV 🚌 ⛷ 👥 £ £££

🕐 Winter sports: Dec–Apr, daily. Weather permitting. Railway: all year round, daily; extended evening hours from late Jun–Aug, Thur–Sun.

Tel 01479 861261
www.cairngormmountain.co.uk

20 Cairngorm Reindeer Centre

Britain's only reindeer herd roam freely in their natural environment. Visitors can join the herder on the hillside where the reindeer graze, and feed and stroke the animals. A centre contains Santa's Bothy and reindeer paddocks.

K5 *Six miles E of Aviemore on the B970.*

P 🚽 E AV ⛷ 👥 £ £££

🕐 Visits to the herd:
May–Sept, daily, 11am & 2.30pm.
Oct–Apr, 11am. (Weather permitting)
Closed mid Jan–early Feb.

Tel: 01479 861228
www.reindeer-company.demon.co.uk

21 Cairngorm Sleddog Centre 🏛 ★

The first and only sleddog centre in the UK, set within panoramic views of the Cairngorms. October to April the centre offers visitors a 'Sleddog Experience' which includes a trip with a 12-dog sleddog team through part of the National Park. Museum dedicated to Alexander 'Scotty' Allan, one of the foremost 'mushers', born in Dundee in 1867. All visitors must book in advance.

K5 *Four miles E of Aviemore on the B970.*

P WC E AV 🎿 👥 £££

⊕ Open all year. Kennel tours: daily, at 2.30pm. Trips: Oct–Apr. Weight restrictions apply. No children under 6 years of age. Booking essential.

Tel 07767 270526
www.sled-dogs.co.uk

22 Caledonian Canal Heritage Centre 🏛

Showcases the history of the Caledonian Canal from its conception to present day refurbishment. The centre is located by the banks of the canal, and overlooks an impressive series of locks.

G5 *Canal Side, Fort Augustus.*

🏛 C 🎿 Free

⊕ Spring & autumn, five days, 10am–5pm. Summer, daily, 10am–5pm.

Tel 01320 366493
www.scottishcanals.co.uk

23 Castle & Gardens of Mey 🏰 ❀

The Queen Mother's home in Caithness. She bought the castle in 1952, restored it and developed the gardens that still flourish. It became her ideal holiday home and she went there every year from 1955 until 2001.

L13 *On the A836 six miles W of John o' Groats.*

P WC 🏛 £££

⊕ May–July & mid Aug–end Sept, Sat–Thur, 10.30am–4pm.

Tel 01847 851473
www.castleofmey.org.uk

CALEDONIAN CANAL

Scotland's longest canal, from Inverness to Corpach, near Fort William, covers a distance of 60 miles (96km) and in its day was a monumental undertaking. The Caledonian Canal by the engineer Thomas Telford was conceived as a through-route for ocean-going vessels to avoid the danger of the northern route between the east and west coasts via the Pentland Firth. (More specifically, at the time of the Napoleonic Wars, the navy was seeking a faster way of getting its ships from coast to coast.) The canal route took advantage of the three lochs – Ness, Oich and Lochy – which lie in the fault-line of the Great Glen. Built between 1804 and 1822, advances in ship design and hence size meant it never truly fulfilled its aim. Today its 29 locks and 42 gates are used mostly by recreational cruising traffic, while its towpaths are popular with cyclists and walkers.

24 Cawdor Castle 🏰 ❀

Cawdor, with its fairytale medieval tower and drawbridge, is one of the most romantic castles in the Highlands. Visitors can tour the house and see the sitting-room, dungeon, freshwater well and kitchens, along with a varied collection of paintings, tapestries, furniture and books. The gardens contain five nature trails, mini golf course and putting green.

K7 *Off B9090, five miles S of Nairn.*

P WC ♿ 🍽 ✕ 🏛 ⛩ 👥 🚲 £££

⊕ May–mid Oct, daily, 10am–5.30pm (last admission 5pm).

Tel 01667 404401
www.cawdorcastle.com

25 Clan Cameron Museum 🏛

A museum devoted to the history of the Clan, with displays relating to Bonnie Prince Charlie and the '45 rising, the Queen's Own Cameron Highlanders, and the Commando training at Achnacarry during the Second World War.

F4   *16 miles N of Fort William on B8004/B8005.*

P �🚻 ⛪ E ♿ £

🕐 Apr–mid Oct, 1.30–5pm.
   Jul–Aug, 11am–5pm; other times on request.

Tel 01397 712090
www.clan-cameron.org

26 Clan Gunn Heritage Centre and Museum 🏛

Studies the history of Clan Gunn, one of Scotland's oldest clans.

L11   *Latheron on A9, S of Wick.*

P �🚻 ⛪ E AV ♿ £

🕐 Jun–Sept, daily, Mon–Sat, 11am–1pm & 2–4pm.

Tel 01593 721325

27 Clan Macpherson Museum 🏛

Houses a range of relics and memorabilia relating to the Macpherson clan.

J4   *Newtonmore main street, on A86, off A9.*

P �🚻 ♿ ⛪ E AV ♿ Free

🕐 Apr–Oct, Mon–Sat, 10am–5pm;
   Sun, 2–5pm.

Tel 01540 673332   www.clan-macpherson.org

28 Clansman Centre 🏛

A reconstructed turf house in which an actor (wearing an authentic clansman's costume) explains how Highland families lived, ate and survived in the seventeenth century. An armoury features swords, sgians, targes, axes and clothing.

G5   *Fort Augustus, adjacent to A82 and Caledonian Canal.*

E ⛪ ⛺ ☀ ♿ £

🕐 Summer, daily, 10am–6pm.
   Winter, reduced hours.
   Please telephone to confirm times.

Tel 01320 366444/07798 761456
www.scottish-swords.com

29 Clynelish Distillery 🍾

Admission includes a guided tour, dram and discount voucher redeemable at the distillery shop.

K10   *Off A9, one mile NW of Brora.*

P ⚧ ⛪ ⛺ ♿ ££

🕐 Easter–Sept, Mon–Fri, 10am–5pm.
   Oct, Mon–Fri, 11am–4pm.
   Nov–Easter, by appointment.

Tel 01408 623000
www.highlandescape.com

30 Colbost Croft Museum 🏛

Located in a black house, the museum shows how people lived back in the eighteenth century; also on show is a replica whisky still.

B7   *On B884, four miles from village of Dunvegan, Skye.*

P E £

🕐 Apr–Oct, daily, 10am–6pm.

Tel 01470 521296

31 Corrieshalloch Gorge 🌲 ☀

This dramatic box canyon is 61 m (200 ft) deep, with the river falling some 46 m (150 ft) over the Falls of Measach. Can be viewed from a suspension bridge or platform downstream.

F8   *Braemore, on A835, 12 miles SE of Ullapool.*

☀ £

🕐 Open access.

Tel 01445 781200
www.nts.org.uk

32 Craig Highland Farm

A rare breeds conservation centre set on a 17 acre holding, with a variety of domestic animals, fowl and birds of prey, including sheep, poultry, rabbits, pigs, llama, goats, geese and ducks. Visitors can make use of a beach, and walk across a coral strand to a heron sanctuary at low tide.

E6   *On Plockton/Achmore road, on shores of Loch Carron.*

P ⚧ E ☀ 🧑 £

🕐 Easter–Oct, daily, 10am–dusk.

Tel 01599 544205
www.geocities.com/t_heaviside

33 Creag Meagaidh National Nature Reserve

Creag Meagaidh is situated along the north-west edge of Loch Laggan and is an ideal area for hill walking. The crags and cliffs, characteristic of the area, are a dramatic geological feature of the reserve, while the moorland is dominated by heather that secretes the reserve's population of red grouse; other wildlife includes ptarmigan and dotterel.

H4 On A96, ten miles W of Laggan.

P E ☀ ⚙ Free

☺ Open access. No dogs allowed.

Tel 01528 544265   www.snh.org.uk

34 Cromarty Courthouse Museum

Focuses on Cromarty's history, with a reconstructed trial in the eighteenth century courtroom, children's costumes, prison cells, video, artefacts and an audio tour of the old town.

J8 Cromarty, on A832, off A9, 22 miles NE of Inverness.

⛩ E AV ⚙ £

☺ Apr–Oct, daily, 10am–5pm.

Tel 01381 600418
www.cromarty-courthouse.org.uk

35 Culloden Battlefield

Site of the last pitched battle fought in Scotland, when the Jacobites were defeated by the Duke of Cumberland and Government forces in April 1746. Turf and stone dykes, used during the fighting, have been rebuilt round the battle area, and there are longterm plans to return the site to its original state. A cottage which stood on the site as fighting went on all around has been restored and opened up to the public who can also see clan graves, the Well of the Dead, a memorial cairn and a visitor centre featuring an exhibition and battle sampler.

J7 Five miles E of Inverness on B9006.

P WC ♿ ⬛ ✕ ⛩ E AV ⚙ ⚙ ££

☺ Site open all year, daily. Visitor Centre: Feb, Nov–Dec, daily, 11am–4pm (closed 24, 25 & 26 Dec). Mar, daily,10am–4pm. Apr–May & Sept–Oct, daily, 9am–5.30pm. Jun–Aug, daily, 9pm–6pm.

Tel 01463 790607   www.nts.org.uk

36 Dalwhinnie Distillery Visitors Centre

Visitors can see whisky being produced in this hundred-year-old distillery which, set in the central Highlands, is also Scotland's 'highest' distillery.

J4 Off A9 at A889; head NW for two miles.

P WC ⛩ E ☀ ⚙ ££

☺ Jan–Mar, Mon–Fri, 1–4pm. Apr–May, Mon–Fri, 9.30am–5pm. Jun–Sept, also Sat. Jul–Aug, also Sun, 12.30–4pm. Oct, Mon–Sat, 11am–4pm.

Tel 01540 672219

37 Dingwall Museum

A small town museum housing a smiddy and old style kitchen, a military room featuring records and medals of the Fourth Seaforth Highlanders and artefacts relating to Fighting Mac, Major General Sir Hector MacDonald. There are occasional special exhibitions and a flower-filled courtyard.

H7 High Street, Dingwall town centre.

P ⛩ E AV ⌐ £

☺ Mid-May–Sept, Mon–Sat, 10am–5pm.

Tel 01349 865366

Culloden Battlefield

38 Dolphins and Seals of the Moray Firth 🏛

A chance to observe dolphins in their natural habitat and listen to them through an underwater microphone system. The visitor centre holds an exhibition with interactives and video footage of local dolphins. Dolphins can also occasionally be seen from Chanonry Point, and from organised boat trips on the Firth (sightings not guaranteed).

J7 *Centre: cross Kessock Bridge northbound, turning off first left; centre located beside Tourist Information car park.*

🅿 ⓦ ♿ 🚻 E ⛱ ♒ 🚶

☻ Centre: Apr–Oct, daily, 10am–5pm. Boat trips: times vary; please contact individual companies for details.

Centre: Tel 01463 731866
Boat trips: Dolphin Ecosse (Cromarty) Tel 01381 600323;
Dolphin Trips (Avoch) Tel 01381 622383;
Moray Firth Cruises (Inverness harbour) Tel 01463 717900

39 Dornoch Cathedral ✚

Founded in 1224 by St Gilbert, the first recorded service was held here in 1239. The cathedral was subsequently destroyed by fire in 1570 and partly restored in the 16th century. The work was finally finished in the 20th century and it now contains interesting stained glass windows.

J9 *Dornoch town centre.*

Free

☻ All year round. Services: Sun, 11am
Tel 01862 810357

40 Dounreay Visitor Centre 🏛

Visitors can learn about the past, present and future of Dounreay Nuclear Power Plant via an exhibition.

K13 *From Thurso on the A836, signposted at Dounreay.*

🅿 ⓦ ♨ E ⛱ Free

☻ May–Oct, daily, 10am–4pm.
Tel 01847 802572   www.ukaea.org.uk

41 Duncansby Head

A line of cliffs and rock stacks with colonies of seabirds in season such as guillemots, kittiwakes and puffins. Clifftop walks require particular care.

Dunvegan Castle

M13 *Two miles E of John O'Groats, off A836/A9.*

♒ Free

☻ Open access. Tel 01955 611448

42 Dunnett Head 🏊

Dunnett Head is the northernmost point of the Scottish mainland, a broad sandstone promontory standing 127 m (417 ft) high, with a lighthouse and views across the Pentland Firth to Orkney. An information point advises visitors on walks and the natural history of the area.

L13 *On the B855, off the A832, 10 miles E of Thurso.*

🅿 ♨ ♒ Free

☻ Open Access. Information point: Apr–Jun & Sept, Thur–Tue, 11am–5pm. Jul & Aug, daily, 11am–5pm.

Tel 01847 851991   www.dunnethead.com

43 Dunrobin Castle and Gardens 🏰 ✿ 🏛

Dunrobin, the home of Clan Sutherland, was established in the thirteenth century, but was altered in the nineteenth century in the style of a chateau. Visitors can see a number of rooms, some of which were designed by Sir Robert Lorimer, and admire the fine furniture, silver, tapestries, family portraits and memorabilia on display. Also of interest are the formal gardens and an eccentric museum which houses Pictish stones and animal trophies. Falconry displays daily.

K9 *Ten miles N of Dornoch on the A9.*

🅿 ⓦ ♨ 🚻 E ♒ ⛱ 🚶 £££

☻ Apr, May–mid Oct, Mon–Sat, 10.30am–4.30pm; Sun, 12 noon–4.30pm. Jun–Sep, daily, 10.30am–5.30pm

Tel 01408 633177   www.highlandescape.com

44 Dunvegan Castle

Dunvegan has been the seat of the MacLeods for 800 years, and contains fine paintings, antiques, rare books and relics relating to Bonnie Prince Charlie and Flora MacDonald. Other features include a clan exhibition, extensive gardens, Dunvegan Castle Pedigree Highland Cattle Fold and boat trips to Dunvegan seal colony.

B7 *E side of Loch Dunvegan, on A850, Skye.*

P WC ♥ ✕ ⊞ E AV ☴ ☼ ☥ ⊞ £££

🕐 Mid Mar–end Oct, daily, 10am–5.30pm (last entrance 5pm).
Nov–mid Mar, castle and gardens only, daily, 11am–4pm (last entrance 3.30pm).

Tel 01470 521206
www.dunvegancastle.com

45 Eilean Donan Castle

Eilean Donan, on an islet in Loch Duich overlooking Skye, is one of the most famous and photographed castles in Scotland. Constructed in the thirteenth century, with later additions, it was virtually destroyed during the eighteenth century Jacobite rising, before being completely rebuilt to its present state in the 1930s. Visitors can cross a causeway and see various rooms including a billeting room, banqueting hall, bedrooms, kitchen and the great hall which contains furniture, portraits and Jacobite relics.

E6 *Dornie, on the A87, nine miles from Skye Bridge.*

P WC ♿ ♥ ⊞ E ☼ ☥ ⊞ ££

🕐 Daily, mid Mar–end Mar, 10am–3.30pm. Apr–Oct, 10am–5.30pm. Beg Nov–mid Mar, 10am–3.30pm.

Tel 01599 555202   www.eileandonancastle.com

46 Falls of Shin

A forestry area with woodland walks, playpark and viewing platforms where visitors can witness wild salmon leap up the waterfalls of the River Shin in season. A centre offers facilities, audio-visual presentation and exhibition.

H9 *Between Lairg and Bonar Bridge on the B837.*

P WC ♿ ♥ ⊞ E AV ☴ ☼ ☥ ⊞ Free

🕐 Apr–Oct, daily, 9.30am–6pm.
Nov–Mar, 10am–5pm; Open all year.

Tel 01549 402231   www.fallsofshin.co.uk

Eilean Donan Castle

Fort George

47 Farigaig Information Centre

The centre is situated amongst copses of large trees, adjacent to a car park, complete with picnic areas. The nearby Farigaig Forest contains a number of waymarked trails. Two routes – the Farigaig walk and the river walk – have been officially sanctioned by the Forestry Commission.

H6 *Off B852, 18 miles SW of Inverness, near Inverfarigaig.*

P WC ﬅ ⚲ ⚘ ⚶ Free

⊕ Apr–Oct, daily, 9am–5pm.

Tel 01320 366322   www.forestry.gov.uk

48 Ferrycroft Countryside Centre

A centre providing information on the history and natural environment of the area, with an archaeological trail up Ord Hill. Internet access.

H10 *Head N along B864, joining A839 to Lairg. Follow the signs.*

P WC ﬅ ⚑ ⚓ E AV ⚲ ⚘ ⚶ Free

⊕ Apr–Jun & Sep–Oct, daily, 10am–5pm; Jun–Aug, Mon–Sat, 9am–6pm; Sun, 10am–6pm.

Tel 01549 402160   www.lairghighlands.org.uk

49 Fort George

This complete eighteenth century artillery fortification, surrounded by sea on three sides, was used by George II's army before being used as a barracks (still in use today). Remarkably well preserved, it has been opened up to the public, and now contains reconstructed barrack rooms from different eras, weaponry and the regimental museum of the Queen's Own Highlanders.

J7 *Ardersier, on the B9006, ten miles NE of Inverness.*

P WC ﬅ ✕ ⚓ E AV ⚲ ⚘ £££

⊕ Apr–Sept, daily, 9.30am–6.30pm. Oct–Mar, daily, 9.30am–4.30pm; (last entry 45 mins before closing).

Tel 01667 460232   www.historic-scotland.gov.uk

50 Gairloch Heritage Museum

Displays in this heritage centre include a typical thatched croft house interior, village shop, classroom and a large lighthouse lens. Visitors can also enjoy hands-on activities, demonstrations, talks and a programme of changing exhibitions.

D8 *Adjacent to the Tourist Office at main road junction of A832/B8021, Gairloch.*

P ✕ ⚓ E £

⊕ Apr–Sept, Mon–Sat, 10am–5pm. Oct, Mon–Fri, 10am–1.30pm.

Tel 01445 712287 www.gairlochheritagemuseum.org.uk

51 Giant Macaskill Museum

A museum telling the story of Giant Macaskill, the tallest Scotsman, who was born in 1825 and grew to a height of 2.2 m (7.9 ft).

B7 *Dunvegan village centre, on A850, Skye.*

P WC E £

⊕ Apr–Oct, daily, 10am–6pm.

Tel 01470 521296

52 Glen Nevis Visitor Centre ★

Houses displays and an audio-visual presentation on Ben Nevis *(see p198)* and Glen Nevis, a mountainous area offering a number of walking and cycling opportunities. Rangers are on hand to advise on the locality and weather conditions.

F3 *At the foot of Glen Nevis, off the A82 Fort William road.*

P WC E AV Free

Apr-Oct, daily, 9am–5pm.

Tel 01397 705922
www.highland.gov.uk

53 Glen Ord Distillery

Visitors can tour the distillery and learn the secrets of distilling, along with the history of the Black Isle and its people over the centuries.

H7 *Muir of Ord, off A832, fifteen miles W of Inverness.*

P WC E ££

Nov–Feb, Wed–Fri, 11.30am–3pm.
Mar–Jun, Mon–Fri, 10am–5pm.
Jul–Sept, Mon–Sat 10am–5pm; Sun, 12 noon–4pm.
Oct, Mon–Fri, 11am–4pm.
Last guided tour 1 hour before closing.

Tel 01463 872004

54 Glencoe and Dalness

One of the most dramatic landscapes in Scotland, famous for its walking/climbing potential and the massacre of 1692, when 38 of the MacDonald Clan were killed on the orders of King William. A visitor centre provides information on the glen's history, local mountaineering and recommended walking routes. (*See also p208*)

P E AV £

F2 *Seventeen miles S of Fort William off A82.*

Site: open access. Visitor centre: Mar, daily, 10am–4pm. Apr-Aug, daily, 9.30am–5.30pm. Sept–Oct, daily, 10am–5pm. Nov–Feb, Thur–Sun, 10am–4pm (last admission half an hour before closing).

Tel 01855 811307/729 www.nts.org.uk

55 Glencoe and North Lorn Folk Museum

Three heather thatched buildings house exhibitions, costumes, tools, weapons and cooking utensils.

F2 *Glencoe village, two miles E of Ballachulish on A82.*

E £

Easter-Sept, Mon-Sat, 10am–5.30pm.

Tel 01855 811314

GLEN AFFRIC

Truly one of Scotland's grandest glens, Glen Affric is noted for its wildlife, autumn colour and access to excellent high-level walking. Its upper reaches are not accessible by the private motorist, though today's track and path through the glen to the west coast at Loch Duich was once the main drove road between Skye and Dingwall.
For the less active, there are short walks to places such as the Dog Falls on the River Affric, easily accessible from the road. The end of the public road, however, is the starting point for major all-day expeditions, including the ascent of the twin Munros Carn Eighe and Mam Sodhail, the highest points north of the Great Glen.

56 Glencoe Ski Centre

Glencoe, the first of Scotland's ski centres to be established, covers an area of around 200 acres. It offers seven lifts, two of which are chairlifts, and 19 runs comprising four green, six blue, seven red and two black. The longest run stretches for a full mile.

G2 *Twenty-six miles S of Fort William on the A82.*

P WC ££

Dec–Apr, daily, 9.30am–4pm. Weather permitting.

Tel 01855 851226 www.ski-glencoe.co.uk

GLENCOE

The sentinel mountain of Buachaille Etive Mor, the great herdsman of Etive, guards the portals of Glencoe on the edge of Rannoch Moor. The glen runs down to the salt water of Loch Leven on the western seaboard. The north side of Glencoe is bounded for 2.5 km (1.5 miles) by the ridge of Aonach Eagach, perhaps the very narrowest on the Scottish mainland. Dizzying drops and a few heart-stopping steps and scrambles make this rocky spine no place for the beginner.

On the south side, Bidean nam Bian, the highest point in Argyll, sends out three long spurs. These, the Three Sisters, loom above the road and block most views of Bidean itself, though it can be glimpsed from Loch Achtriochtan, on the floor of the glen. As on the north side, this is spectacular country, offering challenges for walkers and rock climbers alike. Even from road level, there is a strong sense of endless soaring slopes and a feeling of mountain-ringed containment.

There were other and larger massacres in Scotland's clan story but this setting of wild and silent peaks gathered round the site of a terrible happening lends an extra dimension to Glencoe. The Massacre of Glencoe in February 1692 reverberated around Scotland because it represented murder under trust. It was not just two clans settling a grudge – though the MacDonalds of Glencoe and the Campbells were certainly enemies – but an act of government – approved treachery.

The Campbells were government militia who had sought shelter with the Glencoe MacDonalds. Their host, a minor chief called Alisdair MacDonald, had been a few days late in taking an oath of allegiance to the government and this was enough to seal his clan's fate. The Secretary of State, Sir John Dalrymple of Stair, acting for the king, gave written orders to Captain Robert Campbell of Glenlyon, commanding the troops. The instructions included the words '.... and I hope the soldiers will not trouble the government with prisoners....'

However, the massacre was bungled and several MacDonalds escaped to tell the tale, still remembered today and just one of the themes of the National Trust for Scotland's visitor centre in the glen.

(See page 207)

57 Glendale Toy Museum

A variety of new and old toys are on display, from Barbie and Star Wars, to bears, dolls, trains and games.

A7 *Seven miles from Dunvegan on the Glendale visitor route, Skye.*

P WC 🏛 E ☀ £

⊕ All year round.
Mon–Sat, 10am–6pm.

Tel: 01470 511240   www.toy-museum.co.uk

58 Glenelg Brochs 🄱 🏛

Dun Telve and Dun Troddan are well preserved Iron Age broch towers which stand at over 3 m (10 ft) in height.

E5 *Leave A87 at Shielbridge on to Glenelg unclassified road.*

Free

⊕ Open access.

Tel 01667 460232   www.historic-scotland.gov.uk

59 Glenfinnan Monument ★

Situated at the head of Loch Shiel, the monument was erected in 1815 in tribute to the clansmen who fought and died in the cause of Prince Charles Edward Stuart. The raising of the Standard took place here in 1745 before the Battle of Culloden, the last doomed attempt to reinstate the exiled Stuarts to the throne. A visitor centre houses an exhibition and commentary on the Jacobite campaign.

E3 *On A830, 18 miles W of Fort William.*

P WC ♿ 🍴 🏛 E AV ☀ 🏕 🏕 £

⊕ Site: all year round, daily.
Visitor Centre, monument, shop and snack bar:
Apr–Oct, daily, 10am–5pm. Jul–Aug, daily,
9.30am–5.30pm. Nov, Sat–Sun, 10am–4pm.

Tel 01397 722250   www.nts.org.uk

60 Glenfinnan Station Museum

Relates the history of this rural railway line, with a restored booking office and changing photographic exhibition.

E3 *Glenfinnan Station, off A830.*

P WC ♿ 🍴 🏛 E £

⊕ Jun–Sept, daily, 9.30am–4.30pm.

Tel 01397 722295
www.road-to-the-isles.org.uk/glenfinnan-station

61 Glengarry Visitor Centre

The visitor centre houses an exhibition which tells the story of the MacDonells of Glengarry, the Glengarry emigrations to North America and the Ellice family who built the 'estate village' after the MacDonells left. The centre also acts as a useful information point for the visitors, researchers and the many walkers who explore this area of the Highlands.

G4 *On the A87, seven miles SW of Fort Augustus, in a log cabin next to the Invergarry Hotel.*

P WC ♿ 🍴 ✕ 🏛 E 🏕 ☀ 🦌 🏕 £

⊕ Easter–Sept, daily, 10.30am–4.30pm.

Tel: 01809 501424   www.glengarry.net

62 Glenmorangie Distillery 🍶

Visitors can tour the distillery and learn the history of one of Scotland's most popular whiskies.

J8 *Half a mile N of Tain on A9.*

P WC ♿ 🏛 E AV 🏕 £

⊕ All year round, Mon–Fri, 9am–5pm
(last tour 3.30pm). Jun–Aug, also Sat, 10am–4pm;
Sun, 12 noon–4pm (last tour 2.30pm).
Closed Christmas & New Year.

Tel 01862 892477   www.glenmorangie.com

63 Glenmore Forest Park

Extensive forests, located at the foothills of the Cairngorm National Nature Reserve, offer walking and cycling routes, lochside activities, bird watching and a ranger service. A visitor centre provides facilities and shows an audio-visual presentation relating to the area.

L5 *Seven miles from Aviemore on the ski road.*

🅿 🆆 ♿ 🍴 🏛 E 🆅 🎍 🚶 🚾 Free

🕓 Forest park: open access.
Visitor centre: all year round, daily, 9am–5pm.

Tel 01479 861220

64 Grantown-on-Spey Museum

A permanent exhibition tells the story of Grantown-on-Spey, Sir James Grant's 'planned' town, and brings to life its history using an audio-visual presentation and displays.

L6 *Off the Square, Grantown-on-Spey, on A95/A939.*

🅿 🆆 ♿ 🏛 E 🆅 🎍 £

🕓 Mar–Dec, Mon–Fri, 10am–4pm.

Tel 01479 872478   www.grantownmuseum.co.uk

65 Groam House Museum 🏛

A collection of local Pictish sculpture including a symbol-bearing cross-slab carved in the late eighth to early ninth century. Visitors can also see original Celtic artwork by artist George Bain, temporary exhibitions and videos.

J7 *Rosemarkie, 15 miles NE of Inverness on A832.*

🅿 ♿ 🏛 E 🆅 🚾 Free

🕓 Apr, Sat–Sun, 2–4pm.
May–Oct, Mon–Sat, 10am–5pm;
Sun, 2–4.30pm.
Nov–mid Dec, Sat–Sun, 2–4pm.

Tel 01381 620961

66 Handa Island Wildlife Reserve 🐦 🛶

An uninhabited island with large numbers of seabirds such as puffins, razorbills, kittiwakes and guillemots. There are views from a number of places on the island's circular trail, particularly the northern cliffs. Seals and otters are also regular visitors to the island. Access to the reserve is by boat from Tarbet.

F12 *Travel by ferry from Tarbet,
three miles NW of Scourie.*

🅿 🎍 🚶 £££

🕓 Mid Apr–end Aug, Mon–Sat, ferry runs from 9.30am–2.30pm, and last ferry returns 5pm. Need at least 2–3 hours on the island.

Tel 01463 714746   www.swt.org.uk

67 Highland Folk Museum (1)

Located on sites in Kingussie and Newtonmore (2.5 miles apart), the museum looks at 300 years of Highland social history. The Kingussie collection comprises domestic objects, furniture and farming implements, and features a blackhouse clack mill and salmon smoke-house. Newtonmore houses an eighteenth century farming township with furnished turf houses, an early twentieth century school, a cooking range, clockmaker's shop, joiner's workshop and working croft.

J4 *Kingussie, off A9, on A86.*

🅿 🆆 🏛 E 🎍

🕓 Apr–Aug, Mon–Sat, 9.30am–5pm.
Sept–Oct, Mon–Fri, 9.30am–4pm.

Tel 01540 661307   www.highlandfolk.com

Highland Folk Museum (2) 🏛

J4 *Newtonmore, off A9, on A86.*

🅿 🆆 🍴 🏛 E 🆅 🎍 ££

🕓 Apr–Aug, daily, 10.30am–5.30pm.
Sept–Oct, Mon–Fri, 11am–4.30pm.

Tel 01540 661307   www.highlandfolk.com

68 Highland Museum of Childhood

Located in a restored Victorian Station, the museum relates the history of growing up in the Highlands with photographs, a video, displays, plus doll, toy and costume collections. Children's activities include quizzes, a dressing-up box and toys to play with.

H7 *Strathpeffer, five miles W of Dingwall on A834.*

🅿 🆆 ♿ 🍴 🏛 E 🆅 🎍 🚾 £

🕓 Apr–Oct, Mon–Sat, 10am–5pm. Jul–Aug, Mon–Fri, 10am–7pm; Sat, 10am–5pm; Sun, 2–5pm.

Tel 01997 421031
www.highlandmuseumofchildhood.org.uk

69 Highland Wildlife Park 🐗

Houses a number of Scottish animals in a scenic Highland setting, with information on creatures who roamed the earth hundreds of years ago. A safari area contains herds of red and roe deer, bison, wild horses and Highland cattle, plus a 'wolf territory'.

J4 *On B9152, seven miles S of Aviemore.*

🅿 🆆🅲 ♿ ☕ 🏛 E 🍴 ☀ 🐾 🎫 £££

🕐 Apr–Oct, daily, 10am–6pm.
June–Aug, 10am–7pm. Nov–Mar, 10am–4pm.
Last entry 2 hours before closing.

Tel 01540 651270   www.kincraig.com/wildlife

70 Highland Wineries

A winery making country wines and liqueurs along with marmalades, jellies and sauces. Visitors can tour the winery, sample products and see an audio-visual show on harvesting and wine making.

H6 *Moniack Castle, seven miles W of Inverness on A862.*

🅿 🆆🅲 🏛 🆅 🍴 🎫 £

🕐 Mar–Oct, Mon-Sat, 10am–5pm.
Nov–Feb, Mon-Sat, 11am–4pm.

Tel 01463 831283   www.moniackcastle.co.uk

71 Historylinks

A museum dedicated to the history and development of Dornoch, from the Dornoch Light Railway and the Meikle Ferry Disaster, to Skibo Castle and Dornoch Cathedral. Activities and presentations suitable for all the family.

🅿 🆆🅲 ♿ 🏛 E 🆅 £

J9 *Meadows Road, near the Cathedral.*

🕐 May–Sept, Mon-Sat, 10am–4pm.

Tel 01862 811275   www.visitdornoch.com

72 Hugh Miller's Cottage

This 300-year-old furnished cottage was the birthplace of Hugh Miller, the pioneering naturalist, geologist, stonemason and journalist. Contents include his large fossil collection.

J8 *Cromarty, on A832, 22 miles NE of Inverness.*

E £

🕐 Good Fri–Sept, daily, 12 noon–5pm.
Oct, Sun–Wed, 12 noon–5pm.

Tel 01381 600245   www.nts.org.uk

73 Inverewe Garden

Located on a peninsula by Loch Ewe, these gardens are aided by the warm Gulf Stream, thus allowing a variety of exotic plants to flourish. Himalayan rhododendrons, Tasmanian eucalyptus plus plants from Chile, South Africa and New Zealand are all grown here, along with the national collection of Olearia.

E8 *Six miles NE of Gairloch, by Poolewe on A832.*

🅿 ♿ ✕ 🏛 🐾 ££

🕐 Garden: mid Apr–Oct, daily, 9.30am–9pm.
Nov–Mar, daily, 9.30am–4pm.
Visitor centre: mid Apr-Sept, daily, 9.30am–5pm.
Oct, 9.30am–4pm.

Tel 01445 781200   www.nts.org.uk

74 Inverlochy Castle

Inverlochy, with its square outer walls and round corner towers, is one of Scotland's earliest stone castles, and is particularly well preserved.

F3 *Off the A82, two miles NE of Fort William.*

🅿 Free

🕐 Open access.

Tel 0131 668 8800   www.historic-scotland.gov.uk

75 Inverness Floral Hall and Visitor Centre

The Floral Hall holds a collection of subtropical plants in a climatically controlled environment. Along with a cactus house, are watercourses, fountains and ponds with tropical fish, plus occasional exhibitions by local artists.

J7 *Inverness Aquadome complex, Bught Lane, W of Inverness city centre.*

🅿 🆆🅲 ♿ ☕ £

🕐 Apr–Oct, daily, 10am–5pm.
Nov–Mar, 10am–4pm.
Last admission 30 mins before closing.

Tel 01463 222755

76 Inverness Museum and Art Gallery

Various displays look at the social and natural history of the Highlands, with a full programme of temporary exhibitions and events. The permanent collection contains weaponry, musical instruments, costumes and Jacobite memorabilia.

J7 *Castle Wynd, by the river, Inverness city centre.*

🆆🅲 ♿ ☕ 🏛 E 🎫 Free

🕐 All year round, Mon-Sat, 9am–5pm.

Tel 01463 237114   www.highland.gov.uk

77 Jacobite Cruises ★

Jacobite offer a range of themed cruises and tours on Loch Ness and along the Caledonian Canal. There are audio commentaries from experienced guides on each sailing, and highlights of the cruises include Urquhart Castle and the Loch Ness 2000 Exhibition. Wider tours of the area can also combine a cruise and coach trip. Departure points are located in Inverness and at Clansman Harbour on Loch Ness.

H6 *Off the A82 at Tomnahurich Bridge, 1.5 miles W of Inverness city centre.*

P WC & ☕ ♨ ✲ 🅿 £££

⊕ All year round; departures throughout the day. Telephone or see website for details.

Tel 01463 233999   www.jacobite.co.uk

78 Jacobite Steam Train 🚂

The Jacobite steam train runs the West Highland Line from Fort William, at the foot of Ben Nevis, to the port of Mallaig. Highlights of the journey include a short stop at the restored station of Glenfinnan *(see p209)*, and the journey over Glenfinnan Viaduct, an impressive structure with 21 arches, by the head of Loch Shiel.

F3 *Leaves from Fort William, on A82.*
C4 *Leaves from Mallaig.*

P WC ☕ ♨ ✲ 🅿 ££

⊕ Jun–Oct, Mon–Fri.
End Jul–Aug, also Sun.
Please telephone for timetable information.

Tel 01463 239026   www.steamtrain.info

79 Kerrachar Gardens ✿

Gardens on the shores of Loch a Chairn Bhain containing a range of herbaceous perennials and shrubs, plus plants for sale. Access is via a boat trip from Kylesku.

££

F11 *Sailings from slipway at Kylesku on W coast of Sutherland.*

⊕ Boat sails mid May–mid Sept, Tue, Thur & Sun, 1pm. Additional sailing 1st Sat of each month.

Tel 01571 833288   www.kerrachar.co.uk

KINTAIL

The name of this superb mountain area is from the Gaelic *cean da shaill* meaning head of two seas – those being Loch Long and the better-known Loch Duich whose waters lap the islet on which the well-known Scottish icon of Eilean Donan Castle stands *(see p205)*. The best known mountains amongst this magnificent choice of Munros are the unmistakable Five Sisters of Kintail, at the seaward end of the area. They give a long day's traverse, best done from east to west to enjoy the seaward view.
The National Trust for Scotland looks after the Kintail Estate *(see p213)* which takes in not only the Five Sisters but also the Falls of Glomach. The 112 m (370 ft) drop makes them one of the highest in Britain – well worth the five mile walk from the car park at Dorusduain.

Inverpolly, Wester Ross

80 Kinlochlaich House Garden ❀

A garden plant centre with walled and ornamental gardens, and a woodland walk.

E2 *On A828 between Oban and Fort William; entrance beside Appin police station.*

🅿 ♿ ·🚶 ♿ £

🕐 Apr–mid Oct, Mon–Sat, 9.30am–5.30pm;
Sun, 10.30am–5.30pm.
Mid Oct–Mar, Mon–Sat, 9am–dusk.

Tel 01631 730342 www.kinlochlaich-house.co.uk

81 Kintail and Morvich 🐾 ⚓ ✂

This mountainous area covers the Falls of Glomach and the Five Sisters of Kintail which lie at the head of Loch Duich and make up some of the finest mountain scenery in the country. The western slopes of Sgurr Fhuaran, the highest of the Five Sisters, are reputedly the longest continuous grass slope in the Highlands. The best access to the mountains is via Morvich Farm and its unmanned countryside centre. The Battle of Glen Shiel was fought in 1719 about five miles E of the village, by the main road.

E5 *Sixteen miles E of Kyle of Lochalsh, off A87.*

🚶 🚶 £

🕐 Estate: all year round, daily.
Countryside centre: Apr–Sept, daily, 9am–10pm.

Tel 01599 511231
www.nts.org.uk

82 Knockan Crag Visitor Centre

Knockan Crag is a site of geological importance, providing many clues as to how the landscape of Scotland was formed. Visitors can learn the history of the area in the interpretation centre and enjoy one of two circular walks, designed for a range of abilities, with impressive views across Inverpolly National Nature Reserve.

F10 *On the A835, 13 miles N of Ullapool.*

🅿 ♿ ♿ E 🪑 🚶 🚶 Free

🕐 Open access.

Tel 01854 613418
www.knockan-crag.co.uk

KNOYDART

Lying between Lochs Hourn and Nevis on the western seaboard, the Rough Bounds of Knoydart are sometimes described as the most remote part of the British mainland. Certainly, the local pub at Inverie (the only village) serving the area is 29 km (18 miles) from the nearest public road by land! The raising of Loch Quoich with a hydro-electric scheme made access more difficult from the west via Glen Garry. Most visitors come by boat from Mallaig, though there is also a track in from Barrisdale on Loch Hourn.

Famed for its peerless wild country and choice of Munros, including Ladhar Beinn (1019 m, 3343 ft), Scotland's most westerly, Knoydart is also associated with many of the issues of land ownership in Scotland. It was the scene of a 'land-grab' in 1948 when war veterans took to the land and were successfully evicted by court action taken by the then owner Lord Brocket.

83 Kyle Station Visitor Centre 🚂 🏛

Visitors can leave here for a day trip on one of Scotland's most beautiful coastal rail lines round the shores of Loch Carron via Plockton and Strathcarron. A museum houses information on local rail and maritime history.

D6 *Railway Station, Kyle of Lochalsh, on A87 by the Skye Bridge.*

🅿 ♿ ✕ 🏛 E 📷 🎏 🎫 £

🕐 Museum: Mar–Nov, Mon–Sat, 11am–5pm.
Trains: please contact National Railway Enquiries for timetable information.

Station: Tel 01599 534824.
National Railway Enquiries: 08457 484950

84 Kylerhea Otter Haven

Kylerhea Otter Haven is a hide ideally situated for viewing otters and other species of coastal wildlife. From the car park, there are views across to the Kintail mountains and the Kylerhea narrows between Skye and the mainland. During the summer, the hide is manned by a warden who will answer questions.

D5 *Summer: take the ferry from Glenelg to Kylerhea. Winter: from A850 on Skye, four miles W of the Skye Bridge, follow the road to Kylerhea.*

🅿 🚻 🎏 🎋 🚶 Free

🕐 Summer, daily, 9.30am–9.30pm.
Winter, daily, 9.30am–dusk.

Tel 01320 366322   www.forestry.gov.uk

85 Landmark Forest Heritage Park

Activities include water raft roller coaster rides, trails, timber viewing tower, forest maze and an extensive adventure play area; visitors can also see a working steam-powered sawmill.

K5 *Carrbridge, on B9153, off A95, N of Aviemore.*

🅿 🚻 ♿ ☕ ✕ 🏛 E 🎏 🎋 🚶 🎫 £££

🕐 Nov–Mar, Sept & Oct, daily, 10am–5pm.
Apr–mid Jul, 10am–6pm. Mid Jul–Aug, 10am–7pm (last admission one hour before closing).

Tel 0800 731 3446   www.landmark-centre.co.uk

86 Linnhe Marine Watersports ⚓

Watersports centre with yacht moorings, windsurfing, dinghies, motor boat hire and seal trips. A riding and trekking centre can be found at the same location.

E2 *On A828, 20 miles N of Oban.*

🅿 🚻 ♿ ☕ 🎋 🎏 🚶 Free

🕐 May–Sept, daily, 9am–6pm.

Tel 07721 503981

87 Loch Fleet Wildlife Reserve

Situated amongst the sand dunes and coastal heath, the reserve is an ideal location to watch seals, terns and waders in their natural environment; also features pinewoods and a number of unusual plants.

K10 *By the A9, three miles N of Golspie.*

🅿 🎋 🚶

🕐 Open access.

Tel 01408 633602   www.snh.org.uk

Loch Garten, Strathspey

88 Loch Garten Osprey Centre

The centre overlooks the nest site of the famous Loch Garten ospreys. The birds can be seen at close quarters at their nest through binoculars, telescopes, and live CCTV camera footage. Ospreys arrive in early April, hatch in late May, with the young on view throughout June, July and August, before migrating in late August.

K5 *Off B970, signposted from A9 at Aviemore.*

P WC & ⛢ E AV 斧 £

⊕ Early Apr–early Sept, daily, 10am–6pm.

Tel 01479 821409   www.rspb.org.uk

89 Loch Insh Watersports Centre

Watersports on offer include kayaking, canoeing, sailing and windsurfing; equipment can be hired daily by the hour, and a range of courses are provided by experienced instructors (RYA and BCU recognised). The centre also offers a number of other activities such as archery, mountain biking, fishing and dry slope skiing, plus an adventure area, climbing wall and interpretation trail suitable for children.

K5 *Seven miles S of Aviemore off B970; NE side of Loch Insh.*

P WC & ☕ ✕ ⛢ AV 斧 ⚶ 斧 £ ££

⊕ Watersports: Apr–Oct, 8.30am–5.30pm.
Restaurant: open most of year, times vary.

Tel 01540 651272

www.lochinsh.com

90 Loch Morlich Watersports

A natural sandy beach slopes down into the waters of Loch Morlich, offering a fine setting for canoeing, sailing or windsurfing; instruction and equipment hire available.

K5 *On ski road, E of Aviemore.*

P ☕ ⚶ 斧 斧 £ ££

⊕ Apr–Oct, daily, 9am–5.30pm.

Tel 01479 861221   www.lochmorlich.com

LOCH NESS

Perhaps the most famous of Scotland's lochs as well as its largest by water volume, Loch Ness lies in the Great Glen fault line and is one of the three lochs joined by canal to form the coast to coast connection of the Caledonian Canal *(see p201)*. The hills on either side rise steeply out of the deep water of the loch yet do not inspire and impress as much as other loch and mountain settings. Loch Ness's most impressive feature is its sheer length – around 37 km (23 miles) and also its depth – up to 300 m (1000 ft) in places. This large body of water is said to have local effects on the weather in the area, particularly on warm still days when mirages have been recorded.

The loch has achieved world-wide fame as the home to a phenomenon usually known as the Loch Ness monster – the ancient Highland folk tales of kelpies and water spirits brought up to date and supporting the tourist industry in the vicinity of the loch. The modern version of the story dates from the 1930s, and a report in the local paper about a strange disturbance in the loch. However, the phenomenon's supporters cite Adamnan's *Life of Columba* where the biographer has the saint calming a water beast that threatened one of Columba's companions as he swam in the River Ness (rather than the loch).

Along with the Loch Ness monster themed exhibitions in Drumnadrochit (see Loch Ness 2000 and Loch Ness Monster Exhibition Centre opposite), a popular venue for visitors is Urquhart Castle, the picturesque ruins of what was once one of the largest castles in Scotland *(see p224)*. At the south end of the loch, the locks at Fort Augustus also attract many visitors, who watch the locking operations of the numerous pleasure craft on the Caledonian Canal.

91 Loch Ness 2000

This hi-tech exhibition uses sound, imagery, artefacts and special effects to study the myths and facts surrounding Loch Ness. Much of the original research equipment used in the loch's exploration is on display including the world's smallest crewed submersible and a large inflatable vessel.

H6   *On A82, 14 miles S of Inverness.*

P ᵂᶜ ⅓ ♥ ✕ 🏛 E ᴬⱽ ☰ ☀ ⊞ £££

🕐 Winter, daily, 10am–3.30pm.
Easter–end May, 9.30am–5pm.
Jun & Sept, 9am–6pm.
Jul & Aug, 9am–8pm. Oct, 9.30am–5.30pm.

Tel 01456 450573   www.loch-ness-scotland.com

92 Loch Ness Monster Exhibition Centre (Original)

A wide screen cinema system shows a film on the history and mystery of Loch Ness; language translations include German, French, Spanish, Italian, Japanese, Dutch and Swedish. Visitors can also view the facts and latest news on the Loch Ness Monster, along with information on a variety of supernatural tales from the surrounding area.

H6   *Loch Ness Lodge Hotel, Drumnadrochit; follow signs over bridge.*

P ᵂᶜ ⅓ ✕ 🏛 E ᴬⱽ ☀ ☰ 🚶 ⊞ ££

🕐 Summer, daily, 8.45am–10pm. Winter, 9am–5pm.

Tel 01456 450342   www.lochness-centre.com

93 Lochaber Watersports

Provides offshore sailing and power boat instruction, and hire of dinghies, canoes and kayaks plus equipment.

F2   *Ballachulish on A82, on the shores of Loch Leven.*

P ᵂᶜ ⊞ Free

🕐 Daily, 9am–5.30pm

Tel 01855 821391
www.lochaberwatersports.co.uk

94 Mallaig Heritage Centre

The exhibition covers the history and culture of west Lochaber, from prehistory to the present day. Displays, films and photographs describe Mallaig, the railway, ferries and the remote Highland area of Knoydart *(see also p214)*, and there are activities and quizzes for children.

ᵂᶜ ⅓ E ᴬⱽ 🏛 ⊞ £

D4   *Station Road, Mallaig, adjacent to railway station.*

🕐 Apr, May & Oct, Mon–Sat, 11am–4pm.
Jun–Sept, 9.30am–4.30pm & Sun, 1–4.30pm.
Nov–Mar, open four days a week
(phone or check website for times).

Tel 01687 462085   www.mallaigheritage.org.uk

95 Mallaig Marine World

A marine aquarium featuring Scotland's sea creatures, such as skates and rays, and exhibition of Mallaig's fishing tradition with models, photographs and unique video.

ᵂᶜ ⅓ 🏛 E ⊞ £

D4   *Beside Mallaig Harbour.*

🕐 All year round, daily, 9am–6pm.
Winter, 11am–5.30pm, closed Sun.

Tel 01687 462292   www.road-to-the-isles.org.uk

96 Maryck Memories of Childhood

A collection of dolls, dolls' houses, toys and teddy bears from 1880.

F11   *Unapool, half mile S of Kylesku Bridge on A894.*

P ᵂᶜ ⅓ 🏛 E ♥ ⊞ ☀ £

🕐 Easter–Oct, daily, 10.30am–5.30pm.

Tel 01971 502341

97 Nairn Golf Course

The links of the Nairn Golf Club on the Moray Firth are set among strands of gorse and heather, with views across the water to the Black Isle and Easter Ross. There is classic links golf to be found here played on crisp seaside turf where the greens are firm and fast anywhere.

K7   *On A96, 16 miles E of Inverness.*

P ᵂᶜ ⅓ ✕ 🏛 ⊞

🕐 Booking is advisable. Restricted access to the course at weekends for non-members.

Tel 01667 453208   www.nairngolfclub.co.uk

98 Nairn Museum

Gives the history of the Nairn area and the people who lived and worked there, with fishertown displays, Nairn Burgh and children's rooms plus a number of artefacts.

K7   *Nairn, off A96, at the police station.*

ᵂᶜ ⅓ 🏛 E £

🕐 Apr–Oct, Mon–Sat, 10am–4.30pm.

Tel 01667 456791   www.nairnmuseum.co.uk

THE HIGHLANDS OF SCOTLAND

99 Nevis Range

The Nevis Range features Scotland's highest ski slopes, with 35 runs comprising seven green, twelve blue, eleven red and five black, plus twelve lifts, three of which are chairlifts; ski and snowboard tuition and equipment hire available. Visitors can also take a mountain gondola up 655 m (2150 ft) on Aonach Mor, beside Ben Nevis, and enjoy views, walks and a mountain restaurant, plus a downhill mountain bike track and trails.

F3 *Seven miles N of Fort William, off the A82 to Inverness.*

P WC & ☕ ✕ 🏛 🌲 🚶 ♿ £££

⊕ Summer, daily, 10am–5pm.
July–Aug, 9.30am–6pm.
Winter, daily, 9.30am–3.30pm weather permitting.

Tel 01397 705825   www.nevis-range.co.uk

100 Northlands Viking Centre

A museum devoted to the history of Caithness, with information on the Vikings and Norse settlers, and recreated longship and Viking settlement.

M13 *Auckengill, on the A99, two miles N of Wick.*

P WC & 🏛 E AV 🌲 £

⊕ Jun–Sept, daily, 10am–4pm.

Tel 01847 805518

101 Plockton

Plockton stands at the entrance to Loch Carron, with the Applecross peninsula behind. It was once a fishing and crofting village, but is now popular for its unspoilt, beautiful setting.

D6 *Off A87, N of Kyle of Lochalsh.*

P ☕ ✕ 🏛 🌲 🌿 Free

⊕ Open access.

Tel 01599 534276   www.plockton.com

102 Raasay Outdoor Centre

The outdoor centre is based in a 250 year old Georgian Mansion, set in its own wooded grounds, overlooking Skye. A number of outdoor activities such as kayaking, waterfall abseiling, windsurfing, sailing and orienteering are offered on a daily or residential basis.

C6 *Isle of Raasay; take fifteen minute ferry crossing from Sconser, Skye, on A850.*

P WC ☕ ✕ 🏛 🌲 🌿 🚶 ♿ £

⊕ Apr–Oct, daily.

Tel: 01478 660266
www.raasayoutdoorcentre.co.uk

103 Revack Highland Estate

A visitor centre featuring gardens, a plant centre and children's playground, plus a series of wildlife trails.

L6 *On the B970, between Grantown-on-Spey and Nethy Bridge.*

P WC ✕ 🏛 🌿 🚶 ♿ Free

⊕ All year round, daily, 10am–5pm.

Tel 01479 872234

104 Rothiemurchus Highland Estate

Rothiemurchus Estate stretches south and eastwards of Aviemore, into the Cairngorms, taking in parts of Caledonian pine forest, Loch an Eilein with its island castle and Gleann Einich. A large number of activities are on offer such as walking (trails and ranger-led), tours, fishing, clay pigeon shooting, off-road driving and mountain biking. Visitors are advised to pre-book for all walks, tours and instruction.

K5 *On A951, two miles S of Aviemore.*

P WC & 🏛 🌲 🌿 🚶 ♿ £££

⊕ Visitor centre: daily, 9.30am–5.30pm. Shooting ground: daily, 9am–5pm weather permitting.

Tel 01479 812345   www.rothiemurchus.net

105 Royal Dornoch Golf Course

Classic links and terrain with views of the sea. The holes are strung out along Embo Bay in the mouth of the Firth on a narrow strip of softly contoured duneland where there is just enough room for parallel fairways on two distinct levels.

J9 *Off A9, two miles N of Dornoch bridge.*

P ᵂᶜ ᶜ ✗ ⌂
⊕ Booking is advisable.
Tel 01862 810219   www.royaldornoch.com

106 Rum

Since its designation as a nature national reserve in 1957, Rum has become well known for the diversity of its plant and wildlife, and is an important base for nesting seabirds. Rum's rugged terrain is open to hillwalkers, while visitors can find accommodation and information at Kinloch Castle which was built as a Victorian Mansion but now serves as a hostel *(see p221)*.

B4 *Access from Mallaig by Calmac Ferry and Shearwater Cruises, Arisaig.*

ᵂᶜ ☕ ⌂ ♨ 👫 Free
⊕ Open access.
Tel 01687 462026   www.snh.org.uk   Calmac Ferries: Tel 01687 462403; Shearwater Cruises: Tel 01687 450224.

107 Ruthven Barracks ★

These eighteenth century barracks, built after the 1715 Jacobite rising, were burned down by Prince Charles Edward Stuart's army in 1746. Located on top of a mound, they consist of two ranges of quarters and a stable block.

J4 *On B970, off A86/A9, one mile SE of Kingussie.*

P Free
⊕ Open access.
Tel 01667 460232   www.historic-scotland.gov.uk

108 Scottish Kiltmaker Visitor Centre 🏛

A centre devoted to Scotland's national dress, describing the kilt's history and development, tradition and culture, and how it is worn today. It is set within a large kiltmaking workshop, where visitors can see the kilt being made for export.

J6 *Inverness town centre, W bank of River Ness.*
⊕ Jun–Sept, Mon–Sat, 9am–9pm; Sun, 10am–4pm. Oct–May, Mon–Sat, 9am–5pm.
Tel 01463 222781   www.hector-russell.com

109 Skye Museum of Island Life 🏛

A group of seven thatched cottages illustrating how people lived in Highland crofting areas over a century ago. Each cottage carries a different theme and includes the old croft dwelling house, byre, barn, smithy and ceilidh house. Furniture, implements and photographs are also on display.

B8 *North Skye, 20 miles N of Portree on A855.*

P ᵂᶜ ᶜ E ♨ £
⊕ Apr–Oct, Mon–Sat, 9.30am–5.30pm.
Tel 01470 552206   www.skyemuseum.co.uk

110 Skye Serpentarium ★

A reptile exhibition and breeding centre in a converted watermill containing snakes, lizards, frogs and tortoises in natural surroundings. Frequent handling sessions.

D5 *On the A87 at Broadford, Skye.*

P ᵂᶜ ᶜ ☕ ⌂ E ⊓ ♨ 🅿 £
⊕ Apr–Oct, Mon–Sat, 10am–5pm. Also Sun, Jul–Aug & bank holiday weekends.
Tel 01471 822209   www.skyeserpentarium.org.uk

111 Smoo Cave

A huge limestone cave containing pools fed by a waterfall in the roof.

H13 *Two miles E of Durness, on A838. Access is via a path and gangway into the cave.*

♨ Free
⊕ Open access.
Tel 01971 511259

112 Spey Valley Smokehouse ★

A smokehouse using traditional processes, set close to the banks of the River Spey with a viewing area and factory shop.

L6 *One mile S of Grantown-on-Spey on A95.*

P ᵂᶜ ᶜ ⌂ E AV ♨ 🅿 Free
⊕ All year round, Mon–Fri, 9am–5pm. Apr–end Sept, Sat, 10am–2pm.
Tel 01479 873078

SKYE

The romantic image of Skye owes much to tales of the fugitive Bonnie Prince Charlie after Culloden. After the Jacobite episode however, the island saw increasing emigration because of over-population, then forced clearances in the first half of the nineteenth century. Then there were conflicts over crofting rights which culminated in what became known as the Battle of the Braes (1882). Yet Skye today has a fairly prosperous air, with new houses tucked into the croftlands, and new inhabitants. Gaelic is still spoken here.

The Norsemen first named Skye as Skuy-ö, with the meaning island of cloud, hence today's frequent label of 'the misty isle'. This is a reference to the way that the high Cuillins catch the rain-bearing clouds of the prevailing south-westerlies. Nevertheless, so spectacular are the sharp-toothed ridges of these mountains that they are a huge draw, especially for experienced climbers. Of the 12 Cuillin peaks classified as Munros, only a few can be reached without scrambling or serious rock-work.

Skye does not reveal its scenic spectacle right away to first-time visitors heading for Portree. First comes the Red Hills or Red Cuillin, pink granite slopes rounded and plain. The spikes and spears of the Black Cuillins, with their dark rocks of gabbro, burst on the scene at Sligachan with the end of the main ridge. This mountain spine is also spectacularly viewed from Glen Brittle, while the Elgol road from Broadford is also worthwhile for the panorama across Loch Scavaig.

Aside from the Cuillins, Skye has other interesting landforms. The northern peninsula of Trotternish is made of ancient tilted basalt lava flows. These end abruptly on a cliff-face inland from and running for many miles near the main road. The rock pinnacle of the Old Man of Storr beyond Portree marks a point where the cliff has slipped into a confusion of screes and detached boulders. This same phenomenon can be seen even more spectacularly at the Quiraing further to the north. Here slabs of the ancient cliff have split away infinitesimally slowly – a kind of slow-motion avalanche – to create more weird pinnacles, huge table-topped detached slabs and secret rocky places used in the past to hide stolen cattle. Between Portree and the Quiraing, another popular landscape viewpoint is Kilt Rock, where alternate bands of light and dark rock types resemble the pleats in a kilt. This is seen in a high sea cliff viewed from a specially built platform.

THE SMALL ISLES – RUM, EIGG, CANNA AND MUCK

The Small Isles are conspicuous on the horizon on the road or rail journey to Mallaig. Eigg and Muck lie closest to the mainland, with the blunt crag of the Sgurr of Eigg making that island unmistakable. Eigg also has the largest population of the four – around 70. A three-way partnership between islanders, Highland Council and the Scottish Wildlife Trust form a trust which owns the islands thereby ending the uncertainties which changes of ownership in the latter half of the 20th century had brought. For

Canna

Eigg

puffin, shearwater and the occasional sea eagle, visiting from Rum. Canna has the best protected harbour out of the four islands, sheltered by its near-neighbour, Sanday, joined to it by a bridge. The island, remarkably, also has the world's largest collection of Gaelic literature and poetry in Canna House, thanks to the efforts of a previous owner, the historian and folklorist Dr John Lorne Campbell.

Rum, with its Norse-named peaks high enough to catch the rain clouds, is a national nature reserve owned by Scottish Natural Heritage *(see p219)*. Important research on red deer and other native species is carried out here. The island is associated with the wealthy Lancastrian MP and industrialist John Bullough who bought the island in 1888 as a holiday home. His son built the extraordinary Kinloch Castle in order to live out his Highland fantasies as a laird. Rum also has large colonies of Manx shearwaters – over 60,000 pairs – as well as good numbers of other seabirds, plus corncrake, golden eagle and the rare and re-introduced sea eagle.

visitors today, Eigg has otters, and the elusive corncrake, as well as a colony of Manx shearwaters which burrow into the soils of the Sgurr. On the west side, Laig Beach with its singing sands is just one of the many unspoilt corners of the island.

Contrasting with Eigg, Muck is the smallest of the islands with around 30 of a population and has been owned by the same (resident) family for more than a century. It is the most fertile and hence is quite extensively farmed.

Now in the care of the National Trust for Scotland, Canna has a well wooded appearance above the harbour. This soft air is in contrast to the wild sea cliffs on its western end, with

Rum from Arisaig

113 Speyside Heather Centre ★

An exhibition, show garden, trail and garden centre with a heather theme.

K6 *Between Aviemore and Grantown-on-Spey, off the A95.*

P ᵂᶜ & ✕ ⚓ E ⚞ ⚟ Free

⊕ Summer, daily, 9am–6pm.
   Winter, daily, 10am–4pm.

Tel 01479 851359
www.heathercentre.com

114 Strathnaver Museum

Housed in the former parish church, the museum looks at the Strathnaver Clearances and the history of Clan Mackay.

J12 *Bettyhill, on the A836, 12 miles E of Tongue.*

P E £

⊕ Apr–Oct, Mon–Sat, 10am–1pm & 2–5pm.
   Nov–Mar, by appointment only.

Tel 01641 521418

115 Strathspey Railway 🚂

This steam railway travels the scenic route from Aviemore to Boat of Garten and Broomhill, better known as Glenbogle Station from the TV series *Monarch of the Glen*, providing views of the Cairngorms and offering refreshments on board. Special events run in the summer months, some specifically for children, and December sees a season of 'Santa' trains. Passengers can take Sunday lunch on board, while the 'Dinner on the Diner' service runs on a limited number of evenings during the summer.

K5 *Aviemore Station, Dalfaber Road; Boat of Garten Station, off A95 to Grantown-on-Spey.*

P ᵂᶜ & ☕ ✕ ⚓ E ⛱ ☀ ⚟ £££

⊕ Jun–Sept, daily, 10am–4pm.
   Restricted hours March–May, Oct & Dec.

Tel 01479 810725
www.strathspeyrailways.co.uk

116 Summer Isles Cruises ★

Cruise around the Summer Isles, leaving twice daily, and see the many species of seabirds among the rugged rock formations, visit a seal colony and land for one hour on the Summer Isles.

SUMMER ISLES

The low, bare appearance of this scattering of islands, seen offshore from the road to Achiltibuie, adds to the bleak ambience of this wind-honed corner of Wester Ross. Their name is said to come from the fact that crofters of old would graze their stock on the islands during the summer – and this still takes place today. They were associated with the naturalist Sir Frank Fraser Darling who wrote of his farming experiences here during World War II. The largest island of Tanera Mor lost its last permanent native residents in 1931, though it is now once again lived in all year round. However it is still mostly a place where holidaymakers rent renovated cottages to escape from it all.

E10 *Bardentarbet Pier, Achitibuie.*

P ☀ £££

⊕ May–Sept, Mon–Sat, departs 10.30am,
   returns 2pm & departs 2.15, returns 5.45pm.

Tel 01854 622200
www.summer-isles.com

117 Tain Through Time

This fourteenth century church, once the shrine of Tain's St Duthac, now houses a museum giving a history of Tain. On offer is a sound and light show telling the story of St Duthac, children's activities and temporary exhibitions.

J8 *Tower Street, Tain town centre.*

ᵂᶜ & ⚓ E ᴬⱽ ⚟ ££

⊕ Apr–Oct, daily, 10am–5pm.
   Jul–Aug, 10am–6pm.

Tel 01862 894089
www.tainmuseum.demon.co.uk

TORRIDON

It is hard to say which is the most spectacular approach to Glen Torridon. From the east, via Kinlochewe, the sandstone flanks of Beinn Eighe fill the view and are topped with white quartzite screes, which some mistake for snow. (Beinn Eighe was the very first national nature reserve in Scotland.) The toothed ridge of the mountain curves into the glen, filling its north side, even before the upturned boat-keel shape of Liathach, its neighbour, catches the eye. Along a line near the summit, the sandstone terraces are shattered into pinnacles, a test of head and nerve for confident hillwalkers.

Coming from the west via Shieldaig, the road runs high above Loch Torridon, with Beinn Alligin as the sentinel peak. The red ramparts of its highest point, Sgurr Mhor, are gashed by a diagonal cleft or chimney, which appears as a startling dark shadow on the steep slope as the sun moves round. Further along the road, the tiny village of Torridon is also seen from afar, dwarfed by the summit-ridge to valley floor scree-filled gullies of Liathach. This is Scottish scenery at its dramatic best.

A big day's walk, which reveals a hidden side of the Torridons, goes in between Liathach and Beinn Eighe to curve north and east into Beinn Eighe's magnificently unpronounceable Corrie Mhic Fhearchair (trans: corrie of the son of Farquhar). Beyond the crystal clear corrie loch and forming the corrie headwall (which also gives a route to the summit) is the famous Triple Buttress, soaring with quartzite over sandstone 380 m (1250 ft) from the corrie floor and sometimes described as the finest corrie in Scotland *(see p224)*.

---

118 Talisker Distillery Visitor Centre

Skye's only distillery, founded in 1830, lies on its western shores at Loch Harport. On a guided tour of the distillery visitors can see the production processes involved in whisky making and sample a dram.

B6 *On the B8009, at Carbost, Skye.*

P WC ♿ E 🍴 ♿ ££

🕐 Easter–Oct, 9.30am–4.30pm.
Closed Sunday.
Nov–Easter, by appointment only.
Tel 01478 614308
www.malts.com

119 Tarbat Discovery Centre 🏛

This centre uses touch screens and videos to describe how archaeologists have discovered a Dark Ages monastic settlement. Many Pictish carved stones are on display along with finds from other periods, and a gallery devoted to Tarbat through the centuries.

K9 *Portmahomack, on B9165, turning E off A9 before Tain.*

🅿 [WC] ♿ ♨ E [AV] ££

⊕ Mar, Apr & Oct, daily, 2–5pm.
   May–Sept, daily, 10am–5pm. Nov, Fri–Sat, 2–5pm.

Tel 01862 871351   www.tarbat-discovery.co.uk

120 Timespan Heritage Centre 🏛

Relates the story of the Highlands, from Picts and Vikings, to witch burning and the Highland Clearances via displays featuring models, sets and sound effects, and an audio-visual programme. Also on site is an arts centre and herb garden.

K10 *Helmsdale, off the A9.*

🅿 [WC] ♿ ☕ ♨ E [AV] [£] ££

⊕ Apr–Oct, Mon–Sat, 9.30am–5pm; Sun, 2–5pm.

Tel 01431 821327   www.timespan.org.uk

121 Tomatin Distillery 🍾

After a tour of the building, visitors can try a free dram of Tomatin Single Malt Whisky.

🅿 [WC] ♿ ♨ [AV] [£] Free

J6 *Sixteen miles S of Inverness, off A9.*

⊕ All year round, Mon–Fri, 9am–5pm
   (last tour 3.30pm).
   May–Sept, also Sat, 9am–1pm (last tour 12 noon).

Tel 01808 511444

122 Torridon

One of Scotland's most spectacular mountainous landscapes, which is dominated by Liathach, 1053 m (3456 ft) with its seven tops; the red Torridonian sandstone dates from around 750 million years ago. Displays and an audio-visual presentation on local wildlife can be found in the countryside centre; also on site is a deer museum. *(See also p223)*

E7 *Nine miles SW of Kinlochewe, N of A896. Centre: A896/Diabaig road junction.*

🅿 ♿ ♨ E [AV] ☀ £

⊕ Estate, deer enclosure & deer museum: all year round, daily. Centre: Easter–Sept, daily, 10am–6pm.

Tel 01445 791221   www.nts.org.uk

123 Treasures of the Earth 🏛

A collection of crystals, gemstones, minerals and fossils, including a six foot amethyst, are on display in a simulated cave, cavern and mine.

🅿 [WC] ♿ ♨ E [£] ££

F3 *Corpach, four miles NW of Fort William, on A830.*

⊕ Summer, daily, 9.30am–7pm.
   Winter, daily, 10am–5pm. Closed January.
   Please telephone as times may vary.

Tel 01397 772283

124 Ullapool Museum and Visitor Centre 🏛

This former Telford Parliamentary Church Listed Building is now a museum and visitor centre which looks at Loch Broom using the theme 'The People of the Loch'. Features include interactives, Ullapool's Bicentennial tapestries and quilts worked by local residents and a collection of hand-crafted model ships.

[WC] ♿ ♨ E [AV] £

F9 *West Argyle Street, Ullapool, a few minutes walk from main car park.*

⊕ Apr–end Oct, Mon–Sat, 9.30am–5.30pm.
   Nov–Mar, Sat, 10am–4pm.

Tel 01854 612987

125 Urquhart Castle

The banks of Loch Ness provide a unique setting for the ruins of Urquhart Castle, once one of the largest castles in Scotland. Most of the building, including a well preserved tower, dates from the seventeenth century, but underneath lie the remains of a fortress, possibly visited by St Columba in the 580's. The castle was reduced to its ruined state in 1692 to prevent Jacobite revolutionaries making use of it. A newly established visitor centre houses a short film presentation, display of relics found on the site, a model of how the castle would have looked when newly built, and a variety of interactives, some aimed specifically at children.

H6 *On A82, two miles S of Drumnadrochit, by Loch Ness.*

🅿 [WC] ☕ ♨ E [AV] ☀ ££

⊕ Apr–Sept, daily, 9.30am–6.30pm.
   Oct–Mar, daily, 9.30am–4.30pm.
   Last admission 45 minutes before closing.

Tel 01456 450551   www.historic-scotland.gov.uk

126 Waltzing Waters ★

Water, light and music come together
to form an exciting and unique show.

J4 *Newtonmore, on A86, off the A9.*

🅿 ᵂᶜ ♿ ☕ 🏛 💷 ££

🕐 Please telephone for performance times.

Tel 01540 673752   www.newtonmore.com

127 Waterlines Visitor Centre 🏛

A multi-media exhibition relating the history of
Lybster's herring industry, geology and plantlife.
A remote camera focuses on nearby cliffs,
renowned for their nesting bird colonies.

L11 *Harbour Road, Lybster, on A9.*

🅿 ᵂᶜ ♿ ☕ E AV ⛱ ☀ 🚶 £

🕐 May–Sept, daily, 11am–5pm.

Tel 01593 721520   www.caithness.org

128 West Highland Museum 🏛

Focuses on social and local history,
natural history, archaeology and geology.
Of particular interest are Jacobite and Alexander
Carmichael collections.

F3 *Cameron Square, in centre of Fort William,
off the High Street and adjacent to the Tourist Office.*

ᵂᶜ ♿ 🏛 E £

🕐 May–Sept, Mon–Sat, 10am–5pm.
Jul & Aug, Sun, 2–5pm.
Oct–Apr, Mon–Sat, 10am–4pm.

Tel 01397 702169
www.westhighlandmuseum.org.uk

129 Wildcat Trail and Centre 🏃

A 10 km walk encircling Newtonmore, and taking
in woodland, moorland, views of the Cairngorms
and Monadhliath mountains and the banks of
the River Spey. The centre, manned by
volunteers, advises visitors on the trail together
with walking all over Scotland.

J4 *Main Street, Newtonmore, off A9 on B9150.*

🅿 ᵂᶜ ♿ 🏛 E ⛱ ☀ 🚶

🕐 Wildcat Trail: open access.
Wildcat Centre: Apr–Oct, Mon–Fri,
9.30am–12.30pm & 2.15–5.15pm;
Sat, 9.30am–12.30pm.
Nov–Mar, Mon–Sat, mornings only.

Tel 01540 673131   www.newtonmore.com

Urquhart Castle and Loch Ness

WESTERN ISLES

Out on the Atlantic rim of Europe, the 208km (130 mile) chain of the Western Isles beyond the Minch enjoy a different culture and language from much of the rest of Scotland (though everyone speaks English as well as Gaelic). The landscape is distinctive, windswept and at times almost intimidating. Yet this almost treeless expanse of scoured rock and swelling moor has its own austere beauty and special quality of light. The fertile sands of the machair glow with wildflowers, the yellow flag iris brightens the wetter parts of the grazings and the white and empty beaches simply dazzle.

Most of the Western Isles is made up of some of the world's oldest rocks, Lewisian gneiss, named after the main island of the chain. The various geological processes involving heat and pressure over unimaginable aeons of time have created not just interesting rock shapes and textures for the casual observer but also many variations in the hardness of the rock. Acted on by the scouring glaciers the differences in hardness resulted in the highly characteristic knobbly look of the surface rocks. This process has created the characteristic and bewildering pattern of humps, hollows, lochans, burns and sea inlets which are such a feature of many parts of the islands, for example, North Uist. To overlie the bare bones of the landscape came the gradual formation of peat inland – still widely used as fuel in a land with so little timber – and the shell sand of the machair on the coast.

It is the distribution of machair which has given rise to the curious statistic that the island of Lewis and Harris has three times the surface area of the rest of the islands but less than half the agricultural land. In these marginal and exposed places, the fertility of the machair was all-important – and much of it is found in the southern half of the islands. For example, Barra in the south is typically Hebridean, with croftlands growing hay and potatoes above silvery sands. The largest stretch of sand is Tràigh Mor, which is also the island's airport, with landing times dictated by the tides. Also on Barra is the ferry-port of Castlebay, with Kisimul Castle on an islet in the bay *(see p234)*. This was the stronghold of the MacNeils of Barra, noted in their day for lawlessness and piracy.

Tràigh Seilebost and Luskentyre, Harris

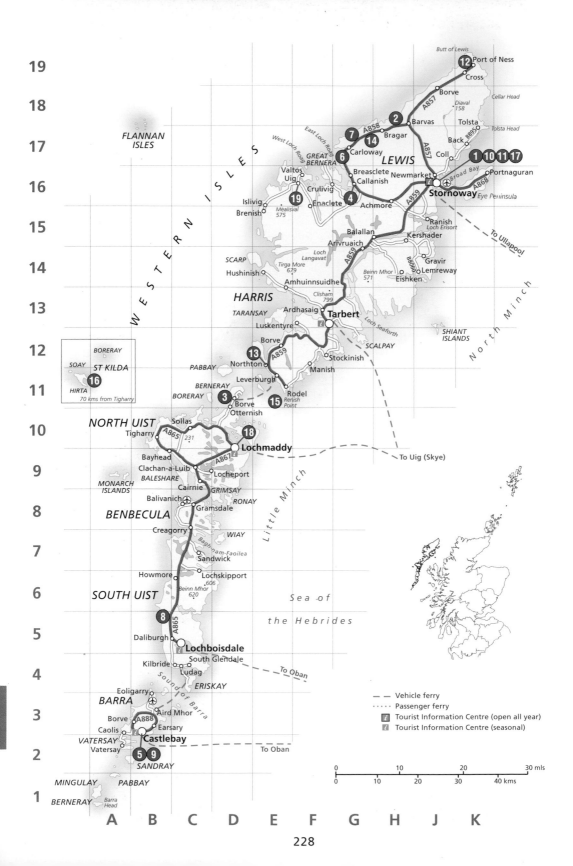

WESTERN ISLES

FLANNAN ISLES

LEWIS

Butt of Lewis
⑫ Port of Ness
Cross
Borve
Diaval 158
Cellar Head
Barvas
Tolsta
②
Back *Tolsta Head*
⑦ ⑭ Bragar
Coll
⑥ Carloway
Breasclete ① ⑩ ⑪ ⑰
Valtos Newmarket
Uig Callanish
Cruilvig ④ Achmore
Islivig ⑲ Enaclete Stornoway
Brenish *Mealisval 575*
Ranish
Loch Erisort
Balallan Kershader
Arivruaich
Gravir
SCARP Loch Lemreway
Langavat Eishken
Hushinish *Tirga More 679* *Beinn Mhor 571*
Amhuinnsuidhe
Clisham 799
HARRIS
TARANSAY Ardhasaig **Tarbert**
Luskentyre *Loch Seaforth*
SCALPAY
Borve *SHIANT ISLANDS*
Stockinish
⑬ Northton
PABBAY Manish
Leverburgh
BERNERAY
BORERAY ③ Borve ⑮ Rodel
Otternish *Rerish Point*

West Loch Roag
East Loch Roag
GREAT BERNERA

North Minch

To Ullapool

NORTH UIST
Sollas
Tigharry *231*
Bayhead
Clachan-a-Luib
BALESHARE
Cairnie
GRIMSAY
Balivanich *RONAY*
Gramsdale
Creagorry *WIAY*
MONARCH ISLANDS
BENBECULA
Baghnam-Faoilea
Sandwick
Howmore Lochskipport
Beinn Mhor 620
SOUTH UIST
⑧
Daliburgh
Lochboisdale
Kilbride South Glendale
Ludag
ERISKAY
Eoligarry
BARRA
Borve *A888* Aird Mhor
Caolis Earsary
VATERSAY **Castlebay**
Vatersay
⑤ ⑨
SANDRAY
MINGULAY
PABBAY
BERNERAY Barra Head

Little Minch

Lochmaddy ⑱
Locheport
A867

Sea of the Hebrides

To Uig (Skye)

To Oban

To Oban

— — — Vehicle ferry
· · · · · Passenger ferry
🛈 Tourist Information Centre (open all year)
🛈 Tourist Information Centre (seasonal)

BORERAY
SOAY **ST KILDA**
⑯
HIRTA
70 kms from Tigharry

0   10   20   30 mls
0   10   20   30   40 kms

VISITOR INFORMATION

MAIN TOURIST INFORMATION CENTRES

Lewis
26 Cromwell Street
Stornoway
Isle of Lewis HS1 2DD
Tel: 01851 703088
Web: www.visitthehebrides.com
E-mail: witb@visitthehebrides.co.uk
Open: all year round

Harris
Pier Road
Tarbet HS3 3DG
Tel: 01859 502011
Web: www.visitthehebrides.com
E-mail: witb@visitthehebrides.co.uk
Open: all year round

SEASONAL TOURIST INFORMATION CENTRES

North Uist
Tel: 01876 500321
E-mail:
witb@visitthehebrides.co.uk
Open: Mid Mar–Oct

South Uist
Tel: 01878 700286
E-mail:
witb@visitthehebrides.co.uk
Open: Mid Mar–Oct

Barra
Tel: 01871 810336
E-mail:
witb@visitthehebrides.co.uk
Open: Mid Mar–Oct

ADDITIONAL INFORMATION

GENERAL TRAVEL INFORMATION
Traveline Scotland
Tel: 0870 608 2608
Provides timetable information for all public transport in Scotland and the rest of Great Britain.

AIR TRAVEL

Highlands & Islands Airports Ltd
Barra Airport
North Bay
Barra HS9 5YD
Tel: 01871 890212
Web: www.hial.co.uk/barra-airport.html
E-mail: hial@hial.co.uk

Highlands & Islands Airports Ltd
Benbecula Airport
Benbecula HS7 5LW
Tel: 01870 602051
Web: www.hial.co.uk/benbecula-airport.html
E-mail: hial@hial.co.uk

Highlands & Islands Airports Ltd
Stornoway Airport
Stornoway
Isle Of Lewis HS2 0BN
Tel: 01851 702256
Web: www.hial.co.uk/stornoway-airport.html
E-mail: hial@hial.co.uk

British Airways PLC (operated by Loganair)
Benbecula Airport
Benbecula HS7 5LW
Tel: British Airways central reservations: 08457 733377
Web: www.britishairways.com
Routes: Glasgow–Benbecula

British Airways PLC (operated by Loganair)
Stornoway Airport
Stornoway
Isle Of Lewis HS2 0BN
Tel British Airways central reservations: 08457 733377
Web: www.britishairways.com
Routes: Edinburgh–Stornoway
Glasgow–Stornoway
Inverness–Stornoway

Highland Airways
Inverness Airport
Inverness
IV2 7JB
Tel: 01851 701282
Web: www.highlandairways.co.uk
E-mail: info@highlandairways.co.uk
Routes: Inverness–Stornoway
Inverness–Stornoway–Benbecula

Airlines

Mainland UK

British Airways PLC (operated by Loganair)
Barra Airport
North Bay
Barra HS9 5YD
Tel: British Airways central reservations: 08457 733377
Web: www.britishairways.com
Routes: Glasgow–Barra

Inter-island flights

British Airways PLC (operated by Loganair)
Tel: British Airways central reservations: 08457 733377
Web: www.britishairways.com
Routes: Barra–Benbecula–Stornoway
Benbecula–Barra–Benbecula
Benbecula–Stornoway–Benbecula

COACHES (TO CONNECT WITH FERRY)

Scottish Citylink Coaches Limited
Buchanan Bus Station
Killermont Street
Glasgow G2 3NP
Tel: 08705 505050
Web: www.citylink.co.uk
E-mail: info@citylink.co.uk
Routes: Inverness–Ullapool
Glasgow–Uig (Skye)
Glasgow–Oban

Rapsons Coaches
1 Seafield Road
Inverness
IV1 1TN
Tel: 01463 710555
Web: www.rapsons.co.uk
E-mail: info@rapsons.co.uk
Route: Inverness–Ullapool

BUS

H Macneil
68 Tangasdale
Castlebay HS9 5XW
Tel: 01871 810262
Route: Barra Circular

W Macvicar
Kiaora
Liniclate HS7 5PJ
Tel: 01870 603197
Routes: Isle of Benbecula
Balivanich Circular

Harris Coaches
Scott Road
Tarbet HS3 3BG
Tel: 01859 502441
Routes: operates all over Harris
Harris–Stornoway (Lewis)

Galson-Stornoway Motor Services
1 Lower Barvas
Stornoway HS2 0QZ
Tel: 01851 840269
E-mail: galson@sol.co.uk
Route: Port of Ness–Barvas–Stornoway

MacLennan Coaches
24 Inclete Road
Stornoway HS1 2RN
Tel: 01851 702114
Routes: West Side Circular:
Stornoway–Barvas–Shawbost–Carloway–Callanish
Stornoway–Uig District
Stornoway Town Service

M Morrison
Timsgarry Filling Station
Timsgarry
Uig
HS2 9JD
Tel: 01851 672444
Route: Uig district
Uig–Garynahine

IA & C Maciver Limited
Units 4-5
Parkend Industrial Estate
Stornoway
HS2 0AN
Tel: 01851 705050
Route: Stornoway–North Lochs

Grenitote Travel
20 Grenitote
HS6 5BP
Tel: 01876 560244
E-mail: grenitotetravel@supernet.com
Routes: operates over North Uist

Hebridean Coaches
2 Howmore
HS8 5SH
Tel: 01870 620345
Routes: operates over the whole island
including to the ferry ports
(Lochboisdale and Lochmaddy) and
the airport

Lindsay Coaches
Lochboisdale
HS8 5TY
Tel: 01878 700206
Route: South Uist–Stornoway

FERRIES

Caledonian MacBrayne
Head Office
The Ferry Terminal
Gourock
PA19 1QP
Tel: Enquiries: 01475 650100
Vehicle Reservations: 08705 650000
Brochure Hotline: 01475 650288

Lochboisdale Office
Tel: 01878 700288

Lochmaddy Office
Tel: 01876 500337

Stornoway Office
Tel: 01851 702361

Tarbert Office
Tel: 01859 502444

Routes: Oban–Castlebay
Oban–Lochboisdale
Uig (Skye)–Lochmaddy
Uig (Skye)–Tarbet
Ullapool–Stornoway

Inter-island ferry

Caledonian MacBrayne
Head Office
The Ferry Terminal
Gourock PA19 1QP
Tel: Enquiries: 01475 650100
Vehicle Reservations: 08705 650000
Brochure Hotline: 01475 650288
Route: Otternish (North Uist)–Leverburgh (Harris)
Lochboisdale–Castlebay

CAR HIRE

Ask Car Hire
Liniclate
Isle of Benbecula
HS7 5PY
Tel: 01870 602818
Web: www.askcarhire.com
E-mail: neil@askcarhire.com

Arnol Car Rentals
Isle of Lewis
HS2 9DB
Tel: 01851 710548
E-mail: arnolmotors@aol.com

Autohire Car and Van Rental
3/5 Bells Road
Stornoway
Isle of Lewis HS1 2SQ
Tel: 01851 706939
E-mail: autohire@btinternet.com

Barra Car Hire
Taigh a 'Dot
Castlebay
Isle of Barra HS9 5XD
Tel: 01871 810243

Lewis Car Rentals
52 Bayhead Street
Stornoway
Isle of Lewis HS1 2TU
Tel: 01851 703760
Web: www.witb.co.uk
E-mail: lewis@carrentkiwi.freeserve.co.uk

Laing Motors
Lochboisdale
Isle of South Uist
HS8 5TH
Tel: 01878 700267

Lochs Motors Car Hire
33 South Beach
Stornoway
Isle of Lewis
HS1 2BN
Tel: 01851 705857
E-mail: lochs@jings.com

MacKinnon Self Drive
18 Inaclete Road
Stornoway
Isle of Lewis
HS1 2RB
Tel: 01851 702984
Web: www.mackinnonselfdrive.co.uk
E-mail: mackinnonhire@hotmail.com

MacLennan Bros. Ltd
Balivanich
Isle of Benbecula
HS7 5LL
Tel: 01870 602191

MacMillan Self Drive
30 Eoligarry
Isle of Barra
HS9 5YD
Tel: 01871 890366

TAXIS

Alba Taxis
(guided tours)
Lewis
Tel: 01851 830433

Central Cabs
Lewis
Tel: 01851 706900

Alda's Taxis/Minibus
North Uist
Tel: 01876 500215

MacIsaac
South Uist
Tel: 01878 710231

BARRA

Barra follows the typical story of the far-flung islands of the west – strong association with one clan, in this case, the MacNeils, then a later shameful episode of clearance (when not in MacNeil hands). Today it follows the typical crofting pattern of scattered smallholdings. Barra is especially noted for its wildflowers and butterflies, owing to the richness of its machair lands. The former herring port of Castlebay is the main and well-equipped centre in the island whose highest point is Heaval (383 m, 1256 ft). There is a white marble statue of the Madonna and Child on its slopes. The hills here are rocky and dramatic, prone to mists and fast weather changes. At the north end of the island is Traigh Mhor (literally in Gaelic: big beach) originally famed for its cockles but now the island's airport, where the plane still lands on the beach.

1 An Lanntair Arts Centre

This arts centre runs a programme of exhibitions and events with an emphasis on local artists and traditional music in the summer. Gaelic is a key part of An Lanntair's identity.

J16 *Corner of South Beach & Kenneth Street, Stornoway.*

P WC ♿ 🏛 E ☀ ☂ Free

⊕ New centre opening Autumn 2005.
Telephone or check website for details.

Tel 01851 703307   www.lanntair.com

2 Arnol Blackhouse

These fine examples of a traditional island thatched house complete with a byre, barn and stackyard, and a fully furnished house dating from the early twentieth century, give visitors an insight into day-to-day life on Lewis in years gone by. On display at the visitor centre are photographs, artefacts and implements.

H18 *Off the A858, Arnol village, Lewis.*

🏛 E £

⊕ Apr–Sept, Mon–Sat, 9.30am–6.30pm.
Oct–Mar, Mon–Sat, 9.30am–4.30pm.

Tel 01851 710395   www.historic-scotland.gov.uk

3 Bosta Iron Age House

On site are the excavated remains of an Iron Age village and a reconstructed Iron Age house, all of which have been built into the sand. A marked walk takes visitors along the scenic coastline.

D11 *Bostadh beach, on the island of Bernera off W coast of Lewis; take B8059 across the bridge and head to NW corner of island.*

P E ☀ 🥾 £

⊕ Jun–Aug, Mon–Fri, 12 noon–4pm.

Tel 01851 612331

Calanais Standing Stones, Lewis

4 Calanais Standing Stones and Visitor Centre

These stones, dating back some 5000 years, make up one of the finest prehistoric sites in Britain. The site consists of a central ring of 13 megaliths with another taller megalith in the centre, and around 35 more stones in the vicinity, forming a cross shape. A distinctive visitor centre, not visible from the site, tells the story of the stones and offers a range of facilities.

G16 *Calanais, on A858, W of Stornoway, Lewis.*

🅿 🆆 ♿ 🍴 ⛪ E 🚶 ♻ £

🕐 Site: all year round, daily.
Visitor centre: Apr–Sept, Mon–Sat, 10am–6pm.
Oct–Mar, Wed–Sat, 10am–4pm.

Tel 01851 621422   www.historic-scotland.gov.uk

5 Dualchas Barra Heritage and Cultural Centre

Focusses on the history and culture of Barra, with exhibitions and activities.

B3 *On A888, Castlebay, S side of Barra.*

🅿 🆆 ♿ 🍴 E £

🕐 Mar–May, Mon, Wed & Fri, 11am–4pm.
June–Aug, Mon–Fri, 11am–4pm.
Sept, Mon, Wed & Fri, 11am–4pm.

Tel 01871 810413
www.isleofbarra.com/heritage

6 Dun Carloway

This well-preserved dry-stone broch, one of the finest in Scotland, measures up to 70 ft in height; the broken wall at one side gives clues as to how the broch was constructed. A visitor centre runs an exhibition on Scenes From the Broch.

G17 *Two miles S of Carloway, on the A858, W side of Lewis.*

🅿 🆆 ♿ ⛪ E ♻ Free

🕐 Site: please ring to confirm times.
Centre: May–Sept, Mon–Sat, 10am–5pm.

Tel 01851 643338

7 Gearrannan Blackhouse Village

The village of Gearrannan and surrounding croft land have been restored to form a typical blackhouse village. Visitors can see the cottages, with their drystone masonry and thatched roofing, and can learn about the traditional rural lifestyle.

G17 *Follow signs for Carloway on A857/A858, 25 miles W of Stornoway.*

🅿 🆆 ♿ 🍴 ⛪ E AV 🪑 🚶 ♻ £

🕐 Easter–Sept, Mon–Sat, 9.30am–5.30pm.
Other times by appointment.

Tel 01851 643416   www.gearrannan.com

8 Kildonan Museum

Contains local crofting and household items dating from 1900 onwards.

B5 *Kildonan, on A865, S Uist.*

E £

Easter–Oct, Mon–Sat, 10am–5pm; Sun, 2–5pm.

Tel 01878 710343/700279

9 Kisimul Castle

Kisimul, the ancestral home of the MacNeil family, is located on a small island off Barra, at Castlebay. The castle dates from the twelfth century, but was fully rebuilt in the mid-twentieth century; features include a great hall, chapel, dungeon and tower. Access is via a small boat; journey time is a few minutes.

B3 *On an island by Castlebay, S coast of Barra, on A888.*

£

Apr–Sept, daily, 9.30am–6.30pm.

Tel 01871 810313
www.historic-scotland.gov.uk

10 Lewis Loom Centre

A centre devoted to weaving, with information on all the processes involved in turning raw wool into Harris tweed, plus demonstrations of hand stake warping and weaving.

J16 *In Stornoway, 100 yards from TIC, Lewis.*

E £

All year round, 9am–6pm;
Winter: please telephone to confirm days.

Tel 01851 704500
www.lewisloomcentre.co.uk

11 Museum Nan Eilean

Houses an array of artefacts, photographs, prints and paintings relating to the history of the Western Isles.

J16 *Francis Street, Stornoway town centre, Lewis.*

E Free

Apr–Sept, Mon–Sat, 10am–5.30pm.
Oct–Mar, Tue–Fri, 10am–5pm; Sat, 10am–1pm.

Tel 01851 703773 www.cne-siar.gov.uk

12 Ness Heritage Centre

Focusses on local history and folklore with artefacts, photographs, plus fishing and crofting equipment.

K19 *Habost, in the far N of Lewis.*

E £

Jun–Sept, Mon–Sat, 10am–5pm.
Oct–May, Mon–Fri, 10am–4pm.

Tel 01851 810377 www.c-e-n.org

13 Seallam! Visitor Centre

A centre devoted to the people and landscape of the Western Isles, with changing exhibitions of arts, crafts and artefacts.

E12 *Northton, 17 miles SW of Tarbert on A859, Harris.*

E £

All year, Mon–Sat, 10am–5pm.

Tel 01859 520258 www.seallam.com

14 Shawbost School Museum

Looks at life in a typical crofting village in the early twentieth century, with an array of equipment and artefacts.

G17 *On NW coast of Lewis.*

E Free

Apr–Sept, Mon–Sat, 9.30am–4.30pm.

Tel 01851 710212

15 St. Clements' Church

This sixteenth century church was built by Alasdair Crotach MacLeod, Lord of Dunvegan and Harris and houses his ornately decorated tomb.

E11 *On A859, Rodel, Harris.*

Free

Open access.

Tel 0131 668 8800 www.historic-scotland.gov.uk

LEWIS AND HARRIS

The only sizeable town on the Western Isles, Stornoway, on Lewis, offers a number of attractions from museum to public park and is the administrative centre for the islands. By taking the road to Tolsta north-east of the town, a flavour of the island can be experienced. The green croft land and the superb beaches towards Tolsta are unusual for the east coast. At the Tolsta road-end there is a well-built bridge constructed by Lord Leverhulme, former landowner and developer. The road stops just beyond, hence the place is known as the 'Bridge to Nowhere'. It was intended to continue the road to Ness on the Butt of Lewis.

Instead, to reach the most northerly point, the route goes across the bleak brown moorland heart of the island, seemingly empty save for peat-cuttings. Lewis is peat covered and its moorland seems to rise and dip in long waves, a feature noticeable particularly on the road which runs via Calanais, past the Dun Carloway broch and northwards. Among a number of prehistoric sites by the road is the Clach an Truseil (at Ballantrushal) – the largest single standing stone in Scotland. It is a grey lichen covered tooth with a definite presence, standing around 6 m (19 ft) high. Ness, the end of the road, stands out to the wild Atlantic. Though the cliffs by the lighthouse at the Butt of Lewis are not as impressive as elsewhere, the trip is well worthwhile just for the wind-blown exhilaration of being at the tip of the island. It is also a good place for whale-watching.

Harris, in contrast to Lewis, is rough and mountainous – its highest point, Clisham, reaches 799m (2620ft). A good way to sample the island ambience is to take the Huisinis road, passing the curious remains of an old whaling station at Bunavoneadar, and switchbacking on beyond Amhuinnsuidhe Castle (strictly private) where a spectacular river cascades over smooth rocks. The end of the road, with its croftland and beach, overlooks the island of Scarp, scene of pre-war rocket experiments which were to be used to deliver mail to the island!

Harris also boasts some breathtaking beaches on the west side, of which Luskentyre is perhaps the best known. These dazzling dune-backed stretches contrast with the lunar landscape of the coast from Rodel north-eastwards. In fact, a suitably enhanced and coloured aerial sequence of part of these islands was used to represent the surface of the planet Jupiter in Stanley Kubrick's 1968 film *2001: A Space Odyssey*.

ST KILDA

On the edge of the Atlantic's continental shelf, 110 miles from the Scottish mainland, eight hour's sailing from the Western Isles, St Kilda qualifies for the most remote part of Britain. First peopled around 4000 years ago its population existed in all but total isolation from Scotland until the mid-nineteenth century, when island and islanders became a tourist curiosity.

The islanders' main food was seabirds, notably fulmars, gannets and puffins. In consequence, islanders were great cliff and rock climbers – as late as 1876 it was said that they caught 89,600 puffins alone. The seabirds were eaten either fresh or cured, and preferred young, when they were harvested from the nest sites. Adult birds were caught with fowling rods and snares. Only farming as a secondary occupation supplemented their diet, though crops did not always prosper in the short seasons.

The last 100 years of occupation until evacuation in 1930 was one of gradual erosion of the traditional way of life, first by mainland missionaries, secondly by tourists and thirdly by increasing contact with the mainland's diseases.

Today, the island archipelago is both a national nature reserve and a World Heritage Site. Some island statistics give an idea of the many unique aspects of St Kilda. It is Europe's most important seabird colony with the world's largest gannet colony on Boreray. It also has the largest colony of fulmars in Britain. (It no longer has the great auk, as the last one recorded in Scotland was killed here in 1840, four years ahead of its global extinction.) Stac an Armin and Stac Lee are the highest sea stacks in Britain and St Kilda also has the highest cliffs. The village in Hirta, along with the many stone-built cleits formerly used as food and fuel stores and found all over the islands, comprise one of Britain's most extensive groups of vernacular buildings.

There are no permanent residents on St Kilda now, though Hirta – the main island – has an all year round army presence. National Trust for Scotland and Scottish Natural Heritage wardens are in residence in the summer. During this time NTS work parties are usually also on the islands.

16 St Kilda

St Kilda is Britain's most remote group of islands. For 4000 years its inhabitants battled with the elements to survive before finally being evacuated in 1930. Now a World Heritage Site, the islands are renowned for their sea-cliffs and stacs, seabird colonies and historic significance. Conservation and archeological work are carried out by National Trust for Scotland work parties during the summer months.

A11 *50 miles W of the Outer Hebrides. Access by charter boat and with NTS work parties.*

🕙 Open all year round; access very difficult during the winter. Limited campsite, booking essential.

Contact any of the Western Isles tourist information centres.
National Trust for Scotland work parties:
Tel 01631 570000
www.nts.org.uk

17 Stornoway Trust Woodland Centre ★

Interactive Centre with guided tours by the Trust Rangers around the grounds of Lews Castle, gifted to the people of Stornoway in 1923.

J16 *In the grounds of Lews Castle, Stornoway.*

🅿 ♿ 🚻 ♨ ☕ 🏛 E 🏃 🎫 Free

🕐 Open all year, Mon-Sat, 10am–5pm.

Tel 01851 706916

18 Taigh Chearsabhagh Museum 🏛 and Arts Centre

Taigh Chearsabhagh was built around 1741, and was believed to be one of the first buildings in North Uist to have a slated roof. The museum displays items relating to the history and culture of North Uist, and houses a collection of over 2000 photographs documenting the social history of the island. The studio/gallery features changing exhibitions by local and mainland artists.

D10 *Short walk from Lochmaddy Pier on NW coast of North Uist.*

🅿 🚻 ♿ ☕ 🏛 E 🏃 🎫 £

🕐 Open all year, Mon-Sat, 10am–5pm.

Tel 01876 500293

www.taigh-chearsabhagh.org

19 Uig Heritage Centre 🏛

A visitor centre featuring local history-related displays and a collection of photographs.

F16 *Uig, W side of Lewis, off B8011 near Gallan Head.*

☕ E Free

🕐 Jun–Sept, daily; please telephone to confirm times. Tel 01851 672456

THE UISTS

South Uist, Benbecula and North Uist have huge stretches of beach along their 50 mile length on their western side, open to the Atlantic waves. Magnificent swathes of machair roll out behind the dunes in South Uist in particular. This southernmost island also has steep rocky hills on its eastern side, with both Beinn Mhor and Hecla around 600m (2000ft). There is a national nature reserve at Loch Druidibeg, where a varied landscape of loch and islands, heather moor and machair is in the care of Scottish Natural Heritage. Loch Druidibeg is an important breeding ground for greylag geese, usually only a winter visitor to Scotland.

Benbecula, the main administrative centre for the southern island grouping, is linked to the other two islands by causeways to north and south. As on the other islands, there are a number of sites of pre-history to visit but modern reality intrudes in the form of the army rocket range on the island. North Uist continues the pattern of rolling hill and loch scenery to the east, contrasting with the machair-lands of the west. The RSPB look after Balranald on North Uist, a varied habitat of loch, marsh, machair and sandy and rocky shore. This is wader and duck country, breeding at high density.

Skara Brae from the air

ORKNEY

First impressions of Orkney from the Scrabster-Stromness connection can be misleading as the ferry sails by way of the great cliffs of Hoy. Even the huge stack known as the Old Man of Hoy *(see p246)* is dwarfed by the cliffs to the north where the cliffs around St John's Head soar vertically in tiers of red and yellow sandstones to 348m (1140ft). This looks like wild country of moor and rock. Only as the boat turns into Hoy Sound is it realised that Hoy of the hills is the exception. Here, instead, on Mainland Orkney are the rolling greens, grazing herds and the tidy field boundaries of a farming landscape.

Though the farming may be as modern as anywhere else in Scotland, Orkney has another intriguing characteristic: past and present exist closely side by side. Cattle graze by standing stones. A band of Vikings, barely ten centuries ago, sheltered from a storm in the chambered cairn at Maes Howe *(see p246)*. They carved runes and a little dragon on slabs which neolithic masons had, with inch-perfect precision, slotted together about 4000 years before them. The Stone Age comes alive at Skara Brae *(see p248)*. This township's dwellings disappeared into the sand for thousands of years and re-emerged after a winter storm in 1850. Hearths and kerbstones, slab-built beds, stone dressers and cupboards bring an immediacy to the lives of folk living as much as five millennia ago. The wealth of prehistoric sites on the islands is almost confusing in its richness and chronology.

Like Shetland, Orkney attracts birdwatchers to a range of bird reserves, for example, Hobbister above Scapa Flow, with its hen harriers and short eared owls on the moor, or to Marwick Head *(see p246)*, where the memorial to Lord Kitchener stands grimly above dizzying vertical seabird cliffs. The RSPB also have a reserve on Hoy which walkers to the Old Man of Hoy will discover (as they are eyed suspiciously by the local great skuas who skulk around the bouldery moor). The Old Man of Hoy walk starts from Rackwick Bay. Here the cliffs sit like book-ends at either end of a beach, part sand, part polished rounded boulders. Here, too, on Hoy the tale of Scapa Flow as an naval anchorage is told at the fascinating Lyness Museum *(see p245)*.

The main town of Kirkwall is a busy place, with local crafts and jewellery shops on its main street. St Magnus Cathedral *(see p249)*, in the town, shows some of the finest Norman work in Scotland. The ferryport of Stromness is also worth exploring. Its narrow shore-side streets wind round the bay, which was a port of call for generations of whalers and Arctic explorers, a story portrayed in the local museum *(see p249)*.

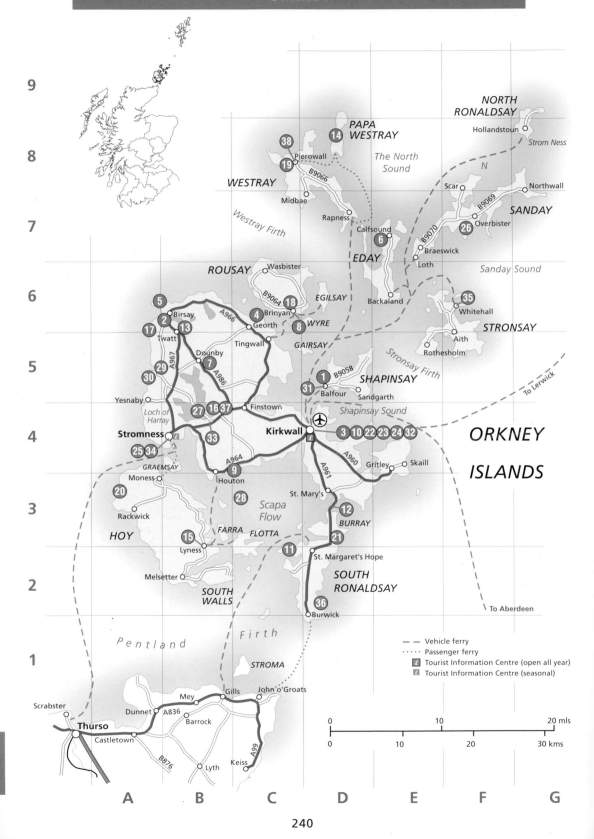

ORKNEY
ISLANDS

NORTH
RONALDSAY

PAPA
WESTRAY

WESTRAY

SANDAY

ROUSAY

EGILSAY

EDAY

STRONSAY

WYRE

GAIRSAY

SHAPINSAY

HOY

SCAPA
FLOW

FARRA

FLOTTA

BURRAY

SOUTH
WALLS

SOUTH
RONALDSAY

GRAEMSAY

STROMA

Pentland   Firth

Westray Firth

The North
Sound

Strom Ness

Sanday Sound

Stronsay Firth

Shapinsay Sound

To Lerwick

To Aberdeen

Hollandstoun
Northwall
Scar
Overbister
Braeswick
Loth
Whitehall
Aith
Rothesholm
Backaland
Calfsound
Rapness
Midbae
Pierowall
Wasbister
Brinyan
Geotth
Tingwall
Birsay
Twatt
Dounby
Finstown
Yesnaby
Stromness
Moness
Rackwick
Lyness
Melsetter
Houton
St. Mary's
Kirkwall
Balfour
Sandgarth
Gritley
Skaill
St. Margaret's Hope
Burwick
Scrabster
Thurso
Dunnet
Mey
Castletown
Barrock
Gills
John o'Groats
Keiss
Lyth

Loch of
Harray

B9066
B9064
B9058
B9069
B9070
A966
A967
A986
A964
A961
A960
A836
A99
B876

Legend

– – Vehicle ferry
····· Passenger ferry
🛈 Tourist Information Centre (open all year)
🛈 Tourist Information Centre (seasonal)

0   10   20 mls
0   10   20   30 kms

VISITOR INFORMATION

MAIN TOURIST INFORMATION CENTRE

Kirkwall
6 Broad Street
Kirkwall
Orkney KW15 1NX
Tel: 01856 872856
Web: www.visitorkney.com
E-mail: info@visitorkney.com
Open: all year round

SEASONAL TOURIST INFORMATION CENTRE

Stromness
The Ferry Terminal
Pier Head
Stromness
Orkney KW16 3BH
Tel: 01856 850716
Web: www.visitorkney.com
E-mail: stromness@visitorkney.com

ADDITIONAL INFORMATION

GENERAL TRAVEL INFORMATION
Traveline Scotland
Tel: 0870 608 2608
Provides timetable information for all public transport in Scotland and the rest of Great Britain.

AIR TRAVEL

Highlands & Islands Airports Limited
Kirkwall Airport
Kirkwall KW15 1TH
Tel: 01856 886210
Web: www.hial.co.uk/
kirkwall-airport.html
E-mail: hial@hial.co.uk

Aberdeen Airport
BAA Aberdeen
Aberdeen Airport
Dyce
Aberdeen AB21 7DU
Tel: 01224 722331
Web: www.baa.co.uk/main/airports/aberdeen

Airlines

British Airways PLC
(operated by Loganair)
Kirkwall Airport
Kirkwall
Orkney KW15 1TH
Tel: British Airways central reservations: 08457 733377
Web: www.britishairways.com
Routes: Aberdeen–Kirkwall
Edinburgh–Kirkwall
Glasgow–Kirkwall
Inverness–Kirkwall
Shetland–Kirkwall
Wick–Kirkwall

COACH / BUS

The Orkney Bus (Operates between May–Sept)
John O'Groats
Caithness KW1 4YR
Tel: 01955 611353
Web: www.jogferry.co.uk
E-mail: info@jogferry.co.uk
Route: Inverness–John O'Groats–Kirkwall

Orkney Coaches
Scotts Road
Hatston Industrial Estate
Kirkwall
Orkney KW15 1GR
Tel: 01856 870555
Web: www.rapsons.co.uk
E-mail: orkney@rapsons.co.uk
Route: operates all over Orkney mainland

Scottish Citylink Coaches Limited
Buchanan Bus Station
Killermont Street
Glasgow G2 3NP
Tel: 08705 505050
Web: www.citylink.co.uk
E-mail: info@citylink.co.uk
Route: Inverness–Scrabster

FERRIES

Booking is strongly recommended during the summer months

John O'Groats Ferries
(Operates between May–Sept)
John O'Groats
Caithness
KW1 4YR
Tel: 01955 611353
Web: www.jogferry.co.uk
E-mail: info@jogferry.co.uk
Route: John O'Groats–Burwick

NorthLink Ferries
NorthLink Orkney and Shetland Ferries Ltd
The New Harbour Building
Ferry Road
Stromness
KW16 3BH
Tel: 01856 851144
Web: www.northlinkferries.co.uk
E-mail: info@northlinkferries.co.uk
Routes: Aberdeen–Kirkwall
Scrabster–Stromness
Kirkwall–Lerwick

Orkney Ferries
Shore Street
Kirkwall
KW15 1LG
Tel: 01856 872044
Web: www.orkneyferries.co.uk
E-mail: info@orkneyferries.co.uk
Routes: operate between Orkney mainland and 13 of the smaller islands including:
South Isles
Shapinsay
Rousay
North Isles

Pentland Ferries Ltd
Pier Road
St Margaret's Hope
South Ronaldsay
KW17 2SW
Tel: 01856 831226
Web: www.pentlandferries.co.uk
E-mail: sales@pentlandferries.co.uk
Route: Gill's Bay (Caithness)–St Margaret's Hope (Orkney)

CAR HIRE

Airport Car Rental
Terminal Building
Kirkwall Airport
Tel: 01856 875500
Web: www.orkneycarrental.co.uk
E-mail: info@wr-tulloch.co.uk

Orkney Car Hire (operated by James D Peace & Co)
Junction Road
Kirkwall
Orkney KW15 1JY
Tel: 01856 872866
Web: www.orkneycarhire.co.uk
E-mail: info@orkneycarhire.co.uk

NW Brass Self Drive Car Hire
Blue Star Filling Station
North End Road
Stromness
Orkney
KW16 3AG
Tel: 01856 850850

John G Shearer & Sons
Ayre Service Station
Kirkwall
Tel: 01856 872950
E-mail: jgshearerandsons@talk21.com

WR Tulloch
Town Office
Castle Street
Kirkwall
Tel: 01856 876262

TAXIS

Bob's Taxis, Kirkwall
Tel: 01856 876543

Brass's Taxis, Stromness
Tel: 01856 850750

Hills of Hoy
Tel: 01856 791240

Kirkwall 5000, Kirkwall
Tel: 01856 875000

Kettletoft Garage, Sanday
Tel: 01857 600321

Mr T Logie, Westray
Tel: 01857 677218

Mr DF Peace, Stronsay
Tel: 01857 616335

Rainbow Taxis, Kirkwall
Tel: 01856 877000

Rousay Traveller, Rousay
Tel: 01856 821234

Mr A Stewart, Eday
Tel: 01857 622206

Stromness Taxis, Stromness
Tel: 01856 850973/851777

Stenness Standing Stones

1 Balfour Castle and Gardens

Tours are given of this mid-nineteenth century family-owned castle (now a hotel), with original furnishings; visitors also have access to an attractive Victorian walled garden.

D5 *Balfour, SW side of Isle of Shapinsay, on B9059.*

May–mid Sept, Sun, ferry departs at 2.15pm. Booking essential.

Tel 01856 711282   www.balfourcastle.co.uk

2 Barony Mills

Now run by the Birsay Heritage Trust, this working water-powered meal mill and kiln was built in 1873, and is the last of it's kind in Orkney. Records indicate that there have been mills on this site and in the area going back to Viking times. The miller is the third generation of his family to operate the mill, which produces bere meal, ground from an ancient form of locally grown barley.

B6 *On A967, main road from Dounby to Earl's Palace, Birsay.*

Free

May–Sept, daily, 10am–1pm & 2–5pm.

Tel 01856 721439
www.orkneyheritage.com

3 Bishop's and Earl's Palaces, Kirkwall

The Bishops' Palace dates back to the twelfth century, with various additions over the years, one of the most significant being a sixteenth century round tower. Patrick Stewart, Earl of Orkney, was responsible for building the elegant Rennaissance-style Earl's Palace (adjacent to the Bishop's Palace) in the early seventeenth century.

D4 *Palace Road, opposite St Magnus Cathedral, Kirkwall town centre, Mainland.*

E £

Apr–Sept, daily, 9.30am–6.30pm.

Tel 01856 875461   www.historic-scotland.gov.

4 Broch of Gurness

The site features a broch, reaching 10 ft in height, surrounded by the remains of an Iron Age settlement, with stone buildings, ditches and ramparts.

C6 *Aikerness on the A966, 14 miles NW of Kirkwall, Mainland.*

Apr–Sept, daily, 9.30am–6.30pm.

Tel 01856 751414   www.historic-scotland.gov.uk

5 Brough of Birsay

Visitors can see the remains of Pictish and Norse settlements, most notably ruins of Norse houses and a twelfth century Romanesque church.

A6 *On a tidal island at Birsay, off the A960, NW side of Mainland. Access is via pedestrian causeway and dependent on tides.*

£

Mid Jun–Sept, daily, 9.30am–6.30pm, when tide permits.

Tel 01856 721205/841815

www.historic-scotland.gov.uk

6 Carrick House

Seventeenth century Laird's house set on the shore of the Bay and Carrick, built by John Stewart, brother of Robert Stewart, 2nd Earl of Orkney. Notorious pirate John Gow was held prisoner here in 1725. Guided tours are given by the owner.

E7 *Ferry runs from Kirkwall twice a day; the house is set at the end of a private road at the N of Eday.*

Mid Jun–Mid Sept, Sun, from 2pm. Groups welcome by arrangement.

Tel 01857 622260

7 Corrigall Farm Museum

A late nineteenth century Orkney farmstead with stone furnishings and heather thatch, along with a working barn, grain kiln and traditional livestock.

B5 *Harray, two miles SE of Dounby on A986.*

Free

Mar–Oct, Mon–Sat, 10.30am–1pm & 2–5pm; Sun, 2–7pm.

Tel 01856 873191   www.orkneyheritage.com

8 Cubbie Row's Castle and St Mary's Chapel

Norseman Kilbein Hruga built this twelfth century rectangular stone tower, with surrounding ditch. The Romanesque remains of St Mary's Chapel date from around the same time.

D6 *Island of Wyre, half a mile from the pier.*

Free

⊕ Open access.

Tel 0131 668 8800   www.historic-scotland.gov.uk
Ferry information: Tel 01856 872044

9 Earl's Bu and Church, Orphir

The Earl's Bu refers to a set of ancient foundations, thought to be an Earl's residence from the Viking era. A medieval round church, unique to Scotland, features a chancel and nave.

C4 *On A964, by Houton, SW side of Mainland.*

P Free

⊕ Open access.

Tel 01856 841815   www.historic-scotland.gov.uk

10 Highland Park Distillery

Highland Park Distillery, established over 200 years ago, welcomes visitors and offers tours, an audio-visual presentation and a dram.

D4 *One mile outside Kirkwall, on Holm Road.*

P WC ⅃ ☕ ⅋ E AV ⅏ £

⊕ Apr–Oct, Mon–Fri, 10am–5pm.
Jul–Aug, Sat–Sun, 2pm–5pm.
Tours every 1/2 hour, last tour 4pm.
Nov–Mar, afternoon tour only at 2pm.

Tel 01856 874619   www.highlandpark.co.uk

11 Hoxa Tapestry Gallery

Studio with shop and work in progress, plus a gallery exhibiting large hand-woven tapestries inspired by the rhythm of life and landscape of Orkney.

C2 *NW of South Ronaldsay, off B9043 at Hoxa Head.*

⊕ Apr–Sept, Mon–Fri, 10am–5.30pm;
weekends, 2–6pm.

Tel 01856 831395
www.hoxatapestrygallery.co.uk

12 Italian Chapel

A beautiful chapel adapted from Nissen huts by Italian prisoners of war who were on Orkney helping to construct the Churchill Barriers during World War Two.

D3 *Off A961, between Mainland and Burray.*

P Free

⊕ All year round, daily, daylight hours.

Tel 01856 872856   www.visitorkney.com

13 Kirbuster Museum

Kirbuster is home to the last surviving 'fire hoose' with central peat hearth in Orkney. Visitors can also make use of the Victorian garden.

B6 *Kirbuster, S of Birsay off A967/A986 junction at Twatt, NW side of Mainland.*

P WC ⅃ ⅋ ⅂ Free

⊕ Mar–Oct, Mon–Sat, 10.30am–1pm & 2–5pm;
Sun, 2–7pm.

Tel: 01856 873191   www.orkneyheritage.com

14 Knap of Howar

Evidence indicates that these two neolothic houses, with stone cupboards and stalls, date from 3600–3100 BC, making them the earliest settlement site in Orkney, and indeed NW Europe. The buildings are well constructed, with the walls still reaching to around ceiling-level.

D8 *Near Holland Farm, Papa Westray.*

Free

⊕ Open access.

Tel 01856 841815   www.historic-scotland.gov.uk
Ferry informations: 01856 872004

15 Lyness Visitor Centre

The pump room of this past naval base now houses an interpretation centre with memorabilia from the first and second world wars.

B2 *Two minutes from ferry terminal.*

P WC ⅃ ⅋ ⅏ E AV ⅏ Free

⊕ May–Oct, daily, 9am–4.30pm.
Oct–May, Mon–Fri, 9am–4.30pm.
If travelling by car, please book ferry in advance.

Tel 01856 791300
Ferry bookings: 01856 811397

16 Maes Howe

Maes Howe, a seemingly ordinary mound from the exterior, is one of the finest megalithic sites in the country. A narrow stone-built passage leads into the centre of the mound to a large burial chamber containing a number of cells set into the walls. Of equal significance are extensive runic inscriptions which were carved on the walls by Vikings during a raid in the twelfth century.

B4 *On the A965, nine miles W of Kirkwall.*

P WC ♥ E ⌂ ££

⊕ Apr–Sept, daily, 9.30am–6.30pm.
  Oct–Mar, Mon–Sat, 9.30am–4.30pm;
  Sun, 2–4.30pm.

Tel 01856 761606   www.historic-scotland.gov.uk

17 Marwick Head RSPB Reserve

Dramatic cliffs at Marwick Head are home to a variety of seabirds such as razorbills, kittiwakes and guillemots. Lying just northwards is the memorial tower dedicated to Lord Kitchener.

A6 *Off B9056, SW of Birsay, Mainland.*

P ☀ 🚶

⊕ Open access.

Tel 01856 872856

18 Midhowe Broch and Midhowe Chambered Cairn

A well preserved broch, surrounded by the remains of later buildings. The nearby Neolithic chambered tomb, built in an oval shape, holds some 25 stalls and is protected by a modern building.

C6 *Five miles from the pier on Rousay.*

Free

⊕ Open access.

Tel 01856 841815   www.historic-scotland.gov.uk
Ferry information: 01856 751360

19 Noltland Castle

Construction of Noltland, a z-plan tower, began during the sixteenth century but was left unfinished. Of particular interest are the gun loops and fine staircase.

C8 *One mile W of Pierowall, on island of Westray.*

£

⊕ Mid Jun–Sept, daily, 9.30am–6.30pm.

Tel 01856 841815   www.historic-scotland.gov.uk
Ferry information: Tel 01856 872044

20 Old Man of Hoy

This 450ft sea stack, off the coast of Hoy, is one of Orkney's most famous landmarks. Walkers can reach the site via a path (steep at times) from Rackwick. A round trip takes approx. three hours.

A3 *NW coast of Hoy.*

☀ Free

⊕ Open access.

Tel 01856 872856   www.visitorkney.com
Ferry information: Tel 01856 850624

21 Orkney Fossil and Vintage Centre

Houses an exhibition of fossils, both local and worldwide, along with archive materials such as old photographs and maps.

D3 *Burray, 12 miles S of Kirkwall, Orkney Mainland.*

P WC ♿ ♥ ⌂ E £

⊕ Apr–Sept, daily, 10am–6pm.

Tel 01856 731255   www.orkneyheritage.com

22 Orkney Museum, Tankerness House and Gardens

Set in the town house and gardens of an Orkney laird, the museum tells the story of Orkney from Medieval times to the present day. Stone Age, Pictish and Viking artefacts are on display, including Neolithic spiral carvings and a Norse whale bone linen smoothing board.

D4 *Kirkwall centre, opposite St. Magnus Cathedral.*

WC ♿ ⌂ E ▣ Free

Old Man of Hoy

🕐 Apr–Sept, Mon–Sat, 10.30am–5pm; Sun 2–5pm.
   Oct–Mar, 10.30am–12.30pm & 1.30–5pm.

Tel 01856 873191   www.orkneyheritage.com

23 Orkney Wireless Museum 🏛

Along with a collection of domestic radio
equipment such as receivers, valves,
gramophones and transistors, is the
history of Orkney's war years, and the
part in which radio and telephones played
in protecting the home fleet in Scapa Flow.

D4 *Near the harbour, Kirkwall town centre.*

WC ♿ 🏛 E £

🕐 Apr–Oct, Mon–Sat, 10am–4pm.

Tel 01856 871400

24 Ortak Visitor Centre 🏛

Visitors can learn how jewellery is made
via a video and demonstrations.

D4 *Hatston Industrial Estate, Kirkwall.*

P WC ♿ 🏛 E AV 🎫 Free

🕐 Easter–Dec, Mon–Sat, 9am–5pm.
   Jan–Easter, Mon–Fri, 9am–5pm.

Tel 01856 872224   www.ortak.co.uk

25 Pier Arts Centre ★

A listed waterfront building which houses
an interesting variety of paintings and
sculptures by a number of British and
Orcadian artists, and runs changing
exhibitions throughout the year.

B4 *Stromness town centre, by the harbour,
SW side of Mainland.*

WC 🏛 E Free

🕐 All year round, Tues–Sat, 10.30am–12.30pm
   & 1.30–5pm.

Tel 01856 850209   www.orkneyheritage.com

26 Quoyness Chambered Cairn 🅱 🏛

Visitors can follow the passage which
runs through this Neolithic tomb into
a large chamber containing six cells.

F7 *Off B9060, S side of Sanday.*

Free

🕐 Open access.

Tel 01856 841815   www.orkneyheritage.com
Ferry information: 01856 872044

27 Ring of Brodgar Stone Circle and Henge

An impressive Neolithic stone circle (103.7 m in diameter), thought to have originally comprised of 60 stones, now has 36, including stumps. A ditch with causeways runs round the site.

B4 *On B9055, five miles NE of Stromness, Mainland.*

P Free

☺ Open access.

Tel 01856 841815   www.historic-scotland.gov.uk

28 Scapa Flow

Displays in Lyness Pumphouse, Scapa Flow Visitor Centre, tell the story of this naval anchorage through the two world wars, in particular, the scuttling of the German fleet here in 1919, and the sinking of the Royal Oak twenty years later. Visitors can take organised boat trips across Scapa Flow and see the scuttled wrecks.

C3 *Visitor centre: off A964 to Houton Ferry; ferry to Lyness, Hoy. Boat trips: run by Roving Eye in the summer months, weather permitting; trips leave from Orphir, off the A964, by Scapa Flow.*

P **WC** 🍵 🏛 E **AV** Free

☺ Visitor centre: All year, Mon–Fri, 9am–4pm. Jun–Sept, Sat, 9am–4pm; Sun, 10am–4pm.

Visitor Centre: Tel 01856 873191
www.orkneyheritage.com
Roving Eye: Tel 01856 811360

29 Skaill House

A handsome seventeenth century family home containing a variety of exhibits such as Captain Cook's dinner service from his ship the Resolution, plus sporting and military items.

B5 *Aith, W side of Mainland on B9056.*

P ♿ 🏛 E 🅱 ££

☺ Apr–Sept, daily, 9.30am–6.30pm.

Tel 01856 841501   www.skaillhouse.com

30 Skara Brae Prehistoric Village

This remarkable Stone Age village, consisting of ten one-roomed houses, is the best preserved Neolithic village in Europe. The rooms contain an array of stone furniture, hearths and drains, and give a valuable insight into how people lived in 3000 BC. A museum provides information on the site and displays a number of artefacts.

A5 *On B9056, 19 miles NW of Kirkwall, Mainland.*

P 🍵 E ££

Skara Brae

🕐 Apr–Sept, daily, 9.30am–6.30pm.
Oct–Mar, Mon–Sat, 9.30am–4.30pm;
Sun, 2–4.30pm.

Tel 01856 841815   www.historic-scotland.gov.uk

31 Smithy

A museum focusing on the history of Shapinsay,
particularly the local herring industry, with an
array of photographs and memorabilia.

D5 *Balfour village, by the pier, Shapinsay.*

[wc] 🍴 ⛪ E £

🕐 Opening times vary; please telephone to confirm.

Tel 01856 711258

32 St Magnus Cathedral ✝

This twelfth century cathedral, with later
additions, was founded by Earl Rognvald Kolson
in honour of his uncle St Magnus. Built from
local red sandstone, it is very well preserved
and still used as a regular place of worship,
with services every Sunday.

D4 *Broad Street, Kirkwall town centre, Mainland.*

Free

🕐 Apr–Sept, Mon–Sat, 9am–6pm; Sun, 2–6pm.
Oct–Mar, Mon–Sat, 9am–1pm & 2–5pm.

Tel 01856 874894

33 Stones of Stenness Circle and Henge

This small but significant circle dates as far
back as 3000 BC; four stones, three of which
are impressive in height, remain from the
original set of twelve.

B4 *On B9055, five miles NE of Stromness, Mainland.*

P Free

🕐 Open access.

Tel 01856 841815   www.historic-scotland.gov.uk

34 Stromness Museum

This restored Victorian museum looks at natural
history including fossils, birds, butterflies, fish
and mammals, along with maritime and social
history such as whaling, shipping and the
German fleet in Scapa Flow.

B4 *Alfred Street, Stromness, Orkney.*

♿ ⛪ E £

🕐 May–Sept, daily, 10am–5pm.
Oct–Mar, Mon–Sat, 10.30am–12.30pm; 1.30–5pm.

Tel 01856 873195   www.orkneyheritage.com

35 Stronsay Fish Mart

An interpretation centre devoted to the herring
fishing days and other aspects of past life
on the island.

F6 *Whitehall, N of Stronsay on B9060,
near the pier.*

[wc] ♿ 🍴 E

🕐 Summer, daily; ring to confirm opening times.

Tel 01857 616360

36 Tomb of the Eagles

A museum, depicting life in Orkney during
the Stone and Bronze Age. Explore the
5000 year old chambered tomb at its clifftop
site and handle some of the artefacts found
within it. Allow sufficient time (1½–2 hours)
to visit the tomb.

D2 *South Ronaldsay, seven miles S of
St Margaret's Hope.*

P [wc] ♿ ⛪ E [AV] ⛱ ☀ 👥 ££

🕐 Daily; Mar, 10am–12noon. Apr–Oct, 9.30am–6pm.
Nov–Feb, by arrangement.

Tel 01856 831339   www.tomboftheeagles.co.uk

37 Tormiston Mill

A late nineteenth century watermill with
original machinery and waterwheel; it now
acts as a reception centre for visitors to
Maes Howe *(see p246).*

B4 *On the A965, nine miles W of Kirkwall, Mainland.*

P [wc] 🍴 ⛪ E Free

🕐 Apr–Sept, daily, 9.30am–6.30pm.
Oct–Mar, Mon–Sat, 9.30am–4.30pm;
Sun, 2–4.30pm.

Tel 01856 761606
www.historic-scotland.gov.uk

38 Westray Heritage Centre 🏛

An ideal place to find out about the island's
history, natural heritage and way of life over
the years. Local artists, crafts people and writers
have designed interpretation panels, models and
interactives to help the visitor find places to
go and things to do while on the island.

C8 *Beside the Pierowall Hotel, Pierowall centre.*

P [wc] ♿ 🍴 ⛪ E 🔊 £

🕐 May–Sept, Sun & Mon, 11.30am–5pm;
Tue–Sat, 10am–12 noon; 2–5pm.

Tel 01857 677414

Eshaness, North Mainland

SHETLAND ISLES

Below the horizon from mainland Scotland, some say Shetland was first settled from the Scottish mainland because Orkney is visible from Caithness. From Orkney, Fair Isle can just be made out and from Fair Isle the cliffs at Sumburgh Head can be seen on the northern horizon. This gave a series of northerly bearings for the early sea-going people to sail on. True or otherwise, Shetland has a sea-going tradition stretching far back in time. It is sometimes described as a kind of crossroads of the northern seas. It certainly has close links with Scandinavia and, overall, feels more Scandinavian than Scottish.

In this island archipelago the taste of the sea is always in the air. Nowhere is more than about five km (three miles) from it. Sea stacks, islets and offshore rocks, cliffs and long sea inlets, (called voes), as well as the narrower gully-like geos, fret the coastline and create habitat for seals and otters, as well as breeding places for spectacular seabird colonies.

Shetland's birds are, however, not confined to cliffs. The moorland rough grazings are patrolled by great skuas, a pirate and predator which will fearlessly dive-bomb anyone approaching its nest site. And there are other northern species of divers and phalaropes which attract birdwatchers. In short, Shetland is a very birdy place.

There is also a good range of prehistoric sites, including the Bronze Age round towers or brochs so characteristic of the Northen Isles. The best preserved is the famous Mousa Broch, on the island of the same name *(see p258)*. Jarlshof on the south end of Mainland (as the largest island is called) is another popular excursion, with its complex overlays of ancient settlements from the Bronze Age to the Vikings and beyond *(see p258)*.

Shetland's main town is Lerwick, with interesting town architecture, including the lodberries at the sea edge, old merchants' houses with their private piers. Scalloway is the island's ancient capital, built around its harbour and guarded by the stark tower of its seventeenth century castle *(see p260)*.

Though there are outstanding seabird encounters to be enjoyed on Noss *(see p259)*, beyond Bressay close to Lerwick, a visit to Hermaness *(see p257)* on Unst is a true northern edge experience. (Like Noss, it is a national nature reserve, with gannet and auk colonies, and great and Arctic skuas.) Inter-island ferries make travel straightforward via Yell. From the top of Hermaness Hill, reached on foot, there are views (and a longer walk) to the cliff edge, beyond which are the lighthouse-topped rocks of Muckle Flugga and the northernmost tip of Britain.

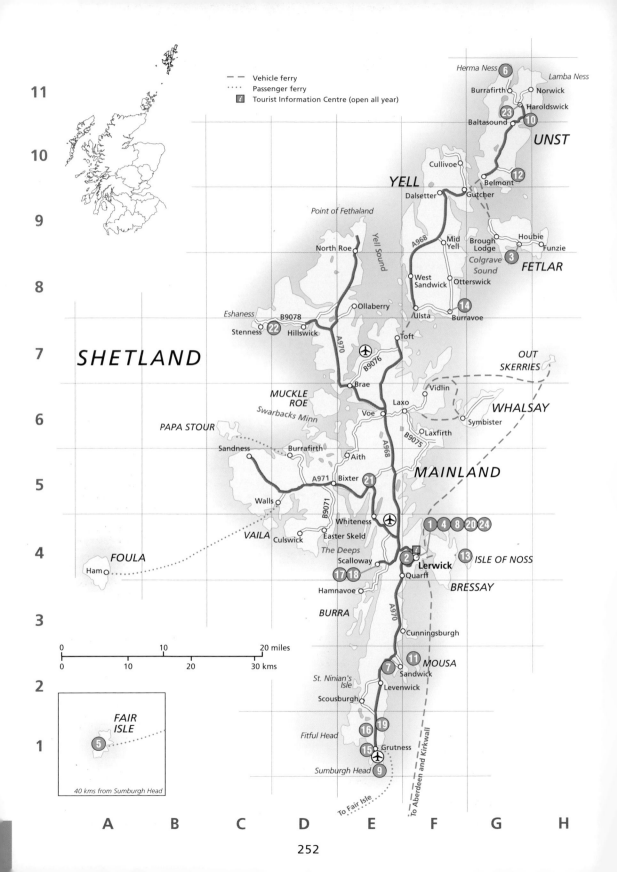

Map Legend

– – – Vehicle ferry
· · · · · Passenger ferry
ℹ️ Tourist Information Centre (open all year)

SHETLAND

YELL

UNST

FETLAR

Herma Ness
Lamba Ness
Burrafirth
Norwick
Haroldswick
Baltasound
Cullivoe
Belmont
Dalsetter
Gutcher
Point of Fethaland
Mid Yell
Brough Lodge
Houbie
Funzie
North Roe
West Sandwick
Otterswick
Colgrave Sound
Yell Sound
Eshaness
Ollaberry
Ulsta
Burravoe
Stenness
Hillswick
B9078
Toft
OUT SKERRIES
Brae
Vidlin
WHALSAY
MUCKLE ROE
Laxo
Swarbacks Minn
Voe
Laxfirth
Symbister
PAPA STOUR
B9075
Sandness
Burrafirth
Aith
MAINLAND
Bixter
A968
A971
Walls
Whiteness
VAILA
Easter Skeld
Culswick
The Deeps
Scalloway
Lerwick
ISLE OF NOSS
FOULA
Ham
Hamnavoe
Quarff
BRESSAY
BURRA
Cunningsburgh
MOUSA
A970
St. Ninian's Isle
Sandwick
Levenwick
Scousburgh
Fitful Head
Grutness
Sumburgh Head
To Fair Isle
To Aberdeen and Kirkwall

FAIR ISLE

40 kms from Sumburgh Head

0   10   20 miles
0   10   20   30 kms

VISITOR INFORMATION

MAIN TOURIST INFORMATION CENTRE

Shetland
Market Cross
Lerwick
Shetland
ZE1 0LU
Tel: 01595 693434
Web: www.visitshetland.com
E-mail: shetland.tourism@zetnet.co.uk
Open: all year round

ADDITIONAL INFORMATION

GENERAL TRAVEL INFORMATION

Traveline Scotland
Tel: 0870 608 2608
Provides timetable information for all public transport in Scotland and the rest of Great Britain.

AIR TRAVEL

Highlands & Islands
Airports Limited
Sumburgh Airport
Wilsmess Terminal
Virkie
ZE3 9JP
Tel: 01950 461000
Web: www.hial.co.uk/
sumburgh-airport.html
E-mail: hial@hial.co.uk

Aberdeen Airport
BAA Aberdeen
Aberdeen Airport
Dyce
Aberdeen AB21 7DU
Tel: 01224 722331
Web:
www.baa.co.uk/main/airports/aberdeen

Airlines

British Airways PLC
(operated by Loganair)
Sumburgh Airport
Virkie
ZE3 9JP
Tel: British Airways central
reservations:
08457 733377
Web: www.britishairways.com
Routes:
Aberdeen–Shetland
Belfast–Shetland
Birmingham–Shetland

Edinburgh–Shetland
Glasgow–Shetland
Inverness–Shetland
Manchester–Shetland
Orkney–Shetland

Inter-island air services

British Airways PLC
(operated by Loganair)
Tingwall Airport
Tingwall
Tel: British Airways central reservations:
08457 733377
Web: www.britishairways.com
Routes:
Fair Isle–Sumburgh
(summer only)
Tingwall–Fair Isle
Tingwall–Out Skerries
Tingwall–Foula
Tingwall–Papa Stour

COACH / BUS

John Leask & Son
Esplanade
Lerwick
ZE1 0LL
Tel: 01595 693162
Web: www.leaskstravel.co.uk
E-mail: leasks@zetnet.co.uk
Routes include:
Lerwick–Sumburgh airport
Lerwick–Toft ferry terminal

Whites Coaches
West Burrafirth
Bridge of Walls
ZE2 9NT
Tel: 01595 809443
Routes include:
Eshaness–Ollaberry–
North Roe–Sullom
Hillswick–Lerwick–
Hillswick
Lerwick–Laxo–Vidlin–Lerwick
Toft–Mossbank–Lerwick

P&T Coaches
Baltasound Industrial Estate
Unst
ZE2 9DS
Tel: 01957 711666
Routes include:
Haroldswick–Baltasound–
Belmont

H Sinclair & Co.
Westsandwick
ZE2 9BH
Tel: 01957 766224
Route: Yell–West Sandwick–
Mid Yell–Ulsta

RJ Jameson
Moarfield
Cullivoe
ZE2 9DD
Tel: 01957 744214
Route: Gutcher–Ulsta

FERRIES

Booking is strongly recommended during the summer months

NorthLink Ferries
NorthLink Orkney and Shetland
Ferries Ltd
The New Harbour Building
Ferry Road
Stromness
KW16 3BH
Tel: 01856 851144
Web: www.northlinkferries.co.uk
E-mail: info@northlinkferries.co.uk
Route: Aberdeen–Lerwick
Aberdeen–Orkney–Lerwick
Scrabster–Stromness–Kirkwall–Lerwick

Inter-island ferries

Shetland Islands Council
Director of Ferries
Marine Operations Department
Sellaness
Graven
Mossbank
ZE2 9QR
Tel: 01806 244219
Web: www.shetland.gov.uk
/ferryinfo/ferry.htm
Routes:
Bressay–Lerwick (Mainland)
Symbister (Whalsay)–Laxo (Mainland)
Ulsta (Yell)–Toft (Mainland)
Gutcher (Yell)–Oddsta (Fetlar)
–Belmont (Unst)
Out Skerries–Vidlin (Mainland)

Inter-island passenger only ferries

Mousa Boat Trips
(Operates between Apr–Sept)
(Mr T Jameson)
Pytaslee
Leebitton
Sandwick
ZE2 9HP
Tel: 01950 431367
Web: www.mousaboattrips.co.uk
E-mail: info@mousaboattrips.co.uk
Route: Sandwick–Mousa

Shetland Islands Council
Director of Ferries
Marine Operations Department
Sellaness
Graven
Mossbank
ZE2 9BD
Operates the following services:

Papa Stour Service
Tel: 01595 810460
Contact: Mr W Clark
Route: West–Burrafirth–Papa Stour–West Burrafirth

Foula Service
Tel: 01595 753226
Contact: Mr B Taylor
Route: Foula–Walls–Foula

Fair Isle Service
Tel: 01595 760222
Contact: Mr JW Stout
Route: Sumburgh–Fair Isle–Sumburgh

CAR HIRE

Bolts Car Hire
Toll Shopping Centre
26 North Road
Lerwick ZE1 0PE
Tel: 01595 693636
www.boltscarhire.co.uk

Grantfield Car Hire
North Road
Lerwick ZE1 0NT
Tel: 01595 692709
Web: www.grantfieldgarage.co.uk
E-mail: admin@grantfieldgarage.co.uk

John Leask & Son
The Esplanade
Lerwick ZE1 0LL
Tel: 01595 693162
Web: www.leaskstravel.co.uk
E-mail: leasks@zetnet.co.uk

Star Rent-a-Car
22 Commercial Road
Lerwick ZE1 0LX
Tel: 01595 692075
Web: www.starrentacar.co.uk
E-mail: admin@starrentacar.co.uk

Wilsness Terminal
Sumburgh Airport
Virkie ZE3 9JP
Tel: 01950 460777
Web: www.boltscarhire.co.uk

TAXIS

Graham Ball
Lerwick
Tel: 01595 696638

Allied Taxis
Lerwick
Tel: 01595 690069

Peca's Taxis
Lerwick
Tel: 07860 465767

Roy's Taxi Service
Lerwick
Tel: 01595 692080

John Halcrow
Hamnavoe
Burra Isles
Tel: 01595 859369

Boddam Cabs
Sumburgh
Tel: 01950 460111

Johnson Transport
Brae
Tel: 01806 522443

R & G Jamieson
Cullivoe
Tel: 01957 744214

R. Robertson & Son
Ulsta
Tel: 01957 722253

Sinclair's Taxis
Lerwick
Tel: 01595 694617

60/50 Cabs
Lerwick
Tel: 01595 696050

Dore Holm, North Mainland

FAIR ISLE

Measuring just four square miles, the Fair Isle is the most southerly of the Shetland Islands, and is owned by the National Trust for Scotland. The community sustains a living through crofting and crafts, particularly the production of items using the famous Fair Isle knitting patterns. The island also attracts tourists, especially bird enthusiasts who come to see the colonies of puffins, guillemots, kittiwakes and other seabirds found around the cliffs and stacks, plus an assortment of migratory birds which arrive in search of shelter. Access is by air from Sumburgh (summer only) and Tingwall, and by ferry from Sumburgh (see p253-254 for travel details, and entry for George Waterston Memorial Centre and Museum on p257).

1 Bod of Gremista Museum

An eighteenth century fishing bod (booth) famous as the birthplace of Arthur Anderson, co-founder of P&O Ferries. On show are period furniture, fittings and artefacts, plus displays on fishing and the life of Anderson.

F4 *Gremista, Lerwick.*

P WC 🏛 E ☕ 🚶 Free

🕑 May–mid Sept, Wed–Sun, 10am–1pm & 2–5pm.

Tel 01595 695057

www.shetland-museums.org.uk

2 Clickimin Broch

A broch on the edge of a loch, with adjacent buildings dating back to the Iron Age.

F4 *One mile SW of Lerwick on the A970.*

Free

🕑 Open access.

Tel 0131 668 8800   www.historic-scotland.gov.uk

3 Fetlar Interpretive Centre

A combined museum/information centre, with an exhibition on the area's history, folklore and geology, plus photographs and films dating from the 1930s onwards.

G9 *Beach of Houbie, Fetlar, four miles from car ferry.*

P WC ♿ 🏛 E AV 🎦 £

🕑 May–Sept, Mon–Fri, 1–5pm.

Tel 01957 733206   www.fetlar.com

4 Fort Charlotte

Fort Charlotte was originally built in the seventeenth century, burned down by the Dutch during a war with England, and finally reconstructed in the 1780s.

F4 *Lerwick town centre, Mainland.*

Free

🕑 Apr–Sept, daily, 9.30am–5.45pm. Oct–Mar, Mon–Sat, 9.30am–3.45pm; Sun, 2–4.30pm. Keys available locally during these times.

Tel 0131 668 8800   www.historic-scotland.gov.uk

FOULA

Foula, lying over 25 miles west of Scalloway, is one of the country's most remote inhabited islands. Great and Arctic skuas breed on the moorland, while extensive seabird colonies can be found around the cliffs, parts of which stretch to a height of some 372 m (1220 ft). Access is by air from Tingwall and ferry from Walls *(see p253-254 for details)*.

5 George Waterston Memorial Centre and Museum

Studies the social history of the Fair Isle, particularly the famous knitting traditions and patterns, plus natural history and archaeology.

A1 *Busta, Fair Isle.*

♿ ⛩ E Free

⏰ May–Sept, Mon, 2–4pm; Wed, 10.30am–12 noon; Fri, 2–4pm. Other times by appointment.

Tel 01595 760244

6 Hermaness National Nature Reserve

Cliffs and stacks are home to thousands of seabirds, with particularly significant numbers of gannets and puffins, while a huge colony of great skuas can be found all over the moorland area. Visitors can also look towards the small island of Muckle Flugga with its automated lighthouse, the most notherly point of the British Isles. Best visited from mid May–mid July, although fog is common around this time.

G11 *N tip of Unst. Follow B9086 to car park.*

P WC E ⛶ 🚶 Free

⏰ Reserve: open access. Visitor centre: Apr–Sept, daily, 9am–5pm.

Tel 01595 693345   www.snh.org.uk

7 Hoswick Visitor Centre

Houses a range of fishing, crofting and weaving artefacts and machines, along with a collection of domestic and military radios.

E2 *Hoswick, off A970, S side of Mainland.*

P WC ♿ ☕ ⛩ E Free

⏰ May–Sept, Mon–Sat, 10am–5pm; Sun, 11am–5pm.

Tel 01950 431406

8 Islesburgh Exhibition of Shetland Crafts and Culture

The exhibition contains a specially constructed stage set depicting a crofthouse in the 1920s, along with photographs, arts and crafts. Volunteers are on hand to demonstrate knitting, carding and spinning. A programme of events include evenings of traditional music and dance, and screenings of old Shetland films.

F4 *Islesburgh Community Centre, Lerwick, Mainland.*

E £

Mid May–mid Sept, Mon & Wed, 7–8.30pm.

Tel 01595 692114 www.islesburgh.org.uk

9 Jarlshof Prehistoric and Norse Settlement

This site of great historical importance is made up of a number of ancient settlements. A Bronze Age village of stone buildings is the oldest part, while lying adjacent is an Iron Age broch and a number of distinctive wheel-houses. Also of significance are the remains of an entire Viking settlement, and a late sixteenth/early seventeenth century mansion house. A visitor centre contains information on prehistoric Scotland and the site.

E1 *At Sumburgh Head, off A970, 22 miles S of Lerwick.*

E ££

Apr–Sept, daily, 9.30am–6.30pm.

Tel 01950 460112 www.historic-scotland.gov.uk

10 Keen of Hamar National Nature Reserve

The rocky terrain allows a number of unusual plants to grow such as the endemic Edmondston's chickweed, which is unique to Unst. Best visited from mid May to early July.

G11 *NE side of Unst. Follow signs on A968 to car park; short walk to the reserve.*

Free

Open access.

Tel 01595 693345 www.snh.org.uk

11 Mousa Broch

Mousa, the finest of all Scotland's brochs, is remarkably well preserved, measuring over 43 ft (13 m) in height. It is located on the small uninhabited island of Mousa, and access is by boat from Sandwick.

F2 *On the island of Mousa off SE Mainland. A boat runs from Sandwick, off A970.*

Free

Ferries run Apr–Sept; please contact operator to confirm days and times.

www.historic-scotland.gov.uk
Ferry: Tel 01950 431367
www.mousaboattrips.co.uk

12 Muness Castle

Muness, the most northerly castle in the British Isles, takes the form of a tower house with circular towers. Dating from the sixteenth century, it has retained a number of fine archtectural details.

G10 *Four miles E of Belmont pier on SE tip of Unst.* *(For ferry details, see p253-254)*

Free

Open access.

www.historic-scotland.gov.uk

Mousa Broch

13 Noss National Nature Reserve

Home to thousands of seabirds such as gannets, guillemots, fulmar, kittiwakes and puffins plus a number of great skuas, best observed from late May to mid July (fog is common in the early summer). A walk around the island takes approx. three hours. Access is by dinghy from the island of Bressay.

F4 *Take ferry from Lerwick to Bressay, travel three miles by car, then take inflatable boat for three-minute crossing.*

P WC E ♨ 🚶 Free

🕐 Late Apr–Aug, Tue–Sun (not Thur), 10am–5pm.
Tel 01595 693345   www.snh.org.uk

14 Old Haa Visitor Centre

Yell's oldest building contains local arts and crafts, plus photographs and eye-witness accounts relating to the German ship Bohus which was wrecked off the island in 1924.

F8 *Burravoe, Yell.*

P WC 🍴 🏛 E AV 🪑 Free

🕐 May–Sept, Tue–Thur, 10am–4pm;
Sat, 10am–4pm; Sun, 2–5pm.
Tel 01957 722339

15 Old Scatness Broch

Guided tours take visitors round this archeological excavation of a broch and Iron Age village where buildings stand up to head height. Also on site is an exhibition, viewing platforms, reconstructed buildings and living history demonstrations.

E1 *On A970, one mile N of Sumburgh Airport.*

P WC ♿ 🏛 E AV ♨ £

🕐 May–Oct, Sat–Thur, 10am–5pm.
Oct–Apr, telephone for details.
Tel 01595 694688   www.shetland-heritage.co.uk

16 Quendale Water Mill

A fully restored nineteenth century over-shot water mill with dam. Along with a guided tour, visitors can watch a video of the working mill and see displays of photographs and artefacts plus various pieces of crofting machinery.

E1 *Dunrossness, three miles W of A970 Sumburgh road.*

P WC ♿ 🍴 🏛 E AV £

🕐 May–Sept, daily, 10am–5pm.
Tel 01950 460969
www.quendalemill.shetland.co.uk

Scalloway Castle

17 Scalloway Castle

Patrick Stewart, Earl of Orkney renowned for his cruelty, built this grand four-storey mansion in 1600. The castle fell into disrepair after his execution in 1615, but the remains still stand impressively by Scalloway harbour.

E4 *Scalloway, six miles from Lerwick on the A970.*

P E Free

⊕ Mon–Sat, 9.30am–5pm.

Tel 0131 668 8800

www.historic-scotland.gov.uk

18 Scalloway Museum

Describes how Shetland helped Norwegian freedom fighters during the Second World War; an exhibition features photographs and artefacts.

E4 *Scalloway, nine miles W of Lerwick off A970.*

E Free

⊕ May–Sept, Mon–Sat, 10am–12 noon & 2–4.30pm.

Tel 01595 880256

19 Shetland Croft House Museum

A museum illustrating the sights, smells and sounds of a thatched croft house with fittings and a water mill from around the 1870s.

E1 *South Voe, near Boddam off A970, Dunrossness.*

P WC ⌂ E ☙ ⚤ Free

⊕ Mid Apr–Sept, daily, 10am–1pm & 2–5pm.

Tel 01595 695057

www.shetland-museum.org.uk

20 Shetland Museum

Shetland's main museum, covering all aspects of over 5000 years of island life. Main display themes are social history, textiles, agriculture, maritime and archaeology, plus exhibitions of local contemporary art.

F4 *Hay's Dock, Lerwick waterfront.*

WC ♿ ⌂ E AV ⚄ Free

⊕ New museum opening summer 2006. Telephone or check website for further details.

Tel 01595 695057

www.shetland-museum.org.uk

21 Shetland Textile Working Museum

A unique collection of textiles and artefacts illustrate the history of spinning and knitting in Shetland. Annual exhibitions show a different aspect of Shetland's textile heritage. Workshops in spinning and knitting can be arranged for group visits.

E5 *Weisdale Mill, Weisdale.*

P WC & ♨ ♨ E £

⊕ Mar–Mid Oct, Tue–Sat, 10.30am–4.30pm; Sun, 12 noon–4.30pm.

Tel 01595 830419

22 Tangwick Haa Museum

This museum, housed in a restored seventeenth century mansion, contains a wedding dress and china dating from around 1840, along with the social history of the area.

D7 *Tangwick, off B9075, NW side of Mainland.*

P WC & ♨ E ⊓ Free

⊕ May–Sept, Mon–Fri, 1–5pm; weekends 11am–7pm.

Tel 01806 503389

23 Unst Heritage Centre

A local history museum with a collection of beautifully made lace items.

G11 *Haroldswick, NE side of Unst off A968 on B9087.*

P E £

⊕ May–Sept, daily, 1.30–5pm.

Tel 01957 711528

24 Up-Helly-Aa Exhibition

An exhibition devoted to this unique fire festival when, on the last Tuesday of January every year, the darkened streets of Lerwick provide a setting for a large torchlit procession, culminating in the burning of a replica galley. Relics, photographs and costumes are on display, along with the ship which is set alight.

F4 *St Sunniva Street, Lerwick, Mainland.*

P WC E AV £

⊕ Mid May–mid Sept, Tue, 2–4pm & 7–9pm; Fri, 7–9pm; Sat, 2–4pm.

Hermaness, Unst

LOCH LOMOND & TROSSACHS NATIONAL PARK

Scotland's first national park became a reality in 2002 with the creation of the Loch Lomond and The Trossachs National Park in an area associated with tourism since the end of the 18th century. Then, at the dawn of the Romantic Age with its cult of the picturesque, daring excursionists started to seek out imposing and wild locations. Around both Loch Lomond and the Trossachs, these first tourists found scenes of unspoilt grandeur in the rugged hills within a day's carriage drive of the cities of Glasgow and Edinburgh. The huge success of Sir Walter Scott's 'block-buster' verse-narrative The Lady of the Lake, published in 1810, which peopled the wooded knolls and lochs with romantic characters, added extra impetus to the area's growing popularity. In short, both Loch Lomond and Trossachs became the byword for Scottish scenery – with their accessibility the key.

The national park here takes in 720 sq miles (1865 sq km) of some of Scotland's most accessible and hence, most vulnerable, wild scenery. Loch Lomond is Scotland's largest loch by surface area and one of the best-known. Hugely popular for all kinds of water sports, from power boating to angling, Loch Lomond attracts large numbers of city-based Scots simply because it is so close to Glasgow. Visitor pressure and the conflicting demands of, for example, powerboat users and conservationists continue to generate a variety of issues. The major development of Loch Lomond Shores at Balloch, with its emphasis on retailing and leisure options, also has the Gateway Centre, designed to orientate and educate visitors. It has a wealth of information on the wildlife and geology of the park area. Meanwhile the impressive Drumkinnon Tower, built on the very edge of the loch like a giant concrete broch-tower, offers a sense of the myths and legends of the area via its audio-visual presentations – and has stunning views as a bonus.

To the east, the Trossachs themselves have miles of walking and routes for all abilities. The hills are clothed in spruce and fir plantations, as well as oak and birch woods. The Duke's Pass, the high road between Aberfoyle and the actual Pass of Trossachs which gives access to Loch Katrine, continues to attract visitors all year round, much as it has done for generations. As well as walking, cycling is also popular, both through the forests and by way of Loch Katrine.

In addition the park spreads westwards into the Argyll Forest Park. In this area alone, 165 miles (264km) of forest roads are open to the public through a landscape split by sea lochs and dominated in the north by the peaks of the Cobbler and the Arrochar Alps. To the north, Breadalbane, from the Gaelic 'the high grounds of Scotland, the area around Crianlarich, also lies within the park boundaries, while, to the south, Dunoon in Cowal is the sea-gateway to the Park.

Loch Lomond & The Trossachs
National Park
National Park Headquarters
The Old Station
Balloch Road
Balloch, G83 8BF
Tel 01389 722600
www.lochlomond-trossachs.org

CAIRNGORMS NATIONAL PARK

At 1467 sq miles (3,800 sq kms) in size, the Cairngorms National Park is the most extensive in Britain. Formally established in 2003 it takes in most of the highest peaks and the largest area of tundra-like plateau in Britain, as well as three out of the five Scottish ski centres (Glenshee, Cairngorm and the Lecht) and the head-waters of two of Scotland's finest salmon rivers, the Dee and the Spey. The National Trust for Scotland's estate of Mar Lodge is also well within the park's boundaries on the eastern side by the upper reaches of the River Dee, in terrain well-traversed by walkers on their way to the high tops of the central Cairngorms.

Some of the other important features of the park include, on the southern side, the rolling plateau of the Mounth between Angus and Deeside, with its old-established through routes crossing the lonely high-level tundra and boulder-fields. The eastern section of the Park takes in the varied landscapes of working estates, such as Glenlivet, with its patchwork of hill farms, grouse moor and forest, as well as the upper waters of the River Don. In many parts of the park, there is also a geology lesson in the effect of glaciation, from the typical U-shaped valleys of Glen Feshie in the west or Glen Mark in the east, to the scooped-out corrie of, say, Lochnagar, or the corries in upper Glen Clova.

Walking, cycling, skiing, angling and watersports top the list of things to do. The river valley of the upper Spey (called variously Spey Valley, Speyside and Strathspey) is noted for its stands of old Scots pinewood, the descendants of the ancient woodlands of Scotland which once covered much of the north. The Royal Society for the Protection of Birds look after much of the woodlands around Abernethy, near Aviemore and, on the sheltered trails deep within the trees, the local birdlife specialities can be seen. Look for species such as crested tit, Scottish crossbill and the increasingly rare capercaillie, a kind of large woodland grouse. The ancient pines, with their characteristic red upper limbs, stand widely spaced, allowing light into the 'understorey' of heather, blueberry and juniper, and re-creating just a hint of the wild wood that a couple of millennia ago was the haunt of bear and wolf.

The 'dissected plateau' of the Cairngorms with its distinct air of wilderness is both threatened by and is a backdrop to much of the leisure activities both on Speyside and the valley of the River Dee. West of the Lairig Ghru, for example, the wild high-level landscape, can be enjoyed on foot on a long day's expedition to the high tops, for example, of Braeriach and Cairn Toul. Eastwards, however, the sense of wilderness is much diminished by the paraphernalia associated with downhill skiing. Visitors can enjoy the views from the funicular railway which offers the highest shop, restaurant and exhibition in Britain at the Ptarmigan top station, below the summit of the mountain of Cairngorm itself. Please note that for environmental reasons, visitors who use the train are not permitted on to the plateau itself.

Cairngorms National Park Authority
12 The Square,
Grantown-on-Spey, PH26 3HG
Tel 01479 873335
Email: enquiries@cairngorms.co.uk
www.cairngorms.co.uk

NATIONAL NATURE RESERVES

A National Nature Reserve is a stretch of land managed for the conservation of its habitat type and, hence, the species of plants and animals which are found there. In Scotland, this is the responsibility of the government agency, Scottish Natural Heritage. The reserves or 'NNRs' are either managed by Scottish Natural Heritage, or are privately owned and managed along with the owners under a Nature Reserve Agreement. SNH also works alongside partner organisations such as the Scottish Wildlife Trust, Forestry Commission Scotland, National Trust for Scotland and RSPB Scotland.

As part of the experience of visiting any of the 50 or so sites promoted by SNH, visitors are likely to find aids to the interpretation of the landscape and habitat by way of information panels or nature trails, as well as leaflets and other publications. The sheer variety of NNRs reflect that, though Scotland is small, there are great contrasts in habitats and landforms.

The very tip of Scotland, for example, is also a NNR. Hermaness in Shetland is home to 100,000 seabirds and like the island of Noss, also in Shetland, offers seabird spectacle in plenty along the awesome cliffs. St Kilda, west of Harris in the Western Isles, is perhaps one of Britain's most remote nature reserves. It supports the largest gannet colony in the world. With much easier access, the island of Handa, close to the north-west mainland seaboard, is another spectacular reserve, noted for its seabirds.

Other well-known reserves featuring birdlife include, for example, the Sands of Forvie, north of Aberdeen, with ducks and waders among the dunes and estuary. In the south-west, Caerlaverock is famous for wintering geese. Some reserves are particularly noted for their woodland habitats. In Glen Tanar on Deeside, there are fine stands of native Scots pine, while the Ariundle Oakwood in the West Highland is a fascinating example of Scotland's equally native 'rainforest'.

Special plantlife is a feature of the Ben Lawers nature reserve, where the high 'base-rich' rocks enable a variety of Arctic-alpine species to thrive. Corrie Fee in the Angus Glens is another site which draws botanists. Inchnadamph, in the north-west, is another famous botanical site, the underlying limestone creating ideal conditions for a range of unusual plants. Sometimes, it is the landforms themselves which are the attraction – for instance, at the spectacular but easily visited Corrieshalloch Gorge by the Ullapool road. On an even larger scale, special wildlife, mountain and woodland spectacle combine at the magnificent Glen Affric reserve west of the Great Glen. Another varied and mountainous reserve is at Creag Meagaidh, between Speyside and the Great Glen. Britain's first ever NNR was Beinn Eighe in Wester Ross, which also offers mountain grandeur, as well as native pinewood and, perhaps, a sighting of the scarce pine marten.

Basically, no matter the reserve you choose, you are sure of getting some special view and insight into Scotland's precious habitats.

www.nnr-scotland.org.uk

Scottish Natural Heritage
12 Hope Terrace
Edinburgh, EH9 2AS
Tel 0131 447 4784
Fax 0131 446 2277
www.snh.org.uk

CYCLING

In much of the Lowlands, from Galloway to Grampian, Scotland has always had a good network of rural roads with low traffic volumes giving cyclists safe passage and a choice of routes. In addition, in a country where forestry is important, the Forestry Commission's extensive plantings and network of access tracks have always been open to all, on foot or by bike. This has been calculated to be at least 1000 miles (1600km) of forest cycling alone!

In addition, environmental concerns in recent years have meant a new emphasis on cycling, so that the route choice for cyclists in Scotland has steadily increased. Old railway trackbeds and canal tow-paths, as well as custom-made dedicated cycleways have taken their place along with the rural roads and forestry track to create an excellent network, with 1300 miles (2080km) already designated as a National Cycle Network.

Cyclists in Scotland can now expect many signposted routes. Notable here are the National Routes, so that signposts with 'NR1' for example, designate a route up to Edinburgh, on to Aberdeen and all round the Moray Firth up to John o' Groats.

Mountain bikers' priorities are different from touring cyclists. Again, the Forestry Commission have opened up many examples of the kind of rugged, off-road routes enjoyed by enthusiasts. Glentress, near Peebles, has become a mountain-biking 'hotspot' with trails of various degrees of difficulty. Mountain biking enthusiasts have superb choice here. Britain's longest downhill track (2150ft/650m descent) is at Nevis Range near Fort William and attracts bikers of all standards. The Mountain Biking World Cup has been held there. The nearby Leanachan Forest has biking trails and also cycle orienteering.
www.cyclingscotland.com

Sustrans is a charity that works on practical projects throughout the UK which encourages people to cycle. The examples of designated cycle routes given below are typical of their work to create a National Cycle Network. www.sustrans.org.uk

Great Glen Cycle Route

This signposted cycleway connects Fort William with Inverness in the Great Glen, the coast-to-coast historic throughway which carries road and canal between the eastern and western seaboards. It takes advantage of the level canal towpath a well as forestry roads to avoid the heavy traffic of the main road.

Clyde to Forth Cycle Route

A west-east crossing of Scotland from Gourock on the Firth of Clyde to the capital, Edinburgh, on the Firth of Forth. This route gives hill views northwards before passing through the heart of Glasgow and on to the Airdrie - Bathgate railway path then links with the Union Canal which goes right into the centre of Edinburgh. The route also covers several linking options: Glasgow - Loch Lomond; Glasgow - Kilmarnock (and Ardrossan) and the Forth Road Bridge to Edinburgh (and Musselburgh).

Lochs & Glens Cycle Route - North

From the outskirts of Glasgow, the route heads for the Queen Elizabeth Forest Park, then goes from loch to loch: Loch Venachar, Loch Lubnaig by Strathyre, continuing to Loch Earn then over Glen Ogle to Loch Tay. The route on through Perthshire and into the Highlands includes a traffic-free section over the high Pass of Drumochter, then by the moors and pinewoods of Strathspey towards Inverness.

WALKING IN SCOTLAND

Scotland is walkers' country, mainly through the sheer variety of terrain which attracts walkers of all grades of experience and fitness. In addition, there is a tradition – though with some exceptions – of tolerance towards walkers and ramblers. In addition, the new Land Reform (Scotland) Act outlines the guidelines for, and gives a right of, responsible access. This is interpreted in the Scottish Access Code which suggests you are exercising 'responsible access' if you, for example:

- Respect people's privacy and peace of mind. When close to a house or garden, keep a sensible distance from the house, use a path or track if there is one.
- Help land managers and others to work safely and effectively. Do not hinder land management operations and follow advice from land managers. Respect requests for reasonable limitations on when and where you can go.
- Care for your environment. Do not disturb wildlife, leave the environment as you find it and follow a path or track if there is one.

Scotland's Munros

The Munros are the collective name for the 284 mountains in Scotland over 3000ft (914m) in height. The name recalls the mountaineer Sir Hugh Munro who compiled them into the famous Munro's Tables in 1881. He was the first to define criteria of descent and re-ascent which allows a summit its Munro status, as opposed to a summit with a number of subsidiary tops. The number of actual summits varies occasionally over the years, depending on mapping and surveying results – as well as changes to the criteria which

defines a Munro in the first place! In fact, modern surveying methods indicate that there are actually 511 tops over the magic figure.

Formerly only the pre-occupation of dedicated hill-folk, 'Munro bagging' has become a major pastime for many Scots and visitors to Scotland, whatever the season. It is now often possible to identify the roadside starting point for a Munro climb by the unofficial car park which has developed there!

In the long days of summer, at least, the majority of Munros can be climbed in one day – one of their most attractive features, along with the fact that, again, the vast majority require only stamina, good sense and strong footwear, rather than rope or rock skills. The exceptions lie mostly in the Cuillins of Skye, though some walkers would also urge caution while traversing, for example, the Aonach Eagach ridge in Glencoe or Liathach in Glen Torridon in anything other than ideal conditions.

Coastal Paths, Forest Trails and Long Distance Footpaths

Aside from high-level walking, there are many low-level and gentler options. Many of these are set in the extensive plantings of the Forestry Commission who encourage access to their woodlands by providing visitor facilities such as marked trails and designated parking areas. Coastal walking is also popular and local authorities in many parts of Scotland have improved access to these unspoilt areas. For example, the Fife Coastal Path extends a full 78 miles (125km) round the old kingdom of Fife between the Forth Bridge and the Tay Bridge. Finally, 'official' long distance footpaths also pass through many areas of high scenic interest.

LONG DISTANCE WALKS

West Highland Way

Distance: 95 miles / 152 km

From one of Scotland's busiest cities to the setting of Scotland's highest mountain, the West Highland Way ranges from Milngavie, on the peripheries of Glasgow, to Fort William. This scenic trail encompasses some of Scotland's most diverse landscapes, from the brooding expanse of Loch Lomond to the majesty of Glencoe, where fortunate walkers may see some of the area's wildlife such as red deer and golden eagles.

Contact: The National Park Gateway Centre
Loch Lomond Shores
Ben Lomond Way, Balloch G83 8LX
Tel: 01389 722199
E-mail: info@west-highland-way.co.uk
www.west-highland-way.co.uk

Great Glen Way

Distance: 73 miles / 117 km

Linking the west coast town of Fort William to the north-east city of Inverness – the capital of the Highlands – this is the newest addition to Scotland's formal Long Distance Routes. The trail traverses through the Great Glen, past the shores of Loch Lochy, Loch Oich and Loch Ness and follows the Caledonian Canal towpaths.

Contact: Great Glen Way Project Office
Auchteraw, Fort Augustus PH32 4BT
Tel: 01320 366633
E-mail: greatglenway@highland.gov.uk
www.greatglenway.com

The Rob Roy Way

Distance: 92 miles / 148 km

This attractive route has as its theme the real-life Highland folk hero Rob Roy Macgregor who died in 1734. It starts at Drymen (on the West Highland Way) and ends at Pitlochry in the heart of Highland Perthshire. Using old through-routes traversed by Rob in his cattle-droving days, it passes by Loch Venachar, turns north via Loch Lubnaig, climbs up and over Glen Ogle and goes east along Loch Tay, through some of the finest landscapes in central Scotland.

Contact: The Rob Roy Way
Email info@scsupport.co.uk
www.robroyway.fsnet.co.uk

Southern Upland Way

Distance: 212 miles / 339 km

This coast-to-coast trail stretches across Dumfries & Galloway and the Borders regions, from Portpatrick on the south-west tip of Galloway to the North Sea coast at Cockburnspath. The walk features the forests, moorland and hills of southern Scotland, with a number of summits exceeding 600 metres (2000 feet).

Contact: Southern Upland Way Office
The Bothy, Ford House
Garroch Estate
St Johns Town of Dalry
Nr Castle Douglas DG7 3XP
E-mail: info@southernuplandway.com
www.southernuplandway.com

Speyside Way

Distance: 84 miles / 134 km

Running from the Moray coast to the edge of the Grampian Mountains, this waymarked trail, for the most part, follows the banks of the River Spey. Walkers will encounter landscape characteristic of the Grampian and Highland areas including forests, birch woodland and moorland. There are a number of Speyside's distilleries en-route.

Contact: The Speyside Way Ranger Service
Speyside Way Visitor Centre
Old Station Building, Aberlour
Banffshire AB38 9QP
Tel: 01340 881266
E-mail: speyside.way@moray.gov.uk
www.speysideway.org

St Cuthbert's Way

Distance: 62 miles / 100 km

Links the abbey-town of Melrose, associated with this saint's early monastic life, with Lindisfarne, over the Border and into England, setting for his later ministry and death.

Contact: St Cuthbert's Way
E-mail: enquiries@st-cuthberts-way.co.uk
www.stcuthbertsway.fsnet.co.uk

Useful website for all aspects of walking
www.walkingwild.com

GOLF IN SCOTLAND

Scotland – and sometimes just St Andrews – is often described as the 'Home of Golf'. This is a reference to the long and continuous tradition of playing a game with ball and sticks which was already popular by the time of the Stewart monarchs. It may have originated as a game played on the short rabbit-nibbled coastal turf using driftwood and rabbit holes. It may even have been imported from Holland, but certainly St Andrews by the coast and several other coastal locations have particular associations with the game, and have evolved the classic Scottish links golf course.

No other country in the world has so many courses per head of population and the golf links has even shaped Scottish towns, with common lands which would otherwise have long ago been built over, preserved for the game. Thus places like Carnoustie, St Andrews, North Berwick or even Aberdeen all have courses close to the town or city centre.

Scotland's golf courses are playable for much of the year, certainly many of links courses. Golfers also take advantage of Scotland's long summer daylight hours – so that 'after dinner' rounds are quite usual.

Booking a round or a day's golf on any of Scotland's courses vary greatly and may depend on the policy of the individual golf club. Especially in the off-season, it can be possible just to turn up and play – but in all cases it is essential to check out the club of your choice by phoning or writing in advance. Visitors are welcome at nearly all clubs in Scotland – but you must find out how and when.

There is also a large choice of specialist operators who arrange golf packages to include accommodation and in addition, a wide variety of discount tickets are available in many parts of Scotland noted for golf. These give reduced prices on a number of local courses.

Scotland and the Open Championship

Golf's oldest national championship was first played in 1860 at Prestwick, then declared 'open to the world' in the following year. There are only seven golf courses in Scotland which have subsequently hosted The Open Championship over the years and only five of them are still on the Open circuit: St Andrews, Turnberry, Muirfield, Royal Troon and Carnoustie. (Prestwick and Musselburgh have been dropped.) In 1894 Sandwich in England became the first non-Scottish venue.

The shortest hole in Open Championship golf is also one of the most famous. The 'Postage Stamp', the 8th hole at Royal Troon, has ended the hopes of many aspiring Open champions. From a high ground tee, a dropping shot is required, played over a gully to a very narrow green set in the side of a sandhill. With no safe route in – bunkers trap any deviation – the ball must find the green from the tee-shot!

Another famous and feared hole on the circuit is the 17th, the Road Hole on the Old Course, St Andrews, where the tee-shot has to be played over part of the nearby hotel, and famously deep bunkers are a hazard by the small green.

Island golf

Even Scotland's islands have plenty of golfing choice. Arran has seven alone. Islay's famous Machrie Golf Course is simply one of Scotland's most highly individualistic links. The course by Scarista Beach in Harris is another hidden gem (though discovered by Nick Faldo, Tom Watson and Sean Connery!) Scotland's most northerly course is on Whalsay, in Shetland – a full 18 holes, with seabirds as a distraction.

http://golf.visitscotland.com/

VISITOR TRAILS

The Castle Trail

Some say that because it lay a little aside from the mainstream of Scotland's warlike story, more castles in Grampian, in Scotland's north-east, were bound to remain intact through the centuries. This may at least in part be true. Craigievar, for example, the finest of the 'Castles of Mar' was built for a successful merchant in the 17th century and remains today virtually in its original condition. However, Craigievar is just one on this well-known and signposted trail. The others featured are Duff House, Delgatie Castle, Huntly Castle, Haddo House, Fyvie Castle, Leith Hall, Tolquhon Castle, Kildrummy Castle, Corgarff Castle, Castle Fraser, Crathes Castle and Drum.
www.agtb.org/castletrail.htm

Scotland's Malt Whisky Trail

The whiskies of Strathspey are the focus of this signposted trail through the Moray countryside. Six working distilleries and world-famous names – Benromach, Cardhu, Glenfiddich, Glen Grant, The Glenlivet and Strathisla, – plus Dallas Dhu as a distillery preserved as an example of its kind, along with the Speyside Cooperage, make up this trail. The signposts take the visitor into some of the finest scenic locations in and around the valley of the Spey, with its birchwood, hill farms and moorland.
www.maltwhiskytrail.com

The Coastal Trail

Discover the unspoilt Grampian coastline. This trail is a reminder of the importance of the maritime heritage in the story of Scotland's north-east. Discover the characteristic little harbour communities with their distinctive gable-ends to the sea. Find secret coves and empty beaches, cliffs and raucous seabird colonies. Look for seals and dolphins. Visit the larger towns to see the awesome catching power of the modern fishing vessel.
www.agtb.org/thecoastaltrail.htm

The Victorian Heritage Trail

Queen Victoria's love affair with the valley of the River Dee is celebrated in this trail centred on the River Dee but including a route 'over the hills' to Fettercairn Distillery. This trail is renminiscent of the Queen's fondness for expeditions all around the area. Look out for the 'By Royal Appointment' signs, notably in Ballater – a reminder of the continuing royal links with the area. The Old Royal Station, also in Ballater, and now a visitor centre, also gives a good background to the Trail.
www.agtb.org/victorianheritage
trail.htm

The Stone Circle Trail

From unknowably old hilltop cairns to much later Pictish carved standing stones, Grampian has many early sites out in its farmlands and moors. More than just old heaps of stones, many of these places have a special atmosphere. Reach out and touch the past.
www.agtb.org/the-stone-circle.htm

Aberdeen and Grampian Tourist Board
Exchange House, 26/28 Exchange Street
Aberdeen, AB11 6PH
Tel: 01224 288828, Fax: 01224 288838
Email: info@agtb.org
www.agtb.org or
www.visitscotland.com
Tel: 0845 2255 121 (UK)
or +44 (0) 1506 832 121 (Outside UK)
Fax: 01506 832 222
Email: info@visitscotland.com

MAIN ANNUAL EVENTS

Up-Helly-Aa   Jan

Every year Shetland holds a series of traditional Viking fire festivals. The biggest occurs in Lerwick where a torch-lit procession, led by the Jarl Squad in full Viking costume, moves through the darkened streets. The spectacle concludes with the burning of a full-size replica galley. Afterwards the town is alive with celebration and parties, although they are strictly invitation only. There are also a number of smaller festivals held between January and March, which are accessible to visitors to the islands.

Contact: Shetland Tourist Information Office
           Market Cross
           Lerwick ZE1 0LU
           Tel: 08701 999 440
           E-mail: info@visitshetland.com
           www.visitshetland.com

Celtic Connections   Jan

Located in venues across Glasgow, Celtic Connections is the biggest winter festival in the world for celebrating Celtic music and culture.

Contact: Box Office
           The Glasgow Royal Concert Hall
           2 Sauchiehall Street
           Glasgow G2 3NY
           Tel: 0141 353 8000
           Email: sales@grch.com
           www.celticconnections.com

Hawick Reivers Festival   Mar

This festival celebrates a period of history when the borderlands of Scotland and England were the home of cattle thieves and outlaws, known as the Border Reivers. Highlights include a spectacular procession as well as concerts and ceilidhs each night, with free street events, a 16th century market, and a torchlight procession.

Contact: Unit 4, Towerdykeside
           Hawick TD9 9EA
           Tel: 01450 372001
           Email: info@teribus.com
www.teribus.com/reivers04.htm

Celtic Food & Drink Festival   Apr

Established in Perthshire, this Iron Age themed food festival includes lamb roasting on a spit, primitive smoking of fish and herbs and local Scottish wine tasting.

Contact: Scottish Crannog Centre
           Kenmore,
           Loch Tay PH15 2HY
           Tel: 01887 830583
           E-mail: info@crannog.co.uk
           www.crannog.co.uk

Aviemore Walking Festival   May

This week-long festival centred in and around Strathspey includes walks with experts to locations such as The Badenoch Way, Ben Macdui, Glen Feshie and The Bacharn Trail at Abernethy.

Contact: Aviemore Walking Festival
           Aviemore Business Association
           PO Box 5349
           Aviemore PH22 1YG
           Email: enquiries@aviemorewalking.com
           www.aviemorewalking.com

Spirit of Speyside Whisky Festival   May

Situated in Scotland's picturesque malt whisky region, the Whisky Festival offers visitors a busy programme of events. Designed to celebrate Speyside's whisky-making heritage, the festival's agenda includes music, distillery tours, competitions, arts and crafts and, of course, whisky tasting.

Contact: Elgin Tourist Information Centre
           17 High Street,
           Elgin IV30 1EG
           Tel: 01343 542666
           E-mail: enquiries@spiritofspeyside.com
           www.spiritofspeyside.com

Burns an a that Festival   May-June

An annual festival celebrating the bard and contemporary Scottish culture. The festival is a week long event in Ayrshire. It offers a series of events including a gala concert, festival club, open air concerts, fireworks displays and theatre productions. There is also a full fringe programme in a range of venues throughout Ayrshire.

Contact: Ayrshire & Arran Tourist Board
           15 Skye Road, Prestwick KA9 2TA
           Tel: 01292 678100
           Email: info@burnsfestival.com
           www.burnsfestival.com

The Highland Festival   May–June

Held annually at a series of venues throughout the Highlands, the Highland Festival features a number of both traditional and contemporary performances devised to celebrate Highland culture.

Contact: Inverness Tourist Information Centre
in person or Highland Festival Office
40 Huntly Street
Inverness IV3 5HR
Tel: 01463 711112
E-mail: info@highlandfestival.org.uk
www.highlandfestival.org.uk

Highland Games   May–Sept

A tradition believed to have originated from the early nineteenth century, gatherings are now held annually at a number of venues throughout Scotland. Spectators can watch competitors take part in a varied programme of events including solo piping and Highland dance competitions, heavyweight contests such as tossing the caber, hammer and stone throwing, tug-of-war, wrestling and athletic and cycling events.

Contact: Local Tourist Information Centres
in person or see local press for details
Tel: 0845 22 55 121
E-mail: info@visitscotland.com
www.visitscotland.com

Pitlochry Festival Theatre   May–Oct

During the festival season, Pitlochry Theatre hosts a variety of plays in the comfortable 544 seat auditorium. Visitors can also attend a number of concerts, art and craft demonstrations and backstage tours.

Contact: Pitlochry Festival Theatre
Pitlochry, Perthshire PH16 5DR
Tel: 01796 484600
E-mail: admin@pitlochry.org.uk
www.pitlochry.org.uk

Scottish Traditional Boat Festival   June

The biggest gathering of traditional boats in Scotland based in and around the 17th century harbour of Portsoy. There are also plenty of on-shore activities as well including live traditional music, a food fair, family activities and even a road run.

Contact: Scottish Traditional Boat Festival
The Mill Office, Burnside Street

Portsoy AB45 2QN
Tel: 01261 842894 (chairman)
Email: contact@scottishtraditional
boatfestival.co.uk
www.thebpl.co.uk/stbf2005/

Talisker Skye & Lochalsh   June
Food & Drink Festival

A very popular food and drink event showcasing the best of Skye and Lochalsh. Try special seafood menus, a 'slow-food' buffet, interactive distillery tours, ceilidhs and even a guided tour through an organic garden.

Contact: Shona MacLennan
Skye & Lochalsh Food & Drink Festival
Co-ordinator
Solas Business Services Ltd.
Kyle Industrial Estate,
Kyle of Lochalsh IV40 8AH
Tel: 01599 555403
Email: shona@skyefood.co.uk or
portreeTIC@host.co.uk
www.skyefood.co.uk

Glasgow International Jazz   Jun–Jul
Festival

The reputation of the International Jazz Festival attracts a diversity of artists from all over the world who perform at a variety of locations throughout Glasgow.

Contact: Royal Bank Glasgow Jazz Festival
81 High Street
Glasgow G1 1NB
Tel: 0141 552 3552
E-mail: glasgow@jazzfest.co.uk
www.jazzfest.co.uk

Hebridean Celtic Festival   July

The Hebridean Celtic Festival is a four-day family-friendly musical celebration. Based in Stornoway. Each of the four main nights have their own musical theme, from Gaelic and Family, to Rock and Party. The festival is mainly held in the beautiful grounds of Lews Castle. Previous performers have been Capercaillie, The Saw Doctors and The Peatbog Faeries.

Contact: PO BOX 9909
Stornoway, Isle of Lewis HS2 0DH
Tel: 01851 621 234
Email: info@hebceltfest.com (for general information), boxoffice@hebceltfest.com (for ticket information)
www.hebceltfest.com

Edinburgh Festival   end Jul–beginning Sept

In 1947, post-war Edinburgh hosted its first International Festival. Since then, the festival has evolved into one of the largest arts festivals in the world, attracting over 100,000 visitors a year from around the world. Music, drama, literature and film have, over the years, become an intrinsic part of the summer in Scotland's historic capital.

Orkney International Science Festival   Sept

A unique and exciting Science-related festival covering many themes that integrate the world of science with the lives of ordinary people with a focus on topics of global interest.

Contact: Orkney International Science Festival
          PO Box 2000
          Kirkwall
          Orkney
          KW15 1WS
          Tel: 01856 876214
          Email: science@orkney.com
          www.oisf.org.uk

St Andrew's Week   Nov

The St Andrew's Week festival features concerts of traditional and classical music, exhibitions of arts and crafts, ceilidhs, dance, drama, a St Andrew's Day Gala Ball and a spectacular fireworks display.

Contact: St Andrew's Week
          St Andrews Local Office
          St Mary's Place
          St Andrews
          Fife
          KY16 9UY
          Tel: 01334 412 674
          Email info@standrewsweek.co.uk
          wwww.standrewsweek.co.uk

Edinburgh International Festival

The UK's annual premier arts festival provides visitors with a unique opportunity to experience a variety of international theatre, dance, opera and music.

Contact: Edinburgh International Festival
          The Hub
          Edinburgh's Festival Centre
          Castlehill
          Royal Mile
          Edinburgh
          EH1 2NE
          Tel: 0131 473 2000
          E-mail: eif@eif.co.uk
          www.eif.co.uk
          www.edinburgh-festivals.com

Edinburgh Festival Fringe

For three weeks every August, Edinburgh is host to the largest arts festival in the world. From comedy to magic, over 1000 shows are performed a day at more than 200 venues across the city.

Contact: The Fringe Office
          180 High Street
          Edinburgh
          EH1 1QS
          Tel: 0131 226 5257
          E-mail: admin@edfringe.com
          www.edfringe.com
          www.edinburgh-festivals.com

The Edinburgh Military Tattoo

Staged on the esplanade of Edinburgh's historic castle, this annual military spectacle combines music and dance with drama and pageantry.

Contact: Tattoo Office
          32 Market Street
          Edinburgh
          EH1 1QB
          Tel: 08707 555 1188
          E-mail: edintattoo@edintattoo.co.uk
          www.edintattoo.co.uk
          www.edinburgh-festivals.com

Edinburgh International Book Festival

Attracting bibliophiles from around the word, the annual Book Festival encompasses a wide range of activities such as readings, demonstrations and workshops, author interviews and literary seminars.

Contact: Scottish Book Centre
          137 Dundee Street
          Edinburgh
          EH11 1BG
          Tel: 0131 228 5444
          E-mail: admin@edbookfest.co.uk
          www.edbookfest.co.uk
          www.edinburgh-festivals.com

Edinburgh International Film Festival

Established in 1947, the Film Festival annually showcases over 300 films, including a number of world premiers.

Contact: Edinburgh International Film Festival
88 Lothian Road
Edinburgh EH3 9BZ
Tel: 0131 228 4051
E-mail: info@edfilmfest.org.uk
www.edfilmfest.org.uk
www.edinburgh-festivals.com

Edinburgh International Jazz & Blues Festival

Staged in a number of venues across Edinburgh, visitors can enjoy a wide range of Scottish and International jazz and blues.

Contact: EIJF
29 St Stephen Street
Edinburgh
EH3 5AN
Tel: 0131 467 5200
www.edinburgh-festivals.com

World Pipe Band Championships   Aug

Held annually, this one day competition attracts over 200 bands from around the world.

Contact: Royal Scottish Pipe Band Association
45 Washington Street
Glasgow
G3 8AZ
Tel: 0141 221 5414
www.rspba.org

Scottish Book Town Festival   Sept

This literary festival features a number of events held in the streets of Wigtown, Bladnoch distillery, the festival marquee and local book shops including readings, book signings and children's entertainment.

Contact: Wigtown Book Town Company
Freepost NAT 5339t
Wigtown DG8 9BR
Tel: 01988 402036
E-mail: mail@wigit.btinternet.com
www.wigtown-booktown.co.uk

The Royal National Mod   Oct

The Royal National Mod is Scotland's principal Gaelic festival. The Mod is an annual competition-based festival designed to celebrate Gaelic language and culture though music, dance, drama, arts and literature.

Contact: The Royal National Mod
109 Church Street, Inverness IV1 1EY
Tel: 01463 709705
E-mail: info@the-mod.co.uk
www.the-mod.co.uk

Glasgay! Gay & Lesbian   Oct–Nov
Arts Festival

The festival programme includes a wide range of events including performing arts, music, literature, film and seminars.

Contact: Glasgay!
Room 320a
74 Victoria Crescent Road
Glasgow G12 9JL
Tel· 0141 334 7126
E-mail: info@glasgay.org.uk
www.glasgay.co.uk

Capital Christmas   Dec

Located in Edinburgh, Capital Christmas includes the Grand Christmas Parade and a festive programme of events featuring Winter Wonderland, Britain's largest open air ice rink, situated in Princes Street Gardens.

Contact: Unique Events Limited
17–23 Calton Road
Edinburgh EH8 8DL
Tel: 0845 22 55 121
www.capitalchristmas.co.uk

Hogmanay   31 Dec–1 Jan

Believed to be derived from the French *aguillanneuf* meaning 'last day of the year', Hogmanay represents Scotland's New Year's eve celebrations. After the stroke of midnight it is customary in Scotland to visit your neighbours – a tradition known as 'first footing' – bearing gifts such as a bottle of whisky, a lump of coal or a food item. However, there are also a number of organised events in Scotland's major cities, including Edinburgh and Glasgow.

Contact: Local Tourist Information Centres
in person or see local press for details
Tel: 0845 22 55 121
E-mail: info@visitscotland.com
www.visitscotland.com
www.edinburghshogmanay.org
www.hogmanay.co.uk

REGION AND ATTRACTION INDEX

The National Wallace Monument, Abbey Craig, near Stirling

ALPHABETICAL INDEX

Entries in **bold** indicate photographs

First published in Great Britain in 2002 by
Colin Baxter Photography Limited, Grantown–on–Spey, PH26 3NA, Scotland
www.colinbaxter.co.uk

Second edition (fully updated) published 2003, Reprinted 2004
Fourth edition (fully updated & expanded) published 2005

Photographs copyright © Colin Baxter 2003, 2004, 2005. Text copyright © Colin Baxter Photography 2003, 2004, 2005.
Special text features written by Gilbert Summers. Regional Scotland maps copyright © Wendy Price 2003, 2004, 2005.
Edinburgh & Glasgow city plans copyright © XYZ Digital Map Company 2003, 2004, 2005

Front cover photograph: *River Avon, Strath Avon, Moray*.
Back cover photograph: *Balmoral Castle, Royal Deeside*.